mathsoft™
mathcad®11

User's Guide

Mathsoft Engineering & Education, Inc.

US and Canada

101 Main Street
Cambridge, MA 02142

Phone: 617-444-8000
FAX: 617-444-8001

http://www.mathsoft.com/

All other countries

Knightway House
Park Street
Bagshot, Surrey
GU19 5AQ
United Kingdom

Phone: +44 (0) 1276 450850
FAX: +44 (0)1276 475552

Contents

Getting Started

About the User's Guide   **1**

1: Welcome to Mathcad   **3**
What Is Mathcad?   3
Highlights of Mathcad 11 Release   4
System Requirements   7
Installation   7
Technical Support   9

2: Getting Started with Mathcad   **11**
The Mathcad Workspace   11
Regions   13
A Simple Calculation   16
Definitions and Variables   17
Entering Text   18
Iterative Calculations   19
Graphs   21
Saving, Printing, and Exiting   22

3: Online Resources   **23**
Mathcad Resources   23
Help   28
Collaboratory User Forums   29
Other Resources   32

4: Working with Math   **33**
Inserting Math   33
Building Expressions   39
Editing Expressions   42
Math Styles   50

5: Vectors, Matrices, and Data Arrays   **53**
Creating Arrays   53
Accessing Array Elements   56
Displaying Arrays   58
Working with Arrays   61
Nested Arrays   63

6: Working with Text   **65**
Inserting Text   65
Text and Paragraph Properties   68
Text Styles   71
Equations in Text   72
Text Tools   73

7: Worksheet Management   **77**

    Worksheets and Templates   77

    Rearranging Your Worksheet   80

    Layout   83

    Safeguarding an Area of the Worksheet   85

    Safeguarding an Entire Worksheet   87

    Worksheet References   88

    Hyperlinks   89

    Distributing Your Worksheets   91

Calculating with Mathcad

8: Calculating in Mathcad   **99**

    Defining and Evaluating Variables   99

    Defining and Evaluating Functions   106

    Units and Dimensions   109

    Working with Results   112

    Controlling Calculation   118

    Animation   121

    Error Messages   123

9: Solving and Data Analysis   **125**

    Solving and Optimization Functions   125

    Differential Equation Solvers   133

    Data Fitting   145

10: Inserting Graphics and Other Objects   **151**

    Overview   151

    Inserting Pictures   151

    Inserting Objects   155

    Inserting Graphics Computationally Linked to Your Worksheet   158

11: 2D Plots   **161**

    Overview of 2D Plotting   161

    Graphing Functions and Expressions   163

    Plotting Vectors of Data   166

    Formatting a 2D Plot   168

    Modifying a 2D Plot's Perspective   171

12: 3D Plots   **175**

    Overview of 3D Plotting   175

    Creating 3D Plots of Functions   176

    Creating 3D Plots of Data   179

    Formatting a 3D Plot   184

    Rotating and Zooming on 3D Plots   193

13: Symbolic Calculation   **195**
     Overview of Symbolic Math   195
     Live Symbolic Evaluation   196
     Using the Symbolics Menu   201
     Examples of Symbolic Calculation   203
     Symbolic Optimization   212

14: Importing and Exporting Data   **215**
     Overview   215
     Functions for Reading and Writing Files   215
     Exchanging Data with Other Applications   216
     Data Input and Output Components   219
     Application Components   222
     230

15: Extending and Automating Mathcad   **231**
     Overview   231
     Programming within Mathcad   231
     Building Function DLLs   243
     Creating Your Own Components   243
     Accessing Mathcad from Within Another Application   248

Functions and Operators

16: Functions   **249**
     Built-in Functions   249
     Function Categories   249
     Mathcad Functions Listed Alphabetically   260
     Functions   260

17: Operators   **391**
     Arithmetic Operators   394
     Vector and Matrix Operators   398
     Calculus Operators   402
     Evaluation Operators   411
     Boolean Operators   415
     Programming Operators   417

18: Symbolic Keywords   **421**
     Accessing Symbolic Keywords   421
     Finding More Information   422
     Keywords   422

Appendices   431

Appendix A: Special Functions   432
Appendix B: SI Units   434
Appendix C: CGS units   436
Appendix D: U.S. Customary Units   438
Appendix E: MKS Units   440
Appendix F: Predefined Variables   442
Appendix G: Suffixes for Numbers   443
Appendix H: Greek Letters   444
Appendix I: Arrow and Movement Keys   445
Appendix J: Function Keys   446
Appendix K: ASCII codes   447
Appendix L: References   448

Index   449

About the *User's Guide*

The Mathcad *User's Guide* is organized as follows:

♦ **Getting Started**

This section contains a quick introduction to Mathcad's features and workspace, including resources available in the product and on the Internet for getting more out of Mathcad. Be sure to read this section first if you are a new Mathcad user.

♦ **Calculating with Mathcad**

This section describes in more detail how to create and edit Mathcad worksheets. It describes how Mathcad interprets equations and explains Mathcad's computational features: units of measurement, complex numbers, matrices, built-in functions, solving equations, programming, and so on. This section also describes how to do symbolic calculations and how to use Mathcad's two- and three-dimensional plotting features.

♦ **Functions and Operators**

This section lists and describes in detail all built-in functions, operators, and symbolic keywords, including how to use them in your calculations.

Notations and Conventions

The *User's Guide* uses the following notations and conventions:

Italics represent scalar variable names, function names, and error messages.

Bold Courier represents keys you should type.

Bold represents a menu command. It is also used to denote vector and matrix valued variables.

An arrow such as that in "**Graph⇒X-Y Plot**" indicates a submenu command.

Function keys and other special keys are enclosed in brackets. For example, [↑], [↓], [←], and [→] are the arrow keys on the keyboard. [**F1**], [**F2**], etc., are function keys; [**BkSp**] is the Backspace key for backspacing over characters; [**Del**] is the Delete key for deleting characters to the right; [**Ins**] is the Insert key for inserting characters to the left of the insertion point; [**Tab**] is the Tab key; and [**Space**] is the space bar.

[**Ctrl**], [**Shift**], and [**Alt**] are the Control, Shift, and Alt keys. When two keys are shown together, for example, [**Ctrl**]V, press and hold down the first key, and then press the second key.

The symbol [↵] and [**Enter**] refer to the same key.

Additionally, in the *Functions and Operators* section of this book, the following specific notation is used whenever possible:

- *x* and *y* represent real numbers.
- *z* and *w* represent either real or complex numbers.
- *m, n, i, j,* and *k* represent integers.
- *S* and any names beginning with *S* represent string expressions.
- **u, v,** and any names beginning with **v** represent vectors.
- **A** and **B** represent matrices or vectors.
- **M** and **N** represent square matrices.
- *f* represents a scalar-valued function.
- **F** represents a vector-valued function.
- *file* is a string variable that corresponds to a filename or path.
- *X* and *Y* represent variables or expressions of any type.

When spaces are shown in an equation, you need not type the spaces. Mathcad automatically spaces equations correctly.

Chapter 1
Welcome to Mathcad

- ♦ What Is Mathcad?
- ♦ Highlights of Mathcad 11 Release
- ♦ System Requirements
- ♦ Installation
- ♦ Technical Support

What Is Mathcad?

Mathcad is the industry standard technical calculation tool for professionals, educators, and college students worldwide. Mathcad is as versatile and powerful as a programming language, yet it's as easy to learn as a spreadsheet. Plus, it is fully wired to take advantage of the Internet and other applications you use every day.

Mathcad lets you type equations as you're used to seeing them, expanded fully on your screen. In a programming language, equations look something like this:

$$x=(-B+SQRT(B**2-4*A*C))/(2*A)$$

In a spreadsheet, equations go into cells looking something like this:

$$+(B1+SQRT(B1*B1-4*A1*C1))/(2*A1)$$

And that's assuming you can see them. Usually all you see is a number.

In Mathcad, the same equation looks the way you might see it on a blackboard or in a reference book. And there is no difficult syntax to learn; you simply point and click and your equations appear.

$$x := \frac{-b + \sqrt{b^2 - 4 \cdot a \cdot c}}{2 \cdot a}$$

But Mathcad equations do much more than look good. You can use them to solve just about any math problem you can think of, symbolically or numerically. You can place text anywhere around them to document your work. You can show how they look with Mathcad's two- and three-dimensional plots. You can even illustrate your work with graphics taken from another application. Plus, Mathcad takes full advantage of Microsoft's OLE 2 object linking and embedding standard to work with other applications, supporting drag and drop and in-place activation as both client and server.

Mathcad comes with online *Tutorials; QuickSheets* to show you working examples of Mathcad functions including working with other applications; and *Reference Tables* with math, science, and engineering formulas all under the **Help** menu. Online *Help* includes the *Author's Reference* and *Developer's Reference* for more advanced usage.

Mathcad simplifies and streamlines documentation, critical to communicating and to meeting business and quality assurance standards. By combining equations, text, and graphics in a single worksheet, Mathcad makes it easy to keep track of the most complex calculations. By printing the worksheet exactly as it appears on the screen, Mathcad lets you make a permanent and accurate record of your work.

Highlights of Mathcad 11 Release

Mathcad 11 features a number of improvements and added capabilities designed to increase your productivity and Web connectivity. For more in-depth details and live examples see *New Features* under **Tutorials** in the **Help** menu.

Usability Features

- **Undo**. Undo in Mathcad now extends far beyond the facility that existed in previous versions. It is now possible to undo and redo edits to most actions and backtrack in as many steps as you need.

- **Copy/Paste Tables with Mixed Data Format**: Data copied and pasted into matrices from tabular applications, such as Excel, or ASCII worksheets that contain rows and columns, will preserve data characteristics, including text, numerics, complex numbers, or empty cells.

- **Menus and Toolbar Changes**: Mathcad menus and toolbars have been updated to include new features and make existing features easier to find and use. You can now add additional buttons to the Standard toolbar by right clicking on it and choosing Customize including new buttons for exchanging data. New Resources and Controls toolbars have been added.

- **Interface Updates**: Pressing [Ctrl] F9 allows you to recalculate an entire worksheet just as F9 recalculates a single region. Regions can be nudged into alignment with arrow keys. The Formatting toolbar now includes subscript and superscript buttons that work in both math and text regions.

- **Save to Web**: There is now a single choice for saving Mathcad documents as HTML under the Save As... choice on the **File** menu and a new Save as Web Page Wizard. All documents saved as HTML will always be readable back into Mathcad, regardless of other choices made. This is accomplished by saving the Content MathML required by Mathcad inside the HTML markup. You can choose how to save your equations, how to save images, and layout preferences including whether or not to use a template.

- **Save for Microsoft Word**: Mathcad documents can now be saved or copied into Microsoft Word through Rich Text Format (RTF) using positioning tables to retain all layout features, particularly side-by-side positioning of regions. Microsoft Word will need to be in the Print Layout view to see all the formatting. We've included a new template with margins set to match Microsoft Word's margins.

Data Input/Output

- **Data File Reading and Writing**: Components for reading and writing data files now preserve data characteristics, including strings, numerics, complex numbers, and empty cells. Reading and writing support a variety of delimiters, including commas, semicolons, tabs, and special characters.

- **Excel Data Exchange**: When reading in from Excel you can now choose a named data range and a specific worksheet within the file.

- **Binary File Reading and Writing**: Two new functions have been introduced to read and write binary data, READBIN and WRITEBIN, allowing you to set various parameters on your data.

Math Enhancements

- **1D Partial Differential Solve Blocks**: One-dimensional parabolic and hyperbolic Partial Differential Equations (PDEs) can now be solved inside solve blocks using the new built-in function **pdesolve()** or with the new function **numol()**. Both the wave equation and the heat equation, systems of PDEs, and PDEs with algebraic constraints, can be solved numerically in Mathcad, as long as they are linear in their highest order time derivatives.

- **New Bessel Functions**: The Bessel functions now accept complex arguments and negative or fractional order. Most Bessel functions now have an exponentially-scaled counterpart, as does the Gamma function. This is useful when trying to evaluate scaled Bessels for large arguments without generating overflow errors.

- **New Hankel Functions**: The new Hankel functions evaluate following their definition.

- **Thresholded Truncation**: New, uppercase versions of the truncation functions (floor, ceil, round, etc.) take a second threshold argument and scale by the threshold before performing the truncation, then rescale after truncation. This is useful if you need to truncate without units. However, the lowercase version of these functions no longer take arguments with units to avoid ambiguity when converting between unit systems. Additionally, all truncation functions now accept complex arguments.

- **Sinc and Seed**: A new function has been added for $\sin(x)/x$ and its behavior at $x = 0$ has improved. The new Seed function resets the seed value used in random number and random distribution functions dynamically in a Mathcad worksheet. It can also be used in a program to set different seeds for different loops through a random generator call.

- **Error functions**: The error function (erf) and complimentary error function (erfc) now accept complex arguments.

- **Strict Boolean Comparison**: When doing comparison operations on floating point numbers that vary beyond the calculation precision of your machine, you may want to implement strict Boolean comparison within your worksheet. If you check this option, the two sides of a Boolean sentence will be compared exactly.

Programming

- **Scriptable Object Improvements**: Mathcad Scriptable Object components can now call other objects and variables in a Mathcad worksheet using the Automation methods outlined in **Help ⇒ Developer's Reference** under *Accessing Mathcad from Another Application.*

- **String Support in User EFIs**: User-written functions for Mathcad may now be programmed to pass strings as arguments and outputs. MCSTRING has been added to define a null-terminated character string pointer.

New Online Resources

- **New Tutorials:** *Getting Started Primers* and *In-depth Features* are entirely new, geared both for new users and users looking for help on more advanced features. They are accessible from the Resources toolbar or directly from the **Help** menu.

- **QuickSheets and Application Samples**: *QuickSheets* provide live examples of most Mathcad functions. They are now all linked from **Help**. In addition, application samples are now included under *Using Mathcad with Other Applications* in the *QuickSheets*. These example files are also accessible directly from the **Help** menu.

- **Developer's Reference**: This online Help now provides more guidance and examples for custom controls, creating scriptable objects, and Automation. Linked sample files have been added to help you use these features.

- **Web Library**: The E-books in the Web Library at www.mathcad.com include helpful resources for using Mathcad. If you are solving differential equations, we recommend downloading *Differential Equation Solve Blocks: ODEs and DAEs in Mathcad.*

If you are upgrading from a version earlier than Mathcad 2001i, you will find many more new features. Online *Help, QuickSheets, Tutorials,* and this *User's Guide* will all help orient you to the current features in Mathcad.

Mathcad Enterprise

- Mathcad 11 Enterprise is designed for organizational use of Mathcad, with additional capabilities to support networked or server-based deployment. Mathcad Enterprise supports Microsoft Sharepoint, including networked accessibility, check-in/check-out, version management, and access control.

System Requirements

In order to run Mathcad 11, the following are recommended or required:

- PC with Pentium/Celeron processor running at 233 MHz. 300 MHz or higher recommended.
- Windows 98 SE, Me, NT 4.0 SP6, 2000 SP2, XP or higher.
- Minimum 96 MB of RAM. 256 MB or higher recommended.
- SVGA or higher graphics card and monitor.
- At least 150 MB disk space.
- Internet Explorer, version 5.5 or higher is required for full functionality of the Help system, accessing HTML content within the Resources window, the opening and saving of web-based files, and automatic product activation. IE 6 can be installed from the CD. IE does not need to be your default browser.
- CD-ROM drive or DVD drive.
- Keyboard and mouse or compatible pointing device.

Direct Internet connection or Internet access through a service provider is recommended.

Installation

Note The installation of Mathcad 11 requires the uninstallation of any previous versions of Mathcad from your computer before installing the new version. We have found that running more than one version of Mathcad from the same computer can lead to instability and unexpected behaviors. To uninstall previous versions of Mathcad, use "Add/Remove Programs" from your Windows **Start** menu under **Settings⇒Control Panel**.

Instructions in this section are intended for single-user editions of Mathcad 11. Enterprise Edition users should refer to the **Installation and License Management Guide** included with your copy of Mathcad for installation instructions.

To Install Mathcad

1. Insert the Mathcad CD into your CD-ROM drive. The first time you do this, the CD will automatically start the installation program. If the installation program does not start automatically, you can start it by choosing **Run** from the Start menu and typing **D:\SETUP** (where "**D:**" is your CR-ROM drive). Click "OK."
2. Click the Mathcad button on the main installation page.
3. When prompted, enter your product code, located on the back of the CD envelope.
4. Follow the remaining on-screen instructions.

To install other items from the Mathcad CD, such as Internet Explorer or Acrobat Reader, click the button for that item on the main installation page.

Activating Your Installation

When you finish installing Mathcad, you will be prompted to activate your installation. If you opt to do so, Mathcad will be launched to activate your installed copy. Activation ensures that you have purchased a valid licensed copy of Mathcad and can be done *automatically* if you have an active Internet connection. If you have Internet access on your computer, but not an active Internet connection, you should initiate one before attempting activation.

If you opt to activate Mathcad *manually*, you will need to provide the following information to Mathsoft Engineering and Education, Inc. by using the form provided in **contact.txt**, available from the Activation Wizard:

- Your email address.
- The product you are registering (in this case, Mathcad 11).
- Your License Number*.
- Your Product Code.
- Your Request Code*.

Entries marked with an "*" are available only from the Activation Wizard. Information submitted during activation is used only to process your request, and is not stored or used for any other purposes.

Once you fill out your copy of **contact.txt**, submit the information to Mathsoft. Users in the US and Canada may do so by either:

- Faxing a copy of **contact.txt** to **1-617-444-8001**.
- Emailing a copy of **contact.txt** to **activation@mathsoft.com**.
- Phoning **1-800-827-1263** and supplying the information from **contact.txt** when prompted.

If you purchased Mathcad outside the U.S. and Canada, please contact your local authorized Mathcad distributor for your activation code. Contact information for Mathcad distributors is available at:

http://www.mathcad.com/buy/International_Contacts.asp

If you do not have Web access you can contact Mathsoft International for assistance at:

- Email: activation@Mathsoft.co.uk
- Fax: +44 (0)1276 475552
- Telephone: +44 (0)1276 450850

Once you receive your Activation Key, return to the Activation Wizard and attempt a manual activation. Click "Next" until you reach the **Enter Your Activation Key** page, then enter the Activation Key you received. Once the Activation Key is accepted, your installation of Mathcad will be activated and ready to use.

Questions about Activation

Mathsoft has implemented activation to ensure that you have purchased a valid licensed copy of Mathcad.

Activation does not transfer any other personal information from your computer. Mathsoft product activation is completely anonymous and is only used to authenticate your license.

Activation allows you to install Mathcad on both your work computer and a home computer used for work or laptop. Most hardware and software upgrades to your computer will not require reactivation, and you can reinstall Mathcad on the same machine without using up an additional activation.

Note Activation installs a **C_DILLA** folder on your C-drive with your license for Mathcad use. If you delete the **C_DILLA** folder you may have to contact to Mathsoft to restore your activation.

If your computer's hardware has changed substantially you may have to contact Mathsoft to reactivate.

Technical Support

Mathsoft provides free technical support for individual users of Mathcad 11. Please visit the Support area of www.mathcad.com for more information regarding our support policies as well as our searchable knowledge base.

U.S. and Canada

*   Web: http://support.mathsoft.com
*   e-mail: support@mathsoft.com
*   automated solution center: 617-444-8102
*   FAX: 617-444-8101

International

If you reside outside the US and Canada, please contact your local authorized Mathcad distributor for technical support. Their contact details can be found at: http://www.mathcad.com/buy/International_Contacts.asp.

If you do not have web access you can contact Mathsoft International direct for assistance at:

*   E-mail: help@Mathsoft.co.uk
*   Fax: +44 (0)1276 475552
*   Telephone: +44 (0)1276 450850

Site Licenses

Contact Mathsoft or your local distributor for information about technical support plans for site licenses.

Chapter 2
Getting Started with Mathcad

- ◆ The Mathcad Workspace
- ◆ Regions
- ◆ A Simple Calculation
- ◆ Definitions and Variables
- ◆ Entering Text
- ◆ Iterative Calculations
- ◆ Graphs
- ◆ Saving, Printing, and Exiting

The Mathcad Workspace

For information on system requirements and how to install Mathcad on your computer, refer to Chapter 1, "Welcome to Mathcad."

When you start Mathcad, you'll see a window like that shown in Figure 2-1. By default the worksheet area is white.

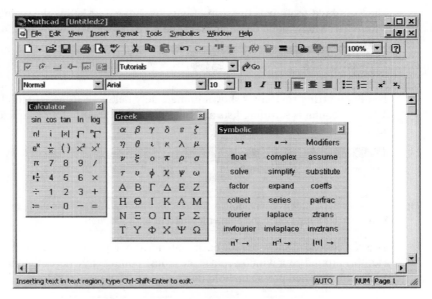

Figure 2-1: Mathcad with various toolbars displayed.

Each button in the **Math toolbar**, shown in Figure 2-1, opens another toolbar of operators or symbols. You can insert many operators, Greek letters, and plots by clicking the buttons found on these toolbars:

Button   Opens math toolbar...

Calculator: Common arithmetic operators.

Graph: Various two- and three-dimensional plot types and graph tools.

Matrix: Matrix and vector operators.

Evaluation: Equal signs for evaluation and definition.

Calculus: Derivatives, integrals, limits, and iterated sums and products.

Boolean: Comparative and logical operators for Boolean expression.

Programming: Programming constructs.

Greek: Greek letters.

Symbolic: Symbolic keywords.

The **Standard toolbar** is the strip of buttons shown just below the main menus in Figure 2-1. Many menu commands can be accessed quickly by using these buttons.

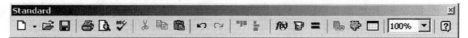

The **Formatting toolbar** is shown immediately below the Standard toolbar in Figure 2-1. This contains scrolling lists and buttons used to specify font characteristics in equations and text.

Tip   To learn what a button on any toolbar does, let the mouse pointer rest on the button momentarily. You'll see a tooltip beside the pointer giving a brief description.

You can choose to show or hide each toolbar from the **View** menu. To detach and drag a toolbar around your window, place the mouse pointer anywhere other than on a button or a text box. Then press and hold down the mouse button and drag.

Tip   You can customize the Standard, Formatting, and Math toolbars. To add and remove buttons, right click on the toolbar and choose **Customize** from the popup menu.

Working with Worksheets

When you start Mathcad, you open up a Mathcad *worksheet*. You can have as many worksheets open as your available system resources allow.

There are times when a Mathcad worksheet cannot be displayed in its entirety because the window is too small. To bring unseen portions of a worksheet into view, you can:

- Expand the window as you do in other Windows applications.

- Choose **Zoom** from the **View** menu or click [100% ▼] on the Standard toolbar and choose a number smaller than 100%.

Tip   Mathcad supports the Microsoft IntelliMouse and compatible pointing devices. Turning the wheel scrolls the window one line vertically for each click of the wheel. When you press [**Shift**] and turn the wheel, the window scrolls horizontally.

See "Appendix I: Arrow and Movement Keys" on page 445 in the Appendices for keystrokes for moving the cursor. If you are working with a longer worksheet, use **Go to Page** from the **Edit** menu to move quickly through the worksheet.

Tip   Mathcad supports standard Windows keystrokes for operations such as file opening, [**Ctrl**]O, saving, [**Ctrl**]S, printing, [**Ctrl**]P, copying, [**Ctrl**]C, and pasting, [**Ctrl**]V. Choose **Preferences** from the **Tools** menu and uncheck "Standard Windows shortcut keys" in the General tab to use shortcut keys supported in early versions of Mathcad.

Regions

Mathcad lets you enter equations, text, and plots anywhere in the worksheet. Each equation, piece of text, or other element is a *region*. Mathcad creates an invisible rectangle to hold each region. A Mathcad worksheet is a collection of such regions. To start a new region in Mathcad:

1. Click anywhere in a blank area of the worksheet. You see a small crosshair. Anything you type appears at the crosshair.

   [+]

2. If the region you want to create is a math region, just start typing anywhere you put the crosshair. By default Mathcad understands what you type as mathematics. See "A Simple Calculation" on page 16 for an example.

3. To create a text region, first choose **Text Region** from the **Insert** menu and then start typing. See "Entering Text" on page 18 for an example.

In addition to equations and text, Mathcad supports a variety of plot regions. See "Graphs" on page 21.

Tip   Mathcad displays a box around any region you are currently working in. When you click outside the region, the surrounding box disappears. To put a permanent box around a region or regions, select them, then right click and choose **Properties** from the popup menu. Click on the Display tab and check the box next to "Show Border."

Selecting Regions

To select a single region, simply click it. Mathcad shows a rectangle around the region.

To select multiple regions:

1. Press and hold down the left mouse button to anchor one corner of the selection rectangle.

2. Without letting go of the mouse button, move the mouse to enclose everything you want inside the selection rectangle.

3. Release the mouse button. Mathcad shows dashed rectangles around the regions you have selected.

Tip   You can also select a single region or disconnected regions anywhere in the worksheet by holding down the [**Ctrl**] key while clicking on each region. If you click one region and [**Shift**]-click another, you select both regions and all regions in between.

Region Properties

The **Region Properties** dialog box allows you to perform the following actions, depending on the type of region you've selected:

• Highlight the region.

• Display a border around the region.

• Assign a tag to the region.

• Restore the region to original size.

• Widen a region to the entire page width.

• Automatically move everything down in the worksheet below the region when the region wraps at the right margin.

• Disable/enable evaluation of the region.

• Optimize an equation.

• Turn protection on/off for the region.

You can change the properties of a region or regions by right clicking and choosing **Properties** from the menu.

Tip   You can change the properties for multiple regions by selecting the regions you want to change, and either selecting **Properties** from the **Format** menu or by right clicking on one of the regions and choosing **Properties** from the menu.

Note   When you select multiple regions, you may only change the properties common to the regions selected. If you select both math and text regions, you will not be able to change text-only or math-only options, such as "Occupy Page Width" or "Disable/Enable Evaluation".

Moving and Copying Regions

Once the regions are selected, you can move or copy them.

Moving regions

You can move regions by dragging with the mouse, *nudging* with the arrow keys, or by using **Cut** and **Paste**.

To drag regions with the mouse:

1. Select the regions.
2. Place the pointer on the border of any selected region. The pointer turns into a small hand.
3. Press and hold down the mouse button.
4. Without letting go of the button, move the mouse. The rectangular outlines of the selected regions follow the mouse pointer.

Dragging regions. To move the selected regions into another worksheet, press and hold down the mouse button, drag the rectangular outlines into the destination worksheet, and release the mouse button.

Nudging Regions. To nudge the regions, first select them to get a dotted line around them. If you want to select a single region, press [**Ctrl**] and then click on the region. Then you can use the arrows keys to nudge them in different directions.

To move the selected regions by using **Cut** and **Paste**:

1. Select the regions.
2. Choose **Cut** from the **Edit** menu, [**Ctrl**] **X**, or click ✄ on the Standard toolbar. This deletes the selected regions and puts them on the Clipboard.
3. Click the mouse wherever you want the regions moved. Make sure you've clicked in an empty space.
4. Choose **Paste** from the **Edit** menu, [**Ctrl**] **V**, or click 📋 on the Standard toolbar.

Note   You can move one region on top of another. To move a particular region to the top or bottom, right click on it and choose **Bring to Front** or **Send to Back** from the popup menu.

Copying Regions

To copy regions by using the **Copy** and **Paste** commands:

1. Select the regions.
2. Choose **Copy** from the **Edit** menu, [**Ctrl**] **C**, or click 📋 on the Standard toolbar to copy the selected regions to the Clipboard.
3. Click the mouse wherever you want to place a copy of the regions. Make sure you've clicked in an empty space and that you see the crosshair.
4. Choose **Paste** from the **Edit** menu, [**Ctrl**] **V**.

Tip   If the regions you want to copy are coming from a locked area (see "Safeguarding an Area of the Worksheet" on page 85) or an E-book, you can copy them simply by dragging them with the mouse into your worksheet.

Deleting Regions

To delete one or more regions:

1. Select the regions.

2. Choose **Cut** from the **Edit** menu, [**Ctrl**] **X**.

Choosing **Cut** removes the selected regions from your worksheet and puts them on the Clipboard. If you don't want to disturb the contents of your Clipboard, or if you don't want to save the selected regions, choose **Delete** from the **Edit** menu or press [**Ctrl**] **D** instead.

A Simple Calculation

Although Mathcad can perform sophisticated mathematics, you can easily use it as a simple calculator. To try your first calculation, follow these steps:

1. Click anywhere in the worksheet. You see a small crosshair. Anything you type appears at the crosshair.

2. Type **15-8/104.5=**. When you type the equal sign or click $=$ on the **Evaluation** toolbar, Mathcad computes the result.

$$15 - \frac{8}{104.5} = 14.923$$

This calculation demonstrates the way Mathcad works:

- Mathcad sizes fraction bars, brackets, and other symbols to display equations the same way you might see them in a book or on a blackboard.

- Mathcad understands which operation to perform first. In this example, Mathcad knew to perform the division before the subtraction and displayed the equation accordingly.

- As soon as you type the equal sign or click $=$ on the Evaluation toolbar, Mathcad returns the result. Unless you specify otherwise, Mathcad processes each equation as you enter it. See the section "Controlling Calculation" in Chapter 8 to learn how to change this.

- As you type each operator (in this case, – and /), Mathcad shows a small rectangle called a *placeholder*. Placeholders hold spaces open for numbers or expressions not yet typed. As soon as you type a number, it replaces the placeholder in the expression. The placeholder that appears at the end of the expression is used for unit conversions. Its use is discussed in "Displaying Units of Results" on page 115.

Once an equation is on the screen, you can edit it by clicking in the appropriate spot and typing new letters, numbers, or operators. You can type many operators and Greek letters by clicking in the math toolbars introduced in "The Mathcad Workspace" on page 11. Chapter 4, "Working with Math," details how to edit Mathcad equations.

Definitions and Variables

Mathcad's power and versatility quickly become apparent once you begin using *variables* and *functions*. By defining variables and functions, you can link equations together and use intermediate results in further calculations.

Defining Variables

To define a variable t, follow these steps:

1. Type **t** followed by a colon **:** or click on the Calculator toolbar. Mathcad shows the colon as the definition symbol **:=**.

$$t := \blacksquare$$

2. Type **10** in the empty placeholder to complete the definition for t.

$$t := 10$$

If you make a mistake, click on the equation and press [**Space**] until the entire expression is between the two editing lines, just as you did earlier. Then delete it by choosing **Cut** from the **Edit** menu ([**Ctrl**] **X**). See Chapter 4, "Working with Math," for other ways to edit an expression.

These steps show the form for typing any definition:

1. Type the variable name to be defined.

2. Type the colon key **:** or click on the Calculator toolbar to insert the definition symbol.

3. Type the value to be assigned to the variable. The value can be a single number or a more complicated combination of numbers and previously defined variables.

Mathcad worksheets read from top to bottom and left to right. Once you have defined a variable like t, you can compute with it anywhere *below and to the right* of the equation that defines it.

Now enter another definition:

1. Press [↵]. This moves the crosshair below the first equation.

2. To define acc as –9.8, type: **acc:-9.8**. Then press [↵] again. Mathcad shows the crosshair cursor below the last equation you entered.

$$t := 10$$
$$acc := -9.8$$
+

Calculating Results

Now that the variables acc and t are defined, you can use them in other expressions:

1. Click the mouse a few lines below the two definitions.

2. Type **acc/2[Space]*t^2**. The caret symbol (^) represents raising to a power, the asterisk (*) is multiplication, and the slash (/) represents division.

3. Press the equal sign [=].

$$t := 10$$
$$acc := -9.8$$
$$\frac{acc}{2} \cdot t^2 = -490 \quad \blacksquare$$

This equation calculates the distance traveled by a falling body in time t with acceleration *acc*. When you enter the equation and press the equal sign [=], or click ▨= on the **Evaluation** toolbar, Mathcad returns the result.

Mathcad updates results as soon as you make changes. For example, if you click on the 10 on your screen and change it to some other number, Mathcad changes the result as soon as you press [**Enter**] or click outside of the equation.

Entering Text

Mathcad handles text as easily as it does equations, so you can make notes while calculating.

Here's how to enter text:

1. Click in the blank space to the right of the equations you entered. You'll see a small crosshair.

2. Choose **Text Region** from the **Insert** menu, or press **"** (the double-quote key), to tell Mathcad that you're about to enter some text. Mathcad changes the crosshair into a vertical line called the insertion point. Characters you type appear behind this line. A box surrounds the insertion point, indicating you are now in a text region. This box is called a text box. It grows as you enter text.

3. Type **Equations of motion**. The text appears in the worksheet.

Note If **Ruler** under the **View** menu is checked when the cursor is inside a text region, the ruler resizes to indicate the size of your text region. To use the ruler to set tab stops and indents in a text region, see "Changing Paragraph Properties" on page 69.

Tip If you click in blank space in the worksheet and start typing, which creates a math region, Mathcad automatically converts the math region to a text region when you press [**Space**].

To enter a second line of text:

1. Press [↵].

2. Then type **for falling body under gravity**.

3. Click in a different spot in the worksheet or press [**Ctrl**][**Shift**][↵] to move out of the text region. The text box disappears and the cursor appears as a small crosshair.

Note Use [**Ctrl**][**Shift**][↵] to move out of the text region to a blank space in your worksheet. If you press [↵], Mathcad inserts a line break in the *current* text region instead.

You can set the width of a text region and change the font, size, and style of the text in it. (See Chapter 6, "Working with Text.")

Iterative Calculations

Mathcad can do repeated or iterative calculations as easily as individual calculations by using a special variable called a *range variable*.

Range variables take on a range of values, such as all the integers from 0 to 10. Whenever a range variable appears in a Mathcad equation, Mathcad calculates the equation not just once, but once for each value of the range variable.

Creating a Range Variable

To compute equations for a range of values, first create a range variable. In the problem shown in "Calculating Results" on page 17, for example, you can compute results for a range of values of *t* from 10 to 20 in steps of 1.

To do so, follow these steps:

1. First, change *t* into a range variable by editing its definition. Click on the **10** in the equation **t:=10**. The insertion point should be next to the 10 as shown.

    $$t := 10$$

2. Type **,11**. This tells Mathcad that the next number in the range will be 11.

    $$t := 10, 11$$

3. Type **;** for the range variable operator, or click 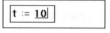 on the Matrix toolbar, and then type the last number, **20**. This tells Mathcad that the last number in the range will be 20. Mathcad shows the range variable operator as a pair of dots.

    $$t := 10, 11 .. 20$$

    $$\frac{acc}{2} \cdot t^2 =$$

-490
-592.9
-705.6
-828.1
-960.4
$-1.103 \cdot 10^3$
$-1.254 \cdot 10^3$
$-1.416 \cdot 10^3$
$-1.588 \cdot 10^3$
$-1.769 \cdot 10^3$
$-1.96 \cdot 10^3$

4. Now click outside the equation for *t*. Mathcad begins to compute with *t* defined as a range variable. Since *t* now takes on eleven different values, there must also be eleven different answers. These are displayed in an *output table* as shown at right.

Defining a Function

Here's how to add a function definition to your worksheet:

1. First delete the table if you are in the same worksheet. Now define the function *d(t)* by typing **d(t):**

    $$d(t) := \blacksquare$$

2. Complete the definition by typing this expression:
    1600+acc/2[Space]*t^2[↵]

The definition you just typed defines a function. The function name is *d*, and the argument of the function is *t*. You can use this function to evaluate the above expression for different values of *t*. To do so, simply replace *t* with an appropriate number. For example:

1. To evaluate the function at a particular value, such as 3.5, type **d (3 . 5) =**. Mathcad returns the correct value as shown at right.

$$d(3.5) = 1.54 \times 10^3$$

2. To evaluate the function once for each value of the range variable *t* you defined earlier, click below the other equations and type **d (t) =**. Mathcad shows a table of values, as shown at right.

$$d(t) =$$

$1.11 \cdot 10^3$
$1.007 \cdot 10^3$
894.4
771.9
639.6
497.5
345.6
183.9
12.4
-168.9
-360

Formatting a Result

You can set the display format for any number Mathcad calculates and displays. This means changing the number of decimal places shown, changing exponential notation to ordinary decimal notation, and so on.

For example, in the example above, the first two values, $1.11 \cdot 10^3$ and $1.007 \cdot 10^3$, are in exponential (powers of 10) notation. Here's how to change the table produced above so that none of the numbers in it are displayed in exponential notation:

1. Click anywhere on the table with the mouse.

2. Choose **Result** from the **Format** menu. You see the Result Format dialog box. This box contains settings that affect how results are displayed, including the number of decimal places, the use of exponential notation, the radix, and so on.

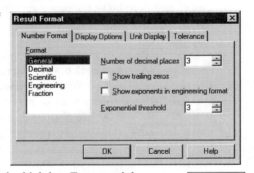

3. The default format scheme is General which has Exponential Threshold set to 3. This means that only numbers greater than or equal to 10^3 are displayed in exponential notation. Click the arrows to the right of the 3 to increase the Exponential Threshold to 6.

4. Click "OK." The table changes to reflect the new result format. (See "Formatting Results" on page 112.)

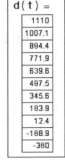

$$d(t) =$$

1110
1007.1
894.4
771.9
639.6
497.5
345.6
183.9
12.4
-168.9
-360

Note When you format a result, only the display of the result is affected. Mathcad maintains full precision internally (up to 15 digits).

Graphs

Mathcad provides two-dimensional Cartesian and polar graphs, contour plots, surface plots, and a variety of other three-dimensional graphs. This section describes how to create a simple two-dimensional graph showing the points calculated in the previous section.

Creating a Basic Graph

To create an X-Y plot:

1. Click in your worksheet.

2. Choose **Graph⇒X-Y Plot** from the **Insert** menu or click 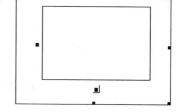 on the Graph toolbar. Alternatively, type **[Shift]2** or **@**. Mathcad inserts a blank X-Y plot.

3. Fill in both the *x*-axis placeholder (bottom center) and the *y*-axis placeholder (left center) with a function, expression, or variable.

4. Click outside the plot or press **[Enter]**.

Mathcad automatically chooses axis limits for you. If you want to specify the axis limits yourself, click in the plot and type over the numbers in the placeholders at the ends of the axes.

Mathcad creates the plot over a default range using default limits. See "Formatting a 2D Plot" on page 168 for how to modify these defaults. For detailed information on graphs, see Chapter 11, "2D Plots."

Formatting a Graph

When you first create a graph it has *default* characteristics: numbered linear axes, no grid lines, and points connected with solid lines. You can change these characteristics by *formatting* the graph. To format the graph created previously:

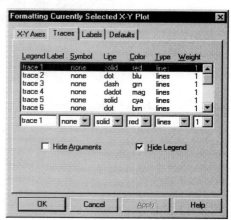

1. Click on the graph and choose **Graph⇒X-Y Plot** from the **Format** menu, or double-click the graph to bring up the formatting dialog box. To learn more about these settings, see Chapter 11, "2D Plots."

2. Click the Traces tab.

3. Click "trace 1" in the scrolling list under "Legend Label." Mathcad places the current settings for trace 1 in the boxes under the corresponding columns of the scrolling list.

4. Click the arrow under the "Type" column to see a drop-down list of trace types. Select "bar" from this drop-down list.

5. Mathcad shows the graph as a bar chart instead of connecting the points with lines. Note that the sample line under the *d*(*t*) now has a bar on top of it.

6. Click outside the graph to deselect it.

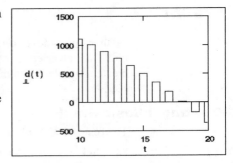

Saving, Printing, and Exiting

Once you've created a worksheet, you will probably want to save or print it.

Saving a Worksheet

To save a worksheet:

1. Choose **Save** from the **File** menu (keystroke: **[Ctrl] S**) or click 🖫 on the Standard toolbar. If the file has never been saved before, the **Save As** dialog box appears.

2. Type the name of the file in the text box provided. To save to another folder, locate the folder using the **Save As...** dialog box.

By default Mathcad saves the file in Mathcad (MCD) format, but you have the option of saving in other formats, such as HTML, as RTF for Microsoft Word, as a template for future Mathcad worksheets, or in a format compatible with earlier Mathcad versions. To save as HTML, choose **Save as Web Page** under the **File** menu. (See Chapter 7, "Worksheet Management.")

Printing

To print, choose **Print** from the **File** menu or click 🖨 on the Standard toolbar. To

preview the printed page, choose **Print Preview** from the **File** menu or click 🔍 on the Standard toolbar.(See Chapter 7, "Worksheet Management.")

Exiting Mathcad

To quit Mathcad choose **Exit** from the **File** menu. If you have moved any toolbars, Mathcad remembers their locations for the next time you open the application.

Note To close an individual worksheet while keeping Mathcad open, choose **Close** from the **File** menu.

Chapter 3
Online Resources

- ◆ Mathcad Resources
- ◆ Resources Window and E-books
- ◆ Help
- ◆ Collaboratory User Forums
- ◆ Other Resources

Mathcad Resources

Note Help resources need to be installed from your CD. If you chose Custom Install and did not install all of these resources, you can find them on your Mathcad CD.

Help Menu Resources:

- **Tutorials** includes both *Getting Started Primers* and *Features In-depth*.

- **QuickSheets** are live examples that you can manipulate to see how to use Mathcad functions, graphs, and programming. *Using Mathcad with Other Applications* helps you connect Mathcad to other applications and use Mathcad custom controls.

- **Reference Tables** provides you with physical constant tables, chemical and physical data, and mathematical formulas.

- **Mathcad Help** contains complete help on every feature of Mathcad with links to live examples.

- The **Author's Reference** covers creating E-books in Mathcad; and exporting Mathcad files in RTF for Microsoft Word and HTML formats for distribution to non-Mathcad audiences.

- The **Developer's Reference** provides information about developing customized Mathcad components, specialized OLE objects, and controls that allow you to access functions from other applications and data from remote sources. The **Developer's Reference** also documents Mathcad's Object Model, allowing you to access Mathcad's functionality from another application or an OLE container.

Resources Window and E-books

If you learn best from examples, want information you can put to work immediately in your Mathcad worksheets, or wish to access any page on the Web from within Mathcad, open the **Resources** toolbar or open *Tutorials, QuickSheets,* or *Reference Tables* from the **Help** menu. The Resources window and Mathcad E-books appear as custom windows with their own menus and toolbar, as shown in Figure 3-1.

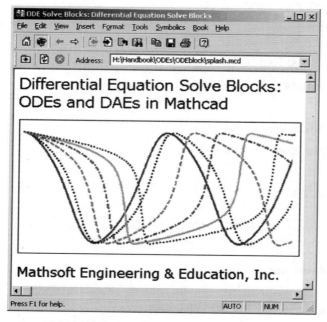

Figure 3-1: E-book window and toolbar.

Note A number of Mathcad E-books, which you can download and use, are available in the Web Library on *www.mathcad.com*. In addition, a variety of Mathcad E-books are available from the Mathsoft Webstore at **http://www.webstore.mathsoft.com** or your local distributor or software reseller. To open an E-book, choose Open Book under **E-books** in the **Help** menu and browse to find the location of the E-book (HBK) file. E-books install to a Handbook folder in the directory where you have installed Mathcad. Once you have restarted Mathcad, they will be listed under E-books in the Help menu. If you create your own E-books, you may have to create a Handbook folder.

Finding Information in an E-book

As in other hypertext systems, you move around a Mathcad E-book simply by clicking on icons or underlined text. You can also use the buttons on the toolbar at the top of the E-book and Resources window to navigate within the E-book:

Button	Function
	Links to the home page or welcome page for the E-book.
	Opens a toolbar for entering a Web address.
	Backtracks to whatever document was last viewed.
	Reverses the last backtrack.
	Goes backward one section.
	Goes forward one section.
	Displays a list of documents most recently viewed.
	Searches the E-book for a particular term.
	Copies selected regions to the Clipboard.
	Saves current section of the E-book.
	Prints current section of the E-book.

Mathcad keeps a record of where you've been in the E-book. When you click ⇐ , Mathcad backtracks through your navigation history in the book. Backtracking is especially useful when you have left the main navigation sequence of a worksheet to look at a hyperlinked cross-reference.

If you don't want to go back one section at a time, click 🔳 to open a History dialog from which you can jump to any section you viewed since you first opened the E-book.

E-book search

In addition to using hypertext links to find topics in an E-book, you can search for topics or phrases. To do so:

1. Click 🔭 to open the Search dialog box.

2. Type a word or phrase in the "Search for" text box. Select a word or phrase and click "Search" to see a list of topics containing that entry and the number of times it occurs in each topic.

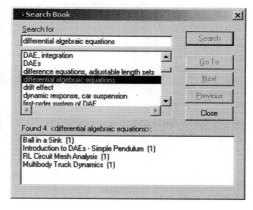

3. Choose a topic and click "Go To." Mathcad opens the section containing the entry you want to search for. Click "Next" or "Previous" to see the next or previous occurrence of the entry.

Annotating an E-book

A Mathcad E-book is made up of fully interactive Mathcad worksheets. You can freely edit any math region in an E-book to see the effects of changing a parameter or modifying an equation. You can also enter text, math, or graphics as *annotations* in any section of your E-book, using the menu commands on the E-book window and the Mathcad toolbars.

Tip By default any changes or annotations you make to the E-book are displayed in an annotation highlight color. To change this color, choose **Color**⇒**Annotation** from the **Format** menu. To suppress the highlighting of E-book annotations, remove the check from **Highlight Changes** on the E-book's **Book** menu.

Saving annotations

Changes you make to an E-book are temporary by default: your edits disappear when you close the E-book, and the E-book is restored to its original state. You can choose to save annotations in an E-book by checking **Annotate Book** on the **Book** menu or by right clicking in the E-book window and selecting Annotate Book on the popup menu. You can also choose:

- **Save Section** from the **Book** menu to save annotations you made in the current section, or choose **Save All Changes** to save all changes.

- **View Original Section** to see the E-book section in its original form or choose **View Edited Section** to see your annotations again.

- **Restore Section** to revert to the original section or **Restore All** to delete all annotations you have made to the E-book.

Copying Information from an E-book

There are two ways to copy information from an E-book into your Mathcad worksheet:

- You can use the Clipboard. Select text or equations in the E-book using one of the

    methods described in "Selecting Regions" on page 14, click on the E-book toolbar or choose **Copy** from the **Edit** menu, click in your worksheet, and choose **Paste** from the **Edit** menu.

- You can drag regions from the E-book window and drop them into your worksheet. Select the regions, then click and hold down the mouse button over one of the regions while you drag the group into your worksheet. Release the mouse button to copy the regions into your worksheet.

Web Browsing

You can also use the Resources window to browse to any location on the Web and open Web pages, in addition to Mathcad worksheets and E-books posted on the Web. The Mathcad Web Library contains a number of useful worksheets and e-books.

Note When the Resources window is in Web-browsing mode, Mathcad is using a Web-browsing OLE control provided by Microsoft Internet Explorer. Web browsing in Mathcad requires Microsoft Internet Explorer version 5.5 or higher to be installed on your system, but it does not need to be your default browser.

Microsoft Internet Explorer 6 is available for installation when you install Mathcad. Refer to Microsoft Corporation's Web site at `http://www.microsoft.com/` for support information and to download the latest version.

To browse to any Web page from within the Resources window:

1. Click 🐾 on the Resources toolbar. As shown below, an additional toolbar with an "Address" box appears below the Resources toolbar to indicate that you are now in a Web-browsing mode:

2. In the "Address" box type a Uniform Resource Locator (URL) for a document on the Web. To visit the Mathsoft home page, for example, type `http://www.mathsoft.com/` and press [**Enter**]. If you have Internet access and the server is available, the requested page is loaded in your Resources window. If you do not have a supported version of Microsoft Internet Explorer installed, you must launch a Web browser.

The remaining buttons on the Web Toolbar have the following functions:

Button	Function
📑	Bookmarks current page.
🔁	Reloads the current page.
❌	Interrupts the current file transfer.

Note When you are in Web-browsing mode and right click on the Resources window, Mathcad displays a popup menu with commands appropriate for viewing Web pages. Many of the buttons on the Resources toolbar remain active when you are in Web-browsing mode, so that you can copy, save, or print material you locate on the Web, or backtrack to pages you previously viewed. When you click 🏠, you return to the Home page for the Resources window or E-book and disconnect from the Web.

Tip You can use the Resources window in Web-browsing mode to open Mathcad worksheets anywhere on the Web. Simply type the URL of a Mathcad worksheet in the "Address" box in the Web toolbar.

Help

Mathcad provides several ways to get support on product features through an extensive online Help system. To see Mathcad's online Help at any time, choose **Mathcad Help** from the **Help** menu, click ![?] on the Standard toolbar, or press **[F1]**. Mathcad's Help system is delivered in Microsoft's HTML Help environment, as shown in Figure 3-2.

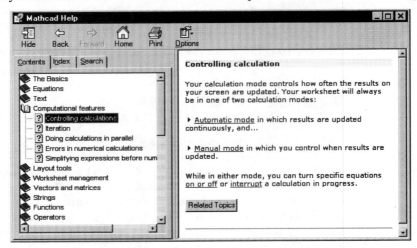

Figure 3-2: Mathcad online Help

You can browse the Explorer view on the Contents tab, look up terms or phrases on the Index tab, or search the entire Help system for a keyword or phrase on the Search tab.

Note To run Help, you must have Internet Explorer 5.5 or higher installed. However, IE does not need to be set as your default browser.

To know what Mathcad menu commands do, hover over the command and read the status bar at the bottom of your window. For toolbar buttons, hold the pointer over the button momentarily to see a tool tip.

Note The status bar in Mathcad is displayed by default. You can hide the status bar by removing the check from **Status Bar** on the **View** menu.

You can also get more detailed help on menu commands, toolbars, built-in functions and operators, and error messages. To do so:

1. Click an error message, a built-in function or variable, or an operator.

2. Press **[F1]** to bring up the relevant Help screen.

To get help on menu commands or on any of the toolbar buttons:

1. Press **[Shift][F1]**. Mathcad changes the pointer into a question mark.

2. Choose a command from the menu. Mathcad opens the relevant Help screen.

3. Click any toolbar button. Mathcad displays the operator's name and a keyboard shortcut in the status bar.

To resume editing, press [**Esc**]. The pointer turns back into an arrow.

| Tip | Choose **Mathcad Tips** from the **Help** menu for a series of helpful hints on using Mathcad. |

Additional Mathcad help

Mathcad includes two other online help references:

*   The **Author's Reference** contains all the information needed to create a Mathcad E-book or to save your files in HTML for posting on the Web.

*   The **Developer's Reference** provides information for using Mathsoft custom Scriptable Object components, Mathsoft Custom Controls, and the Data Acquisition component. See Chapter 14, "Importing and Exporting Data," for details. It also guides advanced Mathcad users through Mathcad's Object Model, which explains the tools needed to access Mathcad's feature set from within another application. Also included are instructions for using C or C++ to create your own functions in Mathcad in the form of DLLs.

Collaboratory User Forums

The Mathcad Collaboratory User Forums consist of a group of forums that allow you to contribute Mathcad or other files, post messages, and download files and read messages contributed by other Mathcad users. You can search the User Forums for messages containing a key word or phrase, be notified of new messages in specific forums, and view only the messages you haven't yet read. You'll find that the User Forums combine some of the best features of an online news group with the convenience of sharing Mathcad worksheets.

Logging in

To open the User Forums, choose **User Forums** from the **Help** menu, or you can open an Internet browser and go directly to the Collaboratory User Forums:

`http://collab.mathsoft.com/~mathcad2000/`

You'll see the Collaboratory User Forums login screen in a browser window:

The first time you come to the login screen of the Collaboratory User Forums, click "New User." This brings you to a form for entering required and optional information.

Note Mathsoft does not use this information for any purposes other than for your participation in the User Forums.

Click "Create" when you are finished filling out the form. Check your email for a message with your login name and password. Go back to the Collaboratory, enter your login name and password given in the email message and click "Log In." You see the main page of the Collaboratory:

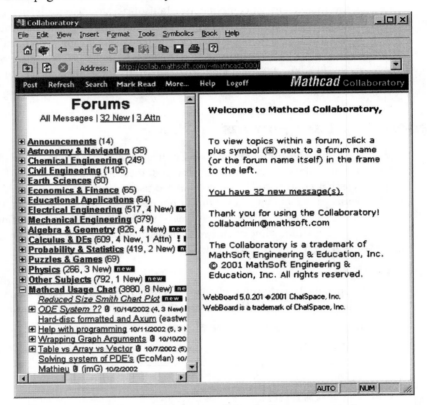

Figure 3-3: Opening the Collaboratory from the Resources window.

A list of forums and messages appears on the left side of the screen. The toolbar at the top of the window gives you access to features such as search and online Help.

Tip After logging in, you may want to change your password to one you will remember. To do so, click **More** on the toolbar at the top of the window, then go to Edit User Profile.

Note Mathsoft maintains the User Forums as a free service, open to all in the Mathcad community. Be sure to read the Agreement posted in the top level of the Collaboratory User Forums for important information and disclaimers.

Reading Messages

When you enter the User Forums Collaboratory, you will see how many messages are new and how many are addressed to your attention. To read any message in any forum:

1. Click on the ⊞ next to the forum name or click on the forum name.

2. Click on a message to read it. Click the ⊞ to the left of a message to see replies underneath it.

3. You can read the message and the replies in the right side of the window.

Messages that you have not yet read are shown in italics. You may also see a "new" icon next to these messages.

Posting Messages

After you enter the User Forums, you can post a new message or reply to existing messages. To do so:

1. Choose **Post** from the toolbar to post a new message. To reply to a message, click **Reply** at the top of the message in the right side of the window. You'll see the post/ reply page in the right side of the window. For example, if you post a new topic message in the Biology forum, you see:

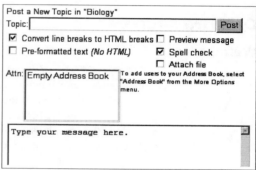

2. Click on the boxes below the title to preview a message, spell check a message, or attach a file.

3. Type your text in the message field.

4. Click "Post" after you finish typing. Depending on the options you selected, the Collaboratory either posts your message immediately or allows you to preview it.

5. If you choose Attach File, a new page will appear. Specify the file type and browse to the file then click "Upload Now."

Note For more information on reading, posting messages, and using other features of the Collaboratory, click **Help** on the Collaboratory toolbar.

To delete a message that you posted, click on it to open it and click Delete in the small toolbar just above the message on the right side of the window.

Searching

You can search the Collaboratory User Forums for messages containing specific words or phrases, messages within a certain date range, or delete messages posted to specific forums.

Changing Your User Information

You may want to change your login name and password or hide your email address. To update this information or change the Collaboratory defaults, you need to edit your profile:

1. Click **More** on the toolbar at the top of the window.
2. Click "Edit Your Profile" and fill out the changed information.

Other Features

To create an address book, mark messages as read, view certain messages, or request automatic email announcements when specific forums have new messages, choose **More** from the toolbar.

The Collaboratory also supports participation via email or a news group. For more information on these and other available features choose **Help** on the toolbar.

Other Resources

Web Library

Accessible at **http://www.mathcad.com/library**, the Mathcad Web Library contains user-contributed documents, E-books, graphics, and animations created in Mathcad. The library is divided into several sections: E-books, Mathcad Files, Gallery, and Puzzles. Files are further categorized as application files (professional problems), education files, graphics, and animations. You can choose a listing by discipline from each section, or you can search for files by keyword or title.

If you wish to contribute files to the library, please email *author@mathsoft.com.*

Online Documentation

The *Mathcad User's Guide* and *Installation Guide* for Enterprise users are available in PDF form from the Windows **Start** menu under **Programs⇒Mathcad**.

Release Notes

Release notes are located in the DOC folder located in your Mathcad folder. They contain the latest information on Mathcad, updates to the documentation, and troubleshooting instructions.

Technical Support

The Technical Support Knowledge Base contains frequently asked questions, samples files, and support resources. These are posted on the Web at www.mathsoft.com/support /

This page has links to past issues of the *Mathcad Advisor Newsletter,* which is filled with useful Mathcad tips.

Downloads on Mathcad.com

Registered users can download updates, Mathcad modules, and other useful tools from the http://www.mathcad.com/download/ site depending on your version of Mathcad.

Chapter 4
Working with Math

♦ Inserting Math
♦ Building Expressions
♦ Editing Expressions
♦ Math Styles

Inserting Math

You can place math expressions anywhere you want in a Mathcad worksheet.

1. Click anywhere in the worksheet. Anything you type appears at the crosshair.

2. Type numbers, letters, and math operators, or insert them by clicking buttons on Mathcad's math toolbars, to create a *math region*.

$$+$$

$$15 - \frac{8}{104.5} = 14.923$$

You'll notice that unlike a word processor, Mathcad by default understands anything you type at the crosshair cursor as math. If you want to create a *text region* instead, see Chapter 6, "Working with Text."

You can also type math expressions in any math *placeholder* that appears. See Chapter 17, "Operators" for more on Mathcad's operators.

Numbers and Complex Numbers

A single number in Mathcad is called a *scalar*. To enter groups of numbers in *arrays*, see "Inserting an Operator" on page 38.

Types of numbers

In math regions, Mathcad interprets anything beginning with one of the digits 0–9 as a number. A digit can be followed by:

• other digits

• a decimal point

• digits after the decimal point

• or appended as a suffix, one of the letters **b**, **h**, or **o**, for binary, hexadecimal, and octal numbers, or **i** or **j** for imaginary numbers. These are discussed in more detail below. See "Appendix G: Suffixes for Numbers" on page 443 for additional suffixes.

Note   Mathcad uses the period (**.**) to signify the decimal point. The comma (**,**) is used to separate values in a range variable definition, as described in "Range Variables" on page 103. So when you enter numbers greater than 999, do not use either a comma or a period to separate digits into groups of three. Simply type the digits one after another. For example, to enter ten thousand, type "**10000**".

Imaginary and complex numbers

To enter an imaginary number, follow it with *i* or *j*, as in **1i** or **2.5j**.

Note You cannot use *i* or *j* alone to represent the imaginary unit. You must always type **1i** or **1j**. If you don't, Mathcad thinks you are referring to a variable named either *i* or *j*. When the cursor is outside an equation that contains 1*i* or 1*j*, however, Mathcad hides the (superfluous) 1.

Although you can enter imaginary numbers followed by either *i* or *j*, Mathcad normally displays them followed by *i*. To have Mathcad display imaginary numbers with *j*, choose **Result** from the **Format** menu, click on the Display Options tab, and set "Imaginary value" to "j(J)." See "Formatting Results" on page 112 for a full description.

Mathcad accepts complex numbers of the form $a + bi$ (or $a + bj$), where *a* and *b* are ordinary numbers.

Binary numbers

To enter a number in binary, follow it with the lowercase letter **b**. For example, **11110000b** represents 240 in decimal. Binary numbers must be less than 2^{31}.

Octal numbers

To enter a number in octal, follow it with the lowercase letter **o**. For example, **25636o** represents 11166 in decimal. Octal numbers must be less than 2^{31}.

Hexadecimal numbers

To enter a number in hexadecimal, follow it with the lowercase letter **h**. For example, **2b9eh** represents 11166 in decimal. To represent digits above 9, use the upper or lowercase letters **A** through **F**. To enter a hexadecimal number that begins with a letter, you must begin it with a leading zero. If you don't, Mathcad will think it's a variable name. For example, use **0a3h** (delete the implied multiplication symbol between **0** and **a**) rather than **a3h** to represent the decimal number 163 in hexadecimal. Hexadecimal numbers must be less than 2^{31}.

Exponential notation

To enter very large or very small numbers in exponential notation, just multiply a number by a power of 10. For example, to represent the number $3 \cdot 10^8$, type **3*10^8**.

Vectors and Matrices

In Mathcad a column of numbers is a *vector* and a rectangular array of numbers is called a *matrix*. The general term for a vector or matrix is an *array*. The term "vector" refers to a *column vector*. A column vector is simply a matrix with one column. You can also create a *row vector* by creating a matrix with one row and many columns. There are a number of ways to create an array in Mathcad. See Chapter 5, "Vectors, Matrices, and Data Arrays" for more information.

Tip You may wish to distinguish between the names of matrices, vectors, and scalars by font. Names of vectors could be set in bold while setting scalars in italic. See "Math Styles" on page 50.

Strings

Although in most cases the math expressions or variables you work with in Mathcad are numbers or arrays, you can also work with *strings* (also called *string literals* or *string variables*). Strings can include any character you can type at the keyboard, including letters, numbers, punctuation, and spacing, as well as a variety of special symbols as listed in "Appendix K: ASCII codes" on page 447. Strings differ from variable names or numbers because Mathcad always displays them between double quotes. You can assign a string to a variable name, use a string as an element of a vector or matrix, or use a string as the argument to a function.

To create a string:

1. Click on an empty math placeholder usually on the right-hand side of a variable definition.

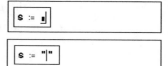

2. Type the double-quote (") key to get a pair of quotes with an insertion line between them.

3. Type any combination of letters, numbers, punctuation, or spaces. Click outside the expression or press the right arrow key (→) twice when you are finished.

s := "The result 5 is valid|"

To enter a special character corresponding to one of the ASCII codes:

1. Click to position the insertion point in the string.

2. Hold down the [**Alt**] key, and type the number "0" followed immediately by the number of the ASCII code *using the numeric keypad* in number-entry mode.

3. Release the [**Alt**] key to see the symbol in the string.

For example, to enter the degree symbol (°) in a string, press [**Alt**] and type "0176" using the numeric keypad.

Note The double-quote key (") has a variety of meanings in Mathcad, depending on the exact location of the cursor in your worksheet. When you want to enter a string, you must *always* have a blank placeholder selected.

Valid strings include expressions such as "Invalid input: try a number less than -5," and "Meets stress requirements." A string in Mathcad, while not limited in size, always appears as a single line of text. Note that a string such as "123" is understood by Mathcad to be a string of characters rather than the number 123.

Tip Strings are especially useful for generating custom error messages in programs, as described in Chapter 15, "Extending and Automating Mathcad." Other string handling functions are listed in "String Functions" on page 256. You can use strings to specify system paths for arguments to some Mathcad built-in functions. (See "File Access Functions" on page 250.)

Names

A *name* in Mathcad is simply a sequence of characters you type referring to a variable or function used in computations. Mathcad distinguishes between two kinds of names:

- Built-in names.
- User-defined names.

Built-in names

Mathcad's built-in names include built-in *variables* and built-in *functions*.

- Some *predefined* or *built-in* variables either have a conventional value, like π (3.14159...) or *e* (2.71828...), or are used as system variables to control how Mathcad performs calculations. (See "Built-in Variables" on page 100.)

- In addition to these predefined variables, Mathcad treats the names of all built-in *units* as predefined variables. For example, Mathcad recognizes the name "A" as the ampere, "m" as the meter, "s" as the second, and so on. Choose **Unit** from the **Insert** menu or click on the Standard toolbar to insert one of Mathcad's predefined units. (See "Units and Dimensions" on page 109.)

- Choose **Function** from the **Insert** menu or click on the Standard toolbar to insert one of Mathcad's built-in functions. (See "Built-in Functions" on page 249.)

User-defined variable and function names

Names in Mathcad can contain any of the following characters:

- Uppercase and lowercase letters.
- The digits 0 through 9.
- The underscore (_).
- The prime symbol ('). Note that this is not the same as an apostrophe. The prime symbol is on the same key as the tilde (~) or press [**Ctrl**][**F7**] to insert it.
- The percent symbol (**%**).
- Greek letters. To insert a Greek letter, click a button on the Greek toolbar or type the equivalent roman letter and press [**Ctrl**]**G**. (See "Greek letters" on page 37.)
- The infinity symbol ∞ is inserted by clicking on the Calculus toolbar or by typing [**Ctrl**][**Shift**]**Z**.
- The following are examples of valid names:

  ```
  alpha               b
  xyz700              A1_B2_C3_D4%%%
  F1'                 a%%
  ```

The following restrictions apply to variable names:

- A name cannot start with one of the digits 0 through 9. Mathcad interprets anything beginning with a digit as either an imaginary number ($2i$ or $3j$), a binary, octal, or hexadecimal number (e.g., 5o, 7h), or as a number *times* a variable ($3 \cdot x$).

- The infinity symbol ∞ can only appear as the first character in a name.

- Any characters you type after a period (.) appear as a subscript. (See "Literal subscripts" on page 37.)

- All characters in a name must be in the same font, have the same point size, and be in the same style (italic, bold, etc.). Greek letters can, however, appear in any variable name. (See "Math Styles" on page 50.)

- Mathcad does not distinguish between variable names and function names. Thus, if you define $f(x)$, and later on you define the variable f, you will find that you cannot use $f(x)$ anywhere below the definition for f.

- Although you can redefine Mathcad's names for built-in functions, constants, and units, keep in mind that their built-in meanings will no longer exist after the definition. For example, if you define a variable *mean*, Mathcad's built-in function *mean*(**v**) can no longer be used.

Note Mathcad distinguishes between uppercase and lowercase letters. For example, *diam* is a different variable from *DIAM*. Mathcad also distinguishes between names in different fonts, as discussed in "Math Styles" on page 50. Thus, *Diam* is also a different variable from **Diam**.

Tip To type symbols such as $ in a name, press [**Ctrl**][**Shift**]**K**, type the symbol(s), and type [**Ctrl**][**Shift**]**K** again.

Greek letters

There are two ways to enter a Greek variable name:

- Click the letter on the Greek toolbar. To see this toolbar, click **αβ** on the Math toolbar or choose **Toolbars⇒Greek** from the **View** menu.

- Type the *Roman equivalent* of the Greek symbol and then press [**Ctrl**]**G**. For example, to enter φ, press **f** [**Ctrl**] **G**. See "Appendix H: Greek Letters" on page 444 in the Appendices for a table of Greek letters and their Roman equivalents.

Note Although many uppercase Greek letters look like ordinary capital letters, they are *not* the same. Mathcad distinguishes between Greek and Roman letters, even if they appear the same.

Tip The Greek letter π can also be typed by pressing [**Ctrl**][**Shift**]**P**.

Literal subscripts

If you include a period in a variable name, Mathcad displays whatever follows the period as a subscript. You can use these *literal subscripts* to create variables with names like vel_{init} and u_{air}.

To create a literal subscript:

1. Type the text that appears before the subscript.

2. Type a period (**.**) followed by text that is to become the subscript.

Note Do not confuse literal subscripts with *array* subscripts, which are generated with the left bracket key ([ ) or by clicking $\times_n$ on the Calculator toolbar. Although they appear similar—a literal subscript appears below the line, like an array subscript, but with a slight space before the subscript—they behave quite differently in computations. A literal subscript is simply a cosmetic part of a variable name. An array subscript represents a reference to an array element. See Chapter 5, "Vectors, Matrices, and Data Arrays".

Operators

Operators are symbols like "+" and "−" that link variables and numbers together to form *expressions*. The variables and numbers linked together by operators are called *operands*. For example, in an expression like:

$$a^{x+y}$$

the operands for the "+" are x and y. The operands for the *exponent* operator are a and the expression $x + y$.

Inserting an Operator

Insert arithmetic operators in Mathcad using standard keystrokes, like * and +, that you use in other applications. Alternatively, all of Mathcad's operators can be inserted from the math toolbars. For example, insert a derivative operator by clicking $\frac{d}{dx}$ on the Calculus toolbar, or by typing **?**. Choose **Toolbars** from the **View** menu to see the math toolbars. See Chapter 17, "Operators" for a complete list of operators, their keystrokes, and descriptions.

Note To use operators in text, first click in the text and choose **Math Region** from the **Insert** menu.

Tip You can find the keyboard shortcut for an operator by hovering the mouse pointer over a button in a math toolbar and reading the tooltip.

When you insert a Mathcad operator into a blank space in your worksheet, a mathematical symbol with empty *placeholders* appears. You must enter a valid math expression in each placeholder of an operator in order to calculate a result.

Here is a very simple example involving Mathcad's addition operator:

1. Click in a blank space in your worksheet and click $+$ on the Calculator toolbar, or simply type **+**. The addition operator with two placeholders appears.

2. Enter **2** in the first placeholder.

3. Click in the second placeholder, or press [**Tab**] to move the cursor, and enter **6**.

4. Press =, or click $=$ on the Evaluation toolbar, to see the numerical result.

Building Expressions

You can create many mathematical expressions by simply typing. For example, you type these characters: **3/4+5^2=** to get the result at the right.

$$\frac{3}{4 + 5^2} = 0.103$$

Mathcad's equation editor is designed to work within the structure of a mathematical expression so that expressions are not so much typed as they are built.

Mathcad assembles the parts that make up an expression using the rules of precedence plus some additional rules to simplify entering denominators, exponents, and expressions in radicals. For example, when you type **/** or click ⊘ on the Calculator toolbar to create a fraction, Mathcad stays in the denominator until you press [**Space**] to select the entire expression.

Typing in Names and Numbers

When you type in names or numbers, Mathcad behaves very much like a standard word processor. As you type, you see the characters you type appear behind a vertical *editing line*. The left and right arrow keys move this vertical editing line to the left or to the right a character at a time. There are, however, two important differences:

- As it moves to the right, the vertical editing line leaves behind a trail. This trail is a "horizontal editing line."

  $$\boxed{abcde|}$$

- Unless the equation you've clicked in already has an operator in it, pressing [**Space**] turns the math region into a text region. It is not possible to turn a text region back into a math region.

Typing in Operators

The key to working with operators is learning to specify what variable or expression is to become an *operand*. There are two ways to do this:

- You can type the operator first, then fill in the placeholders with operands, or
- You can use the editing lines to specify what variable or expression you want to select.

The first method is like building a skeleton and filling in the details later. This method may be easier to use for very complicated expressions, or when you're working with operators like summation that require many operands but don't have a natural typing order.

The second method is more like straight typing so can be much faster when expressions are simple. You may find yourself switching back and forth as the need arises.

Here's how to create the expression a^{x+y} using the first method:

1. Press **^** to create the exponent operator, or click on the Calculator toolbar. You see two placeholders. The editing lines "hold" the exponent placeholder.

2. Click in the lower placeholder and type **a**.

3. Click in the upper placeholder.

$$a^{\blacksquare}$$

4. Type **+**.

$$a^{\blacksquare + \blacksquare}$$

5. Click in the remaining placeholders and type **x** and **y**.

$$a^{x + y}$$

To use the editing lines to create the expression a^{x+y} proceed as follows:

1. Type **a**. The editing lines hold the a indicating that a becomes the first operand of whatever operator you type next.

$$a$$

2. Press **^** to create the exponent operator. a becomes the first operand of the exponent. The editing lines now hold another placeholder.

$$a^{\blacksquare}$$

3. Type **x+y** in this placeholder to complete the expression.

$$a^{x + y}$$

Note that you can type the expression the same way you'd say it out loud. However, even this simple example already contains an ambiguity. When you say "a to the x plus y" there's no way to tell if you mean a^{x+y} or $a^x + y$. For more complicated expressions, the number of ambiguities increases dramatically.

Although you can always resolve ambiguities by using parentheses, doing so can quickly become cumbersome. A better way is to use the editing lines to specify the operands of whatever operator you type. The following example illustrates this by describing how to create the expression $a^x + y$ instead of a^{x+y}.

1. Enter **a^x** as you did in the previous example. Note how the editing lines hold the x between them. If you were to type **+** at this point, the x would become the first operand of the plus.

$$a^{x}$$

2. Press **[Space]**. The editing lines now hold the entire expression a^x.

$$a^{x}$$

3. Now type **+**. Whatever was held between the editing lines now becomes the first operand of the plus.

$$a^{x} + \blacksquare$$

4. In the remaining placeholder, type **y**.

$$a^{x} + y$$

Multiplication

When writing, expressions like ax or $a(x+y)$ are easily understood to mean "a times x" and "a times the quantity x plus y," respectively.

This cannot be done with Mathcad variables for the simple reason that when you type **ax**, Mathcad has no way of knowing whether you mean "a times x" or "the variable named ax." Similarly, when you type **a(x+y)**, Mathcad cannot tell if you mean "a times the quantity x plus y" or whether you mean "the function a applied to the argument $x + y$."

To avoid ambiguity in math expressions, we recommend that you always press *****
explicitly to indicate multiplication, as shown in the following example:

1. Type **a** followed by *****. Mathcad inserts a small dot after the "*a*" to
   indicate multiplication.

2. In the placeholder, type the second factor, **x**.

Note In the special case when you type a numerical constant followed immediately by a variable
name, such as **4x**, Mathcad interprets the expression to mean the constant multiplied by the
variable: $4 \cdot x$. Mathcad displays a space between the constant and the variable to indicate that
the multiplication is implied. This enables you to produce math notation that closely
approximates the notation in textbooks. However, Mathcad reserves certain letters, such as "*i*"
for the imaginary unit and "*o*" for octal, as suffixes for numbers, and in these cases does not
attempt to multiply the number by a variable name but rather treats the expression as a single
number with a suffix.

Tip You can change the display of the multiplication operator to an X, a thin space, or a large dot.
To do so, click on the multiplication operator with the right mouse button and choose **View
Multiplication As...** Or to change all the multiplication operators in a worksheet, choose
Worksheet Options from the **Tools** menu, click on the Display tab, and choose from the
selections next to "Multiplication." See "Changing the Display of an Operator" on page 391.

An Annotated Example

An equation is really *two-dimensional*, with a structure more like a tree with branches
than like a line of text. As a result, Mathcad has to use a *two-dimensional* editing cursor.
That's why there are two editing lines: a vertical line and a horizontal line.

Suppose, for example, that you want to type the slightly more complicated expression

$$\frac{x - 3 \cdot a^2}{-4 + \sqrt{y + 1} + \pi}$$

Watch what happens to the editing lines in the following steps:

1. Type **x-3*a^2**. Since the editing lines contain just the "2,"
   only the "2" becomes the numerator when you press the **/**. To
   make the whole expression, $x - 3 \cdot a^2$, be the numerator, you
   need the editing lines to hold the entire expression.

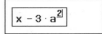

2. Press **[Space]**. Each time you press **[Space]**, the editing lines
   hold more of the expression. You need to press **[Space]** three
   times to enclose the entire expression.

3. Now press **/** to create a division bar. Note that the numerator
   is whatever was enclosed between the editing lines when you
   pressed **/**.

4. Now type **-4+** and click on the Calculator toolbar. Then type **y+1** under the radical to complete the denominator.

$$\frac{x - 3 \cdot a^2}{-4 + \sqrt{y + 1}}$$

5. To add something *outside* the radical sign, press **[Space]** twice to make the editing lines hold the radical. For example, to add the number π to the denominator, press **[Space]** twice.

$$\frac{x - 3 \cdot a^2}{-4 + \sqrt{y + 1}}$$

6. Press **+**. Since the editing lines are holding the entire radical, it is the entire radical that becomes the first operand when you press **+**.

$$\frac{x - 3 \cdot a^2}{-4 + \sqrt{y + 1} + \blacksquare}$$

7. Click π on the Calculator toolbar or press **[Ctrl][Shift]P**.

$$\frac{x - 3 \cdot a^2}{-4 + \sqrt{y + 1} + \pi}$$

Editing Expressions

Changing a Name or Number

To edit a name or number:

1. Click on it with the mouse. The vertical editing line appears.
2. Move the vertical editing line by pressing the [→] and [←] keys.
3. If you type a character, it appears just to the left of the vertical editing line. Pressing **[Bksp]** removes the character to the left. Pressing **[Delete]** removes the character to the right.

Choose **Replace** from the **Edit** menu to change several occurrences of the same name or number. To search for a sequence of characters, choose **Find** from the **Edit** menu. See "Text Tools" on page 73.

Inserting an Operator

The easiest place to insert an operator is between two characters in a name or two numbers in a constant. For example, here's how to insert a plus sign between two characters:

1. Place the editing lines where you want the plus sign to be.

$a\underline{b}$

2. Press the **+** key, or click **+** on the Calculator toolbar.

$a\underline{} + b$

Note Mathcad inserts spaces automatically around operators wherever doing so is appropriate. If you do try to insert a space, Mathcad assumes you meant to type text rather than math and converts your math region into a text region.

When you insert a division sign, Mathcad moves everything that comes after the division sign into the denominator. Here's how you insert a division sign:

1. Place the editing lines where you want the division sign.

$a\underline{b}$

2. Press the **/** key or click on the Calculator toolbar. Mathcad reformats the expression.

$\dfrac{a}{b}$

Some operators require only one operand. Examples are the square root, absolute value, and complex conjugate operators. To insert one of these, place the editing lines on either side of the operand and press the appropriate keystroke. Many of these operators are available on the Calculator toolbar as well. For example, to turn x into $\sqrt{x}$ do the following:

1. Place the editing lines around the "x," either preceding or following the character.

2. Press \ to insert the square root operator, or click on the Calculator toolbar.

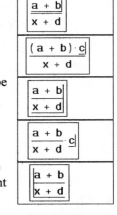

Applying an Operator to an Expression

If you want to apply an operator to an *entire expression:*

- Surround the expression in parentheses, or
- Use the editing lines to specify the expression.

Although the first method may be more intuitive, it is slower since you need to type a pair of parentheses. The more efficient, second method is described below. "Inserting Parentheses" on page 46 describes working with parentheses.

The editing lines consist of a horizontal line and a vertical line that moves left to right along the horizontal line. To make an operator apply to an expression, select the expression by placing it between the two editing lines. The following examples show how typing *c results in completely different expressions depending on what was selected.

- The two editing lines hold only the numerator. Any operator you type will apply only to the numerator.

- Typing *c applies the operation to the numerator only.

- The editing lines hold the entire fraction. Any operator you type will apply to the entire fraction.

- Typing *c applies to the whole fraction.

- The editing lines hold the entire fraction. However, this time the vertical editing line is on the *left* side instead of on the right side.

- Typing *c results in this expression. The c is before the fraction. because the vertical editing line was on the *left* side rather than the right side.

Controlling the editing lines

Use the following techniques to control what's between the editing lines:

- Click on an operator. To move the vertical editing line from one side to the other of the expression, press [**Insert**].

- Use the left and right arrow keys to move the vertical editing line one character at a time. The horizontal editing line selects an operand of the nearest operator. If your expression contains built-up fractions, you can also use the up and down arrow keys to move the editing lines.

- Press [**Space**] to select larger parts of the expression. Each time you press [**Space**], the editing lines enclose more and more of the expression, until they enclose the entire expression. Pressing [**Space**] one more time brings the editing lines back to where they started.

Tip   You can *drag-select* parts of an expression to hold it between the editing lines. The selected expression is highlighted in reverse video. Whatever you type next overwrites the highlighted expression.

The following example walks you through a short cycle of using [**Space**]:

1. This is the starting position. The two editing lines hold just the single variable "*d*."

2. Pressing [**Space**] makes the editing lines grow so that they now hold the entire denominator.

3. Pressing [**Space**] again makes the editing lines grow again so that they now hold the entire expression.

4. At this point, the editing lines can't become any longer. Pressing [**Space**] brings the editing lines back to the starting point of the cycle.

You'll notice there was never an intermediate step in which the editing lines held just the numerator. Nor was there ever a step in which the editing lines held just the *a* or just the *b* in the numerator. The sequence of steps the editing lines go through as you press [**Space**] depends on the starting point of the cycle.

The arrow keys walk the editing lines through the expression in the indicated direction. Keep in mind that the idea of "up" and "down" or "left" and "right" may not always be obvious, particularly when the expression becomes very complicated or if it involves summations, integrals, and other advanced operators.

Note   Editing of strings differs from editing of other math expressions because you must use the arrow keys or click outside the string to move out of a string. Pressing [**Space**], which can be used in other expressions to change the position of the editing lines, is interpreted as just another character in a string.

Deleting an Operator

To delete an operator connecting two variable names or constants:

1. Place the vertical editing line after the operator.

2. Press [**BkSp**].

Now you can insert a new operator to replace the one you deleted just by typing it in.

Tip   You can place the editing lines *before* an operator and press [**Delete**].

In these examples, it is easy to see what "before" and "after" mean because the expressions involved naturally flow from left to right, the same way we read. Fractions behave the same way. Since we naturally say "*a* over *b*," putting the editing lines "after" the division bar means putting them just before the *b*. Similarly, putting the editing lines "before" the division bar means putting them immediately after the *a*. The following example illustrates this:

1. Place the vertical editing lines *after* the division bar.

2. Press [**BkSp**].

To delete an operator having only one operand
(for example, $\sqrt{x}$, $|x|$ or $x!$):

1. Position the editing lines just after the operator.

2. Press [**BkSp**].

For certain operators, it may not be clear where to put the editing lines.
For example, it is not clear when looking at $|x|$ or $\overline{x}$ what "before" and "after" mean.
When this happens, Mathcad resolves the ambiguity by referring to the spoken form of the expression. For example, since you read $\overline{x}$ as "*x* conjugate," the bar is treated as being *after* the *x*.

Replacing an Operator

To replace an operator after deleting it, simply type the new operator after pressing [**BkSp**].

To replace an operator between two expressions:

1. Position the editing lines just after the operator.

2. Press [**BkSp**]. An operator placeholder appears.

3. Type the new operator.

Inserting a Minus Sign

The minus sign that means "negation" uses the same keystroke as the one that means "subtract." To determine which one to insert, Mathcad looks at where the vertical editing line is. If it's on the left, Mathcad inserts the "negation" minus sign. If it's on the right, Mathcad inserts the "subtract" minus sign. To move the vertical editing line from one side to the other, use [**Insert**].

The following example shows how to insert a minus sign in front of "sin(*a*)."

1. Click on the sin(*a*). If necessary, press [**Space**] to select the entire expression.

2. If necessary, press [**Insert**] to move the vertical editing line all the way to the left.

3. Type -, or click $-$ on the Calculator toolbar, to insert a minus sign.

Inserting Parentheses

Mathcad places parentheses automatically to maintain the precedence of operations. You may want to place parentheses to clarify an expression or to change the overall structure of the expression. You can either insert a matched pair of parentheses all at once or insert the parentheses one at a time. We recommend you insert a matched pair since this avoids the possibility of unmatched parentheses.

To enclose an expression with a matched pair of parentheses:

1. Select the expression by placing it between the editing lines. Do this by clicking on the expression and pressing [**Space**] one or more times.

2. Type the single-quote key (**'**), or click **( )** on the Calculator toolbar. The selected expression is now enclosed by parentheses.

It is sometimes necessary to insert parentheses one at a time using the **(** and **)** keys. For example, to change $a - b + c$ to $a - (b + c)$ do the following:

1. Move the editing lines just to the left of the *b*. Make sure the vertical editing line is on the left as shown. Press [**Insert**] if necessary to move it over.

2. Type **(** and click to the right of the *c*. Make sure the vertical editing line is to the right as shown. Press [**Insert**] if necessary to move it over.

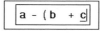

3. Type **)**.

Deleting Parentheses

Whenever you delete one parenthesis, Mathcad deletes the matched parenthesis. This prevents you from inadvertently creating an expression having unmatched parentheses.

To delete a matched pair of parentheses:

1. Move the editing lines to the right of the "(".

2. Press [**BkSp**]. Note that you could also begin with the editing lines to the left of the ")"and press [**Delete**] instead.

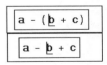

Insert Function

To see an alphabetical or category listing of available built-in functions or to insert a function together with placeholders for its arguments, choose **Function** from the **Insert** menu. The dialog box lists all functions.

1. Click in a blank area of your worksheet or on a placeholder.

2. Choose **Function** from the **Insert** menu or click ***f(x)*** on the Standard toolbar. Mathcad opens the Insert Function dialog box.

3. Choose a Function Category or click "All" to see all functions sorted alphabetically.

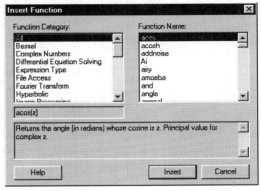

4. Double-click the name of the function you want to insert from the right-hand list, or click "Insert." The function and placeholders for its arguments are inserted into the worksheet.

5. Fill in the placeholders.

To apply a function to an expression you have already entered, select the expression and follow the steps given above. See Chapter 4, "Working with Math."

You can also type the name of a built-in function directly into a math placeholder or in a math region.

Tip   Although built-in function names are not font sensitive, they are case sensitive. If you do not use the Insert Function dialog box to insert a function name, you must enter the name of a built-in function in a math region exactly as it appears in the tables in Chapter 16, "Functions: : uppercase, lowercase, or mixed, as indicated.

Note   Brackets, [ ], around an argument indicate that the argument is optional.

Assistance for Using Built-in Functions

Mathcad includes several sources of assistance for using built-in functions:

- Chapter 16, "Functions" provides details on the syntax, arguments, algorithms, and behavior of all of Mathcad's built-in functions, operators, and keywords.

- The Insert Function dialog box gives you a convenient way to look up a function by category, to see the arguments required, and to see a brief function synopsis. When you click "Help" in the Insert Function dialog box, you immediately open the Help topic associated with the currently selected function.

- Online **Help** or clicking on the Standard toolbar provides both overview and detailed help on functions and function categories.

- QuickSheets under the **Help** menu include working examples of most functions.

Applying a Function to an Expression

To turn an expression into the argument of a function, follow these steps:

1. Click in the expression and press [**Space**] until the entire expression, $w \cdot t - k \cdot z$, is held between the editing lines.

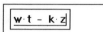

2. Type the single-quote key ('), or click on the Calculator toolbar. The selected expression is enclosed by parentheses.

3. Press [**Space**]. The editing lines now hold the parentheses as well.

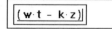

4. If necessary, press the [**Insert**] key so that the vertical editing line switches to the left side.

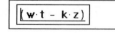

5. Now type the name of the function. If the function you wish to use is a built-in function, you can also choose **Function** from the **Insert** menu or click on the Standard toolbar and double-click the name of the function.

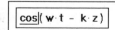

Moving Parts of an Expression

The menu commands **Cut, Copy,** and **Paste** from the **Edit** menu are useful for editing complicated expressions. They function as follows:

- **Cut** deletes whatever is between the editing lines and copies it to the Clipboard.

- **Copy** takes whatever is between the editing lines and copies it to the Clipboard.

- **Paste** takes whatever is on the Clipboard and places it into your worksheet, either into a placeholder or into blank space.

The **Copy** and **Paste** commands use the Clipboard to move expressions from one place to another. You can, however, bypass the Clipboard by using Mathcad's *equation drag and drop* feature.

Suppose you want to build the expression

$$\cos(wt + x) + \sin(wt + x)$$

1. Drag-select the argument to the cosine function so that it is highlighted in reverse video.

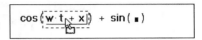

2. Press and hold down **[Ctrl]** and the mouse button. The pointer changes to indicate that it carries the selected expression with it.

3. With the mouse button still held down, drag the pointer over the placeholder.

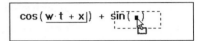

4. Release the mouse button. The pointer drops the expression into the placeholder and recovers its original form.

Tip You can drag and drop expressions, or even entire math regions, into placeholders in other expressions or into any blank space. Don't let go of the mouse button before you've dragged the expression to wherever you want to drop it. If you're trying to drop the expression into a placeholder, be sure to position the pointer carefully over the placeholder.

Deleting Parts of an Expression

You can delete part of an expression by using either the **[Delete]** key or the **[BkSp]** key. If you use this method, whatever you delete is *not* placed on the Clipboard. This is useful when you intend to replace whatever you delete with whatever is currently on the Clipboard.

To delete part of an expression *without* placing it on the Clipboard:

1. Drag-select the part of the expression (in this case, the numerator) so that it is highlighted in reverse video.

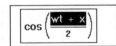

2. Press **[Delete]** or **[BkSp]**. This removes the numerator and leaves behind a placeholder.

Note If you select an expression with the editing lines instead of drag-selecting as shown above, you must press **[Bksp]** or **[Delete]** *twice* to remove it. In this case, **[Bksp]** removes the expression to the left of the editing lines, and **[Delete]** removes to the right.

Math Styles

By making changes to text styles rather than to individual text elements, you can make uniform changes across your files. (See Chapter 6, "Working with Text".) You can get this same kind of leverage by using *math styles* to assign particular fonts, font sizes, font styles and affects, and colors to your math expressions.

Mathcad has predefined math styles that govern the default appearance of all the math in your worksheet, but you can define and apply additional styles.

Mathcad's predefined math styles are:

- **Variables**: all variables, letters, and operators in math regions.
- **Constants**: all numbers in math regions.

Whenever you type a variable name, Mathcad:

- Assigns to it a math style named "Variables."
- Displays the variable name using the characteristics associated with the style named "Variables."

Similarly, when you type a number or when a result is calculated, Mathcad:

- Assigns to it a math style named "Constants."
- Displays the number using the characteristics associated with the style named "Constants."

Editing Math Styles

To change Mathcad's default style for all variables and plots:

1. Click on a variable name in your worksheet.

2. Choose **Equation** from the **Format** menu. The style name "Variables" is selected.

3. Click "Modify" to change the font associated with the "Variables" style. You'll see a dialog box for changing fonts.

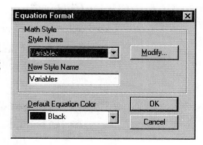

4. Make any changes using the dialog box. Mathcad changes the font of all variables in the worksheet.

If you change the Variables style, you may also want to change the style used for numbers so that the two go together.

1. Click on a number.

2. Choose **Equation** from the **Format** menu to see the Equation Format dialog box. The style name "Constants" is now selected.

3. Follow the procedure given above for modifying the Variables style.

You can also use the Formatting toolbar to change the font, font size, or font style associated with a math style. For example, click on a variable, then click on the appropriate Formatting toolbar button to make variables bold, italic, or underlined or to specify the font or point size in the drop-down lists.

Note Mathcad's line-and-character grid does not respond automatically to changes in the font sizes used in text and math. Changing font characteristics, particularly font sizes, may cause regions to overlap. You can separate these regions by choosing **Separate Regions** from the **Format** menu.

You may wish to have your equations display in a different color than your default text regions to avoid confusing the two. To change the default color of all equations in your worksheet:

1. Choose **Equation** from the **Format** menu.
2. Select a color in the "Default Equation Color" drop-down list.

Applying Math Styles

The "Variables" and "Constants" styles govern the default appearance of all math in your worksheet. These two style names cannot be changed. You may, however, create and apply additional math styles.

To see what math style is currently assigned to a name or number, simply click on the name or number, and look at the style window on the Formatting toolbar.

Alternatively, click the name or number and choose **Equation** from the **Format** menu. The math style associated with whatever you clicked on appears in the drop-down list in the Equation Format dialog box.

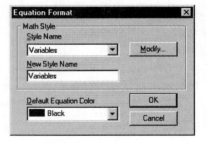

If you click on the button to the right of "Variables" in either the Formatting toolbar or the Equation Format dialog box, you'll see a drop-down list of available math styles. If you now choose "User 1" and click "OK," a new math style is applied to the selected element and its appearance changes accordingly.

You can apply a variety of math styles to:

• individual variable names in an expression, or

• individual numbers in a math expression (but not in computed results, which always display in the "Constants" style).

For example, you may want to show vectors in a bold, underlined font:

1. Choose **Equation** from the **Format** menu.
2. Click the down arrow beside the name of the current math styles to see a drop-down list of available math styles.

3. Click on an unused math style name like "User 1" to select it. The name "User 1" should now appear in the "New Style Name" text box. Click in this text box and change the name to "Vectors."

4. Click "Modify" to change this style to a bold, underlined font.

This creates a math style called "Vectors" with the desired appearance.

Now rather than individually changing the font, font size, and font style for names of vectors, you can simply change the math style for all vectors.

Note All names, whether function names or variable names, are font sensitive. This means that x and x refer to different variables, and $\mathbf{f}(x)$ and $f(x)$ refer to different functions. In deciding whether two variable names are the same, Mathcad actually checks *math styles* rather than fonts. To avoid having distinct variables that look identical, don't create a math style with exactly the same font, size, and other characteristics as another math style.

Saving Math Styles

You can reuse math style information by saving a worksheet as a template. Choose **Save As** from the **File** menu and select Mathcad Template (*.mct) as the file type in the Save As dialog box.

To apply math style information to another worksheet, open your template from the **File** menu and copy the contents of the worksheet to the template. See "Worksheets and Templates" on page 77.

Chapter 5
Vectors, Matrices, and Data Arrays

- ♦ Creating Arrays
- ♦ Accessing Array Elements
- ♦ Displaying Arrays
- ♦ Working with Arrays
- ♦ Nested Arrays

Creating Arrays

This section describes creating and working with arrays of numbers and math expressions. The procedures listed below can be used *only* for creating arrays of numbers, as opposed to arbitrary math expressions.

- Using range variables to fill in the elements. This technique is useful when you have some explicit formula for the array elements in terms of their indices.
- Using the File Input and Output components to import data from external files in a variety of formats.
- Entering numbers manually in a spreadsheet-like input table.

Note The effective array size limit depends on the memory available on your system—usually at least 1 million elements. In no system is it higher than 8 million elements.

Insert Matrix Command

To insert a vector or matrix in Mathcad, follow these steps:

1. Click in either a blank space or on a math placeholder.

2. Choose **Matrix** from the **Insert** menu, or click 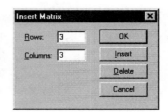 on the Matrix toolbar. A dialog box appears

3. Enter the appropriate number of elements in the text boxes for "Rows" and "Columns." For example, to create a three-element vector, enter **3** and **1**.

4. An array with blank placeholders appears in your worksheet.

Next, fill in the array elements. You can enter any math expression into the placeholders of an array created in this way. Simply click in a placeholder and type a number or expression. Use the [**Tab**] key to move from placeholder to placeholder.

Note Arrays created using the **Matrix** command on the **Insert** menu are limited to 100 elements.

Changing the size of a vector or matrix

You can change the size of a matrix by inserting and deleting rows and columns:

1. Click on one of the matrix elements to place it between the editing lines. Mathcad begins inserting or deleting with this element.

$$\begin{pmatrix} 2| & 5 & 17 \\ 3.5 & 3.9 & -12.9 \end{pmatrix}$$

2. Choose **Matrix** from the **Insert** menu. Type the number of rows and/or columns you want to insert or delete. Then press either "Insert" or "Delete." For example, to delete the column that holds the selected element, type **1** in the box next to "Columns," **0** in the box next to "Rows," and press "Delete."

$$\begin{pmatrix} 5 & 17 \\ 3.9 & -12.9 \end{pmatrix}$$

Note If you insert rows or columns, Mathcad inserts rows *below* the selected element and inserts columns to the *right* of the selected element. If you delete rows or columns, Mathcad begins with the row or column occupied by the selected element and deletes rows from that element downward and columns from that element rightward. To insert a row above the top row or a column to the left of the first column, first place the entire matrix between the editing lines.

Creating Arrays with Range Variables

As introduced in "Range Variables" on page 103, you can use one or more range variables to fill up the elements of an array. If you use two range variables in an equation, for example, Mathcad runs through each value of each range variable. This is useful for defining matrices. For example, to define a 5×5 matrix whose i,jth element is $i + j$, enter the equations shown in Figure 5-1.

$$i := 0 .. 4 \qquad j := 0 .. 4$$

$$x_{i,j} := i + j$$

$$x = \begin{pmatrix} 0 & 1 & 2 & 3 & 4 \\ 1 & 2 & 3 & 4 & 5 \\ 2 & 3 & 4 & 5 & 6 \\ 3 & 4 & 5 & 6 & 7 \\ 4 & 5 & 6 & 7 & 8 \end{pmatrix}$$

Figure 5-1: Defining a matrix using range variables.

Recall that you enter the range variable operator by pressing the semicolon key (**;**) or clicking `m..n` on the Calculator toolbar. You enter the subscript operator by clicking `Xₙ` on the Matrix toolbar.

The $x_{i,j}$ equation is evaluated for each value of each range variable, for a total of 25 evaluations. The result is the matrix shown at the bottom of Figure 5-1, with 5 rows and 5 columns. The element in the ith row and jth column of this matrix is $i + j$.

Note	To be used to define an array element, a range variable can take on only whole-number values.

Tip	You can also define individual array elements using the subscript operator, as described in "Accessing Array Elements" on page 56.

Entering a Matrix as a Data Table

To get the convenience of a spreadsheet-like interface for entering data, you can create an array using a Data Table:

1. Click in a blank spot in your worksheet and choose **Data⇒Table** from the **Insert** menu.

2. Enter the name of the Mathcad variable to which the data will be assigned in the placeholder that appears.

3. Click in the component and enter data into the cells. Each row must have the same number of data values. If you do not enter a number into a cell, Mathcad inserts 0 into the cell.

Figure 5-2 shows two data tables. Notice that when you create a data table, you're actually assigning elements to an array that has the name of the variable you entered into the placeholder.

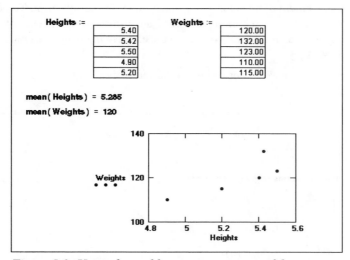

Figure 5-2: Using data tables to create arrays of data.

When you click the table, you can edit the values in it using the scroll bars. To resize the table, move the cursor to one of these handles along the sides of the region so that it changes to a double-headed arrow. Then press and hold down the mouse button and drag the cursor to change the table's dimensions.

Note A component is a specialized OLE object that you insert into a Mathcad worksheet to create a link between the worksheet and either a data source or another application containing data. To see how to create matrices with data from external files using Data Tables and other components, see Chapter 14, "Importing and Exporting Data."

Tip You can copy data from a data table as follows: first select some data, then click with the right mouse button on the component and choose **Copy** from the popup menu. You can paste a single number from the Clipboard into the table by selecting a cell and choosing **Paste** from the popup menu. Choosing **Paste Table** from the popup menu overwrites the entire table with values in the Clipboard.

Accessing Array Elements

You can access all the elements of an array simply by using its variable name, or you can access the elements individually or in groups.

Subscripts

You access individual elements of a vector or matrix by using the subscript operator.

Insert the subscript operator by clicking X_n on the Matrix toolbar or by typing [. To access an element of a vector, enter one number in the subscript. To access a matrix element, enter two numbers separated by a comma. To refer to the ith element of a vector, type **v [i**. In general, to refer to the element in the ith row, jth column of matrix **M**, type **M[i,j**.

Figure 5-3 shows examples of how to define individual matrix elements and how to view them.

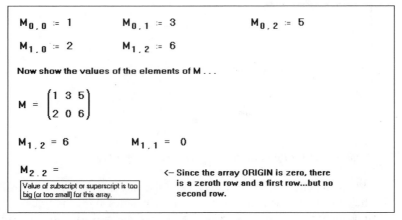

Figure 5-3: Defining and viewing matrix elements.

Note When you define vector or matrix elements, you may leave gaps in the vector or matrix. For example, if **v** is undefined and you define v_3 as 10, then v_0, v_1, and v_2 are all undefined.

Mathcad fills these gaps with zeros until you enter specific values for them, as shown in Figure 5-3. Be careful of inadvertently creating very large vectors and matrices by doing this. Also note that vector and matrix elements by default are numbered starting with row zero and column zero unless the built-in variable ORIGIN has a value other than zero (see page 57).

You can use this kind of subscript notation in Mathcad to perform parallel calculations on the elements of an array. See "Performing Calculations in Parallel" on page 61.

Tip If you want to define or access a group of array elements at once, you can use a range variable in a subscript.

Accessing Rows and Columns

Although you can use a range variable to access all the elements in a row or column of an array, Mathcad provides a column operator for quickly accessing all the elements in a column. Click M⟨⟩ on the Matrix toolbar for the column operator. Figure 5-4 shows how to extract the third column of the matrix **M**.

$$M = \begin{pmatrix} 1 & 3 & 5 \\ 2 & 0 & 6 \end{pmatrix} \qquad M^{\langle 2 \rangle} = \begin{pmatrix} 5 \\ 6 \end{pmatrix}$$

Note: the origin is 0. Thus, the superscript of 2 refers to the third column of the matrix M.

$$M^T = \begin{pmatrix} 1 & 2 \\ 3 & 0 \\ 5 & 6 \end{pmatrix} \qquad w := (M^T)^{\langle 1 \rangle} \qquad w = \begin{pmatrix} 2 \\ 0 \\ 6 \end{pmatrix}$$

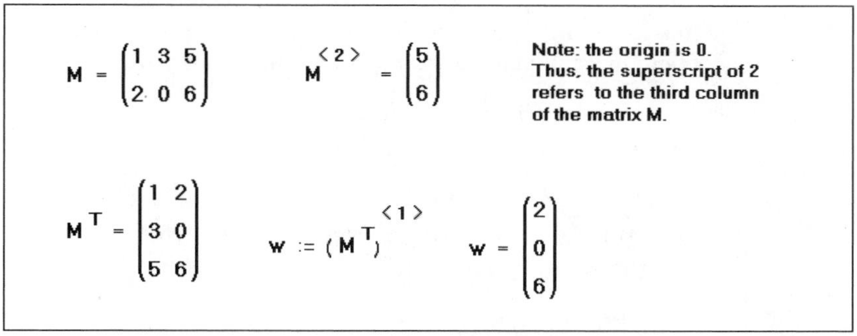

Figure 5-4: Extracting a column from a matrix.

To extract a single row from a matrix, transpose the matrix using the transpose operator (click M^T on the Matrix toolbar) and then extract a column using the column operator. This is shown on the right-hand side of Figure 5-4.

Changing the Array Origin

When you use subscripts to refer to array elements, Mathcad assumes the array begins at the current value of the built-in variable ORIGIN. By default, ORIGIN is 0, but you can change its value. See "Built-in Variables" on page 100 for details.

Figure 5-5 shows a worksheet with the ORIGIN set to 1. If you try to refer to the zeroth element of an array in this case, Mathcad displays an error message.

ORIGIN $\equiv$ 1
Matrices:
$$M := \begin{pmatrix} 1 & 2 & 7 \\ 2 & 4 & 6 \\ 3 & 6 & 9 \end{pmatrix}$$

$M_{1,1} = 1$ $M_{3,3} = 9$ $M_{1,3} = 7$ $M_{0,0} =$

> Value of subscript or superscript is too big (or too small) for this array.

Vectors:

$v_1 := 1$ $v_2 := 3$ $v_3 := 5$ Since the array ORIGIN is now one, there is no longer a zeroth row or column.

$$v = \begin{pmatrix} 1 \\ 3 \\ 5 \end{pmatrix}$$ $v_0 =$

> Value of subscript or superscript is too big (or too small) for this array.

Figure 5-5: Arrays beginning at element one instead of at element zero.

Displaying Arrays

Mathcad automatically displays matrices and vectors having more than nine rows or columns as output tables rather than as matrices or vectors. Smaller arrays are displayed by default in traditional matrix notation. Figure 5-6 shows an example.

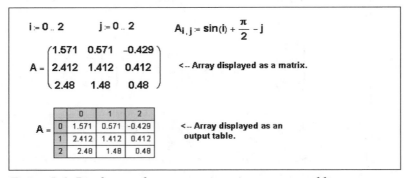

Figure 5-6: Display results as a matrix or in an output table.

Note An output table displays a portion of an array. To the left of each row and at the top of each column, there is a number indicating the index of the row or column. Click with the right mouse button on the output table and select **Properties** from the popup menu to control whether row and column numbers appear and the font used for values in the table. If your results extend beyond the table, you can scroll through the table using scroll bars.

To resize an output table:

1. Click the output table. You'll see handles along the sides of the table.

2. Move the cursor to one of these handles so that it changes to a double-headed arrow.

3. Press and hold down the mouse button and drag the cursor in the direction you want the table's dimensions to change.

Tip You can change the alignment of the table with respect to the expression on the left-hand side of the equal sign. Click with the right mouse button on the table, then choose one of the **Alignment** options from the popup menu.

Changing the Display of Arrays—Table versus Matrix

Although matrices and vectors having more than nine rows or columns are automatically displayed as output tables, you can have Mathcad display them as matrices. You can also change matrices to output tables. To do so:

1. Click on the output table.
2. Choose **Result** from the **Format** menu.
3. Click on the Display Options tab.
4. Choose Matrix or Table in the "Matrix display style" drop-down box.

To display all the results in your worksheet as matrices or as tables regardless of their size, click "Set as Default" in the Result Format dialog box rather than "OK."

Note Mathcad cannot display extremely large arrays in matrix form. You should display a large array as an output table.

Changing the Format of Displayed Elements

You format the numbers in the array the same way you format other numerical results, as described in "Formatting Results" on page 112. Just click on the displayed array and choose **Result** from the **Format** menu, and modify the settings there. When you click "OK," Mathcad applies the selected format to all the numbers in the table, vector, or matrix. It is not possible to format the numbers individually.

Copying and Pasting Arrays

You can copy an array of numbers directly from a tabular application, such as Excel, or an ASCII file that contains rows and columns, into a Mathcad. All data characteristics, including text, numerics, complex numbers, or empty cells are preserved. Once you've performed computations or manipulations on the data, you can paste or export the resulting array of numbers back to its source or into another application.

To copy just one number from a result array, click the number and choose **Copy** from the **Edit** menu, or click 🗐 on the Standard toolbar. Copying multiple numbers from a vector or matrix result differs depending on whether the array is displayed as a matrix or as an output table. See "Displaying Arrays" on page 58 for more information on how vector and matrix results are displayed.

To copy a result array displayed as a matrix:

1. Drag-select the array to the right of the equal sign to place the entire array between the editing lines.
2. Choose **Copy** from the **Edit** menu. This places the entire array on the Clipboard.

3. Click wherever you want to paste the result. If you're pasting into another application, choose **Paste** from that application's **Edit** menu. If you're pasting into a Mathcad worksheet, choose **Paste** from Mathcad's **Edit** menu.

You may only paste an array into a math placeholder or into a blank space in a Mathcad worksheet.

When you display array results as a table, you can copy some or all of the numbers from the table and use them elsewhere:

1. Click on the first number you want to copy.

2. Drag the mouse in the direction of the other values you want to copy while holding the mouse button down.

3. Right click on the selected values then choose **Copy Selection** from the popup menu.

To copy all the values in a row or column, click on the column or row number shown to the left of the row or at the top of the column. All the values in the row or column are selected. Then choose **Copy** from the **Edit** menu.

After you have copied one or more numbers from an output table, you can paste them into another part of your worksheet or into another application. Figure 5-7 shows an example of a new matrix created by copying and pasting numbers from an output table.

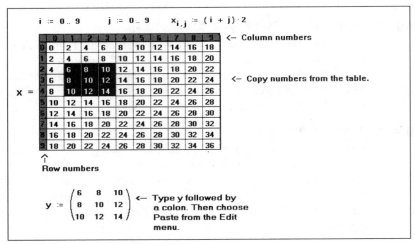

Figure 5-7: Copying and pasting results from an output table.

Tip   When you display an array as an output table, you can export data directly from the table. Right click on the output table, choose **Export** from the popup menu, and enter the name of the file, the format, and the columns and rows to export.

Working with Arrays

There are many operators and functions designed for use with vectors and matrices. See "Vector and Matrix Operators" on page 398 and "Vector and Matrix Functions" on page 256 for an overview. This section highlights the vectorize operator, which permits efficient parallel calculations on the elements of arrays. You can also display the values of an array graphically or export them to a data file or another application.

Performing Calculations in Parallel

Any calculation Mathcad can perform with single values, it can also perform with vectors or matrices of values. There are two ways to do this:

- Iterate over each element using range variables. For example, see "Creating Arrays with Range Variables" on page 54.

- Use the *vectorize operator*, which allows Mathcad to perform the same operation efficiently on each *element* of a vector or matrix.

Mathematical notation often shows repeated operations with subscripts. For example, to define a matrix **P** by multiplying corresponding elements of the matrices **M** and **N**, you would write:

$$\mathbf{P}_{i,j} = \mathbf{M}_{i,j} \cdot \mathbf{N}_{i,j}$$

Note that this is not matrix multiplication, but multiplication element by element. It *is* possible to perform this operation in Mathcad using subscripts, but it is much faster to perform exactly the same operation with a vectorized equation.

Here's how to apply the vectorize operator to an expression like $\mathbf{M} \cdot \mathbf{N}$:

1. Select the whole expression by clicking inside it and pressing [**Space**] until the right-hand side is surrounded by the editing lines.

2. Click 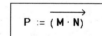 on the Matrix toolbar to apply the vectorize operator. Mathcad puts an arrow over the top of the selected expression.

Properties of the vectorize operator

- The vectorize operator changes the meaning of the other *operators* and *functions* to which it applies. The vectorize operator tells Mathcad to apply the operators and functions with their scalar meanings, element by element. It does not change the meaning of the actual names and numbers. If you apply the vectorize operator to a single name, it simply draws an arrow over the name. You can use this arrow for only cosmetic purposes if you like.

- Since operations between two arrays are performed element by element, all arrays under a vectorize operator must be the same size. Operations between an array and a scalar are performed by applying the scalar to each element of the array.

- You can use any of the following matrix operations under a vectorize operator: dot product, matrix multiplication, matrix powers, matrix inverse, determinant, or magnitude of a vector. The vectorize operator transforms these operations into element-by-element scalar multiplication, exponentiation, or absolute value, as appropriate.

Tip   A number of Mathcad's built-in functions and operators ordinarily take scalar arguments but *implicitly* vectorize arguments that are vectors (one-column arrays): they automatically compute a result element by element, whether you apply the vectorize operator or not. Functions that implicitly vectorize vector arguments include the trigonometric, logarithmic, Bessel, and probability distribution functions. Operators that implicitly vectorize vector arguments include the factorial, square and nth root, and relational operators. You must continue to use the vectorize operator on arrays of other sizes with these functions and operators.

For example, suppose you want to apply the quadratic formula to three vectors containing coefficients a, b, and c. Figure 5-8 shows how to do this with the vectorize operator.

Coefficients as follows . . . $a := \begin{pmatrix} 1 \\ 1 \\ 2 \\ 2 \end{pmatrix}$ $b := \begin{pmatrix} 3 \\ 2 \\ 1 \\ 0 \end{pmatrix}$ $c := \begin{pmatrix} 2 \\ 1 \\ 1 \\ 1 \end{pmatrix}$

Compute a root . . .

$$x := \overrightarrow{\left[\frac{-b + \sqrt{b^2 - 4 \cdot a \cdot c}}{2 \cdot a} \right]}$$

$$x = \begin{pmatrix} -1 \\ -1 \\ -0.25 + 0.661i \\ 0.707i \end{pmatrix}$$

$$\overrightarrow{(a \cdot x^2 + b \cdot x + c)} = \begin{pmatrix} 0 \\ 0 \\ 0 \\ 0 \end{pmatrix} \quad \text{. . . should be zero}$$

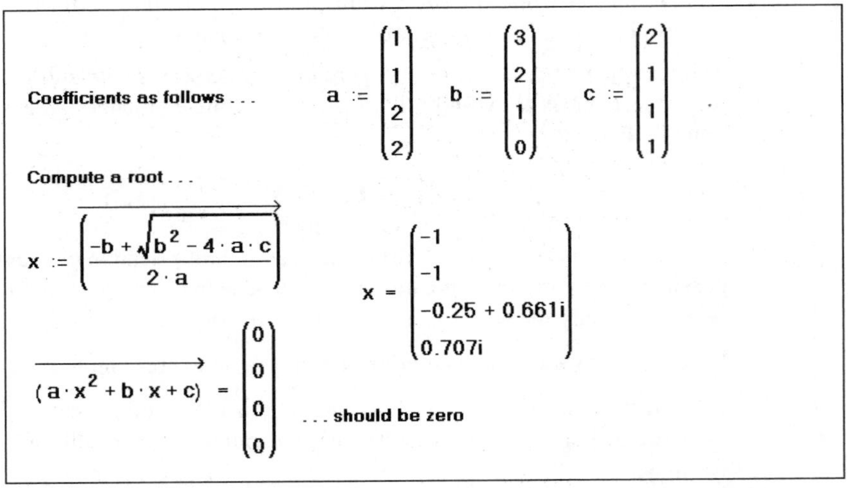

Figure 5-8: Quadratic formula with vectors and the vectorize operator.

The vectorize operator, appearing as an arrow above the quadratic formula in Figure 5-8, is essential in this calculation. Without it, Mathcad would interpret **a** · **c** as a vector dot product and also flag the square root of a vector as illegal. But with the vectorize operator, both **a** · **c** and the square root are performed element by element.

Graphical Display of Arrays

In addition to looking at the actual numbers making up an array, you can also see a graphical representation of those same numbers. There are several ways to do this:

- For an arbitrary array, you can use the various three-dimensional plot types discussed in Chapter 12, "3D Plots."

- For an array of integers between 0 and 255, you can look at a grayscale image by choosing **Picture** from the **Insert** menu and entering the array's name in the placeholder.

- For three arrays of integers between 0 and 255 representing the red, green, and blue components of an image, choose **Picture** from the **Insert** menu and enter the arrays' names, separated by commas, in the placeholder.

See Chapter 10, "Inserting Graphics and Other Objects," for more on viewing a matrix (or three matrices, in the case of a color image) in the picture operator.

Nested Arrays

An array element need not be a scalar. It's possible to make an array element itself be another array. This allows you to create arrays within arrays.

These arrays behave very much like arrays whose elements are all scalars. However, there are some distinctions, as described below.

Note Most of Mathcad's operators and functions do not work with nested arrays, since there is no universally accepted definition of what constitutes correct behavior in this context. Certain operators and functions are nevertheless useful and appropriate for nested arrays. Functions that enumerate rows or columns, or that partition, augment, and stack matrices, can be applied to nested arrays. The transpose, subscript, and column array operators and the Boolean equal sign likewise support nested arrays.

Defining a Nested Array

You define a nested array in much the same way you would define any array. The only difference is that you cannot use the **Matrix** command from the **Insert** menu when you've selected a placeholder within an existing array. You can, however, click on a placeholder in an array and type the *name* of another array. Figure 5-9 shows several ways to define a nested array. Additional methods include using a file access function such as READPRN in the array of placeholders created using the Insert Matrix command, and using the programming operators in Mathcad to build up an array whose elements are themselves arrays.

Note The display of a nested array is controlled by Display Styles settings in the Result Format dialog (see page 112). You can expand a nested array when the array is displayed in matrix form; otherwise, whenever an array element is itself an array, you see bracket notation showing the number of rows and columns rather than the array itself. If the nested array is displayed as an output table, you can see the underlying array temporarily. Click on the array element, then right click and choose **Down One Level** from the popup menu. Choose **Up One Level** from the popup menu to restore the array element to non-expanded form.

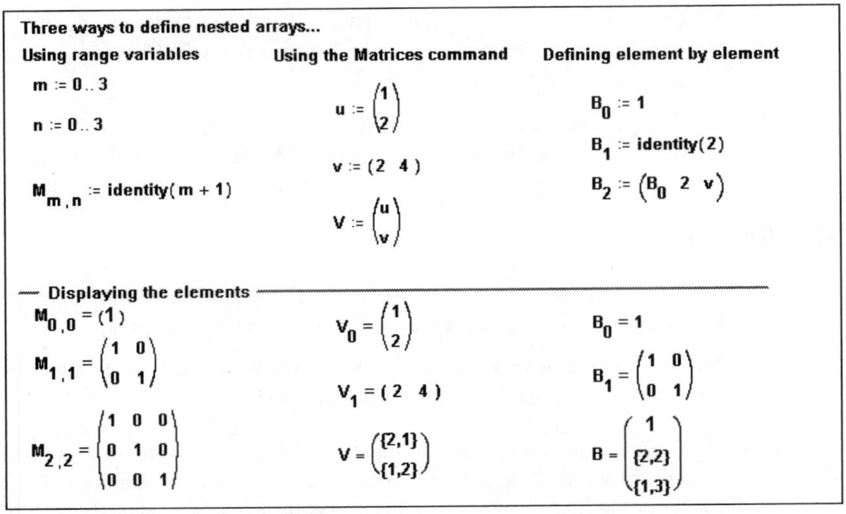

Three ways to define nested arrays...

Using range variables	Using the Matrices command	Defining element by element
$m := 0 .. 3$	$u := \begin{pmatrix} 1 \\ 2 \end{pmatrix}$	$B_0 := 1$
$n := 0 .. 3$		$B_1 := identity(2)$
	$v := (2 \quad 4)$	$B_2 := \begin{pmatrix} B_0 & 2 & v \end{pmatrix}$
$M_{m,n} := identity(m+1)$	$V := \begin{pmatrix} u \\ v \end{pmatrix}$	

—— Displaying the elements ——————————————————

$M_{0,0} = (1)$

$M_{1,1} = \begin{pmatrix} 1 & 0 \\ 0 & 1 \end{pmatrix}$

$M_{2,2} = \begin{pmatrix} 1 & 0 & 0 \\ 0 & 1 & 0 \\ 0 & 0 & 1 \end{pmatrix}$

$V_0 = \begin{pmatrix} 1 \\ 2 \end{pmatrix}$

$V_1 = (2 \quad 4)$

$V = \begin{pmatrix} \{2,1\} \\ \{1,2\} \end{pmatrix}$

$B_0 = 1$

$B_1 = \begin{pmatrix} 1 & 0 \\ 0 & 1 \end{pmatrix}$

$B = \begin{pmatrix} 1 \\ \{2,2\} \\ \{1,3\} \end{pmatrix}$

Figure 5-9: Defining nested arrays.

Chapter 6
Working with Text

- ♦ Inserting Text
- ♦ Text and Paragraph Properties
- ♦ Text Styles
- ♦ Equations in Text
- ♦ Text Tools

Inserting Text

This section describes how to add text to your worksheets. Mathcad ignores text when it performs calculations, but you can insert working math equations into text regions as described in "Equations in Text" on page 72.

Creating a Text Region

To create a text region, follow these steps. First, click in a blank space in your worksheet to position the crosshair where you want the text region to begin. Then:

1. Choose **Text Region** from the **Insert** menu, or press the double-quote (**"**) key. You can also just start typing and once you type a space Mathcad begins a text region. The crosshair changes into an insertion point and a text box appears.

2. Now begin typing some text. Mathcad displays the text and surrounds it with a text box. As you type, the insertion point moves and the text box grows.

3. When you finish typing the text, click outside the text region. The text box disappears.

Note   You cannot leave a text region simply by pressing [↵]. You must leave the text region by clicking outside the region, by pressing [**Ctrl**][**Shift**][↵], or by repeatedly pressing one of the arrow keys until the cursor leaves the region.

To insert text into an existing text region:

- Click anywhere in a text region. A text box now surrounds your text. Anything you type gets inserted at the insertion point.

To delete text from an existing text region, click in the text region and:

1. Press [**BkSp**] to delete the character to the left of the insertion point, or
2. Press [**Delete**] to delete the character to the right of the insertion point.

To overtype text:

1. Place the insertion point to the left of the first character you want to overtype.

2. Press [**Insert**] to begin typing in *overtype* mode. To return to the default *insert* mode, press [**Insert**] again.

You can also overtype text by first selecting it (see "Selecting Text" on page 66). Whatever you type next replaces your selection.

Tip   To break a line or start a new line in a text region, press [↵]. Mathcad inserts a hard return and moves the insertion point down to the next line. Press [**Shift**][↵] to start a new line in the same paragraph. When you rewrap the text by changing the width of the text region, Mathcad maintains line breaks at these spots in the text. We recommend adjusting the width of the text box rather than using returns to shorten a text region.

Moving the Insertion Point

Click with the mouse wherever you want to put the insertion point. The arrow keys can be used to move the insertion point character by character or line by line. Ways of moving the insertion point are summarized below.

Key	Action
[→]	Move right one character.
[←]	Move left one character.
[↑]	Move up to the previous line.
[↓]	Move down to the next line.
[**Ctrl**][→]	Move to the end of the current word. If the insertion point is already there, move to the end of the next word.
[**Ctrl**][←]	Move to the beginning of the current word. If the insertion point is already there, move to the beginning of the previous word.
[**Ctrl**][↑]	Move to the beginning of the current line. If the insertion point is already there, move to the beginning of the previous line.
[**Ctrl**][↓]	Move to the end of the current line. If the insertion point is already there, move to the end of the next line.
[**Home**]	Move to the beginning of the current line.
[**End**]	Move to the end of the current line.

Selecting Text

One way to select text within a text region is:

1. Click in the text region so that the text box appears.

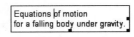

2. Drag across the text holding the mouse button down.

Mathcad highlights the selected text, including any full lines between the first and last characters you selected.

Online Help   You can also select text using arrow keys and multiple clicks of the mouse button, just as you can in most word processing applications. For more information, refer to the topic "Selecting text" in online Help.

Once text is selected, you can delete it, copy it, cut it, check the spelling, or change its font, size, style, or color.

To select and move an entire text region or group of regions, follow the same steps that you would use with math regions, described on "Moving and Copying Regions" on page 15.

Greek Letters in Text

To type a Greek letter in a text region, use one of these two methods:

• Click on the appropriate letter on the Greek toolbar. To see this toolbar, click on the Math toolbar, or choose **Toolbars⇒Greek** from the **View** menu, or

• Type the *Roman equivalent* of the Greek symbol and then press **[Ctrl]G**. For example, to enter ϕ, press **f[Ctrl]G**. See "Appendix H: Greek Letters" on page 444 in the Appendices for a table of Greek letters and their Roman equivalents.

Tip   Typing **[Ctrl]G** after a letter in a math region also converts it to its Greek equivalent. In addition, **[Ctrl]G** converts a non alphabetic character to its Greek symbol equivalent. For example, typing **[Shift]2[Ctrl]G** in a text region produces the "≅" character.

To change a text *selection* into its Greek equivalent, select the text and then:

1. Choose **Text** from the **Format** menu.

2. From the Font list select the Symbol font.

You can also change the font of a text selection by using the Formatting toolbar.

Changing the Width of a Text Region

When you start typing in a text region, the region grows as you type, wrapping only when you reach the right margin or page boundary. (The location of the right margin is determined by the settings in the Page Setup dialog box, which you can modify by choosing **Page Setup** from the **File** menu.) To set a width for your whole text region and have lines wrap to stay within that width as you type:

1. Type normally until the first line reaches the width you want.

2. Type a space and press **[Ctrl][↵]**.

All other lines break to stay within this width. When you add to or edit the text, Mathcad rewraps the text according to the width set by the line at the end of which you pressed **[Ctrl][↵]**.

To change the width of an existing text region, do the following:

1. Click anywhere in the text region. A selection box encloses the text region.

2. Move the pointer to the middle of the right edge of text region until it hovers over the "handle" on the selection rectangle. The pointer changes to a double-headed arrow. You can now change the size of the text region the same way you change the size of any window—by dragging the mouse.

Tip You can specify that a text region or regions occupy the full page width by selecting them and choosing **Properties** from the **Format** menu. Click the Text tab and check "Occupy Page Width." As you enter more lines of text into a full-width text region, any regions that are below are automatically pushed down in the worksheet.

Text and Paragraph Properties

This section describes changing various font properties and changing the alignment and indenting of *paragraphs* within a text region.

Changing Text Properties

To change the font, size, style, position, or color of a portion of the text within a text region, first select the text. Then choose **Text** from the **Format** menu to access the Text Format dialog box or right click and choose **Font** from the popup menu.

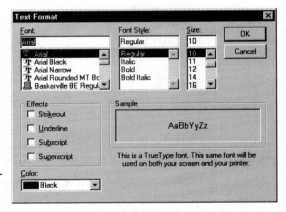

Many of the options of the Text Format dialog box are also available via the buttons and drop-down lists on the **Formatting** toolbar:

When you first insert text, its properties are determined by the defaults for the style called "Normal." See "Text Styles" on page 71 to find out about creating and modifying text styles. Any properties that you change for selected text *override* the properties associated with the style for that text region.

Tip If you place the insertion point in text and then change the text properties, any new text you type at that insertion point will have the new properties.

You can change the following properties of selected text:

- Font
- Font style
- Font size
- Effects such as subscripts and superscripts
- Color

Font sizes are in points. Remember that if you choose a bigger font, the text region you're in may grow and overlap nearby regions. Choose **Separate Regions** from the **Format** menu if necessary.

Tip   You can specify that a text region or regions automatically push down following regions as they grow by selecting them and choosing **Properties** from the **Format** menu. Click the "Text" tab and select "Push Regions Down As You Type."

Tip   As a shortcut for creating subscripts and superscripts in text, use the **Subscript** and **Superscript** button on the Formatting toolbar. pop upThese work in both math and text regions.

Changing Paragraph Properties

A paragraph in a text region is any stream of characters followed by a hard return, which is created when you type **[↵]**. You can assign distinct properties to each paragraph in a text region, including *alignment, indenting* for either the first or all lines in the paragraph, *tab stops*, and *bullets* or *sequential numbering* to begin the paragraph.

Text paragraph properties are determined by the defaults for the style called "Normal." See "Text Styles" on page 71. Any paragraph properties that you change as described below *override* the Normal style for that text region.

Note   When you type **[Shift][↵]** Mathcad inserts a new line within the current paragraph; it does not create a new paragraph.

To change the properties for a paragraph within a text region:

1. Select the paragraph by clicking in it to place the insertion point, by drag-selecting it, or by triple-clicking it.

2. Choose **Paragraph** from the **Format** menu, or right click on it and choose **Paragraph** from the popup menu. Mathcad displays the Paragraph Format dialog box.

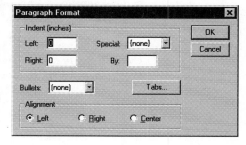

You can change the following paragraph properties:

Indent

To indent every line in the paragraph the same amount, enter numbers in the "Left" and "Right" text boxes. To indent the *first* line of the paragraph a different amount than the rest of the lines, as for a conventional or hanging indent, select "First Line" or "Hanging" from the "Special" drop-down list and enter a value below.

You can also set indents using the text ruler. Click in a paragraph and choose **Ruler** from the **View** menu. Move the top or bottom arrow in the ruler to set a different indent for the first line, or move both arrows to indent all the lines in the paragraph.

Bullets and numbered lists

To begin the paragraph with a bullet, select "Bullets" from the "Bullets" drop-down list. Select "Numbers" from the drop-down list to have Mathcad number successive

paragraphs in the region automatically. Alternatively, click  or on the Formatting toolbar.

Alignment

To align the paragraph at either the left or right edge of the text region, or to center the text within the text region, use the three alignment buttons in the Paragraph Format dialog box. Alternatively, click one of the three alignment buttons on the Formatting

toolbar: , , or .

Tab stops

To specify tabs, click the "Tabs" button in the Paragraph Format dialog box to open the Tabs dialog box. Enter numbers into the "Tab stop position" text box. Click "Set" for each tab stop then click "OK."

Or you can set tab stops using the text ruler. Click in a paragraph and choose **Ruler** from the **View** menu. Click in the ruler where you want a tab stop to be. A tab stop symbol appears. To remove a tab stop, click on the tab stop symbol, hold the mouse button down, and drag the cursor away from the ruler.

Tip   To change the measurement system used in the Paragraph Format dialog box or in the text ruler, choose **Ruler** from the **View** menu to show the text ruler. Then right click on the ruler and choose **Inches**, **Centimeters**, **Points**, or **Picas** from the popup menu.

Text Styles

Text styles give you an easy way to create a consistent appearance in your worksheets. Rather than choosing particular text and paragraph properties for each individual region, you can apply an available text style.

Every worksheet has a default "Normal" text style with a particular choice of text and paragraph properties. You can also modify existing text styles, create new ones of your own, and delete ones you no longer need.

Applying a Text Style to a Paragraph in a Text Region

When you create a text region in your worksheet, the region is tagged by default with the "Normal" style. You can, however, apply a different style to each paragraph—each stream of characters followed by a hard return—within the text region:

1. Click in the text region of the paragraph where you want to change the style.

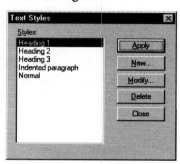

2. Choose **Style** from the **Format** menu, or right click on the paragraph and choose **Style** from the popup menu, to see a list of the available text styles. Available text styles depend on the worksheet template used.

3. Select a text style and click "Apply." The default text in your paragraph acquires the text and paragraph properties associated with that style.

Tip You can apply a text style to a text paragraph simply by clicking in the paragraph and choosing a style from the left-most drop-down list in the Formatting toolbar. To apply a text style to an entire text region, first select all the text in the region. For information on selecting text, refer to "Selecting Text" on page 66.

Modifying an Existing Text Style

You can change the definition of a text style by modifying it:

1. Choose **Style** from the **Format** menu. Mathcad brings up the Text Styles dialog box showing the currently available text styles.

2. Select the name of the text style you want to modify and click "Modify."

3. The Define Style dialog box displays the definitions of that text style.

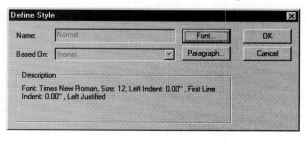

4. Click "Font" to modify text formats such as the font, font size, font styling, special effects, and color. Click "Paragraph" to modify the indenting, alignment and other paragraph properties.

Any text regions previously created with the text style will be modified accordingly.

Creating and Deleting Text Styles

You can create new text styles or delete ones you no longer use; any text style changes are saved with your worksheet. A new text style can be based on an existing text style, such that it inherits text or paragraph properties. For example, you may want to base a new "Subheading" style on an existing "Heading" style, but choose a smaller font size, keeping other text and paragraph properties the same.

Creating a text style

To create a new text style:

1. Choose **Style** from the **Format** menu. Mathcad brings up the Text Styles dialog box.

2. Click "New" to bring up the Define Style dialog box.

3. Enter a name for the new style in the "Name" text box. If you want to base the new style on one of the existing styles, select a style from the "Based on" drop-down list.

4. Click the "Font" button to make your choices for text formats for the new style. Click the "Paragraph" button to choose paragraph formats for the new style.

Your new style now appears in the Text Styles dialog box and can be applied to any text region. When you save the worksheet, the new text style is saved with it. To use the new text style in future worksheets, save your worksheet as a template as described in Chapter 7, "Worksheet Management." You may also copy the text style into another worksheet simply by copying and pasting a styled region into the new worksheet.

Note If you base a new text style on an existing text style, any changes you later make to the original text style will be reflected in the new text style as well.

Deleting a text style

To delete a text style:

1. Choose **Style** from the **Format** menu. Mathcad brings up the Text Styles dialog box showing the currently available text styles.

2. Select one of the available text styles from the list and click "Delete."

Any text regions in your worksheet whose text and paragraph properties were defined in terms of that text style will continue to display the properties of that style.

Equations in Text

This section describes how to insert equations into your text regions. Equations inserted into text have the same properties as those in the rest of your worksheet.

Inserting an Equation into Text

Place an equation into text either by creating a new equation inside a text region or by pasting an existing equation into a text region.

To add a new equation into text:

1. Click to place the insertion point where you want the equation to start.

> The universal gravitational constant, G, has the value │and can be used to determine the acceleration of a less massive object toward a more massive object.

2. Choose **Math Region** from the **Insert** menu or press [**Ctrl**][**Shift**]**A**. A math placeholder appears.

> The universal gravitational constant, G, has the value ▯ and can be used to determine the acceleration of a less massive object toward a more massive object.

3. Type in the equation just as you would in a math region.

4. When you've finished typing in the equation, click on any text to return to the text region. Mathcad adjusts the line spacing in the text region to accommodate the embedded math region.

> The universal gravitational constant, G, has the value $G := 6.67259 \cdot 10^{-11} \cdot \dfrac{m^3}{kg \cdot s^2}$ and can be used to determine the acceleration of a less massive object toward a more massive object.

To paste an existing equation into a text region, follow these steps:

1. Select the equation you want to paste into the text.

2. Choose **Copy** from the **Edit** menu, or click ▣ on the Standard toolbar.

3. Click in the text region to place the insertion point where you want the equation to start.

4. Choose **Paste** from the **Edit** menu, or click ▣ on the Standard toolbar.

Text Tools

Mathcad's text tools are similar to those in word processors.

Find and Replace

Mathcad's **Find** and **Replace** commands on the **Edit** menu are capable of working in both text and math regions. By default, however, Mathcad finds and replaces text in text regions only.

Searching for text

To find a sequence of characters:

1. Choose **Find** from the **Edit** menu. Mathcad brings up the Find dialog.

2. Enter the sequence of characters you want to find.

3. Click "Find Next" to find the next occurrence of the characters after the current insertion point. You can search upward or downward in the worksheet, match whole words only, match the case exactly of the characters you entered, and specify whether Mathcad should search in text or math regions or both.

Online Help   The Help topic "Characters You Can Find and Replace" details the characters you can find in math and text regions, including Greek symbols. Many special characters, including punctuation and spaces, can be located only in text or math strings.

Replacing characters

To search and replace text:

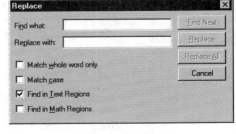

1. Choose **Replace** from the **Edit** menu to bring up the Replace dialog box.

2. Enter the character string you want to find in the "Find what" box.

3. Enter the string you want to replace it with in the "Replace with" box. You can match whole words only, match the case exactly of the characters you entered, or specify whether Mathcad should search in text or math regions or both.

You now have the following options:

- Click "Find Next" to find and select the next instance of your character string.

- Click "Replace" to replace the currently selected instance of the string.

- Click "Replace All" to replace all instances of the string.

Spell-Checking

Mathcad can search the text for misspelled words and suggest replacements. You can also add commonly used words to your personal dictionary.

Note Mathcad spell-checks text regions only, not math or graphics regions.

To begin spell-checking:

- Click at the beginning of wherever you want to spell-check. Mathcad spell-checks starting from this point and continues to the end of the worksheet. You can then either continue the spell-check from the beginning of the worksheet or quit.

- Alternatively, select the text you want to spell-check.

Once you've defined a range over which to check spelling:

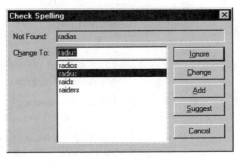

1. Choose **Spelling** from the **Tools** menu, or click ABC on the Standard toolbar.

2. When Mathcad finds a misspelled word, it opens the Check Spelling dialog box. The misspelled word is shown along with a suggested replacement(s). If Mathcad does not have a suggestion, it shows only the misspelled word.

Tip To determine whether a word is misspelled, Mathcad compares it with the words in two dictionaries: a general dictionary of common English words supplemented by mathematical terms and a personal dictionary. If Mathcad detects correctly spelled words throughout your worksheet you can add them to your personal dictionary.

After the Check Spelling dialog box appears:

- Click "Change" to change the word to the suggested replacement or to another word you select from the list of possible replacements.

- Click "Suggest" to see additional but less likely replacements. If Mathcad can offer no additional suggestions, "Suggest" is grayed.

- Click "Change" and type the replacement into the "Change to" box to change the word to one not listed

- Click "Ignore" or "Add" to leave the word as is. If you click "Ignore," Mathcad leaves the word alone, continues spell-checking, and ignores all future occurrences of the word. If you click "Add," the word is added to your personal dictionary.

Note To choose a dialect associated with the English dictionary, choose **Preferences** from the **Tools** menu, click on the Language tab, and choose an option below "Spell Check Dialect."

Chapter 7
Worksheet Management

- ◆ Worksheets and Templates
- ◆ Rearranging Your Worksheet
- ◆ Layout
- ◆ Safeguarding an Area of the Worksheet
- ◆ Safeguarding an Entire Worksheet
- ◆ Worksheet References
- ◆ Hyperlinks
- ◆ Distributing Your Worksheets

Worksheets and Templates

As you use Mathcad you create a worksheet file. Mathcad uses MCD as the file extension for worksheets.

When you create a new worksheet in Mathcad, you can start with Mathcad's default choices, or you can use a *template* that contains customized formats. Mathcad comes with a variety of predefined templates. You can extend this set by saving any of your Mathcad worksheets as a new template. Mathcad uses MCT as the file extension for templates.

You can save a worksheet in Hypertext Markup Language (HTML), so that the file can be viewed through a Web browser, or in rich-text format (RTF), so that it can be opened by most word processors. You can also save a worksheet in a previous version of Mathcad.

Creating a New Worksheet

When you first open Mathcad or click on the Standard toolbar, you see an empty worksheet based on a *worksheet template* (NORMAL.MCT). You can enter and format equations, graphs, text, and graphics in this space, as well as modify worksheet attributes such as numerical format, headers and footers, and text and math styles. The normal template is only one of the built-in templates Mathcad provides.

To create a new worksheet based on a template:

1. Choose **New** from the **File** menu. Mathcad displays a list of available worksheet templates. The exact templates available differ depending on the templates you have developed.

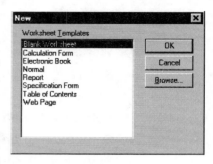

2. Choose a template other than "Blank Worksheet." By default Mathcad displays worksheet templates saved in the TEMPLATE folder of the directory you used to install Mathcad. Click "Browse" to find a template in another directory or on another drive.

Opening a Worksheet

Open an existing worksheet by choosing **Open...** [**Ctrl**]**O** from the **File** menu. You will be able to browse for files anywhere on your desktop or network. You can type a path directly into the File Name box, including URLs, e.g.

http://www.mathcad.com/librarycontent/convol.mcd

Note   If you open files online, you will create a temporary file locally on your machine, but the original URL will still be displayed in the Title bar. You may get a warning that the file is Read-only, depending on the permissions of the directory from which you read it.

If you are running Windows 2000 or XP, you can set up a Web directory as one of your Network Places (if you have permission to write to that directory), and you'll be able to browse directories online within Mathcad.

Saving Your Worksheet

To save a worksheet, choose either **Save** or **Save As...** from the **File** menu and enter a file name with the extension MCD. After the first time you save the worksheet, simply

choose **Save** from the **File** menu or click 🖫 on the Standard toolbar.

Saving your worksheet in an earlier format

Worksheets created in an earlier version of Mathcad will open in the current version, but files in the current version of Mathcad will *not* open in earlier versions. Mathcad does allow you to save a worksheet as a previous version. Regions or features that won't work in an earlier version appear as bitmap images.

To save a worksheet that can be read by an earlier version of Mathcad:

1. Choose **Save As** from the **File** menu.

2. In the "Save as type" drop-down list, select the earlier version and provide a file name.

Creating a New Template

When you create a worksheet based on a template, all of the formatting information and any text, math, and graphic regions from the template are copied to the new worksheet. Templates allow you to maintain consistency across multiple worksheets.

The template specifies:

- Definitions of all math styles (Chapter 4).
- Definitions of all text styles (Chapter 6).
- Margins for printing (see "Layout" on page 83).
- Numerical result formats and values for Mathcad's built-in variables (Chapter 8).
- Names of Mathcad's basic units and the default unit system (Chapter 8).
- The default calculation mode (Chapter 8).
- Ruler visibility and measurement system (see "Aligning Regions" on page 80).

To create a new template, first create a new worksheet setting the options listed above the way you want. The worksheet can also contain any equations, text, and graphics that you want repeated in new files. Then save this worksheet as a template. To do so:

1. Choose **Save As** from the **File** menu.
2. Browse to the TEMPLATE folder within the directory where you installed Mathcad.
3. In the "Save as type" drop-down list, select "Mathcad Templates (*.mct)."
4. Type a name in the "File name" box."

Your template will be added to the list of templates that appears when you choose **New** from the **File** menu. To make a new worksheet based on a template, choose **New** from the **File** menu and select a template from the list. If you did not save your template to the TEMPLATE folder, you will need to browse to find the template.

Modifying a Template

To modify an existing worksheet template:

1. Choose **Open** from the **File** menu or click ![icon] on the Standard toolbar.
2. In the "Files of type" drop-down list, select "All Files."
3. Type the name of the template in the "File name" box or browse to locate it in the dialog box. Worksheet templates are saved by default in the TEMPLATE folder.
4. Click "Open." The template opens in the Mathcad window.

You may now edit the template as you would modify any Mathcad worksheet. If you want to give a new name to the modified template, choose **Save As** from the **File** menu and enter a new name for the template.

Tip   To modify the default template for a blank worksheet, modify the template file NORMAL.MCT. You may want to save the original NORMAL.MCT elsewhere in case you need to retrieve it.

> **Note** When you modify a template, your changes affect only new files created from the modified template. The changes do not affect any worksheets created with the template before the template was modified.

Rearranging Your Worksheet

This section describes how to rearrange math, graphics, and text in your worksheets. See the section "Regions" on page 13 for the basics on selecting, copying, moving, and deleting regions.

> **Note** You can get an overall view of how your worksheet looks by choosing **Zoom** from the **View** menu or clicking `100%` on the Standard toolbar and choosing a magnification. Or you can use the **Print Preview** command.

Aligning Regions

Once you've inserted regions into your worksheet, you can align them vertically or horizontally using menu commands, nudging with the arrow keys, or by using the worksheet ruler.

Using commands

To align regions horizontally or vertically using commands:

1. Select regions as described on page 14.

2. Choose **Align Regions**⇒**Across** (to align horizontally) or **Align Regions**⇒**Down** (to align vertically) from the Format menu. Or choose these commands by clicking  and on the Standard toolbar.

When you align the regions down, Mathcad moves selected regions so that their left edges are aligned vertically. Aligning regions across moves all selected regions so that their top edges are aligned horizontally.

> **Note** Aligning regions may inadvertently cause regions to overlap. Mathcad warns you when this will occur. See "Separating Regions" on page 82.

Nudging Regions with Arrow Keys

To "nudge," or move, a region or regions with the arrow keys, the regions must be dotted-line selected. Dotted-line selection can be achieved in two ways:

- **Multiple regions**: Click and drag over multiple regions to select all dragged regions with a dotted line.

- **Single regions**: Press [**Ctrl**] or [**Shift**] and then click on the region to get a dotted line selection box.

Once selected, the region(s) can be moved an arbitrary number of grid spaces up, down, right, or left using the arrow keys. Pressing an arrow once will move the regions one grid space in that direction. Clicking and holding a key will move repeatedly until the key is released.

Hovering the mouse over the edge of the selected region(s) results in the grabbing hand icon. Clicking and holding allows the region(s) to be dragged freely.

Using the worksheet ruler

Choosing **Ruler** from the **View** menu while the cursor is in a blank spot or in a math region, opens the worksheet ruler at the top of the window. You can use alignment guidelines on the ruler to align regions at particular measurements along the worksheet.

To set alignment guidelines on the ruler:

1. Click on the ruler wherever you want the alignment guideline to appear. A tab stop symbol appears on the ruler.

2. Click on the tab stop symbol with the right mouse button and choose **Show Guideline** from the popup menu. A check appears next to the command. You can add as many guidelines as you need.

You can also set Tabs and Guidelines by selecting **Tabs** from the **Format** menu. Type the location for any tabs or guides you'd like to place, then check the "Show Guidelines" checkbox. You must be viewing the **Ruler** for guidelines to show up.

The alignment guideline appears as a green vertical line. Select and move regions to the guideline. Figure 7-1 shows how you can use an alignment guideline to align math regions.

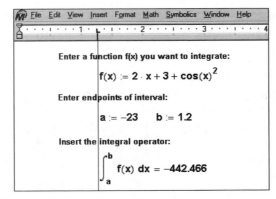

Figure 7-1: Using an alignment guideline to align regions vertically.

Note The tab stops you insert on the ruler specify where the cursor should move when you press the [**TAB**] key. To remove a tab stop, click on its symbol, hold the mouse button down, and drag the the stop off the ruler.

To move a guideline, click on the tab stop on the ruler and drag it. To remove an alignment guideline, click on the ruler with the right mouse button where the guideline is located and uncheck **Show Guideline** in the dialog.

To automatically place the next region you create on a guide, press the [**TAB**] key in a blank region of the worksheet. The red crosshair will move to the next tab/guideline.

> **Tip** You can change the measurement system used in the ruler by clicking on the ruler with the right mouse button, and choosing **Inches**, **Centimeters**, **Points**, or **Picas** from the popup menu. To change the ruler measurement for all documents, make this change to NORMAL.MCT.

Inserting or Deleting Blank Lines

You can easily insert one or more blank lines into your worksheet:

1. Click in blank space below which you want to insert one or more blank lines. Make sure the cursor looks like a crosshair.

2. Press [**Enter**] to insert a blank line and move the cursor to the left margin.

To delete one or more blank lines from your worksheet:

1. Click above the blank space you want to delete. Make sure the cursor looks like a crosshair and that there are no regions to the right or left of the cursor.

2. Press [**Delete**]. Mathcad deletes blank lines below your cursor. Alternatively, press [**BkSp**] to remove blank lines *above* your cursor.

If you press either [**Delete**] or [**BkSp**] and nothing seems to be happening, check to make sure that the cursor is on a line all by itself. If any region in your worksheet extends into the line you are trying to delete, Mathcad won't be able to delete that line.

> **Tip** To quickly insert or delete a *specific number* of lines from your worksheet, right click in a blank part of the worksheet, choose **Insert Lines** or **Delete Lines** from the popup menu, and enter the number of lines in the dialog box.

Separating Regions

As you move and edit the regions in a Mathcad worksheet, they may end up overlapping one another. Overlapping regions don't interfere with each other's calculations, but they may make your worksheet hard to read.

A good way to determine whether regions overlap is to choose **Regions** from the **View** menu. As shown at right, Mathcad displays blank space in gray and leaves the regions in your default background color. To return to the default background color, choose **Regions** from the **View** menu again.

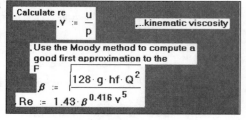

To separate all overlapping regions, choose **Separate Regions** from the **Format** menu. Wherever regions overlap, this command moves the regions in such a way as to avoid overlaps.

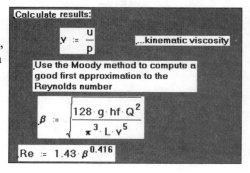

Note Be careful with the **Separate Regions** command since moving regions can change the order of calculation. You can also drag regions individually, add lines by pressing [**Enter**], or cut and paste the regions so they don't overlap.

Highlighting Regions

Mathcad allows you to highlight regions so that they stand out from the rest of the equations and text in your worksheet:

To apply a highlight color to a region:

1. Click in the region or select multiple regions.
2. Choose **Properties** from the **Format** menu.
3. Click the Display tab.
4. Check "Highlight Region." Click "Choose Color" to choose a highlight color other than the default choice.

Mathcad colors the region with the color you chose. This is a purely cosmetic change with no effect on any math regions.

Note The appearance of a highlighted region when printed depends on the capabilities of your printer and the choice of highlight color. Some black and white printers render a color as black, obscuring the equation or text. Others render just the right gray to highlight the equation without obscuring it. Still other printers will disregard the background highlight color.

Changing the worksheet background color

To change the color of the background of your worksheet:

1. Choose **Color** from the **Format** menu.
2. Pull right and choose **Background** to see a palette of colors. Click the appropriate color, then click "OK."

Layout

Before printing a worksheet, you may need to adjust the margins, paper options, page breaks, and headers and footers so that pages of the worksheet are printed appropriately.

Setting Margins, Paper Size, Source, and Orientation

Mathcad worksheets have user-specifiable margins at the left, right, top, and bottom of the worksheet. To set these margins, choose **Page Setup** from the **File** menu.

Use the four text boxes in the lower right of the Page Setup dialog to specify the distances from the margin to the corresponding edge of the actual sheet of paper on which you are printing.

You can also use Page Setup settings to change the size, source, or orientation of the paper on which you print your worksheet. See "Printing" on page 91 for more about printing your Mathcad worksheets.

Tip To use the margin and other page setup settings in the current worksheet in new worksheets, save the worksheet as a template as described in "Creating a New Template" on page 79.

Page Breaks

Mathcad provides two kinds of page breaks:

- **Soft page breaks**. Mathcad uses your default printer settings and your top and bottom margins to insert these page breaks automatically. These show up as dotted horizontal lines, which you see as you scroll down in your worksheet. You cannot add or remove soft page breaks.

- **Hard page breaks**. You can insert a hard page break by placing the cursor at a place in your worksheet and choosing **Page Break** from the **Insert** menu. Hard page breaks display as solid horizontal lines in your worksheets.

To delete a hard page break:

1. Drag-select the hard page break as you would select any other region in your Mathcad worksheet. A dashed selection box appears around the page break.

2. Choose **Delete** from the **Edit** menu or press the [**Delete**] key.

Tip Because Mathcad is a WYSIWYG environment, any region that overlaps a soft or hard page break prints by default in pieces on successive pages. To separate a region from a hard page break, choose **Separate Regions** from the **Format** menu. However, this command does not separate regions from any overlapping *soft* page breaks. Choose **Repaginate Now** from the **Format** menu to force Mathcad to insert a soft page break above any region that otherwise would print in pieces on successive pages.

Headers and Footers

To add a header or a footer to every printed page, to create a different header or footer for the first page of a worksheet, or to modify an existing header or footer, choose **Header and Footer** from the **View** menu.:

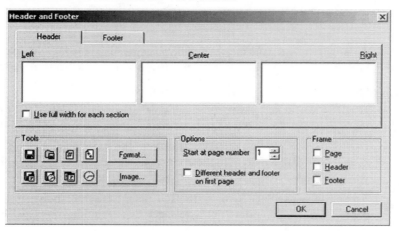

To add or edit a header or footer:

1. Click the Header or Footer tab to modify the header or footer for the worksheet. To create a different header or footer for the first page of your worksheet, check the "Different header and footer on first page" option and click the Header–Page 1 or Footer–Page 1 tab.

2. Type the header or footer information into the text boxes. Whatever you type into the Left, Center, and Right text boxes will appear in these positions on the page. Click "Format" in the Tools group to change the header or footer font, font style, size, or alignment. Click "Use full width for each section" if you want text in any of the boxes to extend beyond the width of that third of the worksheet.

3. Click the buttons in the Tools group to insert items such as the file name, page number, current date, or time automatically wherever the insertion point is. To insert an image, click "Image" in the Tools group and browse to locate a bitmap (.BMP format) file.

Tip Mathcad by default begins numbering at page 1. You can set a different starting page number in the Options group in the Header and Footer dialog box.

Safeguarding an Area of the Worksheet

Sometimes you want to protect areas of your worksheet. For example, if you've developed a set of equations, you may want to prevent readers of your worksheet from tampering with them. To avoid unintended edits to your worksheet, you can safeguard an area of your worksheet by locking it such that you can still edit it even though nobody else can.

Once a region is safely inside a locked area, nobody can edit it. Any math regions inside a locked area continue, however, to affect other equations in the document. For example, if you define a function inside a locked area, you can still use that function anywhere below and to the right of its definition. You cannot, however, change the function's definition unless you unlock the area first.

Inserting an Area

To insert a lockable area into your worksheet:

1. Choose **Area** from the **Insert** menu. Mathcad inserts a pair of lines into the worksheet. These mark the boundaries of the lockable area.

2. Select either of these boundary lines just as you'd select any region: by dragging the mouse across the line or by clicking the line itself.

3. Now you can drag the boundary line to increase or decrease the area or select both to move the entire area.

You should position the boundaries so that there's enough space between them for whatever regions you want to lock. You can have any number of lockable areas in your worksheet. The only restriction is that you cannot have one lockable area inside another.

Tip   To name an area in your worksheet, click on an area boundary, choose **Properties** from the **Format** menu, and enter a name on the Area tab. The Area tab also lets you modify other display attributes of an area, such as whether a border or icon appears.

Locking and Collapsing an Area

You can lock the area to preserve what's inside of it. You can choose to use a password to prevent unauthorized editing of the regions in a locked area. You can also collapse the area, either with or without locking it, so that the regions are hidden from view.

To lock an area:

1. Click in the area.

2. Choose **Area⇒Lock** from the **Format** menu.

3. In the Lock Area dialog box, enter a password if you want to lock the area with a password. Type any combination of letters, numbers, and other characters. You must re-enter the password to confirm it.

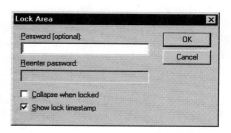

4. Check "Collapse when locked" to hide the locked regions from view. Check "Show lock timestamp" to display the date and time the area was last locked above and below the boundary lines.

5. To hide the collapsed area, right click on it and choose Properties, then the Area tab. You can uncheck all the boxes to totally hide the area. If you drag over a hidden area, you will see two dashed lines above and below it.

The area is now locked and by default shows padlocks on the boundaries and a timestamp.

Note   If you choose to password protect an area, make sure you remember your password. If you forget it, you will find yourself permanently locked out of that area. Keep in mind also that the password is case sensitive.

To collapse an area without locking it first:

1. Click in the area.

2. Choose **Area⇒Collapse** from the **Format** menu.

A collapsed area appears by default as a single line in your worksheet.

Unlocking and Expanding an Area

If you want to make changes to a region inside a locked area, you have to unlock it. If the area is collapsed, you must also expand it.

To unlock a locked area:

1. Click in the area you want to unlock.

2. Choose **Area⇒Unlock** from the **Format** menu.

3. If a password is required, you are prompted for the password.

To expand a collapsed area:

1. Click on the boundary line.

2. Choose **Area⇒Expand** from the **Format** menu.

Once an area is unlocked and expanded, you can make whatever changes you want to just as freely as you would elsewhere in your worksheet.

Tip When you lock an area without a password, anyone can unlock it by simply choosing **Area⇒Unlock** from the **Format** menu.

Deleting an Area

You can delete an area just as you would any other region. To do so:

1. Make sure the area is unlocked. You cannot delete a locked area.

2. Select either of the two lines indicating the extent of the locked area by dragging the mouse across it.

3. Choose **Cut** from the **Edit** menu or click ✂ on the Standard toolbar.

Safeguarding an Entire Worksheet

Worksheet Protection

When distributing a worksheet, you may wish to restrict user access to most regions. Rather than locking an area, you may opt instead to *protect* your worksheet.

Mathcad provides three levels of worksheet protection:

-   **File**. The worksheet can only be saved as either a Mathcad file or an HTML file. No restrictions are placed on any regions.

-   **Content**. The worksheet can only be saved as either a Mathcad file or an HTML file. Existing regions cannot be changed. New regions can be created and protected regions can be copied.

-   **Editing**. The worksheet can only be saved as either a Mathcad file or an HTML file. Existing regions cannot be changed. Protected regions cannot be edited or copied. No new regions can be created in the worksheet.

To protect your worksheet, choose **Protect Worksheet** from the **Tools** menu; to turn off Worksheet Protection, choose **Unprotect Worksheet** from the **Tools** menu. To disable protection for a specific region when the rest of the worksheet is protected, right click on the region, choose Properties from the dialog, and deselect "Protect region from editing" on the Protect tab *before* protecting the worksheet.

When enabled and set at the content or editing level, worksheet protection prohibits access to any region not explicitly left unprotected; by default, a region is flagged for protection.

Note Regions added while worksheet protection is enabled (content level) cannot be flagged for protection until the worksheet is unprotected.

Tip Disabling protection for an area, when the rest of the worksheet is protected, can be set either before or after the area is collapsed. Right click either of the area boundaries when expanded or right click the collapsed area; then choose **Properties** from the dialog, and uncheck region protection on the Protect tab. Your setting will be preserved when the area is either collapsed or expanded. Once you've enabled Worksheet Protection, areas cannot be expanded or collapsed.

Worksheet References

There may be times when you want to use formulas and calculations from one Mathcad worksheet inside another. You may have calculations and definitions that you re-use frequently. You can, of course, simply use **Copy** and **Paste** from the **Edit** menu to move whatever you need to move, or drag regions from one worksheet and drop them in another. However, when entire worksheets are involved, this method can be cumbersome.

Mathcad allows you to *reference* one worksheet from another—that is, to access the computations in a worksheet without opening it. When you insert a reference to a worksheet, you won't see the formulas of the referenced worksheet, but the current worksheet behaves as if you could.

Tip An alternative described in "Safeguarding an Area of the Worksheet" on page 85 is to create a collapsible *area* to hide calculations in your worksheet. This method, while it does not let you re-use calculations in the same way as a worksheet reference, does give you the option of password protecting or locking an area of calculations.

To insert a reference to a worksheet:

1. Click the mouse wherever you want to insert the reference. Make sure you click in empty space and not in an existing region. The cursor should look like a crosshair.

2. Choose **Reference** from the **Insert** menu.

3. Click "Browse" to locate and select a worksheet. You can also enter an Internet address (URL) to insert a reference to a Mathcad file that is located on the Web.

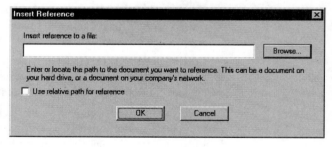

To indicate that a reference has been inserted, Mathcad pastes a small icon wherever you had the crosshair. The path to the referenced worksheet is to the right of the icon. All definitions in the referenced worksheet are available below or to the right of the icon. If you double-click the icon, Mathcad opens the referenced worksheet in its own window for editing. You can move or delete the icon just as you would any other Mathcad region.

Reference:http://www.mathsoft.com/mcad60/ug/

Note By default, the location of the referenced file is stored in the worksheet as an absolute system path or URL. This means that if you move the main worksheet or the referenced worksheet to a different location, Mathcad cannot locate the referenced file. If you want the location of the referenced file to be stored relative to the Mathcad worksheet containing the reference, click "Use relative path for reference" in the Insert Reference dialog box. The reference is then valid even if you move the referenced file and the main worksheet to a different drive but keep the *relative* directory structure intact. To use a relative path, you must first save the file containing the reference.

To update a worksheet containing a reference, make the change on the referenced worksheet, save the sheet, return to the referencing worksheet, click on the reference and press the [**F9**] key ("Calculate"). The calculation will then incorporate the change.

Hyperlinks

Mathcad allows you to create *hyperlinks* in your Mathcad worksheets that, when double-clicked, open Mathcad worksheets, jump to other regions of a Mathcad worksheet, or link to other files.

Creating Hyperlinks Between Worksheets

You can create a hyperlink from any Mathcad region, such as a text region or image, to any other Mathcad region, either within the same worksheet or in another worksheet. Hyperlinks allow you to connect groups of worksheets or simply cross-reference related areas of a worksheet or worksheets.

Creating hyperlinks from worksheet to worksheet

When you create a hyperlink from one worksheet to another you have two options:

- The target worksheet can open in a full-sized Mathcad worksheet window that allows you to edit its contents.
- The target worksheet can open in a small *popup window* that displays the contents of the worksheet, but does not allow you to edit its contents.

Mathcad can follow a hyperlink to any worksheet, whether it is stored on a local drive, a network file system, or the internet.

To create a hyperlink from one worksheet to another, first specify the hyperlink by:

1. Selecting a piece of text, or
2. Clicking anywhere in image, or
3. Placing the insertion point anywhere within an entire text region.

Tip When you select text, Mathcad underlines the text to show a hyperlink. The arrow cursor changes to a hand cursor when you hover over any hyperlink.

The next step is to specify the target worksheet:

1. Choose **Hyperlink** from the **Insert** menu. Mathcad opens the Insert Hyperlink dialog box.

2. Click "Browse" to locate and select the target worksheet. You can enter an Internet address (URL) to create a hyperlink to a file on the Internet.

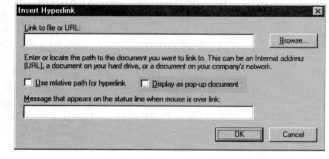

3. Check "Use relative path for hyperlink" to store the location of the target worksheet relative to the Mathcad worksheet containing the hyperlink. This allows the hyperlink to be valid even if you move the target file and the worksheet containing the hyperlink, but keep the relative directory structure between the two the same.

Note In order for "Use relative path for hyperlink" to be available, you must first save the worksheet in which you are inserting the hyperlink.

4. Check "Display as popup document" if you want the target worksheet to open in a small popup window.

5. Enter a message to appear on the status line at the bottom of the window when the mouse hovers over the hyperlink.

To revise a hyperlink—for example, if you move the target worksheet and still want the hyperlink to work—click the hyperlinked item and choose **Hyperlink** from the **Insert** menu. Make any changes you wish in the Edit Hyperlink dialog box.

To remove a hyperlink, click the hyperlink and choose **Hyperlink** from the **Insert** menu. Click "Remove Link" in the dialog box. Mathcad removes the link.

Creating hyperlinks from region to region

Before you can link to a specific region in a worksheet, you must mark it with a *tag*. A tag can be any collection of words, numbers, or spaces, but not symbols.

To create a region tag:

1. Right click on the region and select Properties.

2. In the Properties dialog box, under the Display tab, type a tag in the text box provided.

Note You can not include a period in the tag name such as Section1.3, you must write Section1-3.

To create a hyperlink to a region that has been *tagged*:

1. Click a region or select words in your worksheet and choose **Hyperlink** from the **Insert** menu.

2. Click "Browse" to locate and select the target worksheet or enter an Internet address (URL). You must enter the name of the target worksheet even if you are creating a hyperlink to a region within the same worksheet.

At the end of the worksheet path type "#" followed by the region tag. The complete path for your target region will look something like this: **C:\filename#region tag**.

Note When you link from region to region within or between Mathcad worksheets, you cannot use the popup window option.

Creating Hyperlinks to Other Files

You can create a hyperlink not only from one Mathcad worksheet to another, but also from a Mathcad worksheet to any other file type, either on a local or network file system or on the Internet. Use this feature to create E-books, as described in "Distributing Your Worksheets," or compound documents that contain not only Mathcad worksheets but word processing files, animation files, web pages—any file type that you want.

Note When you double-click a hyperlink to a file other than a Mathcad worksheet, you launch either the application that created the file or an application associated with a file of that type in the Windows Registry. You cannot display such hyperlinked files within a popup window.

Distributing Your Worksheets

Mathcad worksheets can be distributed in a variety of media including the Internet, through email, in Microsoft Word, in print format, and, of course, as individual Mathcad documents or as a Mathcad E-book. You can print Mathcad worksheets to PDF files if you have the appropriate applications on your computer.

Printing

To print a Mathcad worksheet, choose **Print** from the **File** menu. The Print dialog box lets you control whether to print the entire worksheet, selected pages, or selected regions. The particular dialog box you see depends on the printer you've selected.

Printing Wide Worksheets

Mathcad worksheets can be wider than a sheet of paper, since you can scroll as far to the right as you like in a Mathcad worksheet and place equations, text, and graphics wherever you like. As you scroll horizontally, however, you see dashed vertical lines appearing to indicate the right margins of successive "pages" corresponding to the settings for your printer. The sections of the worksheet separated by the dashed vertical lines print on separate sheets of paper, yet the page number at the bottom of the Mathcad window does not change as you scroll to the right.

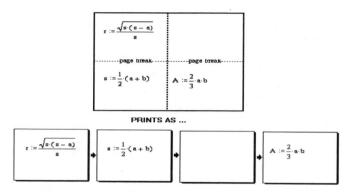

You can think of the worksheet as being divided into vertical strips. Mathcad begins printing at the top of each strip and continues until it reaches the last region in this strip. It prints successive strips left to right. Note that certain layouts will produce one or more blank pages.

Tip   You can control whether a wide worksheet is printed in its entirety or in a single page width. To do so, choose **Page Setup** from the **File** menu to open the Page Setup dialog box. Then, to suppress printing of anything to the right of the right margin, check "Print single page width."

Tip   Mathcad allows you to change the display of some operators including the **: =**, the bold equals, the derivative operator, and the multiplication operator. Before you print, you can choose **Worksheet Options** from the **Tools** menu and click on the Display tab to change the appearance of these operators. This can make your printout clearer to someone unfamiliar with Mathcad notation.

Print Preview

To check your worksheet's layout before printing, choose **Print Preview** from the **File** menu or click [icon] on the Standard toolbar. The Mathcad window shows the current section of your worksheet in miniature, as it will appear when printed, with a strip of buttons across the top of the window:

Click "Close" to go back to the main worksheet screen. The remaining buttons give you more control over the preview.

Tip   You can use the "Zoom In" and "Zoom Out" buttons to magnify the worksheet or you can magnify the worksheet by moving the cursor onto the previewed page so that the cursor changes to a magnifying glass. T hen click the mouse. Click again to magnify your worksheet even more. Once you're at the maximum magnification, clicking on the page de-magnifies it.

Note   You cannot edit the current page or change its format in the Print Preview screen. To edit the page or change its format, return to the normal worksheet view by clicking "Close."

Creating PDF Files

If you wish to distribute your documents electronically in a format which mimics the original exactly, but without requiring Mathcad to open it, you can save documents in Adobe's Portable Document Format (PDF). You can purchase Acrobat Pro from Adobe or use one of the various PDF tools on the market. Once a PDF printer driver is installed, you can choose Print and select the PDF driver from your list of printers. Then choose Print to File in the print dialog box to create a PDF file that can be distributed as is, or further manipulated in Acrobat Distiller.

Creating E-books

As described in Chapter 3, "Online Resources," an E-book is a hyperlinked collection of Mathcad worksheets. When you open an E-book in Mathcad, it opens in its own window. An E-book has a table of contents, an index, and search features accessible through buttons on the toolbar in the book window. The worksheets in an E-book are live, so a reader can experiment directly within the book.

If you have several Mathcad worksheets that you want to collect together, you can create your own E-book. There are several steps to creating an E-book:

1. Creating individual Mathcad files
2. Preparing a Table of Contents
3. Adding hyperlinks between appropriate files
4. Creating an HBK file to specify the order of the files in the book
5. Developing an index (optional)
6. Checking the index, HBK file, and worksheets for errors.

For more details about each step of this process, see the online **Author's Reference** under the **Help** menu in Mathcad. There you will find tips and techniques for creating E-books, as well as other details associated with turning a collection of worksheets into a navigable book.

After you have created an E-book, others can open it in Mathcad and navigate through it using the toolbar buttons of the E-book window. For more information on E-books and the navigation tools, refer to Chapter 3, "Online Resources."

Creating Web Pages and Sites

Mathcad worksheets can be output as HTML files for viewing in a Web browser. Any HTML file created by Mathcad 11 can be read back into Mathcad 11, then can be calculated like a native Mathcad worksheet. The only exception to this is protected documents, which will only be saved as flat HTML files that will not calculate.

There are a variety of options for specifying how worksheet regions are represented in HTML files. All Mathcad text regions are output as standard HTML, but you must choose the format in which you would like equations, graphs, and other types of regions to be stored on a web page.

Choose **Save as Web Page...** from the **File** menu to save a file in HTML format. Once you have chosen a file name and location to store your file, click **Save**, and you will be presented with a set of options for saving your file:

Preferences for Web page output

You can save equations as images or in Mathematical Markup Language (MathML). If you select images, then all equation regions will be inserted in the HTML document using <IMG> tags. If you select MathML, equation regions will be encoded as presentation MathML, and you'll be able to select from a variety of supported renderers from the dropdown menu.

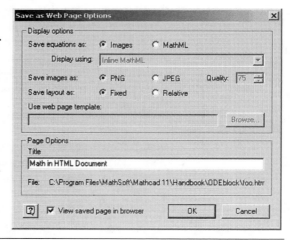

Note You can save equations as images or *presentation* MathML. This choice does not affect Mathcad's ability to read the document for live calculation, only how the Web browser will display equations. Presentation MathML display typically requires a plug-in. For pages that require only a Web browser for display, save your equations as images. Mathcad region information is simultaneously stored as *content* MathML for subsequent rendering and calculation back into Mathcad.

Choose a format for image export, either JPEG or PNG. PNG is a lossless format so may result in clearer images for graphs and drawings, while JPEG images may be smaller or compatible with older browser versions. All graphs, embedded images, and tables will be displayed as images in the output HTML document, as well as equations, if you have chosen this method of export.

Fixed or relative positioning and templates

Choose whether a document will use relative or fixed layout when exported to HTML. When the **Save Layout As** radio button is set to **Relative**, regions will be stored in an HTML table that attempts to retain the relative horizontal and vertical placement of your regions. This arrangement makes it possible to edit the Web page outside of Mathcad to include additional HTML — navigation links, images, etc. This attribute must selected to use HTML templates.

When the **Relative** button is selected, you can browse for an HTML template file. Templates are used to wrap HTML content exported from a Mathcad file. You can use them to add headers, footers, navigation links, and images, creating a uniform layout for many files. This facilitates large Web site production. Template files must be saved with MLT extensions and use the same structure as the HTML template.MLT sample in your Templates folder within the Mathcad directory. Note that these MLT templates are *output* templates, not input templates like those used to format Mathcad document styles for display in Mathcad.

If you check the **Fixed** radio button, each Mathcad region image or block of text will be precisely positioned on a web page, mimicking the original Mathcad document as closely as possible, but making it difficult to add new items to the page outside of Mathcad. For further instructions and tips on publishing Web sites with Mathcad, see the online **Author's Reference** under the **Help** menu in Mathcad.

Tip Relative positioning creates a much more flexible MathML document, but it does require some thought about region layout to be effective. Keeping your Mathcad regions aligned horizontally and vertically will result in a much better-displaying file. See "Aligning Regions" on page 80 for ways to make this easier.

Finally, you can choose a new title for your page, and choose, if you wish, to open the page immediately in your default Web browser.

You can also save Mathcad documents in HTML by choosing **Save As...** from the **File** menu, and selecting "HTML/MathML File" from the "Save as type" drop-down list. This will not display the special properties dialog shown above. Options for HTML can be set by choosing **Preferences** from the **Tools** menu, and modifying choices on the "HTML Options" tab.

Round-Trip HTML/MathML

Using Microsoft's Internet Explorer, you can activate Mathcad to edit worksheets that have been saved in HTML/MathML format. To edit HTML files generated by Mathcad through the Internet Explorer browser:

1. Load a Mathcad worksheet that has been saved in HTML/MathML format into Internet Explorer.

2. Select **Edit with Mathcad Application** under the **File** menu.

Edit your file as usual and then save it. The file will be saved in HTML/MathML format.

Note When you save a Mathcad worksheet in HTML/MathML format, an HTM file is created and a subdirectory with the name "(filename)_images" is also created to contain all the associated image files. When copying files to your server, don't forget to include the associated image directory.

Saving Your Worksheet to Microsoft Word

To save a worksheet so you can distribute it in Microsoft Word:

1. Scroll to the bottom of your worksheet to update all calculated results.

2. Choose **Save As** from the **File** menu.

3. In the Save As dialog box, choose "Rich Text Format File" (.rtf) from the "Save as type" drop-down list.

4. Enter a file name and then click "Save."

Regions that are past the right margin will not be visible in Word. When you open an RTF file with Microsoft Word, you will be able to edit the text. However, you'll no longer be able to edit math regions and graphs, which have become pictures. The regions will not appear in their correct position across the page unless you choose **Print Layout** from Word's **View** menu.

Tip   Any regions that are to the right of the right margin in Mathcad will not be visible in Microsoft Word. For optimal conversion to Word, you should set your margins in Mathcad to the same defaults as Word (1.25" on left and right, and 1" top and bottom) or start with the Mathcad template, "Microsoft Word.mct," from **File⇒New**.

Drag and dropping a region(s) from Mathcad to Microsoft Word inserts a Mathcad object into Word. See "Inserting Objects" on page 155.

You can also just simply select text in a Mathcad text region, copy the text by choosing

Copy from the **Edit** menu or clicking 🖹 on the Standard toolbar, and choose **Paste** from the **Edit** menu in Microsoft Word to move your text to Word.

Storing Worksheets in a SharePoint Repository

SharePoint is a document storage and management system from Microsoft, which grants you control over the dissemination and modification of files stored within a repository. Mathcad Enterprise customers who have access to a SharePoint server can access worksheets directly from a SharePoint repository.

You can open worksheets from the repository just as you would any other location, by navigating to the file in the **Open** dialog and clicking "OK,"or typing its URL, if you know it. When you open a worksheet from a SharePoint Repository, you will have the option to either open the file on a *Read Only* or *Check Out* basis.

- **Read Only**. You will notice an extra item in the **File** menu, called **Check Out**. Until you check out your worksheet, it will behave just like any worksheet opened from your hard drive, and you will not be able to save it to the repository.

- **Check Out**. If you have checked your worksheet out, Mathcad adds an additional entry to the **File** menu, **Check In**, which allows you to update the version in your repository.

When you *Check In* a worksheet, you will have the option to publish your worksheet. Publishing your worksheet makes it visible to users with Reader access. Only users with Author or higher access can see unpublished worksheets.

Closing a checked out worksheet will prompt you to:

- Check the file back into the repository, thereby saving your edits, or

- Discard your changes and undo the check out, thus allowing another user to check out the worksheet, or

- Close the worksheet and keep it checked out. In this last case, the file will reopen with all your edits intact, but SharePoint still considers it to be one checkout so that discarding changes the next time you edit the worksheet will discard any changes made in any session since you checked the file out.

Tip   File functions such as READBIN can read from data files stored in a SharePoint Repository, as long as you use either the full URL to the file or a relative path in the function call. Functions that write data files, such as WRITEBIN, will only work if you have checked out the data file.

Mailing

If you're connected to a mail system that's compatible with Microsoft's Mail API (MAPI), you can use Mathcad to direct that system to send an electronic mail message and your current Mathcad worksheet.

Tip The settings in your mail system determine how Mathcad worksheets are attached to or encoded in the mail message. We recommend that you use a compression method such as ZIP to attach Mathcad worksheets to mail messages.

To send a Mathcad worksheet by electronic mail, :

1. Open the worksheet you want to send.

2. Choose **Send** from the **File** menu.

Your mail system will launch and creates a new message with your worksheet as an attachment.

Chapter 8
Calculating in Mathcad

- ♦ Defining and Evaluating Variables
- ♦ Defining and Evaluating Functions
- ♦ Units and Dimensions
- ♦ Working with Results
- ♦ Controlling Calculation
- ♦ Animation
- ♦ Error Messages

Defining and Evaluating Variables

When you type an expression into a worksheet, you are usually doing one of two things:

- Typing a variable or function name and assigning some value to it.
- Typing an equation and asking Mathcad to solve it.

These topics are discussed in the next two sections.

Defining a Variable

A variable definition defines the value of a variable everywhere below and to the right of the definition. To define a variable:

1. Type the variable name. Chapter 4, "Working with Math" contains a description of valid variable names.

2. Press the colon (**:**) key, or click  on the Calculator toolbar. The definition symbol (:=) appears with a blank placeholder to the right.

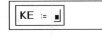

3. Type an expression to complete the definition. This expression can include numbers and any previously defined variables and functions.

The left-hand side of a ":=" can contain any of the following:

- A simple variable name like x.

- A subscripted variable name like v_i.

- A matrix whose elements are either of the above. For example, $\begin{bmatrix} x \\ y_1 \end{bmatrix}$. This technique allows you to define several variables at once: each element on the right-hand side is assigned simultaneously to the corresponding element on the left-hand side.

- A function name with an argument list of simple variable names. For example, $f(x, y, z)$. This is described further in the next section.

- A superscripted variable name like $\mathbf{M}^{\langle 1 \rangle}$.

Built-in Variables

Built-in variables can have a conventional value, like π and e, or be used as system variables to control how Mathcad works. See "Appendix F: Predefined Variables" on page 442 for a list of built-in variables in Mathcad.

Note Mathcad treats the names of all built-in *units* as predefined variables. See "Units and Dimensions" on page 109.

Although Mathcad's predefined variables already have values when you start Mathcad, you still can redefine them. For example, if you want to use a variable called e with a value other than the one Mathcad provides, enter a new definition, like $e := 2$. The variable e takes on the new value everywhere in the worksheet below and to the right of the new definition. Or create a global definition for the variable as described in "Global Definitions" on page 102.

Note Mathcad's predefined variables are defined for all fonts, sizes, and styles. This means that if you redefine e as described above, you can still use e, for example, as the base for natural logarithms. Note, however, that Greek letters are not included.

You can modify many of Mathcad's built-in variables without having to explicitly define them in your worksheet. To do so, choose **Worksheet Options** from the **Tools** menu, and click the Built-In Variables tab.

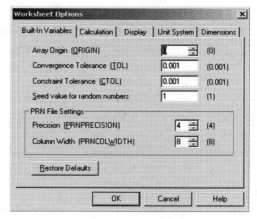

You can enter new values for any of these variables. Then choose **Calculate⇒Worksheet** from the **Tools** menu to ensure that all existing equations use the new values.

The numbers in brackets to the right of the variable names represent the default values for those variables. To restore these default values for the built-in variables listed in the dialog box, click "Restore Defaults."

Evaluating Expressions Numerically

To evaluate an expression numerically:

1. Type an expression containing any valid combination of numbers, variables, and functions. Any variables or functions should be defined earlier in the worksheet.

$$\frac{1}{2} \cdot m \cdot v^2$$

2. Press the "=" key, or click $\boxed{=}$ on the Calculator toolbar. Mathcad computes the value of the expression and shows it after the equal sign.

$$\frac{1}{2} \cdot m \cdot v^2| = 567.108 \quad \blacksquare$$

Tip Whenever you evaluate an expression, Mathcad shows a final placeholder at the end of the equation. You can use this placeholder for unit conversions, as explained in "Working with Results" on page 112. As soon as you click outside the region, Mathcad hides the placeholder.

Figure 8-1 shows some results calculated from preceding variable definitions.

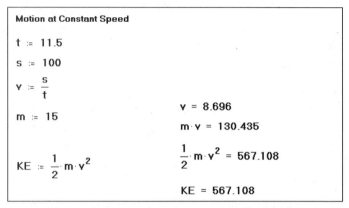

Motion at Constant Speed

$t := 11.5$

$s := 100$

$v := \dfrac{s}{t}$

$m := 15$

$KE := \dfrac{1}{2} \cdot m \cdot v^2$

$v = 8.696$

$m \cdot v = 130.435$

$\dfrac{1}{2} \cdot m \cdot v^2 = 567.108$

$KE = 567.108$

Figure 8-1: Calculations based on simple variable definitions.

How Mathcad Scans a Worksheet

Mathcad scans a worksheet the same way you read it: left to right and top to bottom. This means that a variable or function definition involving a "**:=**" affects everything below and to the right of it.

To see the placement of regions more clearly in your worksheet, choose **Regions** from the **View** menu. Mathcad displays blank space in gray and leaves regions in your background color.

Figure 8-2 shows examples of how placement of equations in a worksheet affects the evaluation of results. In the first evaluation, both x and y are highlighted (Mathcad shows them in red on screen) to indicate that they are undefined. This is because the definitions for x and y lie below where they are used. Because Mathcad scans from top to bottom, when it gets to the first equation, it doesn't know the values of x and y.

The second evaluation, on the other hand, is below the definitions of x and y. By the time Mathcad gets to this equation, it has already assigned values to both x and y.

Note You can define a variable more than once in the same worksheet. Mathcad simply uses the first definition for all expressions until the variable is redefined, then uses the new definition.

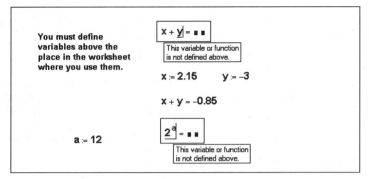

Figure 8-2: Mathcad evaluates equations from top to bottom in a worksheet. Undefined variables are highlighted.

Global Definitions

Global definitions work exactly like local definitions except that they are evaluated before any local definitions. If you define a variable or function with a global definition, that variable or function is available to all local definitions in your worksheet, regardless of whether the local definition appears above or below the global definition.

To type a global definition, follow these steps:

1. Type a variable name or function.

2. Press the tilde (~) key, or click $\blacksquare$ on the Evaluation toolbar. The global definition symbol appears.

3. Type an expression. The expression can involve numbers or other globally defined variables and functions.

You can use global definitions for functions, subscripted variables, and anything else that normally uses the definition symbol ":=".

This is the algorithm that Mathcad uses to evaluate all definitions:

1. First, Mathcad takes one pass through the entire worksheet from top to bottom. During this first pass, Mathcad evaluates global definitions only.

2. Mathcad then makes a second pass through the worksheet from top to bottom. This time, Mathcad evaluates all definitions made with ":=" as well as all equations containing "=" and "≡". Note that during this pass, global definitions do not use any local definitions.

Note A global definition of a variable can be overridden by a local definition of the same variable name with the definition symbol ":=".

Figure 8-3 shows the results of a global definition for the variable *R* which appears at the bottom of the figure.

Although global definitions are evaluated before any local definitions, Mathcad evaluates global definitions the same way it evaluates local definitions: top to bottom and left to right. This means that whenever you use a variable to the right of a "≡":

Start with these definitions and calculations . . .

$V := 1000$ $n := 3$ $T := 373$

$$P := \frac{n \cdot R \cdot T}{V}$$ $P = 0.092$

Now change the definitions of V and T . . .

$V := 500$ $T := 323$

$$P := \frac{n \cdot R \cdot T}{V}$$ $P = 0.159$

Since R is defined globally, its definition applies everywhere in the document . . .

$R \equiv .0820562$

Figure 8-3: Using the global definition symbol.

- that variable must also have been defined with a "$\equiv$," *and*
- the variable must have been defined *above* the place where you are trying to use it.

Otherwise, the variable is marked in red to indicate that it is undefined.

Tip   It is good practice to allow only one definition for each global variable. Although you can do things like define a variable with two different global definitions or with one global and one local definition, this may make your worksheet difficult to revise or understand in the future.

Range Variables

Iterative processes in Mathcad worksheets depend on *range variables*. A range variable looks just like a conventional variable. The difference is that a conventional variable takes on only one value while a range variable takes on a range of values.

Range variables are crucial to exploiting Mathcad's capabilities to their fullest. This section shows how to define and use range variables to perform iteration. For a description of more advanced iterative operations made possible by the programming operators in Mathcad, turn to Chapter 15, "Extending and Automating Mathcad."

Defining and using range variables

To define a range variable, type the variable name followed by a colon and a range of values. For example, here's how to define the variable *j* ranging from 0 to 15 in steps of 1:

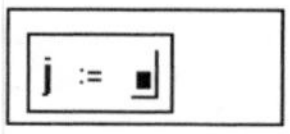

1. Type **j** and then press the colon key (**:**), or click 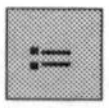 ▦ on the Calculator toolbar. The empty placeholder indicates that Mathcad expects a definition for *j*. At this point, Mathcad does not know whether *j* is to be a conventional variable or a range variable.

$j := \blacksquare$

2. Type **0**. Then press the semicolon key (**;**), or click [m..n] on the Matrix toolbar. This tells Mathcad that you are defining a range variable.
   Mathcad displays the semicolon as two periods ".." to indicate a range. Complete the range variable definition by typing **15** in the remaining placeholder.

$$j := 0 .. 15$$

This definition indicates that j now takes on the values $0, 1, 2 \ldots 15$. To define a range variable that changes in steps other than 1, see the section "Types of ranges" on page 105.

Once you define a range variable, it takes on its complete range of values *every time you use it*. If you use a range variable in an equation, for example, Mathcad evaluates that equation once for each value of the range variable.

You must define a range variable exactly as shown above.

Note You *cannot* define a variable in terms of a range variable. For example, if after having defined j as shown you now define $i := j + 1$, Mathcad assumes you are trying to set a scalar variable equal to a range variable and marks the equation with an appropriate error message.

One application of range variables is to fill up the elements of a vector or matrix. You can define vector elements by using a range variable as a subscript. For example, to define x_j for each value of j:

- Type **x[j:j^2[Space]+1**.

$$x_j := j^2 + 1$$

Figure 8-4 shows the vector of values computed by this equation. Since j is a range variable, the entire equation is evaluated once for each value of j. This defines x_j for each value of j from 0 to 15.

```
j := 0 .. 15
       2
x  :=  j  + 1
 j

x
 j
┌─────┐
│  1  │
├─────┤
│  2  │          x  = 1
├─────┤           0
│  5  │
├─────┤          x  = 2
│ 10  │           1
├─────┤
│ 17  │          x  = 10
├─────┤           3
│ 26  │
├─────┤          x  = 50
│ 37  │           7
├─────┤
│ 50  │          x   = 122
├─────┤           11
│ 65  │
├─────┤          x   = 226
│ 82  │           15
├─────┤
│ 101 │
├─────┤
│ 122 │
├─────┤
│ 145 │
├─────┤
│ 170 │
└─────┘
```

Figure 8-4: Using a range variable to define the values of a vector.

To understand how Mathcad computes with range variables, keep in mind this fundamental principle:

If you use a range variable in an expression, Mathcad evaluates the expression once for each value of the range variable.

If you use two or more range variables in an equation, Mathcad evaluates the equation once for each value of each range variable.

Tip   Mathcad takes longer to compute equations with ranged expressions since there may be many computations for each equation. While Mathcad is computing, the mouse pointer changes its appearance. See "Interrupting Calculations" on page 120.

Types of ranges

The definition of j in the previous section, ranging from 0 to 15, is an example of the simplest type of range definition. But Mathcad permits range variables with values ranging from any value to any other value, using any constant increment or decrement.

To define a range variable with a step size other than 1, type an equation of this form:

$$\mathtt{k:1,1.1;2}$$

This appears in your worksheet window as:

$$k := 1, 1.1 .. 2$$

In this range definition:

- The variable k is the name of the range variable itself.
- The number 1 is the first value taken by the range variable k.
- The number 1.1 is the second value in the range. *Note that this is not the step size.* The step size in this example is 0.1, the difference between 1.1 and 1. If you omit the comma and the 1.1, Mathcad assumes a step size of one in whatever direction (up or down) is appropriate.
- The number 2 is the last value in the range. In this example, the range values are constantly increasing. If instead you had defined $k := 10 .. 1$, then k would count down from 10 to 1. If the third number in the range definition is not an even number of increments from the starting value, the range will not go beyond it. For example, if you define $k := 10, 20 .. 65$ then k takes values 10, 20, 30, . . ., 60.

Note   You can use arbitrary scalar expressions in range definitions. However, these values must always be *real* numbers. Also note that if you use a fractional increment for a range variable, you will not be able to use that range variable as a subscript because subscripts must be integers.

Defining and Evaluating Functions

Although Mathcad has an extensive set of built-in functions (see Chapter 16, "Functions") you may want to define your own functions.

Define a function in much the same way as you define a variable. The name goes on the left, followed by a definition symbol, then an expression on the right. The main difference is that the name includes an *argument list*. The example below shows how to define a function called *dist(x, y)* that returns the distance between the point *(x, y)* and the origin.

To make a function definition:

1. Type the function name.

2. Type a left parenthesis followed by one or more names separated by commas. Complete this argument list by typing a right parenthesis.

Note It makes no difference whether or not the names in the argument list have been defined or used elsewhere in the worksheet. What is important is that these arguments *must be names*. They cannot be more complicated expressions.

- Press the colon (**:**) key, or click ⬛ on the Calculator toolbar to enter the definition symbol (:=).

$$dist(x, y) := \blacksquare$$

- Type an expression to define the function. The expression can contain a name or any previously defined functions and variablesl.

$$dist(x, y) := \sqrt{x^2 + y^2}$$

Once you have defined a function, you can use it anywhere below and to the right of the definition, just as you would use a variable.

When you evaluate an expression containing a function, as shown in Figure 8-5, Mathcad:

3. evaluates the arguments you place between the parentheses,

4. replaces the dummy arguments in the function definition with the actual arguments you place between the parentheses,

5. performs whatever arithmetic is specified by the function definition,

6. returns the result as the value of the function.

Note As shown in Figure 8-5, if you type only the name of a function without its arguments, Mathcad returns the word "function."

The arguments of a user-defined function can represent scalars, vectors, or matrices.

For example, you could define the distance function as $dist(v) := \sqrt{v_0^2 + v_1^2}$. This is an example of a function that accepts a vector as an argument and returns a scalar result. See Chapter 5, "Vectors, Matrices, and Data Arrays" for more information.

```
Computing distances between points
    x1 := 0            y1 := 1.5
    x2 := 3            y2 := 4
    x3 := -1           y3 := 1            dist(x, y) := √(x² + y²)
Compute distance from origin:
    dist(x1, y1) = 1.5                        dist = function
    dist(x2, y2) = 5
    dist(x3, y3) = 1.414
```

Figure 8-5: A user-defined function to compute the distance to the origin.

Note   User-defined function names are font and case sensitive. The function **f**(*x*) is different from the
function f(*x*) and SIN(*x*) is different from sin(*x*). Mathcad's built-in functions, however, are
defined for all fonts (except the Symbol font), sizes, and styles. This means that **sin**(*x*), *sin*(*x*),
and `sin`(*x*) all refer to the same function.

Variables in User-Defined Functions

When you define a function, you don't have to define any of the names in the argument
list since you are telling Mathcad *what to do* with the arguments, not what they are.
When you define a function, Mathcad doesn't even have to know the types of the
arguments—whether the arguments are scalars, vectors, matrices, and so on. It is only
when Mathcad *evaluates* a function that it needs to know the argument types.

However, if in defining a function you use a variable name that *is not* in the argument
list, you must define that variable name above the function definition. The value of that
variable at the time you make the function definition then becomes a permanent part
of the function. This is illustrated in Figure 8-6.

```
Using Variables in User Functions:
        a := 2
        f(x) := xᵃ
The value of f depends on its argument . . .
        f(2) = 4            t := -4
        f(3) = 9
        f(√5) = 5           f(t) = 16

. . . but not on the value of a.         f(2) = 4
        a := 3
                                         f(2) = 4
        a := 5
                                         f(2) = 4
Since a is not an argument of f, the value of f depends on the value of a
at the point where f is defined.
```

Figure 8-6: The value of a user function depends on its arguments.

If you want a function to depend on the value of a variable, you must include that variable as an argument. If not, Mathcad just uses that variable's fixed value at the point in the worksheet where the function is defined.

Recursive Function Definitions

Mathcad supports *recursive* function definitions—you may define the value of a function in terms of a previous value of the function. As shown in Figure 8-7, recursive functions are useful for defining arbitrary periodic functions, as well as elegantly implementing numerical functions like the factorial function

Note that a recursive function definition should always have at least two parts:

• An initial condition that prevents the recursion from going forever.

• A definition of the function in terms of some previous value(s) of the function.

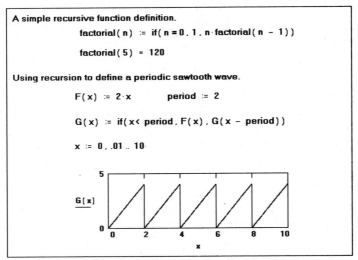

Figure 8-7: Mathcad allows recursive function definitions.

Note If you do not specify an initial condition that stops the recursion, Mathcad generates a "stack overflow" error message when you try to evaluate the function.

The programming operators in Mathcad also support recursion. See the section "Programming within Mathcad" in Chapter 15.

Units and Dimensions

Mathcad includes a complete set of units for your calculations. You can treat these units just like built-in variables. To assign units to a number or expression, just multiply it by the name of the unit.

Mathcad recognizes most units by their common abbreviations. Lists of all of Mathcad's built-in units in several systems of units are in the Appendices. By default Mathcad uses units from the SI unit system (also known as the International System of Units) in the *results* of any calculations, but you may use any supported units you wish in creating your expressions. See "Displaying Units of Results" on page 115 for how to set a unit system for results.

For example, type expressions like the following:

```
mass:75*kg
acc:100*m/s^2
acc_g:9.8*m/s^2
F:mass*(acc + acc_g)
```

Figure 8-8 shows how these equations appear in a worksheet.

$$mass := 75 \cdot kg$$

$$acc := 100 \cdot \frac{m}{s^2}$$

$$acc\_g := 9.8 \cdot \frac{m}{s^2}$$

$$F := mass \cdot (acc + acc\_g)$$

$$F = 8.235 \times 10^3 \, N$$

$$mass := 75kg$$ <--Mathcad treats the multiplication as implied when you type an expression like **mass:75kg**

$$mass = 75 \, kg$$

Figure 8-8: Equations using units.

Tip   If you define a variable which consists of a number followed immediately by a unit name, you can omit the multiplication symbol; Mathcad inserts a very small space and treats the multiplication as implied. See the definition of mass at the bottom of Figure 8-8.

You can also use the Insert Unit dialog box to insert one of Mathcad's built-in units into any placeholder.

To use the Insert Unit dialog box:

1. Click in the empty placeholder and choose **Unit** from the **Insert** menu, or click 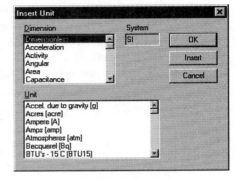 on the Standard toolbar. Mathcad opens the Insert Unit dialog box.

2. The list at the bottom shows built-in units, along with their Mathcad names, corresponding to the physical quantity selected in the top list. When "Dimensionless" is selected, a list of all available built-in units shows on the bottom.

3. You can use the top list to display only those units corresponding to a particular physical quantity to see what choices are appropriate.

4. In the bottom list, double-click the unit you want to insert, or click the unit you want and then click "Insert." Mathcad inserts that unit into the empty placeholder.

Note Mathcad performs some dimensional analysis by trying to match the dimensions of your selected result with one of the common physical quantities in the top list. If it finds a match, you'll see all the built-in units corresponding to the highlighted physical quantity in the bottom list. If nothing matches, Mathcad simply lists all available built-in units on the bottom.

Dimensional Checking

Whenever you enter an expression involving units, Mathcad checks it for dimensional consistency. If you add or subtract values with incompatible units, or violate other principles of dimensional analysis, Mathcad displays an appropriate error message.

For example, suppose you had defined *acc* as $100 \cdot m/s$ instead of $100 \cdot m/s^2$ as shown at right. Since *acc* is in units of velocity and *acc_g* is in units of acceleration, it is inappropriate to add them together. When you attempt to do so, Mathcad displays an error message.

$$mass := 75 \cdot kg$$

$$acc := 100 \cdot \frac{m}{s}$$

$$acc\_g := 9.8 \cdot \frac{m}{s^2}$$

$$F := mass \cdot (acc + acc\_g)$$

The units in this expression do not match.

Other unit errors are usually caused by one of the following:

• An incorrect unit conversion.

• A variable with the wrong units.

• Units in exponents or subscripts (for example $v_{3 \cdot acre}$ or $2^{3 \cdot ft}$).

• Units as arguments to inappropriate functions (for example, $\sin(0 \cdot henry)$).

Tip If you want to temporarily remove units from an argument, *x*, divide *x* by *UnitsOf*(*x*). For example, if *p* is defined as $2\,ft$ then $\sin(p)$ gives an error but $\sin\left(\frac{p}{UnitsOf(p)}\right) = 0.573$.

Defining Your Own Units

Although Mathcad recognizes many common units, you may need to define your own unit if that unit isn't one of Mathcad's built-in units or if you prefer to use your own abbreviation instead of Mathcad's abbreviation.

Note Although absolute temperature units are built into Mathcad, the Fahrenheit and Celsius temperature units are not. See the QuickSheet "Temperature Conversions" under the **Help** menu for samples of defining these temperature scales and converting between them.

You define your own units in terms of existing units in exactly the same way you would define a variable in terms of an existing variable. Figure 8-9 shows how to define new units as well as how to redefine existing units.

$Å := 10^{-10} \cdot m \qquad μs := 10^{-6} \cdot s$

$week := 7 \cdot day \qquad kilo := 1 \cdot kg$

Results are displayed by default in terms of the base units of the current unit system, but you can type other units into the units placeholder to see the result in different units.

$Å = 1 \times 10^{-10}\ m \qquad week = 6.048 \times 10^{5}\ s$

$week = 0.019\ yr \qquad μs = 1.667 \times 10^{-8}\ min$

$kilo = 1\ kg$

Figure 8-9: Defining your own units.

Note Since units behave just like variables, you may run into unexpected conflicts. For example, if you define the variable *m* in your worksheet, you won't be able to use the built-in unit *m* for meters anywhere below that definition. However, Mathcad automatically displays the unit *m* in any results involving meters, as described in "Displaying Units of Results" on page 115.

Working with Results

Formatting Results

The way that Mathcad displays numbers (the number of decimal places, whether to use *i* or *j* for imaginary numbers, and so on) is called the *result format.* You can set the result format for a single calculated result or for an entire worksheet.

Setting the format of a single result

When you evaluate expressions numerically in Mathcad, results are formatted in the worksheet according to the worksheet default result format. To modify the format for a single result

1. Click anywhere in the equation.

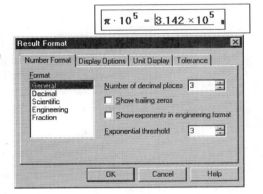

2. Choose **Result** from the **Format** menu or double-click the result. The Result Format dialog box appears.

3. Change the desired settings. See below for the various settings in the dialog box. To display a result with six decimal places, you would increase "Number of decimal places" from 3 to 6.

To redisplay a result using the worksheet default result format settings, click on the result to enclose the result between the editing lines, delete the equal sign, and press = to replace the equal sign. The result is now restored to the default worksheet settings.

Note When the format of a result is changed, only the *appearance* of the result changes in the worksheet. Mathcad continues to maintain full precision internally for that result. To see a number as it is stored internally, click on the result, press [Ctrl][Shift]N, and look at the message line at the bottom of the Mathcad window. If you copy a result, however, Mathcad copies the number only to the precision displayed.

Setting worksheet default format

To change the default display of numerical results:

1. Click in a blank part of your worksheet.

2. Choose **Result** from the **Format** menu.

3. Change the desired settings in the Result Format dialog box.

Mathcad changes the display of all results whose formats have not been explicitly specified.

Alternatively, you can change the worksheet default by clicking on a particular result, choosing Result from the **Format** menu, changing the settings in the Result Format dialog box, and clicking "Set as Default."

Tip　Changing the worksheet default result format affects only the worksheet you are working in when you make the change. Any other worksheets open at the time retain their own default result formats. If you want to re-use your default result formats in other Mathcad worksheets, save your worksheet as a template as described in Chapter 7, "Worksheet Management."

The Result Format dialog box

The **Number Format** page lets you control the number of decimal places, trailing zeros, and other options. Depending on the format scheme you choose under the Format section, you see different options.

- **General** lets you control the number of digits to the right of the decimal point, trailing zeros, and exponential threshold. A result is displayed in exponential notation or engineering format when the exponential threshold is exceeded. You can display trailing zeros to the right of the decimal until you exceed 15 digits total.

- **Decimal** lets you control the number of digits to the right of the decimal point and never display the results in exponential notation. You can display trailing zeros to the right of the decimal point beyond 15 digits total, but only the first 15 digits are accurate.

- **Scientific** or **Engineering** lets you control the number of digits to the right of the decimal point and always display results in exponential notation. For Engineering, the exponents are displayed in multiples of three. You can use E-notation for the exponents by choosing "Show exponents as ± E 000." You can display trailing zeros to the right of the decimal point beyond 15 digits total, but only the first 15 digits are accurate.

- **Fractional** lets you display results as fractions or mixed numbers. Use the level of accuracy setting to control the number of decimal places of accuracy of the fraction displayed. You can display a fraction that is accurate to up to 15 decimal places.

Note　Settings that are grayed can only be changed for the entire worksheet, as described in "Setting worksheet default format" on page 112.

The **Display Options** page lets you control whether arrays are displayed as tables or matrices, whether nested arrays are expanded, and whether i or j is used to indicated imaginary. You can also specify another radix such as Binary or Octal.

The **Unit Display** page gives you options to format units (as fractions) or simplify the units to derived units.

The **Tolerance** page allows you to specify when to hide a real or imaginary part of a result and how small a number has to be for it to display as zero.

Online Help　Click the Help button at the bottom of the dialog box to see more details of options in the Result.

Figure 8-10 shows some examples of formatting options.

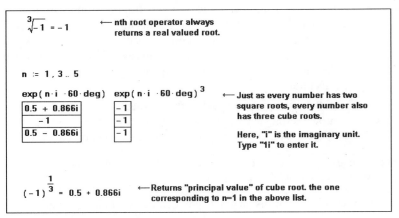

Figure 8-10: Several ways to format the same number.

Complex Results

Results can have complex numbers if you enter an expression that contains a complex number. Even a Mathcad expression that involves only real numbers can have a complex value. For example, if you evaluate $\sqrt{-1}$, Mathcad returns i. See Figure 8-11 for examples.

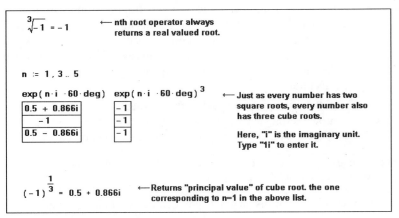

Figure 8-11: Examples of complex results.

Note   When complex numbers are available, many functions and operators we think of as returning unique results become multivalued. In general, when a function or operator is multivalued, Mathcad returns the *principal value:* the value making the smallest positive angle relative to the positive real axis in the complex plane. For example, when it evaluates $(-1)^{1/3}$, Mathcad returns $.5 + .866i$ despite the fact that we commonly think of the cube root of -1 as being -1. This is because the number $.5 + .866i$ makes an angle of only 60 degrees from the positive real axis. The number -1, on the other hand, is 180 degrees from the positive real axis. Mathcad's *n*th root operator returns -1 in this case, however.

Displaying Units of Results

Mathcad by default displays results in the fundamental units of the unit system you're working with.

Tip Check "Simplify units when possible" in the Result Format dialog box (see page 112) to see units in a result expressed in terms of derived units rather than in base units. Check "Format units" to see units in a result displayed as a built-up fraction containing terms with positive exponents only rather than as a product of units with positive and negative exponents.

You can have Mathcad redisplay a particular result in terms of any of Mathcad's built-in units. To do so:

1. Click in the result. You'll see an empty placeholder to its right. This is the *units placeholder*.

2. Click the units placeholder and choose **Unit** from the **Insert** menu, or click on the Standard toolbar. Mathcad opens the Insert Unit dialog box. This is described in "Units and Dimensions" on page 109.

3. Double-click the unit in which you want to display the result. Mathcad inserts this unit in the units placeholder.

Note For some engineering units—such as *hp*, *cal*, *BTU*, and *Hz*—Mathcad adopts one common definition for the unit name but allows you to insert one of several alternative unit names, corresponding to alternative definitions of that unit, in your results. In the case of horsepower, for example, Mathcad uses the U.K. definition of the unit *hp* but gives you several variants, such as water horsepower, metric horsepower, boiler horsepower, and electric horsepower.

Another way to insert a unit is to type its name directly into the units placeholder. This method works for built-in units, for units you've defined yourself, and for combinations of units.

Unit systems

Mathcad's uses SI as the default unit system. When you use the equal sign to display a result having units, Mathcad automatically displays the units in the result in terms of base or derived SI units.

You can have Mathcad display results in terms of the units of any of the other built-in unit systems in Mathcad: CGS, US customary, MKS, or no unit system at all. To do so, choose **Worksheet Options** from the **Tools** menu and click the Unit System tab.

Select the default unit system in which you want to display results. The SI unit system provides two additional base units over the other systems, one for luminosity (*candela*) and one for substance (*mole*), and the base SI electrical unit (*ampere*) differs from the base electrical unit in the other systems (*coulomb*).

The following table summarizes the base units available in Mathcad:

Unit System	Base Units
SI	*m, kg, s, A, K, cd*, and *mole*
MKS	*m, kg, sec, coul*, and *K*
CGS	*cm, gm, sec, coul*, and *K*
U.S.	*ft, lb, sec, coul*, and *K*
None	Displays results in terms of fundamental dimensions of length, mass, time, charge, and absolute temperature. All built-in units are disabled.

The standard SI unit names—such as *A* for *ampere*, *L* for *liter*, *s* for *second*, and *S* for *siemens*—are generally available only in the SI unit system. Many other unit names are available in all the available systems of units. For a listing of which units are available in each system, see the Appendices. Mathcad includes most units common to scientific and engineering practice. Where conventional unit prefixes such as *m-* for *milli-*, *n-* for *nano-*, etc. are not understood by Mathcad, you can easily define custom units such as μm as described in "Defining Your Own Units" on page 111.

Tip For examples of units with prefixes not already built into Mathcad, see the Unit QuickSheets under the **Help** menu.

If you click "None" in the Unit System tab of the Worksheet Options dialog box, Mathcad doesn't understand any built-in units and displays answers in terms of the fundamental dimensions of *length*, *mass*, *time*, *charge*, and *temperature*. However, even if you are working in one of Mathcad's built-in unit systems, you can always choose to see results in your worksheet displayed in terms of fundamental dimension names rather than the base units of the unit system. To do so:

1. Choose **Worksheet Options** from the **Tools** menu.
2. Click the Dimensions tab.
3. Check "Display dimensions" and click "OK."

Unit conversions

There are two ways to convert from one set of units to another:

• By using the Insert Unit dialog box, or
• By typing the new units in the units placeholder itself.

To convert units using the Insert Unit dialog box:

1. Click the unit you want to replace.
2. Choose **Unit** from the **Insert** menu, or click on the Standard toolbar.
3. Double-click the unit in which you want to display the result.

As a quick shortcut, or if you want to display the result in terms of a unit not available through the Insert Unit dialog box—for example, a unit you defined yourself or an algebraic combination of units—you can edit the units placeholder directly.

Figure 8-12 shows *F* displayed both in terms of fundamental SI units and in terms of several combinations of units.

When you enter an inappropriate unit in the units placeholder, Mathcad inserts a combination of base units that generate the correct units for the displayed result. For example, in the last equation in Figure 8-12, $kW \cdot s$ is not a unit of force. Mathcad therefore inserts m^{-1} to cancel the extra length dimension.

mass := 75kg   acc := 100 $\cdot$ m $\cdot$ s^{-2} acc_g := 9.8 $\cdot$ m $\cdot$ s^{-2}

F := mass $\cdot$ (acc + acc_g)

F = 8.235 × 10^3 $\cdot$ kg $\cdot$ m $\cdot$ s^{-2} ∎   ←—— Default display using fundamental SI units. Click on result to see the "units placeholder."

F = 8.235 × 10^3 N   ←—— Type desired unit in the units placeholder.

F = 8.235 × 10^8 dyne

F = 82.35 $\dfrac{\text{J}}{\text{cm}}$ ←—— You can type combinations of units in the units placeholder.

F = 8.235 m^{-1} kW $\cdot$ s   ←—— Since kW s is not a force unit, Mathcad inserts an extra m^{-1} to make the units come out right.

Figure 8-12: A calculated result displayed with different units

Whenever you enter units in the units placeholder, Mathcad divides the value to be displayed by whatever you enter in the units placeholder. This ensures that the complete displayed result—the number *times* the expression you entered for the placeholder—is a correct value for the equation.

Note Conversions involving an offset in addition to a multiplication, for example gauge pressure to absolute pressure, or degrees Fahrenheit to Celsius, cannot be performed directly with Mathcad's unit conversion mechanism. You can, however, perform conversions of this type by defining suitable functions. See the QuickSheet "Temperature Conversions" under the **Help** menu.

You can enter *any* variable, constant, or expression in a units placeholder. Mathcad then redisplays the result in terms of the value contained in the units placeholder. For example, you can use the units placeholder to display a result as a multiple of π or in engineering notation (as a multiple of 10^3, 10^6, etc.).

Tip You can also use the units placeholder for dimensionless units like degrees and radians. Mathcad treats the unit *rad* as a constant equal to 1, so if you have a number or an expression in radians, you can type *deg* into the units placeholder to convert the result from radians to degrees.

Copying and Pasting Numerical Results

You can copy a numerical result and paste it either elsewhere in your worksheet or into a new application.

To copy a single number appearing to the right of an equal sign:

1. Click on the result to the right of the equal sign putting the result between the editing lines.

2. Choose **Copy** from the **Edit** menu.

3. Click wherever you want to paste the result. If you're pasting into another application, choose **Paste** from that application's **Edit** menu. If you're pasting into a Mathcad worksheet, choose **Paste** from Mathcad's **Edit** menu.

When you paste a numerical result into a Mathcad worksheet, it appears as:

- A math region consisting of a number if you paste it into empty space.

- A number if you paste it into a placeholder in a math region.

- A number if you paste it directly into text or into a placeholder in text created using the **Math Region** command on the **Insert** menu.

To copy more than one number, follow the steps for copying from an array. See "Displaying Arrays" on page 58.

Note The **Copy** command copies the numerical result only to the precision displayed. To copy the result in greater precision, double-click it and increase "Displayed Precision" on the Result Format dialog box. **Copy** does not copy units and dimensions from a numerical result.

Controlling Calculation

Mathcad starts in *automatic mode* meaning results are updated automatically. You can tell you're in automatic mode because the word "Auto" appears in the message line at the bottom of the window.

You can disable automatic mode by choosing **Calculate⇒Automatic Calculation** from the **Tools** menu. The word "Auto" disappears from the message line and the check beside **Automatic Calculation** disappears. You are now in *manual mode.*

Tip The calculation mode—either manual or automatic—is a property saved in your Mathcad worksheet. As described in Chapter 7, "Worksheet Management" the calculation mode is also a property saved in Mathcad template (MCT) files.

Calculating in Automatic Mode

Here is how Mathcad works in automatic mode:

- As soon as you press the equal sign, Mathcad displays a result.

- As soon as you click outside of an equation having a ":=" or a "≡," Mathcad performs all calculations necessary to make the assignment statement.

When you process a definition in automatic mode by clicking outside the equation region, this is what happens:

- Mathcad evaluates the expression on the right side of the definition and assigns it to the name on the left.

- Mathcad then takes note of all other equations in the worksheet that are in any way affected by the definition.

- Finally, Mathcad updates any of the affected equations that are currently visible in the worksheet window.

Note Although the equation you altered may affect equations throughout your worksheet, Mathcad performs only those calculations necessary to guarantee that whatever you can see in the window is up-to-date. This optimization ensures you don't have to wait for Mathcad to evaluate expressions that are not visible. If you print or move to the end of the worksheet, however, Mathcad automatically updates the whole worksheet.

Whenever Mathcad needs time to complete computations, the mouse pointer changes its appearance and the word "WAIT" appears on the message line. This can occur when you enter or calculate an equation, when you scroll, during printing, or when you enlarge a window to reveal additional equations. In all these cases, Mathcad evaluates pending calculations from earlier changes.

As Mathcad evaluates an expression, it surrounds it with a green rectangle. This makes it easy to follow the progress of a calculation.

Calculating in Manual Mode

In manual mode, Mathcad does not compute equations or display results until you specifically request it to recalculate. This means that you don't have to wait for Mathcad to calculate as you enter equations or scroll around a worksheet.

Mathcad keeps track of pending computations while you're in manual mode. As soon as you make a change that requires computation, the word "Calc" appears on the message line. This is to remind you that the results you see in the window are not up-to-date and that you must recalculate them before you can be sure they are updated.

You can update the screen by choosing **Calculate Now** from the **Tools** menu, clicking ▬ on the Standard toolbar, or pressing [**F9**]. Mathcad performs whatever computations are necessary to update all results visible in the worksheet window. When you move down to see more of the worksheet, the word "Calc" reappears on the message line to indicate that you must recalculate to see up-to-date results.

To force Mathcad to recalculate all equations throughout the whole worksheet, choose **Calculate Worksheet** from the **Tools** menu or press [**Ctrl**] [**F9**].

Note When you print a worksheet in manual calculation mode, the results on the printout are not necessarily up-to-date. In this case, make sure to choose **Calculate Worksheet** from the **Tools** menu before you print.

Interrupting Calculations

To interrupt a computation in progress:

1. Press [**Esc**]. The dialog box shown at right appears.

2. Click "OK" to stop the calculations or "Cancel" to resume calculations.

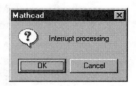

If you click "OK," the equation that was being processed when you pressed [**Esc**] is marked with an error message (see "Error Messages" on page 123) indicating that calculation has been interrupted. To resume an interrupted calculation, first click in the equation having the error message, then press [F9] or click $\blacksquare$ on the Standard toolbar.

Tip   If you find yourself frequently interrupting calculations to avoid having to wait for Mathcad to recalculate as you edit your worksheet, you should switch to manual mode.

Disabling Equations

You can *disable* a single equation so that it no longer calculates along with other regions in your worksheet. Disabling an equation does not affect Mathcad's equation editing, formatting, and display capabilities.

To disable calculation for a single equation in your worksheet, follow these steps:

1. Click on the equation you want to disable.

2. Choose **Properties** from the **Format** menu, and click the Calculation tab.

3. Under "Calculation Options" check "Disable Evaluation."

4. Mathcad shows a small rectangle after the equation to indicate that it is disabled. An example is shown at right.

$$KE := \frac{1}{2} \cdot m \cdot v^2 \ \blacksquare$$

Tip   An easy shortcut for disabling evaluation is to right click on an equation and select **Disable Evaluation** from the popup menu.

To re-enable calculation for a disabled equation:

1. Click on the equation to select it.

2. Choose **Properties** from the **Format** menu, and click the Calculation tab.

3. Remove the check from "Disable Evaluation."

Animation

You can use Mathcad to create and play short animation clips by using the built-in variable FRAME. Anything that can be made to depend on this variable can be animated. This includes not only plots but numerical results as well. You can play back the animation clips at different speeds or save them for use by other applications.

Creating an Animation Clip

Mathcad comes with a predefined constant called FRAME whose sole purpose is to drive animations. The steps in creating any animation are as follows:

1. Create an expression or plot, or a group of expressions, whose appearance ultimately depends on the value of FRAME. This expression need not be a graph. It can be anything at all.

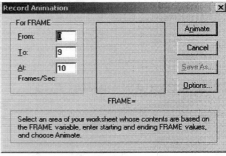

2. Choose **Animation**⇒ **Record** from the **Tools** menu to bring up the Record Animation dialog box.

3. Drag-select the portion of your worksheet you want to animate as shown in Figure 8-13. Draw a rectangle around as many regions as you want to appear in the animation

4. Set the upper and lower limits for FRAME in the dialog box. When you record the animation, the FRAME variable increments by one as it proceeds from the lower limit to the upper limit.

5. Enter the playback speed in the Frames/Sec. box.

6. Click "Animate." You'll see a miniature rendition of your selection inside the dialog box. Mathcad redraws this once for each value of FRAME. This won't necessarily match the playback speed since at this point you're just *creating* the animation.

7. To save your animation clip as a Windows AVI file, suitable for viewing in other Windows applications, click "Save As" in the dialog box. .

Tip Since animation clips can take considerable disk space, Mathcad saves them in compressed format. Before creating the animation, you can choose what compression method to use or whether to compress at all. To do so, click "Options" in the Animate dialog box.

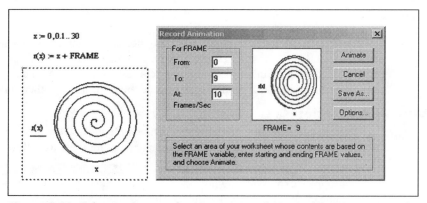

$x := 0, 0.1 .. 30$

$x(x) := x + FRAME$

Figure 8-13: Selecting an area for animation and seeing the animation inside the dialog box.

Playing an Animation Clip

As soon as you've created an animation clip as described in the previous section, Mathcad opens a Playback window:

The first frame of the animation clip you just created is already in the window. To play back the animation clip, click the arrow at the lower left corner of the window. You can also play back the animation clip on a frame by frame basis, either forward or backward. To do so, drag the slider below the animated picture to the left or right.

Tip You can control the playback speed by clicking the button to the right of the play button, which then opens a popup menu. Choose "Speed" from the menu and adjust the slider control.

Playing a Previously Saved Animation

If you have an existing Windows AVI file, you can play it within Mathcad. To do so:

1. Choose **Animation⇒Playback** from the **Tools** menu to bring up the Playback dialog box. The window is collapsed since no animation clip has been opened.

2. Click on the button to the right of the play button and choose "Open" from the menu. Use the Open File dialog box to locate and open the AVI file you want to play.

Tip To launch an animation directly from your worksheet, you can insert a hyperlink to an AVI file by choosing **Hyperlink** from the **Insert** menu. You can also embed a shortcut to the AVI file in your worksheet by dragging the icon for the AVI file from the Windows Explorer and dropping it into your worksheet. Finally, you can embed or link an OLE animation object in your worksheet (see "Inserting Objects" on page 155.)

Error Messages

If Mathcad encounters an error when evaluating an expression, it marks the expression with an error message and highlights the offending name or operator in red.

An error message is visible only when you *click on* the associated expression, as shown to the right.

Mathcad cannot process an expression containing an error. If the expression is a definition, the variable or function it is supposed to define remains undefined. Any expressions that reference that variable will be undefined as well.

$$g(x) := \frac{3}{x}$$
$$f(x) := g(x) \cdot 10$$
$$f(0) = \blacksquare$$
Found a singularity while evaluating this expression. You may be dividing by zero.

Tip You can get online help about many error messages by clicking on them and pressing [**F1**].

Finding the Source of an Error

When working with an expression dependent upon one or more existing definitions, an error you receive in your expression may actually originate in one of those definitions.

For example, in the figure above, the error appears on the third region, *f(0)*. However, *f(x)* is based on the definition of *g(x)*. When x is zero, *g(x)* is the first region that exhibits the error.

You can try to find the source of an error yourself simply by examining your worksheet to see where the error began, or you can use Mathcad to trace the error back through your worksheet. To find the source of an error using Mathcad:

1. Right click on the region showing the error and choose Trace Error from the popup menu or you can click on the region and choose **Trace Error** from the **Tools** menu. The Trace Error dialog box appears.

2. Use the buttons in the dialog box to navigate through the regions associated with the region showing the error. For example, click "Previous" to step back to the previous dependent region.

Or click "First" to jump to the region causing the error.

$$g(x) := \frac{3}{x}$$
$$f(x) := g(x) \cdot 10$$
$$f(0) = \blacksquare$$
Found a singularity while evaluating this expression. You may be dividing by zero.

$$g(x) := \frac{3}{x}$$
Found a singularity while evaluating this expression. You may be dividing by zero.
$$f(x) := g(x) \cdot 10$$
$$f(0) = \blacksquare$$

Fixing Errors

Once you have determined which expression caused the error, edit that expression to fix the error or change the variable definitions that led to the error. When you click in the expression and begin editing, Mathcad removes the error message. When you click outside the equation Mathcad recomputes the expression. Then Mathcad recomputes any expressions affected by the fixed expression.

Note When you define a function, Mathcad does not try to evaluate it until you subsequently use it in the worksheet. If there is an error, the use of the function is marked in error, even though the real problem may lie in the definition of the function itself, possibly much earlier in the worksheet.

Chapter 9
Solving and Data Analysis

- ◆ Solving and Optimization Functions
- ◆ Differential Equation Solvers
- ◆ Data Fitting

This chapter shows methods for solving equations and mapping data to equations. Mathcad supports many functions for solving a single equation in one unknown through large systems of linear, nonlinear, and differential equations, with multiple unknowns. There are also a host of fitting and interpolation routines to generate functions and approximations to data. The techniques described here generate numeric solutions. Chapter 13, "Symbolic Calculation," describes a variety of techniques for solving equations symbolically.

Solving and Optimization Functions

Finding Roots

Finding a Single Root

The *root* function solves a single equation in a single unknown, given a guess value for the unknown. Alternatively, *root* can take a range [a,b] in which the solution lies, and no guess is required. The function returns the value of the unknown variable that makes the equation equal zero, and lies in the specified range, by making successive estimates of the variable and calculating the value of the equation.

The guess value you supply for x becomes the starting point for successive approximations to the root value. If you wish to find a complex-valued root, start with a complex guess. When the magnitude of $f(x)$ evaluated at the proposed root is less than the value of the tolerance parameter, *TOL*, a result is returned. If you increase *TOL*, the function will converge more quickly, but the answer will be less accurate, and vice versa. Plotting the function is a good way to determine how many roots there are, where they are, and what initial guesses are likely to find them.

Tip   As described in "Built-in Variables" on page 100, you can change the value of the tolerance, and hence the accuracy of the solution found by *root*, by including definitions for *TOL* in your worksheet. You can also change the tolerance by using the Built-in Variables tab when you choose **Worksheet Options** from the **Tools** menu.

Note   When you specify the optional arguments a and b for the root function, Mathcad will only find a root for the function f if $f(a)$ is positive and $f(b)$ is negative or vice versa. (See Figure 9-1.)

If, after many approximations, Mathcad still cannot find an acceptable answer, it marks the *root* function with an error message indicating its inability to converge to a result. This error can be caused by any of the following:

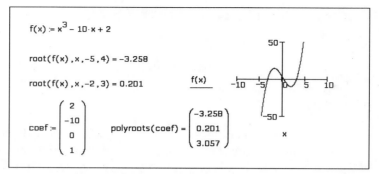

Figure 9-1: Finding roots with root and polyroots.

- The expression has no roots.
- The roots of the expression are far from the initial guess.
- The expression has local maxima or minima between the initial guess and the roots.
- The expression has discontinuities between the initial guess and the roots.
- The expression has a complex root but the initial guess was real (or vice versa).
- To find the cause of the error, try plotting the expression. This will help determine whether or not the expression crosses the x-axis and if so, approximately where. In general, the closer your initial guess is to where the expression crosses the x-axis, the more quickly the root function will converge on an acceptable result.

Here are some more tips on root-finding:

- Solving an equation of the form $f(x) = g(x)$ is equivalent to using *root* as follows: $root(f(x) - g(x), x)$
- If two roots are close together, you may have to reduce *TOL* to distinguish between them.
- If $f(x)$ has a small slope near its root, then $root(f(x), x)$ may converge to a value r that is relatively far from the actual root. In such cases, even though $|f(r)| < TOL$, r may be far from the point where $f(r) = 0$. To find a more accurate root, decrease the value of *TOL*. Or, try finding $root(g(x), x)$, where $g(x) = \dfrac{f(x)}{\dfrac{d}{dx}f(x)}$.
- For an expression $f(x)$ with a known root r, solving for additional roots of $f(x)$ is equivalent to solving for roots of $h(x) = (f(x))/(x-r)$. Dividing out known roots like this is useful for resolving two roots that may be close together. It's often easier to solve for roots of $h(x)$ as defined here than it is to try to find other roots for $f(x)$ with different guesses.

The *root* function can solve only one equation in one unknown. To solve several equations simultaneously, use *Find* or *Minerr*, described below.

Finding all Roots

To find the roots of a polynomial or an expression having the form:

$$v_n x^n + \dots + v_2 x^2 + v_1 x + v_0$$

you can use *polyroots* rather than *root*. *polyroots* does not require a guess value, and *polyroots* returns all roots at once, whether real or complex. It does require that you type the coefficients of the polynomial into a separate vector. Figure 9-1 shows an example.

By default, *polyroots* uses a LaGuerre method of finding roots. If you want to use the companion matrix method instead, click on the *polyroots* function with the right mouse button and choose **Companion Matrix** from the popup menu.

Note *root* and *polyroots* can solve only one equation in one unknown, and they always return numerical answers. To solve several equations simultaneously, use the techniques described in the next section. To solve an equation symbolically, or to find an exact numerical answer in terms of elementary functions, choose **Variable⇒Solve** from the **Symbolics** menu or use the **solve** keyword. See Chapter 13, "Symbolic Calculation."

Linear/Nonlinear System Solving and Optimization

Mathcad includes numerical solving functions that solve problems such as:

- Linear systems of equations with constraints (equalities or inequalities).
- Nonlinear systems of equations with constraints.
- Optimization (maximization or minimization) of an objective function.
- Optimization (maximization or minimization) of an objective function with constraints.
- Linear programming, in which all constraints are either equalities or inequalities that compare linear functions to constants and the objective function is of the form:

$$c_0 x_0 + c_1 x_1 + \dots + c_n x_n$$

- If you have the *Solving and Optimization Extention Pack* installed, you can also use Quadratic programming, in which all constraints are linear but the objective function contains linear terms and quadratic terms, and Mixed Integer Programming, in which variables are further constrained to be integers, floating point numbers, or boolean values.

Solving a Linear System of Equations

Use the *lsolve* function to solve a linear system of equations whose coefficients are arranged in a matrix **M**. The argument **M** for *lsolve* must be a matrix that is neither singular nor nearly singular. An alternative to *lsolve* is to solve a linear system by using matrix inversion.

Solve Blocks

The general form for using system solving functions in Mathcad is within the body of a *solve block*. There are four general steps to creating a solve block. These are:

1. Provide an initial guess (definition) for each of the unknowns. Mathcad solves equations by making iterative calculations that ultimately converge on a valid solution. The initial guesses you provide give Mathcad a place to start searching for solutions. If you expect your solutions to be complex, provide complex guess values. Guess values are required for most systems.

2. Type the word **Given** in a separate math region below the guess definitions. This tells Mathcad that what follows is a system of constraint equations. Be sure you don't type "Given" in a text region.

3. Now enter the constraints (equalities and inequalities) in any order below the word *Given*. Make sure you use the bold equal symbol (click $\boxed{=}$ on the Boolean toolbar or press [**Ctrl**]=) for any equality. You can separate the left and right sides of an inequality with any of the symbols <, >, ≤, and ≥.

4. Enter any equation that involves one of the functions *Find*, *Maximize*, *Minimize*, or *Minerr* below the constraints.

Tip   Solve blocks cannot be nested inside each other—each solve block can have only one *Given* and one *Find* (or *Maximize*, *Minimize*, or *Minerr*). You can, however, define a function like $f(x) := \text{Find}(x)$ at the end of one solve block and refer to this function in another solve block.

Solve Blocks Functions

Figure 9-2 shows a solve block with several kinds of constraints and ending with a call to the *Find* function. There are two unknowns. As a result, the *Find* function here takes two arguments, *x* and *y*, and returns a vector with two elements.

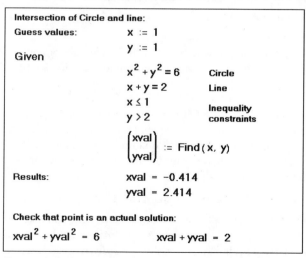

Figure 9-2: A solve block with both equalities and inequalities.

Note   Unlike most Mathcad functions, the solving functions *Find*, *Maximize*, *Minerr*, and *Minimize* can be entered in math regions with either an initial lowercase or an initial capital letter.

Solve blocks can be used to solve parametric systems. In Figure 9-3, the solution is cast in terms of several parameters in the solve block besides the unknown variable.

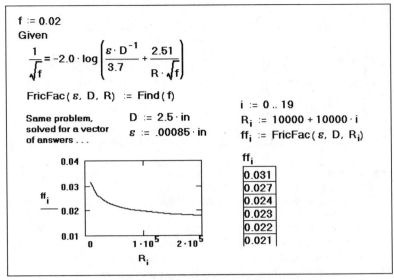

$f := 0.02$

Given

$$\frac{1}{\sqrt{f}} = -2.0 \cdot \log\left(\frac{\varepsilon \cdot D^{-1}}{3.7} + \frac{2.51}{R \cdot \sqrt{f}}\right)$$

$FricFac(\varepsilon, D, R) := Find(f)$

Same problem, solved for a vector of answers . . .

$D := 2.5 \cdot in$

$\varepsilon := .00085 \cdot in$

$i := 0 .. 19$

$R_i := 10000 + 10000 \cdot i$

$ff_i := FricFac(\varepsilon, D, R_i)$

ff_i

ff_i
0.031
0.027
0.024
0.023
0.022
0.021

Figure 9-3: Solving an equation parametrically.

Solve blocks can also take matrices as unknowns, and solve matrix equations. (See Figure 9-4 and Figure 9-5.)

$$M := \begin{pmatrix} 13 & 4 & 4 \\ 4 & 9 & -3 \\ 4 & -3 & 57 \end{pmatrix}$$

Two methods for computing a matrix square root (nonunique).

Using eigenanalysis:

$Vec := eigenvecs(M)$ $Vals := diag(eigenvals(M))$

$$S := Vec \cdot \overrightarrow{\sqrt{Vals}} \cdot Vec^T$$

$$S = \begin{pmatrix} 3.528 & 0.639 & 0.38 \\ 0.639 & 2.915 & -0.31 \\ 0.38 & -0.31 & 7.534 \end{pmatrix} \qquad S^2 = \begin{pmatrix} 13 & 4 & 4 \\ 4 & 9 & -3 \\ 4 & -3 & 57 \end{pmatrix}$$

Using a solve block:

$X := M$ initial guess

Given

$X^2 = M$

$S1 := Find(X)$

$$S1 = \begin{pmatrix} 2.095 & 2.867 & 0.623 \\ 2.867 & -0.55 & -0.69 \\ 0.623 & -0.69 & 7.492 \end{pmatrix} \qquad S1^2 = \begin{pmatrix} 13 & 4 & 4 \\ 4 & 9 & -3 \\ 4 & -3 & 57 \end{pmatrix}$$

Figure 9-4: A solve block for computing the square root of a matrix.

State matrices:

$$A := \begin{pmatrix} 0 & 0 \\ 0 & 1 \end{pmatrix} \quad B := \begin{pmatrix} 0 & 1 \\ 0 & -1 \end{pmatrix} \quad C := \begin{pmatrix} 1 & 0 \\ 0 & 0 \end{pmatrix} \quad P := \text{identity}(2) \quad \text{initial guess}$$

Given

$$-P \cdot A \cdot P + P \cdot B + B^T \cdot P + C = 0 \quad \text{The Riccati Equation from control theory.}$$

$$\text{Find}(P) = \begin{pmatrix} 1.732 & 1 \\ 1 & 0.732 \end{pmatrix}$$

Figure 9-5: A solve block for computing the solution of a matrix equation.

Note Mathcad Solve Blocks can solve linear and nonlinear systems of up to 400 variables. Adding the *Solving and Optimization Extension Pack* increases this number to linear systems of up to 1000 variables, nonlinear systems of up to 250 variables, and quadratic systems of up to 1000 variables.

The table below lists the kinds of constraints that can appear in a solve block between the keyword *Given* and one of the functions *Find*, *Maximize*, *Minerr*, and *Minimize*. In the table, x and y represent real-valued expressions, and z and w represent arbitrary expressions. The Boolean constraints are inserted using buttons on the Boolean toolbar. Constraints are often scalar expressions but can also be vector or array expressions.

Condition	Button	Description
$w = z$	=	Constrained to be equal.
$x > y$	>	Greater than.
$x < y$	<	Less than.
$x \geq y$	≥	Greater than or equal to.
$x \leq y$	≤	Less than or equal to.
$x \wedge y$	∧	And
$x \vee y$	∨	Or
$x \otimes y$	⊕	Xor (Exclusive Or)
$\neg x$	¬	Not

Mathcad does not allow the following between the Given and Find in a solve block:

- Constraints with "$\neq$."
- Range variables or expressions involving range variables of any kind.
- Assignment statements (statements like `x:=1`).

You can, however, include compound statements such as $1 \le x \le 3$.

Note Mathcad returns only one solution for a solve block. There may, however, be multiple solutions to a set of equations. To find a different solution, try different guess values or enter an additional inequality constraint that the current solution does not satisfy.

Tolerances for solving

Mathcad's numerical solvers make use of two tolerance parameters in calculating solutions in solve blocks:

*   **Convergence tolerance.** The solvers calculate successive estimates of the values of the solutions and return values when the two most recent estimates differ by less than the value of the built-in variable *TOL*. A smaller value of *TOL* often results in a more accurate solution, but the solution may take longer to calculate.

*   **Constraint tolerance.** This parameter, determined by the value of the built-in variable *CTOL*, controls how closely a constraint must be met for a solution to be acceptable. For example, if the constraint tolerance were 0.0001, a constraint such as $x < 2$ would be considered satisfied if, in fact, the value of x satisfied $x < 2.0001$.

Procedures for modifying the values of these tolerances are described in "Built-in Variables" on page 100.

Tip If you use *Minerr* in a solve block, you should always include additional checks on the reasonableness of the results. The built-in variable ERR returns the size of the error vector for the approximate solution returned by *Minerr*. There is no built-in variable for determining the size of the error for individual solutions to the unknowns.

Getting past errors

If the solver cannot make any further improvements to the solution but the constraints are *not* all satisfied, then the solver stops and marks Find with an error message. This happens whenever the difference between successive approximations to the solution is greater than *TOL* and:

*   The solver reaches a point where it cannot reduce the error any further.

*   The solver reaches a point from which there is no preferred direction. Because of this, the solver has no basis on which to make further iterations.

*   The solver reaches the limit of its accuracy. Round-off errors make it unlikely that further computation would increase accuracy of the solution. This often happens if you set TOL to a value below 10^{-15}.

The following problems may cause this sort of failure:

*   There may actually be no solution.

*   You may have given real guesses for an equation with no real solution. If the solution for a variable is complex, the solver will not find it unless the starting value for that variable is also complex.

*   The solver may have become trapped in a local minimum for the error values. To find the actual solution, try using different starting values or add an inequality to keep Mathcad from being trapped in the local minimum.

- The solver may have become trapped on a point that is not a local minimum, but from which it cannot determine where to go next. Again, try changing the initial guesses or adding an inequality to avoid the undesirable stopping point.

If you can not solve the constraints to within the desired tolerance, try defining *TOL* with a larger value somewhere above the solve block. Increasing the tolerance changes what Mathcad considers close enough to call a solution.

Solving algorithms and AutoSelect

When you solve an equation, by default Mathcad uses an *AutoSelect* procedure to choose an appropriate solving algorithm. You can override Mathcad's choice of algorithm and select another available algorithm yourself.

Here are the available solving methods:

Linear

Applies a linear programming algorithm to the problem. Guess values for the unknowns are not required.

Nonlinear

Applies either a conjugate gradient, Levenberg-Marquardt, or quasi-Newton solving routine to the problem. Guess values for all unknowns must precede the solve block. Choose **Nonlinear⇒Advanced Options** from the popup menu to control settings for the conjugate gradient and quasi-Newton solvers.

Note   The Levenberg-Marquardt method is not available for the *Maximize* and *Minimize* functions.

You can override Mathcad's default choice of solving algorithm as follows:

1. Create and evaluate a solve block, allowing Mathcad to AutoSelect an algorithm.

2. Click with the right mouse button on the name of the function that terminates the solve block, and remove the check from **AutoSelect** on the popup menu.

3. Check one of the available solving methods on the popup menu. Mathcad recalculates the solution using the method you selected.

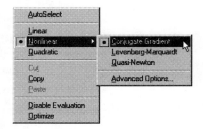

Solving and Optimization Extension Pack

If you have the SOEP installed, the following options are also available:

- **Quadratic**: Applies a quadratic programming algorithm to the problem. Guess values for the unknowns are not required.

- **Reports:** Generates sensitivity analysis reports for linear optimization problems.

- **Mixed integer programming** : Forces the solution for an unknown variable to be a binary number (1 or 0) or an integer. For more information refer to online Help.

Differential Equation Solvers

In solving differential equations, you solve for an unknown function rather than a variable. In ordinary differential equations (ODEs), the unknown function is a function of one variable. In partial differential equations (PDEs) the unknown function is a function of two or more variables. All Mathcad differential equations solvers can be used to solve first-order or higher-order derivative functions or systems of functions.

The easiest way to solve differential equations is to use a Solve Block and the functions *Odesolve* or *Pdesolve*. If you need to solve ODEs or PDEs in programs, or have specialized boundary value problems, you can use the command-line differential equation solvers detailed on subsequent pages.

Solving an ODE Using a Solve Block

Odesolve([**vf**], *x*, **vb**/*b*, [*step*])

Returns a function (or vector of functions **vf**) of the variable *x* which solve an ODE or system of ODEs, subject to either initial value or boundary value constraints. **vf** is only required when a system of ODEs is being solved, to specify order of solutions. **vb** is a two-element column vector that specifies the initial and terminal points of the integration interval; alternatively, *b* is the terminal point of the integration interval, assumed to start at 0. *step* (optional) is the number of steps.

There are three steps to creating a differential equation solve block:

1. Type the keyword **Given**. You can type either **Given** or **given**, and it must be a math region, not a text region.

2. Type the ODE and constraints in any order below the word *Given*. Use the bold equal sign (click ☐ **=** ☐ on the Boolean or Evaluation toolbars or press [**Ctrl]=**) for an equality. The independent variable *x* must be explicitly indicated throughout, that is, use *y(x)* or *y'(x)* when specifying the unknown function and its derivatives, not just *y* or *y'*. A typical initial value or boundary value constraint might be *y(0)=c* or *y'(a)=d*. Mathcad also allows algebraic constraints, such as *y(x) + z(x) = w(x)*; Mathcad does not allow more complicated constraints like *y(a)+y'(a)=d*. ODEs can be written using either the derivative operators d/dx, d^2/dx^2, d^3/dx^3, ... (press **?** or [**Ctrl]?** to insert the derivative or *n*th derivative operators), or using prime notation *y'(x), y''(x), y'''(x)*, ... (Press [**Ctrl][F7]** for the prime symbol.) Initial and boundary conditions must be specified using prime notation.

3. Finally, type the *Odesolve* function. The terminal point *b* must be larger than the starting point for the ODE variable *x*, as implied by the initial conditions, or you can set the range of integration explicitly by using a two-element column vector. The entire process is demonstrated in Figure 9-6.

Tip   Prime notation is only allowed inside a solve block. If you use it outside of a solve block, you see an error.

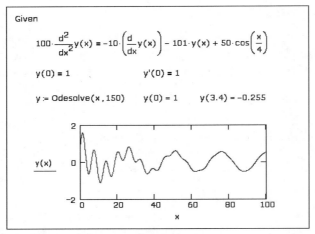

Figure 9-6: Solving a single differential equation.

The output of *Odesolve* is a function, or vector of functions, of *x*, interpolated from a table of values. The algorithm is the fixed-step method employed by *rkfixed*, described on page 137. If you prefer to use an adaptive step or stiff method, click on *Odesolve* with the right mouse button and make your choice from the menu that appears. More information on the available algorithms and the types of systems for which they are best used is available in the section on "Specialized Initial-Value Differential Equation Solvers" on page 140:

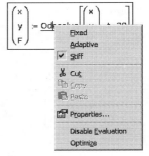

Mathcad is very specific about the types of expressions that can appear between *Given* and *Odesolve*. The lower derivative terms can appear nonlinearly in the differential equation (e.g., they can be multiplied together or raised to powers), but the highest derivative term must appear linearly. Inequality constraints are not allowed.

Note Boundary value problems can be solved for a single equation, but for systems of equations, only initial value constraints are accepted.

The rules of mathematics for solving these systems must be followed, or Odesolve will produce errors:

- There must be *n* independent equality constraints for an *n*th order differential equation.

- For an initial value problem, the values for *y(x)* and its first *n*−1 derivatives at a single initial point *a* are required.

- For a boundary value problem, the *n* equality constraints should prescribe values for *y(x)* and certain derivatives at exactly two points *a* and *b*.

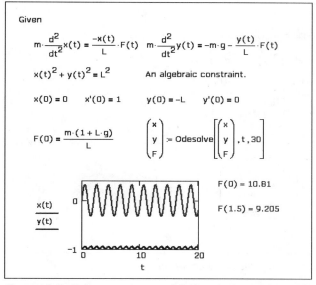

Given

$$m \cdot \frac{d^2}{dt^2} x(t) = \frac{-x(t)}{L} \cdot F(t) \quad m \cdot \frac{d^2}{dt^2} y(t) = -m \cdot g - \frac{y(t)}{L} \cdot F(t)$$

$$x(t)^2 + y(t)^2 = L^2 \qquad \text{An algebraic constraint.}$$

$$x(0) = 0 \quad x'(0) = 1 \qquad y(0) = -L \quad y'(0) = 0$$

$$F(0) = \frac{m \cdot (1 + L \cdot g)}{L} \qquad \begin{pmatrix} x \\ y \\ F \end{pmatrix} := \text{Odesolve} \left[\begin{pmatrix} x \\ y \\ F \end{pmatrix}, t, 30 \right]$$

$$F(0) = 10.81$$

$$F(1.5) = 9.205$$

$$\frac{x(t)}{y(t)}$$

Figure 9-7: Solving a system of differential equations with an algebraic constraint.

Solving a PDE using a Solve Block

Pdesolve([**vf**], *x*, **vb**, *t*, **vc**, [*xstep*], [*tstep*])   Returns a function (or vector of functions **vf**) of the variables *x* and *t* which solve a PDE or system of PDEs, subject to either initial value or boundary value constraints. **vb** is a two-element column vector that specifies the initial and terminal points of the spatial integration interval; **vc** is a two-element column vector that specifies the initial and terminal points of the temporal integration interval; *xstep* (optional) is the number of spatial steps. *tstep* (optional) is the number of temporal steps.

As with Odesolve, are three steps to creating a PDE solve block:

1. Type the keyword **Given**. You can type either **Given** or **given**, and it must be a math region, not a text region.

2. Type the PDE and constraints in any order below the word *Given*. Use the bold equal sign (click ▣= on the Boolean or Evaluation toolbars or press [**Ctrl**]=) for an equality. Use subscript notation to indicate the partial derivative in either x or t, and explicitly specify the independent variables throughout, that is, use *y(x,t)* or $y_{xx}(x,t)$, not just *y* or y_{xx}. Either Dirichlet (*y(0,t) = a*) or Neumann ($y_x(0,t) = a$) boundary conditions are accepted. Mathcad also allows algebraic constraints, such as *y(x,t) + z(x,t) = 2.*

3. Finally, type the *Pdesolve* function. The two-element column vectors vb and vc, ranges over *x* and *t*, respectively, must agree with values assigned in the boundary conditions. (See Figure 9-8.)

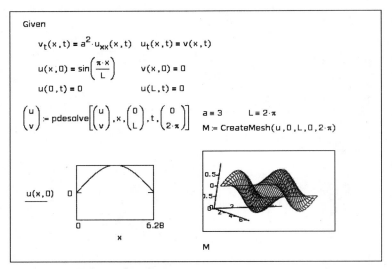

Given

$$v_t(x,t) = a^2 \cdot u_{xx}(x,t) \quad u_t(x,t) = v(x,t)$$

$$u(x,0) = \sin\left(\frac{\pi \cdot x}{L}\right) \qquad v(x,0) = 0$$

$$u(0,t) = 0 \qquad\qquad u(L,t) = 0$$

$$\begin{pmatrix} u \\ v \end{pmatrix} := \text{pdesolve}\left[\begin{pmatrix} u \\ v \end{pmatrix}, x, \begin{pmatrix} 0 \\ L \end{pmatrix}, t, \begin{pmatrix} 0 \\ 2\cdot\pi \end{pmatrix}\right] \qquad a \equiv 3 \qquad L \equiv 2\cdot\pi$$

$$M := \text{CreateMesh}(u,0,L,0,2\cdot\pi)$$

$$\underline{u(x,0)} \quad 0$$

x

M

Figure 9-8: Solving the wave equation.

Note Mathcad uses the numerical method of lines to compute PDEs. This method allows the solution of parabolic (heat), hyperbolic (wave), and parabolic-hyperbolic (advection) equations. It does not accommodate elliptic equations, such as Poisson's equation. To solve other types of systems, try the *relax* function (described on page 145) and the *multigrid* function (described on page 145).

The output of *Pdesolve* is a function, or vector of functions, of *x* and *t*, interpolated from a table of values. The algorithm is the numerical method of lines employed by the function *numol*, described on page 139.

Tip To view each solution in *x* over time, create a graph of the function *u(x,FRAME)* vs. *x*, and use Mathcad's animation tools to capture images of the graph for *FRAME = 0* to the maximum calculated value of *t*.

Command-line Differential Equation Solvers

If you wish to include a differential equation solver within another construct, such as a program loop, you can use the command-line differential equation solvers: *rkfixed*, *rkadapt*, *numol*, etc. A complete list can be found in Chapter 16, "Functions," in the reference section of this book. The general use of the differential functions is the same. Each one uses a different algorithm, so some may be better suited to your application or system of equations than others.

Runge-Kutta initial-value solver for ODEs

rkfixed uses the fourth order Runge-Kutta method to solve a first order differential equation and return a two-column matrix in which:

- The left-hand column contains the points at which the solution to the differential equation is evaluated.

- The right-hand column contains the corresponding values of the solution.

rkfixed(**y0**, *x1*, *x2*, *npoints*, **D**)

y0 = real vector of initial values, whose length depends on the order of the DE or the size of the system of DEs. For a first order DE, the vector degenerates to one point, $y(0) = y(x1)$. For higher order DEs, the vector has n elements for specifying initial conditions of y, $y', y'', ..., y^{(n-1)}$. For a first order system, the vector contains initial values for each unknown function. For higher order systems, the vector contains initial values for the $n-1$ derivatives of each unknown function in addition to initial values for the functions themselves.

x1, *x2* = The endpoints of the integration region.

npoints = Number of solution points between the endpoints (the grid).

D(*x*, **y**) = real vector-valued function containing derivatives of the unknown functions. This vector will be of the same length as **y**, and follow similar rules.

The complicated step in this process is creating the vector of derivatives for each unknown function. This is the step which is transparent in ODE solve blocks. The derivative vector is the way in which each differential equation is specified to *rkfixed*.

Examine the example in Figure 9-9 comparing a system of linear second-order equations solved by a Solve Block vs. *rkfixed*. The part of the setup process which is not explicit is the creation of a vector **y** of all unknown functions and their derivatives in the system. For the case shown, **y** has four elements: u, u', v, v'. So, when referring to the first derivative of u, which is the first element of **D**, the value y_1 is used. The ODEs in the original problem appear as the 2nd and 4th elements in the vector **D**, specifying the second derivatives of $u(x)$ and $v(x)$ in terms of elements of **y**. At no point in this process do we specifically create a vector **y**.

Note The subscripts on elements of y in the definition of **D** are vector subscripts, that is, they are created with the [key. The derivative vector must be defined as a function of x and **y**, since we don't have specific values for these until the solution is created.

Given

$$u''(x) = 2 \cdot v(x) + x \qquad v''(x) = 4 \cdot v(x) - 2 \cdot u(x)$$

$$u(0) = 1.5 \qquad u'(0) = 1.5$$

$$v(0) = 1 \qquad v'(0) = 1$$

$$\binom{u}{v} := \text{Odesolve}\left[\binom{u}{v}, x, 1\right]$$

For rkfixed, the initial condition vector and derivitive vectors are given by

$$IC := \begin{pmatrix} 1.5 \\ 1.5 \\ 1 \\ 1 \end{pmatrix} \quad \begin{matrix} u(0) = 1.5 \\ u'(0) = 1.5 \\ v(0) = 1 \\ v'(0) = 1 \end{matrix} \qquad D(x,y) := \begin{pmatrix} y_1 \\ 2 \cdot y_2 + x \\ y_3 \\ 4 \cdot y_2 - 2 \cdot y_0 \end{pmatrix} \quad \begin{matrix} u' \\ u'' \\ v' \\ v'' \end{matrix}$$

SOLN := rkfixed(IC, 0, 1, 100, D)

SOLN =

x	u(x)	u'(x)	v(x)	v'(x)
0	1.5	1.5	1	1
0.01	1.515	1.52	1.01	1.01
0.02	1.53	1.541	1.02	1.02
0.03	1.546	1.561	1.03	1.03
0.04	1.562	1.582	1.041	1.041
0.05	1.578	1.604	1.051	1.051
0.06	1.594	1.625	1.062	1.062
0.07	1.61	1.647	1.073	1.072

Compare the Odesolve solution with rkfixed:

$$u(0.05) = 1.578$$
$$v(0.06) = 1.062$$

Figure 9-9: Solving a second-order system of differential equations with both Odesolve *and* rkfixed.

The first row of the solution matrix, SOLN, is identical to the initial conditions. The results given by Odesolve are identical to those in the matrix, since they use the same algorithm, but the Odesolve results are functions, while *rkfixed* provides a grid of solution points. The functions returned by *Odesolve* are really just interpolations of the same matrix of solutions. One by-product of using *rkfixed* is that the values of the derivatives are also returned.

Method of Lines Solver for PDEs

Just as initial-value ODE problems can be solved at the command line using *rkfixed*, (or other specialized functions described below) one-dimensional PDEs can be solved using *numol*. *numol* uses the numerical method of lines to solve hyperbolic or parabolic partial differential equations or systems of equations, and returns a matrix of solutions where each column represents a solution over 1-D space at a single solution time.

numol(**x_endpts**, *xpoints*, **t_endpts**, *tpoints*, *num_pde*, *num_pae*, **pfunc**, **pinit**, **bc_func**))

x_endpts =	the column vector *(x1, x2)* giving the start and end of the spatial integration region.
xpoints =	number of spatial discretization points.
t_endpts =	the column vector *(t1,t2)* giving the start and end of the spatial integration region.
tpoints =	number of temporal discretization points.
num_pde =	number of PDEs in the system (at least 1)
num_pae =	number of Partial Algebraic Equations (algebraic constraints, e.g., $0 = u(x)+v(x)-w(x)$ for all *x*. Can be 0.
pfunc =	vector function of *x, t, u, u_x, u_{xx}* of length *num_pde + num_pae* for evaluating right-hand sides (rhs) of the PDEs/PAEs. The unknown solution matrix **u** is assumed to contain solutions for all unknown functions, so systems of equations should be cast in terms of vector-index subscripts, u_0, u_{x0}, u_{xx0}, u_1, u_{x1}, and so on.
pinit =	vector function of *x* of length *num_pde + num_pae* for evaluating initial conditions
bc_func =	The boundary condition (BC) matrix **bc_func** is a *num_pde x 3* matrix function. If the PDE for a row contains 2nd-order spatial derivatives, specify

(left_cond(t) right_cond(t) "D") (for Dirichlet), or
(left_cond(t) right_cond(t) "N") (for Neumann).

If the PDE contains only first order spatial derivatives, use "NA" for either the right or left BC. If no spatial derivatives are present, use "NA" for both BCs (the row will be ignored).

numol returns an *xpoints* by *tpoints* matrix for a single PDE, or, in the case of a system of equations, an *xpoints* by *tpoints*(num_pde+num_pae)* matrix. That is, each column of the matrix represents a snapshot of the solution over all x at a particular point in time. If you want to graph multiple solution functions from a system of equations, add *tpoints* to the index of the column for each successive solution function. (See Figure 9-10.)

Note   At most, two boundary functions per PDE must be declared, based on the order of spatial derivatives in the PDE, so the correct number of conditions to guarantee unique solutions is always met.

The *numol* function requires that the time derivative on the left-hand side of the PDEs is always of first order. If you have equations of second order in time (such as the wave

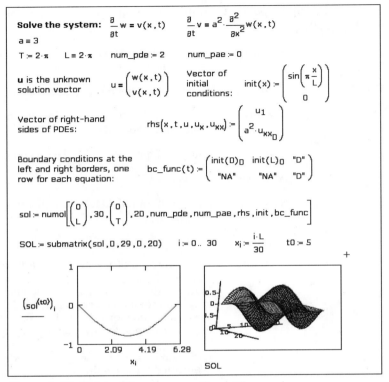

Figure 9-10: Solving the wave equation with numol.

equation), you'll need to recast them as a system of equations, introducing dummy variables to stand in for first-order time derivatives.

Specialized Initial-Value Differential Equation Solvers

Mathcad includes several specialized functions for solving differential equations, which you may want to use rather than the general-purpose *rkfixed*. If your system is stiff, smooth, or has both high and low rates of change over the solution interval, one of these specialized solvers may yeild faster or more accurate results than rkfixed. Each of these functions returns a matrix containing the values of the function evaluated over a set of points.

Tip   When solving a differential equation it is a good idea to try more than one differential equation solver because one method might suit your differential equation better than another method.

Smooth systems

When you know the solution is smooth, use *Bulstoer*, which uses the Bulirsch-Stoer method rather than the Runge-Kutta method used by *rkfixed*.

Bulstoer(**y**, *x1*, *x2*, *npoints*, **D**)

The argument list and the matrix returned by *Bulstoer* are identical to that for *rkfixed*.

Systems with varying rates of change

Given a fixed number of points, you can approximate a function more accurately if you evaluate it frequently wherever it's changing fast and infrequently wherever it's changing more slowly.

Rkadapt($\mathbf{y}$, $x1$, $x2$, $npoints$, $\mathbf{D}$)

The argument list and the matrix returned by *Rkadapt* are identical in form to that for *rkfixed*.

If you know that the solution has this property, you may be better off using *Rkadapt*. Unlike *rkfixed*, *Rkadapt* examines how quickly the solution is changing and adapts its step size accordingly.

Note Although *Rkadapt* uses nonuniform step sizes internally when it solves the differential equation, it nevertheless returns the solution at equally spaced points.

Stiff systems

A system of differential equations expressed in the form $\mathbf{y} = \mathbf{A} \cdot \mathbf{x}$ is a *stiff system* if the matrix $\mathbf{A}$ is nearly singular. Under these conditions, the solution returned by *rkfixed* may oscillate or be unstable. When solving a stiff system, you should use one of the three differential equation solvers specifically designed for stiff systems, *Radau*, *Stiffb* and *Stiffr*, which use the implicit Runge-Kutta RADAU5 method, the Bulirsch-Stoer method and the Rosenbrock method, respectively. They take the same arguments as *rkfixed*. *Stiffb* and *Stiffr* each have one additional argument.

Radau($\mathbf{y}$, $x1$, $x2$, $npoints$, $\mathbf{D}$)
Stiffb($\mathbf{y}$, $x1$, $x2$, $npoints$, $\mathbf{D}$, $\mathbf{J}$)
Stiffr($\mathbf{y}$, $x1$, $x2$, $npoints$, $\mathbf{D}$, $\mathbf{J}$)

$\mathbf{J}(x, \mathbf{y}) =$ A function you define that returns the $n \times (n + 1)$ matrix whose first column contains the derivatives $\partial \mathbf{D} / \partial x$ and whose remaining rows and columns form the Jacobian matrix $(\partial \mathbf{D} / \partial y_k)$ for the system of differential equations. For example, if:

$$\mathbf{D}(x, \mathbf{y}) = \begin{bmatrix} x \cdot y_1 \\ -2 \cdot y_1 \cdot y_0 \end{bmatrix} \quad \text{then} \quad \mathbf{J}(x, \mathbf{y}) = \begin{bmatrix} y_1 & 0 & x \\ 0 & -2 \cdot y_1 & -2 \cdot y_0 \end{bmatrix}$$

See *rkfixed* for a description of other parameters.

Evaluating only the final value

If you only care about the value of the solution at the endpoint, $y(x2)$, rather than over a number of uniformly spaced x values in the integration interval, use the functions listed below. Each function corresponds to the capitalized versions already discussed. The properties of each of these functions are identical to those of the corresponding function in the previous sections, except for the arguments below:

bulstoer(**y**, *x1*, *x2*, *acc*, **D**, *kmax*, *save*)
rkadapt(**y**, *x1*, *x2*, *acc*, **D**, *kmax*, *save*)
radau(**y**, *x1*, *x2*, *acc*, **D**, *kmax*, *save*)
stiffb(**y**, *x1*, *x2*, *acc*, **D**, **J**, *kmax*, *save*)
stiffr(**y**, *x1*, *x2*, *acc*, **D**, **J**, *kmax*, *save*)

acc = Controls the accuracy of the solution. A small value of *acc* forces the algorithm to take smaller steps along the trajectory, thereby increasing the accuracy of the solution. Values of *acc* around 0.001 generally yield accurate solutions.

kmax = The maximum number of intermediate points at which the solution will be approximated. The value of *kmax* places an upper bound on the number of rows of the matrix returned by these functions.

save = The smallest allowable spacing between the values at which the solutions are to be approximated. This places a lower bound on the difference between any two numbers in the first column of the matrix returned by the function.

Boundary Value Problems

The specialized differential equation solvers discussed above are useful for solving *initial value problems*. In some cases, however, you may know the value taken by the solution at the *endpoints* of the interval of integration, which is a *boundary value problem*.

To solve boundary value problems in Mathcad, use *Odesolve*, described in "Solving an ODE Using a Solve Block ," or *sbval* or *bvalfit* as described here.

Two-point ODE boundary value problems

Two-point boundary value problems are one-dimensional systems of differential equations in which the solution is a function of a single variable and the value of the solution is known at two points. You can use *sbval* in the following case:

- You have an *n*th order differential equation.

- You know some, but not all, of the values of the solution and its first $n - 1$ derivatives at the beginning of the interval of integration, *x1,* and at the end of the interval of integration, *x2*.

- Between what you know about the solution at *x1* and at *x2*, you have *n* known values.

sbval returns a vector containing those initial values left unspecified at the first endpoint of the interval. Once you know the missing initial values at *x1*, you have an initial value problem that can be solved using any of the functions discussed earlier in this section.

sbval(**v**, *x1*, *x2*, **D**, **load**, **score**)

v= Vector of guesses for initial values left unspecified at *x1*.

x1, *x2* = The endpoints of the interval on which the solution to the differential equations will be evaluated.

D(*x*, **y**) = An *n*-element vector-valued function containing the first derivatives of the unknown functions.

load(*x1*, **v**) = A vector-valued function whose *n* elements correspond to the values of the *n* unknown functions at *x1*. Some of these values will be constants specified by your initial conditions. Others will be unknown at the outset but will be found by *sbval*. If a value is unknown, you should use the corresponding guess value from **v**.

score(*x2*, **y**) = A vector-valued function having the same number of elements as **v**. Each element is the difference between an initial condition at *x2*, as originally specified, and the corresponding estimate from the solution. The *score* vector measures how closely the proposed solution matches the initial conditions at *x2*. A value of 0 for any element indicates a perfect match between the corresponding initial condition and that returned by *sbval*.

Note As shown in Figure 9-11, *sbval* does not actually return a solution to a differential equation. It merely computes the initial values the solution must have in order for the solution to match the final values you specify. You must then take the initial values returned by *sbval* and solve the resulting initial value problem using a function such as *rkfixed*.

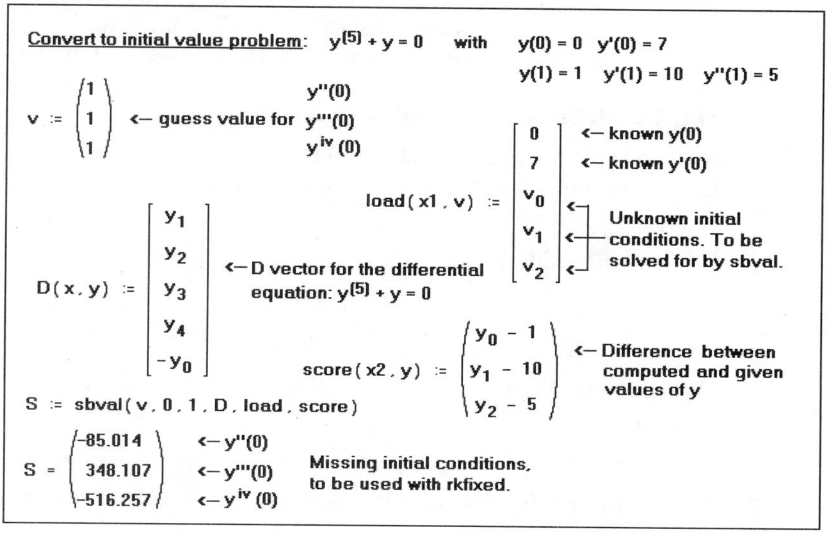

Figure 9-11: Using sbval *to obtain initial values corresponding to given final values of a solution to a differential equation.*

It's also possible that you don't have all the information you need to use *sbval* but you do know something about the solution and its first $n-1$ derivatives at some intermediate value, *xf*. In this case, the function *bvalfit* solves a two-point boundary value problem by shooting from the endpoints and matching the trajectories of the solution and its derivatives at an intermediate point. This method becomes especially useful when the derivative has a discontinuity somewhere in the integration interval.

bvalfit(**v1**, **v2**, *x1*, *x2*, *xf*, **D**, **load1**, **load2**, **score**)

> **v1**, **v2** = Vector **v1** contains guesses for initial values left unspecified at *x1*.
> Vector **v2** contains guesses for initial values left unspecified at *x2*.

> *x1*, *x2* = The endpoints of the interval on which the solution to the differential equations will be evaluated.

> *xf* = A point between *x1* and *x2* at which the trajectories of the solutions beginning at *x1* and those beginning at *x2* are constrained to be equal.

> **D**(*x*, **y**) = An *n*-element vector-valued function containing the first derivatives of the unknown functions.

> **load1**(*x1*, **v1**) = A vector-valued function whose *n* elements correspond to the values of the *n* unknown functions at *x1*. Some of these values will be constants specified by your initial conditions. If a value is unknown, you should use the corresponding guess value from **v1**.

> **load2**(*x2*, **v2**) = Analogous to *load1* but for values taken by the *n* unknown functions at *x2*.

> **score**(*xf*, **y**) = An *n* element vector valued function that specifies how the solutions match at *xf*. You'll usually want to define *score*(*xf*, **y**) := **y** to make the solutions to all unknown functions match up at *xf*.

Elliptic PDEs with boundary values

A second type of boundary value problem arises when you are solving Poisson's PDE. Rather than being fixed at two points, the solution is fixed at a whole continuum of points representing some boundary.

Poisson's Equation is given by:

$$\frac{\partial^2 u}{\partial x^2} + \frac{\partial^2 u}{\partial y^2} = \rho(x, y)$$

These solvers also address the homogeneous form, Laplace's equation, where $\rho(x, y) = 0$.

Tip   To type a partial differential equation symbol such as $\frac{\partial}{\partial x}$, insert the derivative operator $\frac{d}{dx}$ by typing **?**, click on the derivative operator with the right mouse button, and choose **View Derivative As** $\Rightarrow$ **Partial Derivative** from the popup menu.

Mathcad has two functions for solving these equations over a square boundary. You should use *relax* if you know the value taken by the unknown function $u(x, y)$ on all four sides of a square region.

If $u(x, y)$ is zero on all four sides of the square, you can use *multigrid*, which often solves the problem faster than *relax*. Note that if the boundary condition is the same on all four sides, you can simply transform the equation to an equivalent one in which the value is zero on all four sides.

relax returns a square matrix in which:

- An element's location in the matrix corresponds to its location within the square region, and

- Its value approximates the value of the solution at that point.

This function uses the relaxation method to converge to the solution. Poisson's equation on a square domain is represented by:

$$a_{j, k}u_{j + 1, k} + b_{j, k}u_{j - 1, k} + c_{j, k}u_{j, k + 1} + d_{j, k}u_{j, k - 1} + e_{j, k}u_{j, k} = f_{j, k}$$

relax(**a, b, c, d, e, f, u,** *rjac*)

$\quad$ **a . . . e** = Square matrices all of the same size containing coefficients of the above equation.

$\quad$ **f** = Square matrix containing the source term at each point in the region in which the solution is sought.

$\quad$ **u** = Square matrix containing boundary values along the edges of the region and initial guesses for the solution inside the region.

$\quad$ *rjac* = Spectral radius of the Jacobi iteration. This number between 0 and 1 controls the convergence of the relaxation algorithm. Its optimal value depends on the details of your problem.

multigrid(**M,** *ncycle*)

$\quad$ **M** = $(1 + 2^n)$ row square matrix whose elements correspond to the source term at the corresponding point in the square domain.

$\quad$ *ncycle* = The number of cycles at each level of the *multigrid* iteration. A value of 2 generally gives a good approximation of the solution.

Data Fitting

Interpolation

Interpolation involves using existing data points to predict values between these data points. Mathcad allows you to connect the data points either with straight lines (linear interpolation) or with sections of a cubic polynomial (cubic spline interpolation). Unlike the regression functions discussed in the next section, these interpolation functions return a curve which must pass through the points you specify. If your data is noisy, you should consider using regression functions instead (see page 147).

Cubic spline interpolation passes a curve through a set of points in such a way that the first and second derivatives of the curve are continuous across each point. This curve is assembled by taking three adjacent points and constructing a cubic polynomial passing through those points. These cubic polynomials are then strung together to form the completed curve. In the case of "traditional" cubic splines, the data points to be interpolated define the "knots" where the polynomials are joined, but B-splines (implemented in the function *bspline*) join the polynomials at arbitrary points.

Linear prediction involves using existing data values to predict values beyond the existing ones.

The coefficients returned by the spline interpolation functions *bspline*, *cspline*, *lspline*, and *pspline* and the regression functions *regress* and *loess* described in the next section are designed to be passed to Mathcad's *interp* function. *interp* returns a single interpolated *y* value for a given *x* value, but as a practical matter you'll probably be evaluating *interp* for many different points, as shown in Figure 9-12. Store the coefficients returned by the spline or regression functions in a vector (such as **vs** in Figure 9-12) that can be passed to *interp* for evaluation, plotting, or further calculation.

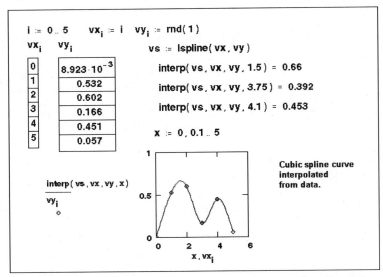

Figure 9-12: Spline curve for the points stored in vx and vy. Since the random number generator gives different numbers every time, you may not be able to recreate this example exactly as you see it.

Tip   For best results with spline interpolation, do not use the *interp* function on values of *x* far from the fitted points. Splines are intended for interpolation, not extrapolation.

Note Mathcad handles *two-dimensional* cubic spline interpolation in much the same way as the one-dimensional case illustrated: in this case the spline function takes two matrix arguments, **Mxy** and **Mz**. The first is an $n \times 2$ matrix specifying the points along the diagonal of a rectangular grid, and the second is an $n \times n$ matrix of z-values representing the surface to be interpolated. Mathcad passes a *surface* through the grid of points. This surface corresponds to a cubic polynomial in x and y in which the first and second partial derivatives are continuous in the corresponding direction across each grid point. For an example see the "Data Analysis" QuickSheets from the **Help** menu.

Regression and Smoothing Functions

Mathcad includes a number of functions for performing *regression*. Typically, these functions generate a curve or surface of a specified type in some sense minimizes the error between itself and the data you supply. The functions differ primarily in the type of curve or surface they use to fit the data. Unlike interpolation functions, these functions do not require that the fitted curve or surface pass through points you supply, and they are therefore less sensitive to spurious data.

Smoothing involves taking a set of y (and possibly x) values and returning a new set of y values that is smoother than the original set. Unlike the regression and interpolation functions, smoothing results in a new set of y values, not a function that can be evaluated between the data points you specify. Thus, if you are interested in y values *between* the y values you specify, you should use a regression or interpolation function.

Polynomial functions are useful when you have a set of measured y values corresponding to x values (or possibly multiple x values) and you want to fit a polynomial through those y values.

Use *regress* when you want to use a *single* polynomial to fit all your data values. The *regress* function lets you fit a polynomial of any order. However as a practical matter, you rarely should go beyond $n = 4$.

The *loess* function performs a more localized regression. Instead of generating a single polynomial the way *regress* does, *loess* generates a different second order polynomial depending on where you are on the curve. It does this by examining the data in a small neighborhood of a point you're interested in.

As in the case of Mathcad's spline interpolation functions, the coefficients returned by *regress* and *loess* are designed to be passed to Mathcad's *interp* function. *interp* returns a single interpolated y value for a given x value, but as a practical matter you'll probably be evaluating *interp* for many different points.

Note Mathcad also allows *multivariate* polynomial regression with *regress* or *loess* to fit y values corresponding to two or more independent variables. In this case, the regression function's first two arguments are **Mx** and **vy**: the first is an $n \times m$ matrix specifying the m values of n predictor variables, and the second is a vector of response data corresponding to the factors in **Mx**. For an example see the "Data Analysis" **QuickSheets** under the **Help** menu. You can add independent variables by simply adding columns to the **Mx** array and a corresponding number of rows to the vector you pass to the *interp* function.

Specialized regression

expfit(**vx, vy, vg**)   **vg**, the guess value for **expfit,** is optional.

lgsfit(**vx, vy, vg**)

lnfit(**vx, vy**)

logfit(**vx, vy, vg**)

pwrfit(**vx, vy, vg**)

sinfit(**vx, vy, vg**)

Use these functions when you have a set of measured y values corresponding to x values and you want to fit a special type of curve through those y values. Although you can use the *genfit* function described on page 148 to perform a curve fit on any function, the functions outlined above are designed for ease of use. Use them if they address the particular function curve to which you are fitting your data.

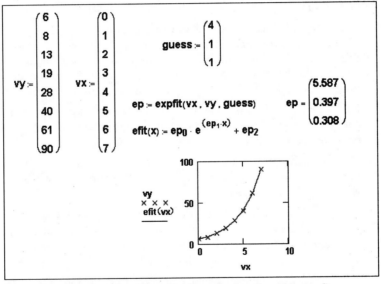

Figure 9-13: Using the specialized regression function expfit.

Generalized regression

linfit(**vx, vy, F**)

genfit(**vx, vy, vg, F**)

linfit is designed to model your data by a linear combination of arbitrary functions:

$$y = a_0 \cdot f_0(x) + a_1 \cdot f_1(x) + \ldots + a_n \cdot f_n(x)$$

genfit is designed to model your data by some arbitrary (possibly nonlinear) function whose parameters must be chosen. For example, if your data is to be modeled by the sum

$$f(x) = 2 \cdot \sin(a_1 x) + 3 \cdot \tanh(a_2 x)$$

and you wish to solve for the unknown parameters a_1 and a_2, you would use *genfit*. An example of using *genfit* is given in Figure 9-14.

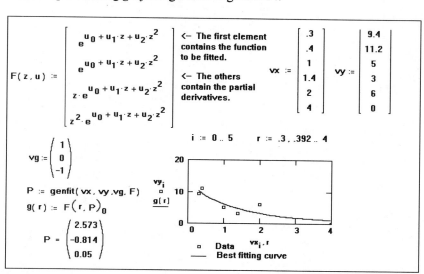

Figure 9-14: Using genfit *for finding the parameters of a function so that it best fits the data.*

Anything you can do with *linfit* you can also do, albeit less conveniently, with *genfit*. The difference between these two functions is the difference between solving a system of linear equations and solving a system of nonlinear equations. The latter generally must be solved by iteration, which explains why *genfit* needs a vector of guess values as an argument and *linfit* does not.

Smoothing functions

medsmooth(**vy**, *n*)

ksmooth(**vx**,**vy**, *b*)

supsmooth(**vx**,**vy**)

medsmooth is the most robust of the three smoothing functions since it is least likely to be affected by spurious data points. This function uses a running median smoother, computes the residuals, smooths the residuals the same way, and adds these two smoothed vectors together. Note that *medsmooth* leaves the first and last $(n-1)/2$ points unchanged. In practice, the length of the smoothing window, *n*, should be small compared to the length of the data set.

ksmooth uses a Gaussian kernel to compute local weighted averages of the input vector **vy**. This smoother is most useful when your data lies along a band of relatively constant width. If your data lies scattered along a band whose width fluctuates considerably, you should use an adaptive smoother like *supsmooth*. *supsmooth* uses a symmetric *k* nearest neighbor linear least-squares fitting procedure to make a series of line segments through your data. Unlike *ksmooth* which uses a fixed bandwidth for all your data, *supsmooth* adaptively chooses different bandwidths for different portions of your data.

Chapter 10
Inserting Graphics and Other Objects

- ◆ Overview
- ◆ Inserting Pictures
- ◆ Inserting Objects
- ◆ Inserting Graphics Computationally Linked to Your Worksheet

Overview

To illustrate your Mathcad calculations visually, you many want to add graphs, pictures, or other objects. You can include the following in your Mathcad worksheet:

- 2D graphs
- 3D graphs
- Pictures based on values in a matrix, pasted from another application, or based on an image file
- Objects created by another application (.AVI files, .DOC files, .MDI files, etc.)
- Graphics computationally linked to your calculations

This chapter describes how to insert pictures and objects into a Mathcad worksheet and format them. The last section introduces how to insert a graphic that is computationally linked to your calculations. See also Chapter 14, "Importing and Exporting Data."

Inserting Pictures

This section describes techniques for creating and formatting *pictures*—static images—in your worksheet.

Creating a Picture

You can create a picture in a worksheet by:

- Creating a *picture region* and supplying either the name of a Mathcad matrix (or matrices) or the name of an external image file.
- Importing an image from another application via the Clipboard.

Creating pictures from matrices

You can view as a grayscale picture any single matrix by creating a picture region:

1. Click in a blank space in your worksheet.
2. Choose **Picture** from the **Insert** menu or click on the **Matrix** toolbar.
3. Type the name of a matrix in the placeholder at the bottom of the picture region.

Mathcad creates a 256-shade grayscale representation of the data in the matrix, with each matrix element corresponding to a *pixel* in the picture.

Note Mathcad's picture region assumes a 256-color model with the value 0 represented as black and 255 as white. Numbers outside the range 0–255 are reduced modulo 256, and any noninteger value is treated as if its decimal part has been removed.

To create a color picture in Mathcad, you must define three matrices of the same size that describe either:

- The red, green, and blue (RGB) components,
- The hue, saturation, and value (Smith's HSV color model) components, or
- The hue, lightness, and saturation (Otswald's HLS color model) components of each pixel in the picture.

To view as a color picture in Mathcad any three same-size matrices:

1. Click in a blank space and choose **Picture** from the **Insert** menu.
2. Type the names of the three matrices, separated by commas, in the placeholder at the bottom of the picture region.

By default, Mathcad creates a 3-layer, 256-color, or RGB, representation of the data in the matrices. This setting can be changed, however, through the Properties dialog box and the Picture toolbar. See "Modifying a picture" on page 153.

Since the matrices used in picture rendering are usually quite large, this technique of creating a picture is most useful when you import graphics files into Mathcad as matrices as described in "File Access Functions" on page 250. For example, you can use the READBMP function to read an external graphics file into a matrix, and then view it as a picture in Mathcad.

Creating a picture by reference to an image file

Mathcad can create a picture directly from an external image file in a number of image file formats, including BMP, JPEG, GIF, TGA, PCX, and more. To do so, click in a blank space and then:

1. Choose **Picture** from the **Insert** menu, or click

    on the Matrix toolbar, to insert a picture.

2. In the placeholder, type a string containing the name of an image file in the current directory, or type a full path to an image file. You create a string in the placeholder by first typing the double-quote (**"**) key.

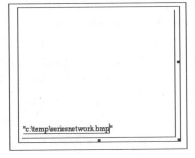

"c:\temp\seriesnetwork.bmp"

3. Click outside the picture region. The bitmap appears in your worksheet.

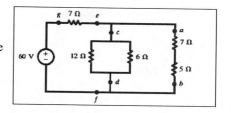

Each time you open the worksheet or calculate the worksheet, the image file is read into the picture region.

Note If you modify the source image file, you must recalculate your worksheet to see the modified image. If you move the source image file, Mathcad can no longer display the picture.

Modifying a picture

You can modify the orientation, view (zoom and pan factors), brightness, contrast, and grayscale mapping of a picture in Mathcad using the Picture toolbar. To do so:

1. Click on the picture so you see hash marks around the picture's border, as shown at the right.

2. The Picture toolbar will pop up. To find out what operation each tool performs, hover over it briefly to see its tooltip.

For example, to zoom in on the picture, click on the Picture toolbar and then repeatedly click the picture until you reach the desired resolution. To zoom out, zoom to window, or reset the zoom factor, click the toolbar buttons , , and , respectively, to activate those commands.

Note If you have the Image Processing Extension Pack or the Communication System Design (CSD) Pack, then you already have an Image Viewer component that behaves in a manner similar to a picture region. Both the Image Viewer component and a picture region allow you to import image files and manipulate them with specialized toolbar options.

You can change your color model or select an output option under the Properties dialog box. To do so:

1. Right click on the picture and select **Properties** from the popup menu.

2. Under the Input and Output tab of the Properties dialog box, make your adjustments in the Input and Output panels.

For example, you can send the color map information for a selected rectangle of the picture to a variable. You might do this if you want to create another picture that only captures part of the whole image. In the Properties dialog box, check "Output Selected Rectangle" in the output pane and select a color map option. Once you click "OK," you need to type a variable name in the placeholder at the left of the picture region.

Creating a picture by importing from another application

You can copy an image from another application and paste it into Mathcad. This section describes using the **Paste Special** command on the **Edit** menu to paste an image into Mathcad in a noneditable format: as a metafile or bitmap. A metafile, which is strictly a Windows graphic format, can be resized in Mathcad without undue loss of resolution, whereas a bitmap is usually viewed best only at its original size. A device-independent bitmap, or DIB, is stored in a bitmap format that is portable to other operating systems.

Note If you use the **Paste** command on Mathcad's **Edit** menu to paste in an image or use drag-and-drop from another application, you are pasting a linked OLE *object* into your Mathcad worksheet, ("Inserting Objects" on page 155.) When you double-click a linked OLE object, you activate the application that created the object and are able to edit the object directly in your Mathcad worksheet.

To paste an image from another application into Mathcad, do the following:

1. Open the application and select and **Copy** it. Many Windows applications have this feature.

2. Click the mouse in your Mathcad worksheet.

3. Choose **Paste Special** from the **Edit** menu, and choose "Picture (metafile)" or "Device Independent Bitmap."

4. Mathcad creates a picture region and puts the image into it.

The format choices in the Paste Special dialog box will vary, depending on the application from which you originally copied a picture.

Mathcad stores the color depth—the number of colors in the image—at the time you paste it into a worksheet. This means that you can safely resave any worksheets that contain color images on systems that have different color displays, either fewer or more colors. The images continue to display at the proper color depth on the systems that created the worksheets.

Note When you import directly by pasting, the picture information is stored as part of the Mathcad worksheet. This makes the file size larger. It also means that when you copy the worksheet, the picture information travels along with it.

Note To avoid making your Mathcad file too large, paste bitmaps that have been saved in as few colors as possible such as 16 or 256 colors and crop them as close as possible to the actual image rather than importing white space.

Formatting a Picture

This section describes options for formatting a picture.

Resizing a picture

To resize a picture region, do the following:

1. Click the mouse inside the picture region to select it.

2. Move the mouse pointer to one of the handles along the edge of region. The pointer changes to a double-headed arrow.

3. Press and hold down the left mouse button. With the button still held, drag the mouse in the direction you want the picture region to be stretched.

Tip When you change the size of the picture region, the picture inside may be distorted. If you resize the picture by dragging diagonally on the handle in the lower right corner, you preserve the aspect ratio—the ratio of height to width—of the original picture. To restore a picture to its original size, click on the picture and choose **Properties** from the **Format** menu. On the display tab of the Properties dialog box, check "Display at Original Size."

Framing a picture

Mathcad allows you to place a border around a picture region. To do so:

1. Double-click the picture, or choose **Properties** from the **Format** menu to bring up the Properties dialog box.

2. Click "Show Border."

3. Mathcad draws a border around the picture region.

Controlling color palettes

If you are using a 256-color display and have color bitmaps in your Mathcad worksheets, Mathcad by default uses a single 256-color palette to display all the bitmaps in your worksheets. This is the same default color palette Mathcad uses for displaying the rest of the Mathcad screen and is suitable for most pictures.

This default color palette, however, may not be the exact one that any color bitmaps in a worksheet were designed to use. To improve the appearance of bitmaps in your worksheet, you can tell Mathcad to optimize its default color palette so that it chooses the best possible 256 colors to display bitmaps in the worksheet. To do so:

1. Choose **Color⇒Optimize Palette** from the **Format** menu. Mathcad surveys the pictures in the worksheet and generates an optimal 256-color palette to use for all of them.

2. Make sure that **Color⇒Use Default Palette** in the **Format** menu is checked. Then Mathcad uses the new default palette it generates.

Note If your display driver supports more than 256 colors, the palette-setting options on the **Format** menu are grayed.

Inserting Objects

This section describes inserting and editing *objects* created by other applications into Mathcad. OLE (Object Linking and Embedding) technology in Microsoft Windows makes it possible to insert static pictures of objects into Mathcad (or Mathcad objects into other applications), so that they can be fully edited in their originating applications.

An object can be either *embedded* in or *linked* to a Mathcad worksheet. An object that is linked must exist in an external saved file. An object that you embed may be created at the time of insertion. When you edit a linked object, any changes you make to the object also update the original file containing the object. When you edit an embedded object, any changes you make to the object affect it only in the Mathcad worksheet. The original object in the source application is unchanged.

Tip For information about *components* to import and export data, as well as setting dynamic connections between Mathcad and other applications see Chapter 14, "Importing and Exporting Data."

Inserting an Object into a Worksheet

You insert an object into Mathcad, which is an OLE 2–compatible application, by using the **Object** command from the **Insert** menu, by copying and pasting, or by dragging and dropping. The method you choose depends on whether you want to create the object on the fly, whether the object has already been created, or whether you want the object to be an entire file. You can edit objects in a Mathcad worksheet simply by double-clicking them, causing *in-place activation* of the originating application in most cases.

Tip You use the same methods to insert a *Mathcad object* into another application and edit it inside that application as you do to insert objects into a Mathcad worksheet. However, the details depend on the extent to which the application receiving a Mathcad object supports OLE 2. Once you've inserted a Mathcad object into a compatible application, you can edit it by double-clicking it. If the application supports in-place activation, as current releases of Microsoft Office applications do, the menus and toolbars will change to Mathcad's.

Insert Object command

The **Object** command from the **Insert** menu allows you to insert an object that you create at the time of insertion or an existing file.

To insert an object or a saved file:

1. First click in your worksheet so that you see the crosshair.

2. Choose **Object** from the **Insert** menu to bring up the Insert Object dialog box. By default "Create New" is selected:

3. Check "Display As Icon" if you want an icon to appear in your worksheet. The icon is typically the icon of the application that created the object.

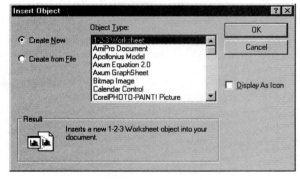

To create a new object:

1. Select an application from the "Object Type" list, which depends on the applications you have installed.

2. The source application opens so that you can create the object. When you are finished, exit the source application. The object you created is then embedded in your Mathcad worksheet.

If you want to insert a previously created file:

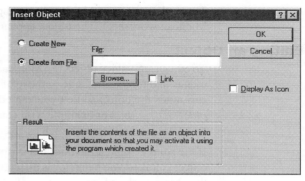

1. Click "Create from File" in the Insert Object dialog box. The dialog box then changes appearance.

2. Type the path to the object file or click "Browse" to locate it.

3. Check "Link" to insert a linked object. Otherwise, the object is embedded.

Pasting an object into a worksheet

You can copy an object from a source application and paste it directly into Mathcad. This method is particularly useful when you've already created the object in another application and you don't want to insert an entire file.

To insert an embedded or linked object into a worksheet by copying:

1. Open the source application containing the object.

2. Copy the object from the source application. You typically do this by choosing **Copy** from the **Edit** menu or by pressing [**Ctrl**]**C**.

3. Click in the Mathcad worksheet.

4. Choose **Paste** or **Paste Special** from Mathcad's **Edit** menu.

If you choose **Paste**, the object is pasted in your Mathcad worksheet in a format that depends on what the source application has placed on the Clipboard. The behavior differs depending on whether you have selected a math placeholder or are pasting into a blank space in the worksheet. Mathcad creates one of the following:

- A *matrix,* if you are pasting numeric data into an empty math placeholder.

- A *text region,* if you are pasting text that does not contain numeric data exclusively.

- A *bitmap* or *picture (metafile),* if the originating application generates graphics.

- An embedded object, if the originating application supports OLE.

If you choose **Paste Special**, you have the option of pasting the object in one of the several formats. You can choose to paste the object as an embedded or linked OLE object (if the object was stored in a saved file in an OLE-compatible source application), a picture (metafile), or a bitmap. See "Creating a picture by importing from another application" on page 153 for pasting metafiles and bitmaps.

Dragging and dropping an object into a worksheet

A third way to insert an OLE object into a Mathcad worksheet is to drag it from the source application and drop it into the worksheet. This is very similar to copying and pasting, but does not allow you to create a link to an object. To do so, open both Mathcad and the source application and arrange the two windows side by side on the screen.

Then select the object in the source application and drag it with the mouse into your Mathcad worksheet. The object appears when you release the mouse button.

Editing an Object

To edit an embedded object in a Mathcad worksheet, double-click the object. Mathcad's menus and toolbars change to those of the source application, and a hatched border surrounds the object so that you can edit it. This OLE editing mechanism is called *in-place activation*. For example, you can use in-place activation to edit objects created by Microsoft applications such as Excel and Word inside Mathcad.

If the source application does not support in-place activation inside Mathcad or the object is linked, the behavior is different. In the case of an embedded object, a copy of the object is placed into a window from the other application. If the object is linked, the source application opens the file containing the object.

Editing a Link

If you've inserted a linked object into a Mathcad worksheet, you can update the link, eliminate it, or change the source file to which the object is linked. To do so, choose **Links** from the **Edit** menu.

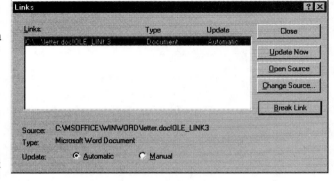

Choose the link you want to edit from the list of links. Then make changes using the available options.

Online Help   See the online Help topic "Links dialog box" for information on each option in the dialog box.

Inserting Graphics Computationally Linked to Your Worksheet

If you want to insert a drawing or other kind of graphic that is computationally linked to your Mathcad worksheet, you can insert a *component*. A component is a specialized OLE object. Unlike other kinds of OLE objects you can insert into a worksheet, a component can receive data from Mathcad, return data to Mathcad, or both, linking the object dynamically to your Mathcad computations.

The SmartSketch component, for example, allows you to insert SmartSketch drawings whose dimensions are computationally linked to your Mathcad calculations.

An example using the SmartSketch component is shown in Figure 10-1. In addition to the SmartSketch component, Mathcad includes several components for exchanging data with applications such as Excel, MATLAB, and ODBC databases. For more information see Chapter 14, "Importing and Exporting Data."

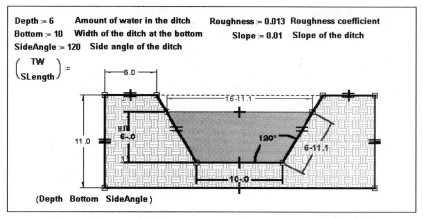

Figure 10-1: The SmartSketch component inserted into a Mathcad worksheet.

Chapter 11
2D Plots

♦ Overview of 2D Plotting

♦ Graphing Functions and Expressions

♦ Plotting Vectors of Data

♦ Formatting a 2D Plot

♦ Modifying a 2D Plot's Perspective

Overview of 2D Plotting

To visually represent a function or expression of a single variable or X-Y data in Mathcad, you can create either a Cartesian X-Y plot or a polar plot. A typical polar plot shows angular values, θ, versus radial values, r. Figure 11-1 shows several examples of 2D plots.

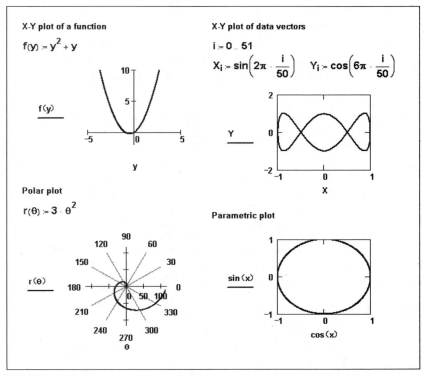

Figure 11-1: Examples of 2D plots.

Creating an X-Y Plot

To create an X-Y plot:

1. Click in your worksheet.

2. Choose **Graph**⇒**X-Y Plot** from the **Insert** menu or click 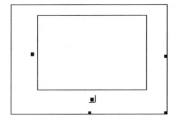 on the Graph toolbar. Alternatively, type [**Shift**]2 or **@**. Mathcad inserts a blank X-Y plot.

3. Fill in both the *x*-axis placeholder (bottom center) and the *y*-axis placeholder (left center) with a function, expression, or variable.

4. Click outside the plot or press [**Enter**].

Mathcad automatically chooses axis limits for you. If you want to specify the axis limits yourself, click in the plot and type over the numbers in the placeholders at the ends of the axes.

Mathcad creates the plot over a default range using default limits. See "Formatting a 2D Plot" on page 168 for how to modify these defaults.

Resizing a graphf

To resize a plot, click in the plot to select it. Then move the cursor to a handle along the edge of the plot until the cursor changes to a double-headed arrow. Hold the mouse button down and drag the mouse in the direction that you want the plot's dimension to change.

Note If a point is complex, Mathcad does not graph it. To graph the real or imaginary part of a point or expression, use the *Re* and *Im* functions to extract the real and imaginary parts, respectively.

To resize a plot, click in the plot to select it. Then move the cursor to a handle along the right or bottom edge of the plot until the cursor changes to a double-headed arrow. Hold the mouse button down and drag the mouse in the direction that you want the plot's dimension to change.

Note If some points in a function or expression are valid and others are not, Mathcad plots only the valid ones. If the points are not contiguous, Mathcad does not connect them with a line. You may therefore see a blank plot if none of the points are contiguous. To see the points, format the trace to have symbols. See "Formatting a 2D Plot" on page 168.

Creating a polar plot

To create a polar plot:

1. Choose **Graph**⇒**Polar Plot** from the **Insert** menu or click 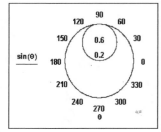 on the Graph toolbar.

2. Fill in both the angular-axis placeholder (bottom center) and the radial-axis placeholder (left center) with a function, expression, or variable.

3. Click outside the plot or press [**Enter**].

Mathcad creates the plot over a default range using default limits.

Graphing Functions and Expressions

2D QuickPlots

A 2D *QuickPlot* is a plot created from an expression or function which represents the *y*-coordinates of the plot. With a *QuickPlot*, there is no need to define the independent or *x*-axis variable.

To create an X-Y plot of a single expression or function:

1. Type the expression or function of a single variable you want to plot. Make sure the editing lines remain in the expression.

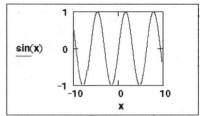

2. Choose **Graph⇒X-Y Plot** from the **Insert** menu or click on the Graph toolbar.

3. Click outside the graph or press [**Enter**].

Mathcad automatically produces a plot over a default domain for the independent variable, from –10 to 10.

To change the default domain for the independent variable in a 2D QuickPlot, change the axis limits on the plot.

Defining an independent variable

If you don't want Mathcad to use a default range for the independent variable, you can define the independent variable as a range variable before creating the plot. For example:

1. Define a range variable, such as x, that takes on the values you want to graph. See "Range Variables" on page 103.

$$x := 0, 0.1 .. 2\pi$$

2. Enter an expression or function you want to plot using that variable. Make sure the editing lines remain in the expression.

3. Choose **Graph⇒X-Y Plot** from the **Insert** menu

4. Type the name of the variable into the x-axis placeholder.

5. Click outside the graph or press [**Enter**].

Mathcad graphs one point for every value of the range variable, and, unless you specify otherwise, connects each pair of points with a straight line.

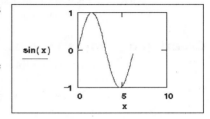

Tip   To override Mathcad's choices for the axis limits on a plot, click in the plot and type over the limits in the placeholders at the ends of the axes (see "Setting Axis Limits" on page 169).

Plotting Multiple 2D Curves

You can graph several traces on the same X-Y or polar plot. A graph can show several *y*-axis (or radial) expressions against the same *x*-axis (or angular) expression. See Figure 11-3. Or it can match up several *y*-axis (or radial) expressions with the corresponding number of *x*-axis (or angular) expressions. See Figure 11-2.

To create a *QuickPlot* containing more than one trace:

1. Enter the expressions or functions of a single variable you want to plot, separated by commas. Make sure the editing lines remain in the expression.

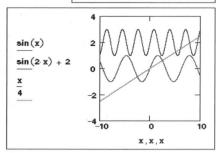

2. Choose **Graph⇒X-Y Plot** from the **Insert** menu or click on the Graph toolbar.

3. Click outside the graph or press [**Enter**].

Mathcad produces a single graph containing plots of all the expressions or functions, over a default range for the independent variable(s), from −10 to 10.

In a *QuickPlot* with multiple traces, you need not use the same independent variable in every *y*-axis (or radial-axis) expression. Mathcad will provide the appropriate corresponding variable in the *x*-axis (or angular-axis) placeholder.

To create a graph containing several independent curves:

1. Choose **Graph⇒X-Y Plot** from the **Insert** menu.

2. Enter two or more expressions separated by commas in the *y*-axis placeholder.

3. Enter the same number of expressions separated by commas in the *x*-axis placeholder.

Mathcad matches up the expressions in pairs—the first *x*-axis expression with first *y*-axis expression, the second with the second, and so on. It then draws a trace for each pair. Figure 11-2 shows an example.

Note All traces on a graph share the same axis limits. For each axis, all expressions and limits on that axis must have compatible units.

Creating a parametric plot

A parametric plot is one in which a function or expression is plotted against another function or expression that uses the same independent variable. You can create either an X-Y or polar parametric plot.

To create an X-Y parametric plot:

1. Choose **Graph⇒X-Y Plot** from the **Insert** menu.

2. In both the *x*-axis and *y*-axis placeholders, enter a function or expression.

3. Press [**Enter**].

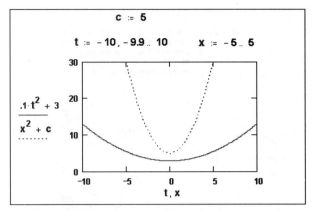

Figure 11-2: Graph with multiple expressions on both axes.

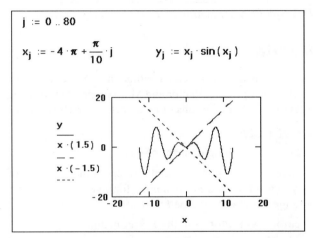

Figure 11-3: Graph with multiple y-axis expressions.

Mathcad produces a *QuickPlot* over a default range for the independent variable. Figure 11-1 shows an example of a parametric plot.

If you don't want Mathcad to use a default range for the plot, define the independent variable as a range variable before creating the plot. Mathcad graphs one point for each value of the independent variable and connects each pair of points with a straight line. Figure 11-4 shows two functions of θ plotted against each other. The range variable θ was previously defined. See "Range Variables" on page 103.

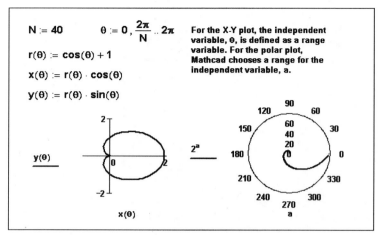

Figure 11-4: Graphing one function against another.

Plotting Vectors of Data

To graph a vector of data, you can create either an X-Y plot or a polar plot. You need to use the vector subscript (see "Vector and Matrix Operators" on page 398) to specify which elements to plot. Some graphs of data vectors are shown in Figure 11-5.

Plotting a single vector of data

To create an X-Y plot of a single vector of data:

1. Define a range variable, such as *i*, that references the subscript of each element of the vector you want to plot. For example, for a vector with 10 elements, your subscript range variable would be $i := 0 .. 9$.
2. Choose **Graph⇒X-Y Plot** from the **Insert** menu.
3. Enter *i* in the bottom placeholder and the vector name with the subscript (y_i for example) in the placeholder on the left. Type [as a shortcut to create the subscript.

Note   Subscripts must be integers greater than or equal to ORIGIN. This means that the *x*-axis or angular variable used in the graphs in Figure 11-5 can run through whole number values only. If you want to graph fractional or negative values on the *x*-axis, graph a function or graph one vector against another, as described in the next section.

Tip   If you have a handful of data points, you can use a data table to create a vector as shown in the second graph in Figure 11-5 or Figure 11-7. See "Entering a Matrix as a Data Table" on page 55.

Plotting one data vector against another

To graph all the elements of one data vector against all the elements in another, enter the names of the vectors in the axis placeholders of an X-Y plot or polar plot.

To create an X-Y plot of two data vectors *x* and *y*:

1. Define the vectors *x* and *y*.

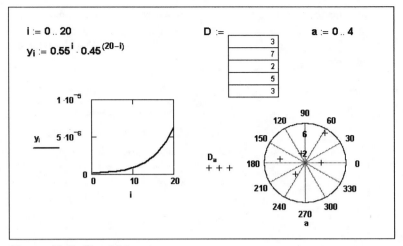

Figure 11-5: Graphing a vector.

2. Choose **Graph⇒X-Y Plot** from the **Insert** menu.

3. Enter *y* in the *y*-axis placeholder and *x* in the *x*-axis placeholder.

Mathcad plots the elements in the vector *x* against the elements in the vector *y*.

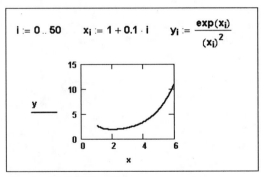

Figure 11-6: Graphing two vectors.

Note If the vectors being plotted are not the same length, Mathcad plots the number of elements in the shorter vector.

If you want to plot only certain vector elements, define a range variable and use it as a subscript on the vector names. In the example above, to plot the fifth through tenth elements of *x* and *y* against each other:

1. Define a range variable, such as *k*, going from 4 to 9 in increments of 1. (Note that the first elements of the vectors *x* and *y* are x_0 and y_0 by default.)

2. Enter y_k and x_k in the axis placeholders.

Note If you have a set of data values to graph, create a vector by reading in data from a data file, by pasting in the data from the Clipboard, or by typing data directly into a data table. See Chapter 5, "Vectors, Matrices, and Data Arrays." See Figure 11-7 for an example showing the use of a data table.

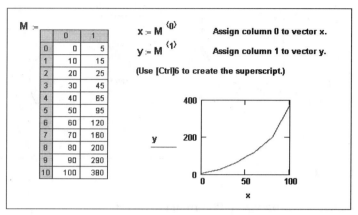

Figure 11-7: Plotting vectors from a data table.

Formatting a 2D Plot

You can override Mathcad's default settings for axes and traces. You can also add titles and labels and control the default settings of the graph.

To format a 2D graph:

1. Double-click the graph. Or click once on the graph and choose **Graph⇒X-Y Plot** or **Graph⇒Polar Plot** from the **Format** menu. You'll see the dialog box for formatting a selected graph.

2. Use the Axes tab to determine the appearance of the axes and grid lines. Use the Traces tab to set the color, type, and width of the traces. Use the Labels tab to insert labels on the axes. Use the Defaults tab to specify the default appearance of your graphs.

3. Make the appropriate changes in the dialog box.

4. Click Apply to see the effect of your changes *without* closing the dialog box.

Note In the X-Y Axes page, make sure you turn options on and off in the appropriate axis column. In the Traces page, click on a trace's name in the Legend Label column and change characteristics by clicking on the arrow beside each of the drop-down options.

Tip	If you double-click an axis on a graph, you'll see a formatting dialog box for that axis alone.

Online Help	Click Help in the dialog box for details on particular formatting options.

Setting Axis Limits

When you create a 2D graph, the Autoscale option is turned on. Use the Axes page of the plot formatting dialog box to turn Autoscale on or off:

- With Autoscale on, Mathcad automatically sets each axis limit to the first major tick mark beyond the end of the data. This is a reasonably round number large enough to display every point being graphed.
- With Autoscale off, Mathcad automatically sets the axis limits exactly at the data limits.

Specifying Other Limits

You can override Mathcad's automatic limits by entering limits directly on the graph. To do so:

1. Click the graph to select it. Mathcad displays four additional numbers, one by each axis limit. These numbers are enclosed within corner symbols, as illustrated in the selected plot in Figure 11-8.

2. Click on each of these numbers and type a number to replace it.

3. Click outside the graph. Mathcad redraws it using the new axis limits you specified. The corner symbols below the limits you changed disappear. Figure 11-8 shows the effect of manually setting limits on a graph.

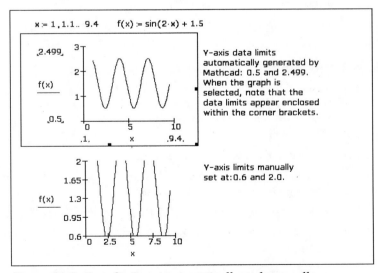

Figure 11-8: Data limits set automatically and manually.

Setting Default Formats

Mathcad uses default settings to format the axes and traces of new graphs you create.

Copying Defaults from an Existing Graph

One way to create a new set of defaults is to use the format settings of an existing graph. To do so:

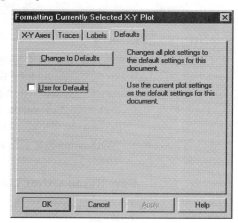

1. Double-click the graph, or click in the graph and choose **Graph⇒X-Y Plot** (or **Graph⇒Polar Plot**) from the **Format** menu. Mathcad displays the dialog box for formatting a selected graph.

2. Click the Defaults tab to see the Defaults page.

3. Check Use for Defaults. When you click OK, to close the dialog box, Mathcad saves these settings as your default settings.

Setting Defaults Without Using a Graph

You can use the Setting Default Formats dialog box to change default plot settings. To do so:

1. Make sure that you don't have any graphs selected.

2. Choose **Graph⇒ X-Y Plot** (or **Graph⇒Polar Plot**) from the **Format** menu. You'll see the Setting Default Formats dialog box.

3. Change the appropriate settings on the Axes and Traces pages.

4. Click OK to accept your changes and close the dialog box.

Adding Custom Titles, Labels, and Other Annotations

One way to add titles and labels to your 2D graph is to use the options on the Labels tab of the 2D Plot Format dialog box. A second way to add titles and labels, as well as annotations, is to create text or some other object in your worksheet and then move it on top of the graph.

To create an annotation for your 2D graph:

1. Create a text region, or insert a graphic object in your worksheet by pasting it in or by choosing **Object** from the **Insert** menu.

2. Drag the text or object onto your 2D graph and position it appropriately.

Figure 11-9 shows a graph containing both a text region ("inflection pt") and a graphic object (an arrow).

Note   If you choose **Separate Regions** from the **Format** menu, all overlapping regions in your worksheet will separate. In the case of annotated graph, such as the one shown above, all annotations move below the graph when you separate regions.

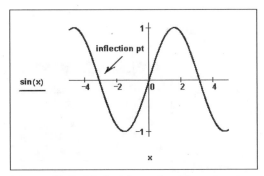

Figure 11-9: Mathcad graph with annotations.

Modifying a 2D Plot's Perspective

Mathcad provides zoom and trace on 2D plots.

Zooming in on a Plot

To zoom in on a portion of a graph, follow these steps:

1. Click in the graph and choose **Graph⇒Zoom** from the **Format** menu, or click [icon] on the Graph toolbar. The Zoom dialog box appears. The X-Y Zoom dialog box is shown to the right.

2. If necessary, reposition the Zoom dialog box so that you can see the entire region of the graph you want to zoom.

3. Click the mouse at one corner of the region in the graph you want to magnify.

4. Press and hold down the mouse button and drag the mouse. A dashed selection outline emerges from the anchor point. The coordinates of the selected region are listed in the Min and Max text boxes (or the Radius text box of the Polar Zoom dialog box).

5. When the selection outline just encloses the region you want to magnify, let go of the mouse button. If necessary, click on the selection outline, hold the mouse button down, and move the outline to another part of the graph.

6. Click Zoom to redraw the graph. The axis limits are temporarily set to the coordinates specified in the Zoom dialog box. To make these axis limits permanent, click OK.

Tip   If you're working with a graph that has already been zoomed, you can restore the default appearance of the graph. To do so, click Full View in the Zoom dialog box.

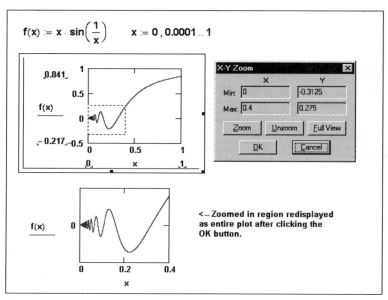

$$f(x) := x \cdot \sin\left(\frac{1}{x}\right) \qquad x := 0, 0.0001 .. 1$$

Figure 11-10: A zoomed-in region of an X-Y plot.

Getting a Readout of Plot Coordinates

To see a readout of coordinates of the specific points that make up a trace, follow these steps:

1. Click in the graph and choose **Graph**⇒**Trace** from the **Format** menu, or click 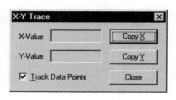 on the Graph toolbar. The X-Y Trace dialog box appears as shown. Check Track Data Points if it isn't already checked. If necessary, reposition the Trace dialog box so that you can see the entire graph.

2. Click and drag the mouse along the trace whose coordinates you want to see. A dotted crosshair jumps from one point to the next as you move the pointer along the trace.

3. If you release the mouse button, you can use the left and right arrows to move to the previous and next data points. Use the up and down arrows to select other traces.

4. As the pointer reaches each point on the trace, Mathcad displays the values of that point in the X-Value and Y-Value boxes (or the Radius and Angle boxes in the Polar Trace dialog box).

5. The values of the last point selected are shown in the boxes. The crosshair remains until you click outside the plot.

Tip When Track Data Points is unchecked in the Trace dialog box, you can see a readout of coordinates for any location in a graph, not just the data points that created an individual plot.

Figure 11-11 shows an example of a plot whose coordinates are being read.

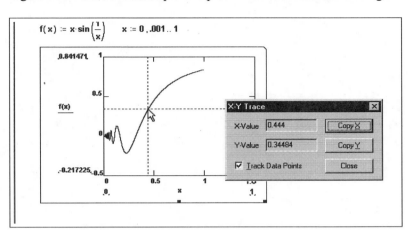

Figure 11-11: Reading coordinates from a graph.

To copy and paste a coordinate:

1. Click Copy X or Copy Y (or Copy Radius or Copy Angle in the case of a polar plot).

2. You can then paste that value into a math or text region in your Mathcad worksheet, into a spreadsheet, or into any other application that allows pasting from the Clipboard.

Chapter 12
3D Plots

♦ Overview of 3D Plotting

♦ Creating 3D Plots of Functions

♦ Creating 3D Plots of Data

♦ Formatting a 3D Plot

♦ Rotating and Zooming on 3D Plots

Overview of 3D Plotting

To visually represent in three dimensions a function of one or two variables or to plot data in the form of *x*-, *y*-, and *z*-coordinates, you can create a surface plot, a contour plot, a 3D bar plot, a 3D scatter plot, or a vector field plot. Mathcad renders 3D plots with sophisticated, high performance OpenGL graphics.

Inserting a 3D Plot

To create a three-dimensional plot:

1. Define a function of two variables or a matrix of data.

2. Choose **Graph** from the **Insert** menu and select a 3D plot. Alternatively, click one of the 3D graph buttons on the Graph toolbar. Mathcad inserts a blank 3D plot with axes and an empty placeholder.

3. Enter the name of the function or matrix in the placeholder.

4. Click outside the plot or press [**Enter**]. Mathcad creates the plot according to the function or matrix of data.

For example, the surface plot shown below was created in Mathcad from the function:

When you create a 3D plot from a function, it's called a *QuickPlot*. A *QuickPlot* uses default ranges and grids for the independent variables. To change these settings, double-click on the graph and use the QuickPlot Data page of the 3D Plot Format dialog. (See "Formatting a 3D Plot" on page 184.)

To learn how to create a plot from a matrix of values, see Figure 12-2 on page 179.

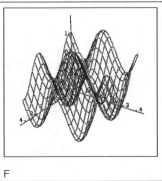

$$F(x, y) := \sin(x) + \cos(y)$$

F

3D Plot Wizard

The *3D Plot Wizard* gives you more control over the format settings of the plot as you insert it. To use the Wizard:

1. Choose **Graph**⇒**3D Plot Wizard** from the **Insert** menu.

2. Select the type of three-dimensional graph you want to see and click "Next."

3. Make your selections for the appearance and coloring of the plot on subsequent pages of the Wizard. Click "Finish" and a graph region with a blank placeholder appears.

4. Enter appropriate arguments (a function name, data vectors, etc.) for the 3D plot into the placeholder.

5. Click outside the plot or press [**Enter**].

The plot is created using the settings you specified in the Wizard. (See "Formatting a 3D Plot" on page 184.)

Creating 3D Plots of Functions

This section describes how to create various 3D plots from functions in Mathcad, also known as *QuickPlots*. Although the instructions focus on using commands on the **Insert** menu and changing settings through the 3D Plot Format dialog box, you can also use the 3D Plot Wizard, as described above.

Tip   To see a variety of two- and three-dimensional functions and data sets visualized in plots, visit the Graphics Gallery section of the Mathcad Web Library at http://www.mathcad.com.

Creating a Surface, Bar, Contour, or Scatter Plot

You can visualize any function of two variables as a surface, bar, contour, or scatter plot in three dimensions.

Step 1: Define a function or set of functions

First, define the function in your worksheet in any one of the following forms:

$$F(x, y) := \sin(x) + \cos(y) \qquad G(u, v) := \begin{pmatrix} 2 \cdot u \\ 2 \cdot u \cdot \cos(v) \\ 2 \cdot \cos(v) \end{pmatrix} \qquad \begin{aligned} X(u, v) &:= v \\ Y(u, v) &:= v \cdot \cos(u) \\ Z(u, v) &:= \sin(u) \end{aligned}$$

F(x,y) is a function of two variables. In this type of function, the *x*- and *y*-coordinates of the plot vary, by default, from –5 to 5 with a step size of 0.5. Each *z*-coordinate is determined by the function using these *x*- and *y*-values.

G(u,v) is a vector-valued function of two variables. In this type of function, the independent variables *u* and *v* vary, by default, from –5 to 5 with a step size of 0.5. The *x*-, *y*-, and *z*-coordinates are plotted parametrically according to the definitions in the three elements of the vector using these *u*- and *v*-values.

X(u,v), *Y(u,v)*, and *Z(u,v)* are functions of two variables. In this type of function triple, the independent variables *u* and *v* vary, by default, from –5 to 5 with a step size of 0.5. The *x*-, *y*-, and *z*-coordinates are plotted parametrically according to the three function definitions using these *u*- and *v*-values.

Note The function descriptions above assume that you are working in Cartesian coordinates. If your function represents spherical or cylindrical coordinates, you can automatically convert the function to Cartesian coordinates. Double-click on the plot, go to the QuickPlot Data page of the 3D Plot Format dialog box, and click "Spherical" or "Cylindrical" under Coordinate System.

Step 2: Insert a 3D plot

After you define a function or set of functions to plot, choose **Graph** from the **Insert** menu and select a 3D plot type.

For example, to create a surface plot from the functions X, Y, and Z, defined above:

1. Choose **Graph⇒Surface Plot** from the **Insert** menu. Mathcad inserts a blank 3D plot.

2. Enter the name of the functions in the placeholder. When you have more than one function definition for a single surface, separate the function names by commas and enclose the function names in parentheses. For this example, type: (X,Y,Z)

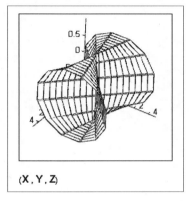

3. Press [**Enter**].

(X,Y,Z)

To change your plot to a different plot type:

1. Double-click on the graph to bring up the 3D Plot Format dialog box.

2. In the Display As section on the General tab, select Bar Plot, Contour Plot, or Data Points from the array of plot types.

Figure 12-1 shows a 3D scatter plot created from the function G, and a contour plot created from the function F, both defined above:

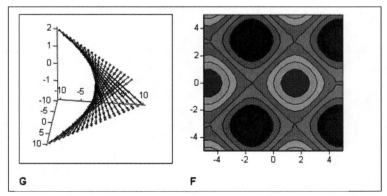

G   F

Figure 12-1: A scatter plot and a contour plot created from functions of two variables.

Note All 3D *QuickPlots* are parametric curves or surfaces. In other words, all *QuickPlots* are created from three vectors or matrices of data representing the *x*-, *y*-, and *z*-coordinates of the plot. In the case of a single function of two variables, Mathcad internally creates two matrices of *x*- and *y*-data over the default range −5 to 5 with a step size of 0.5, and then generates *z*-data using these *x*- and *y*-coordinates.

To change the default ranges and grids for the independent variables, double-click on the graph and use the QuickPlot Data page of the 3D Plot Format dialog. (See "Formatting a 3D Plot" on page 184.)

Creating a Space Curve

You can visualize any parametrically-defined function of one variable as a scatter plot in three dimensions.

Step 1: Define a function or set of functions

First, define the function in your worksheet in one of the following forms:

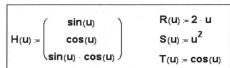

$$H(u) := \begin{pmatrix} \sin(u) \\ \cos(u) \\ \sin(u) \cdot \cos(u) \end{pmatrix} \qquad \begin{aligned} R(u) &:= 2 \cdot u \\ S(u) &:= u^2 \\ T(u) &:= \cos(u) \end{aligned}$$

H(u) is a vector-valued function of one variable. In this type of function, the independent variable *u* varies, by default, from −5 to 5 with a step size of 0.5. The *x*-, *y*-, and *z*-coordinates of the plot are determined by the functions in each element of the vector using these *u*-values.

R(u), *S(u)*, and *T(u)* are functions of one variable. In this type of function triple, the independent variable *u* varies, by default, from −5 to 5 with a step size of 0.5. The *x*-, *y*-, and *z*-coordinates are plotted according to the function definitions using these *u*-values.

Note A space curve often represents the path of a particle in motion through space where *u* is a time parameter.

Step 2: Insert a 3D scatter plot

To create a space curve from a single function or set of functions:

1. Choose **Graph⇒3D Scatter Plot** from the **Insert** menu. Mathcad inserts a blank 3D plot.

2. Enter the name of function or functions in the placeholder. When you have more than one function definition, separate the function names by commas and enclose the function names in parentheses. To create a space curve from the functions R, S, and T, defined above, type (R, S, T).

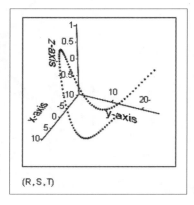

For specific information on formatting a scatter plot, refer to "Scatter Plots" in online Help.

Creating 3D Plots of Data

You can also create various 3D plots from data in Mathcad. Although theses instructions focus on using commands on the **Insert** menu and changing settings through the 3D Plot Format dialog, you can also use the 3D Plot Wizard, as described on page 175.

Creating a Surface, Bar, or Scatter Plot

Surface, bar, and scatter plots are useful for visualizing two-dimensional data contained in an array as either a connected surface, bars above and below the zero plane, or points in space.

For example, to create a surface plot from data:

1. Create or import a matrix of values to plot. The row and column numbers represent the x- and y-coordinate values. The matrix elements themselves are the z-coordinate values plotted as heights above and below the xy-plane (at $z = 0$).

2. Choose **Graph⇒Surface Plot** from the **Insert** menu.

3. Enter the name of the matrix in the placeholder.

Figure 12-2 shows a 3D bar plot created from a matrix, M:

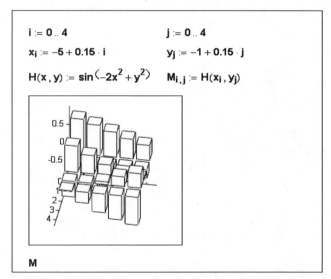

Figure 12-2: Defining a matrix of data and plotting it as a 3D bar plot.

In the default perspective, the first row of the matrix extends from the back left corner of the grid to the right, while the first column extends from the back left corner out toward the viewer. See "Formatting a 3D Plot" on page 184 to change this default view.

Creating a Parametric Surface Plot

A parametric surface plot is created by passing three matrices representing the x-, y-, and z- coordinates of your points in space to the surface plot.

To create a parametric surface plot:

1. Create or import three matrices having the same number of rows and columns.
2. Choose **Graph⇒Surface Plot** from the **Insert** menu.
3. Type the names of the three matrices separated by commas and enclosed in parentheses in the placeholder.

Figure 12-3 shows a parametric surface plot created from the matrices, X, Y, and Z, defined above the plot.

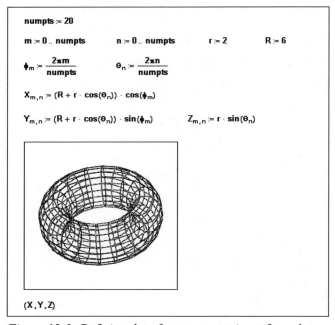

Figure 12-3: Defining data for a parametric surface plot.

Note   The underlying parameter space is a rectangular sheet covered by a uniform mesh. The three matrices map this sheet into three-dimensional space. For example, the matrices **X**, **Y**, and **Z** defined in Figure 12-3 carry out a mapping that rolls the sheet into a tube and then joins the ends of the tube to form a torus.

For specific information on formatting a parametric surface plot, refer to the topic "Surface Plots" in online Help.

Creating a Three-dimensional Parametric Curve

A three-dimensional parametric curve is created by passing three vectors representing the x-, y-, and z-coordinates of your points in space to the surface plot.

To create a three-dimensional parametric curve:

1. Create or import three vectors having the same number of rows.
2. Choose **Graph⇒Scatter Plot** from the **Insert** menu.
3. Type the names of the three vectors separated by commas and enclosed in parentheses in the placeholder.

Figure 12-4 shows a three-dimensional parametric curve created from the vectors, P, Q, and R, defined above the plot:

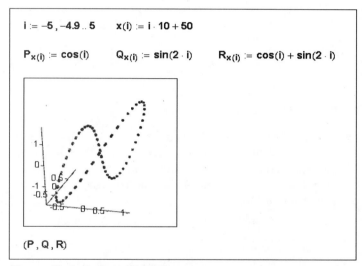

Figure 12-4: Defining data for a space curve.

For specific information on formatting a scatter plot, see "Scatter Plots" in online Help.

Creating a Contour Plot

To view three-dimensional data as a two-dimensional contour map, you can create a contour plot:

1. Define or import a matrix of values to plot.
2. Choose **Graph⇒Contour Plot** from the **Insert** menu. Mathcad shows a blank plot with a single placeholder.
3. Type the name of the matrix in the placeholder.

Figure 12-5 shows a contour plot created from the matrix, C, defined above the plot:

The contour plot is a visual representation of the matrix's level curves. Mathcad assumes that the rows and columns represent equally spaced intervals on the axes, and then linearly interpolates the values of this matrix to form level curves or contours.

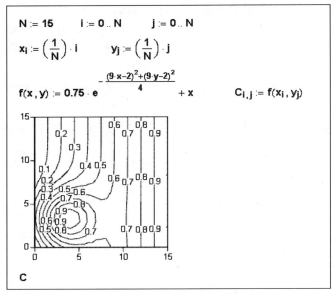

$N := 15 \qquad i := 0 .. N \qquad j := 0 .. N$

$$x_i := \left(\frac{1}{N}\right) \cdot i \qquad y_j := \left(\frac{1}{N}\right) \cdot j$$

$$f(x, y) := 0.75 \cdot e^{-\frac{(9 \cdot x - 2)^2 + (9 \cdot y - 2)^2}{4}} + x \qquad C_{i,j} := f(x_i, y_j)$$

Figure 12-5: Defining data for a contour plot.

Each level curve is formed such that no two cross. By default, the *z*-contours are shown on the *x-y* plane. Mathcad plots the matrix such that the element in row 0 and column 0 is in the lower left corner. Thus the rows of the matrix correspond to values on the *x*-axis, increasing to the right, and the columns correspond to values along the *y*-axis, increasing toward the top.

For information on formatting a contour plot, see "Contour Plots" in online Help.

Note If you create a contour plot of a function as described above, the positive *x*-axis of the plot extends to the right and the positive *y*-axis extends toward the top of the plot.

Creating a Vector Field Plot

In a vector field plot, each point in the *x-y* plane is assigned a two-dimensional vector. There are two ways to set up the data needed for a vector field plot:

1. Create a matrix of complex numbers in which the following conditions exist:
   - The row and column numbers represent the *x*- and *y*-coordinates
   - The real part of each matrix element is the *x*-component of the vector associated with that row and column
   - The imaginary part of each element is the *y*-component of the vector associated with that row and column.

2. Create two matrices having the same number of rows and columns. The first matrix should have the *x*-components of the vectors, the second the *y*-components.

Once you have defined your data to create a vector field plot:

1. Choose **Graph⇒Vector Field Plot** from the **Insert** menu.

2. Type the name(s) of the matrix or matrices in the placeholder. If you have more than one matrix for a vector field plot, separate the matrix names by commas and enclose the matrix name set in parentheses.

Figure 12-6 shows a vector field plot created from the matrix, Q, defined above the plot:

$m := 0 .. 11$ $n := 0 .. 11$

$Q_{m,n} := 0.2i \cdot (m - 5) - 0.1 - 0.1i$ $g(z) := \dfrac{z^2}{0.1 + |z|}$

$M := \overrightarrow{g(Q)}$

M

Figure 12-6: Defining data for a vector field plot.

For specific information on formatting a vector field plot, see "Vector field plots" in online Help.

Graphing Polyhedra

The uniform polyhedra are regular polyhedra whose vertices are congruent. Each has a name, a number, a dual (the name of another polyhedron), and a Wythoff symbol associated with it. To look up the name, Wythoff symbol, and dual name of a polyhedron, use *PolyLookup*.

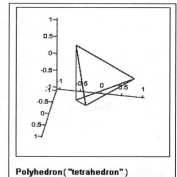

Polyhedron("tetrahedron")

To graph a uniform polyhedron:

1. Click in a blank spot of your worksheet. Choose **Graph⇒Surface Plot** from the **Insert** menu.

2. In the placeholder, enter the *Polyhedron* function with an appropriate string argument.

3. Click outside the plot or press [**Enter**].

Graphing Multiple 3D Plots

Just as you can plot more than one trace on a two-dimensional graph, you can place more than one surface, curve, contour, bar, or scatter plot on a three-dimensional graph.

For example, to create a 3D graph with a contour plot and a surface plot:

1. Define two functions of two variables or any combination of two acceptable argument sets for a 3D plot (two matrices, two sets of three vectors, etc.).

2. Choose **Graph⇒Contour Plot** from the **Insert** menu.

3. Enter the name of the function or matrix for the contour plot into the placeholder. Then type **,** (a comma).

4. Enter the name of the function or matrix for the surface plot.

5. Press [**Enter**]. You see two contour plots.

6. Double-click the graph to bring up the 3D Plot Format dialog box. In the Display As section of the General tab, click the tab labeled Plot 2 and select Surface from the array of plot types. Click "OK."

Both the contour plot and the surface plot, with default format settings, appear in a single graph.

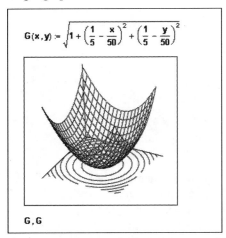

$$G(x,y) = \sqrt{1 + \left(\frac{1}{5} - \frac{x}{50}\right)^2 + \left(\frac{1}{5} - \frac{y}{50}\right)^2}$$

G,G

Figure 12-7: Two plots, one contour and one surface, shown on the same graph.

Tip   As a general rule, you will not want to create a 3D graph with more than two or three plots together since they may obscure each other and make the graph difficult to interpret.

Formatting a 3D Plot

A three-dimensional plot's default appearance depends on how you insert it. When you choose **Graph⇒3D Plot Wizard** from the **Insert** menu, you make selections in the pages of the Wizard that determine a plot's appearance. When you insert a plot by choosing a plot type from the **Insert** menu, however, the plot acquires default characteristics.

You can change the appearance of any 3D plot by using the many options available in the 3D Plot Format dialog box. For example, you can use the options to change a plot's color, format the axes, add backplanes, and format the lines or points.

To bring up the 3D Plot Format dialog box:

1. Click once on the plot to select it and choose **Graph⇒3D Plot** from the **Format** menu. Alternatively, double-click the plot itself. Mathcad brings up the 3D Plot Format dialog box. The General page is shown at right.

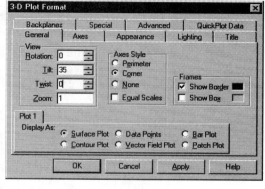

2. Click the tabs to go to each page.

3. Make the appropriate changes in the dialog box.

4. Click Apply to see the effect of your changes *without* closing the dialog box.

5. Close the dialog by clicking OK.

The 3D Plot Format Dialog Box

Some options available on certain pages in the dialog box depend on the kind of plot you are formatting. Options on other pages are available for any three-dimensional graph.

- The **General** page options control the overall appearance of the graph. You can control the position of a plot, set the axis style, draw a border or a box, or convert a plot to another type.

- The **Axes** page options control exactly how each axis looks. You can specify the weight of each axis and whether it has numbers or tick marks. You can also specify the axis limits and label each axis with text. Use the tabs at the top of the page to format the x-, y-, or z-axis.

- The **Backplanes** page options specify whether a backplane is filled with a color, has a border, or has grid lines or tick marks. Use the tabs at the top of the page to format the xy-, yz-, or xz-backplane.

Note Both the Backplanes page and the Axes page have options for setting and formatting grid lines. When you set the grid lines for an axis on the Axes tab, you set them for the two backplanes shared by the axis. When you set the grid lines on the Backplanes tab, you set them for one backplane only.

- Use the options on the **Appearance** page to format the surfaces, lines, and points that make up a plot. For example, you can apply color directly to a plot's surface, its contours, or its lines and points.

- The **Lighting** page options control both the overall lighting of the plot as well as individual lights directed onto it. See "Lighting" on page 190.

- The **Title** page provides a text box for entering a title for the graph and options for specifying the location of the title on the graph.

- The **Special** page allows you to control options related to specific kinds of plots. For example, the Bar Plot Layout options let you specify the way the bars are arranged in a 3D bar plot.

- The **Advanced** page is used only when you need very fine control over the appearance of a plot, such as the vertical scale.

- The **QuickPlot Data** page contains the range and grid settings for the independent variables that control a 3D QuickPlot. Additionally, you can specify whether your function(s) are in Cartesian, spherical, or cylindrical coordinates.

Online Help   For details on the options available on a particular page in the 3D Plot Format dialog box, click the Help button at the bottom of the dialog box.

Some options in the 3D Plot Format dialog box work together to control the appearance of a plot. For example, the choices on the Appearance page, the Lighting page, and the Special and Advanced pages together control the color of a plot.

Note   When you format a graph containing more than one plot, some options in the 3D Plot Format dialog box apply to an entire graph while others apply to individual plots. For example, all the options on the Axes, Backplanes, and Lighting pages are for the graph as a whole: each plot on the graph uses common axes, backplanes, and lighting. However, options on the Appearance tab are specific to each plot on the graph. That is, each plot can be filled with its own color, have its own lines drawn, etc. The tabs labeled Plot 1, Plot 2, etc. control the settings for individual plots.

Fill Color

The color of a plot is primarily determined by its fill color. This section describes the ways to apply color to a plot by filling its surfaces or contours. A plot's color and shading are also affected by *lighting*, as described on page 190.

Mathcad allows you to apply either a solid color or a colormap to the surface or contours of a plot. A solid color is useful when you don't want to overcomplicate a plot with many colors or when you want to use lighting to shade a plot. A colormap applies an array of color to a plot according to its coordinates.

Note   Mathcad comes with a variety of colormaps for applying rainbow colors and shades of gray, red, green, and blue. You can also create and load custom colormaps in Mathcad by using the *SaveColormap* function (page 308) and *LoadColormap* function (page 368). By default, a colormap is applied in the direction of the z-values, or according to the height of the plot. You can apply the colormap in the direction of the x-values or y-values by clicking the Advanced tab and choosing a direction in the Colormap section. For more information, see online Help.

Filling the Surface

The options on the Appearance page of the 3D Plot Format dialog box allow you to fill the plot's surface with a solid color or a colormap. For example, to color the bars in a 3D bar plot according to a colormap:

1. Double-click the graph to bring up the 3D Plot Format dialog box.

2. Click the Appearance tab.

3. Click both Fill Surface in Fill Options and Colormap in Color Options.

4. Click Apply to preview the plot.

Figure 12-8 shows an example.

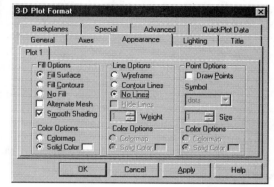

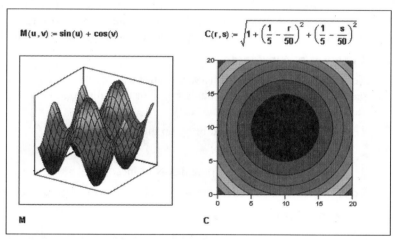

Figure 12-8: Filling the surface or contours of a plot.

The plot is shaded using the default colormap "Rainbow." To choose a different colormap, click the Advanced tab of the 3D Plot Format dialog box and select a colormap from the Choose Colormap drop-down menu.

If you wanted to fill the bars of the plot with a solid color, choose Solid Color instead of Colormap and click the color box next to Solid Color to select a color.

Filling Contours

When you format a surface plot, you can choose Fill Contours instead of Fill Surface in the Fill Options section of the Appearance page. If you fill the contours of a surface plot, the plot is filled according to its contours rather than directly by its data. You can fill according to the x-, y-, or z-contours or two at the same time. For a contour plot, you must choose Fill Contours instead of Fill Surface to fill the contours of the plot.

For example, to fill a contour plot with color:

1. Double-click the graph to bring up the tabbed dialog box.
2. Click the Appearance tab.
3. In the Fill Options section, click Fill Contours.
4. Click Apply to preview the plot.

The plot is shaded using the default colormap Rainbow. To choose a different colormap, click the Advanced tab of the 3D Plot Format dialog box and select a colormap from the Choose Colormap drop-down menu.

Note If you have a contour plot projected on a plane other than the x-y plane, you can fill the contour using options on the Special page of the 3D Plot Format dialog box. To do so, click the Special tab, then choose a contour direction from the drop-down menu. Click Fill for each contour you want to color. For example, if you have Fill checked for the z-contours and x-contours, you will see contour color on both the x-y backplane and the y-z backplane.

Lines

Mathcad provides many ways to control the appearance of the lines on a three-dimensional plot. You can draw the lines so they form a wireframe, or you can draw only the contour lines. You can also control the weight and color of the lines on a plot.

Drawing a Wireframe

To control whether lines form a wireframe on a plot, use the options on the Appearance page of the 3D Plot Format dialog box. For example, to remove the wireframe on a surface plot as shown in Figure 12-9:

1. Double-click the graph to bring up the tabbed dialog box.
2. Click the Appearance tab.
3. In the Line Options section, click No Lines.

To turn lines on again later, choose Wireframe on the Appearance page.

Drawing Contour Lines

When you format a surface plot, you can choose Contour instead of Wireframe in the Line Options section of the Appearance page. Contour lines are those drawn according to the contours of a surface. You can draw either the x-, y-, or z- contour lines, two of these contours lines, or all three.

Note For contour plots, Mathcad always chooses Contour instead of Wireframe to draw contour lines.

For example, to draw lines showing the x-contours of a surface plot:

1. Double-click the graph to bring up the tabbed dialog box.
2. Click the Appearance tab.
3. Click Contour in the Line Options section.
4. Click the Special tab.

5. Verify that Z-Contours is selected in the drop-down menu at the bottom of the Contour Options section. Click Draw Lines to remove the check mark. This turns lines off for the z-contours.

6. Choose Z-Contours from the drop-down menu on the Special page.

7. Check Draw Lines.

The surface plot is drawn with contour lines perpendicular to the z-axis, as shown in Figure 12-9.

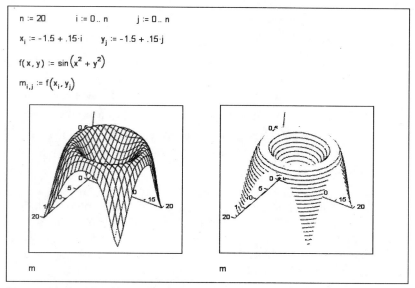

Figure 12-9: A wireframe vs. contour lines on a surface plot.

Note When you format a contour plot on a multi-plot graph (see page 176), the options in the drop-down menu on the Special tab determine on which backplane the contour lines are drawn. For example, if you have Draw Lines checked for the z-contours and x-contours, you will see contour lines on both the x-y backplane and the y-z backplane.

Line Color

You can control the color of the lines in a plot using the color options in the Line Options section of the Appearance page. Just as you can fill a plot's surface with a colormap or a solid color, described on page 187, you can also apply a colormap or solid color to the lines in a plot.

For example, to make the lines of a contour plot orange:

1. Double-click the graph to bring up the tabbed dialog box.

2. Click the Appearance tab.

3. In the Line Options section, click Contour to draw contour lines and Solid Color.

4. Click the color box next to Solid Color, click the orange box, and click OK.

Points

You can draw and format points on most three-dimensional plots, since all 3D plots are constructed from discrete data points. (The exceptions are vector field plots, contour plots, bar plots, and patch plots.) Points are most useful, however, on a 3D scatter plot in which points are the main focus of the plot. Mathcad allows you to control the symbol used for the points in a plot as well as the color and size of the symbol.

To draw or remove points on a surface plot:

1. Double-click the graph to bring up the 3D Plot Format dialog box.
2. Click the Appearance tab.
3. In the Points Options section, check (or uncheck) Draw Points.

To format the symbol, color, and size of the points on your 3D scatter plot using the Points Options section of the Appearance tab:

- Choose a Symbol from the drop-down list to change the symbol displayed.
- Use the arrows next to Size to increase or decrease the size of the symbol.
- Click the color box next to Solid Color and choose a hue from the color palette, or click Colormap to change the coloring of the symbols.

Lighting

The color of a three-dimensional plot is a result of color you use to fill its surface, lines, and points as well as the color of any ambient light or directed lights shining on it. This behavior is identical to the affect of light on object color in the real world. Objects reflect and absorb light depending on their color. For example, a yellow ball reflects mostly yellow light and absorbs others, and it can look grayish under dim lighting, green under blue lighting, and bright yellow in bright lighting.

Light is controlled using the options on the Lighting page of the 3D Plot Format dialog box. If you are content to fill a plot with a colormap, you may not need to use lighting at all. However, if you want to shade the plot differently, or if you fill the plot with a solid color and want to shade it, you can enable lighting.

Note If your 3D graph contains multiple plots, lighting affects all the plots in a graph, but you can fill individual plots with color independently.

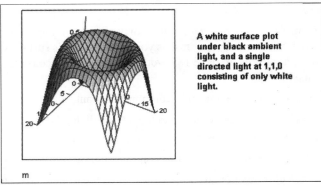

A white surface plot under black ambient light, and a single directed light at 1,1,0 consisting of only white light.

Figure 12-10: A white surface plot with lighting enabled.

Note   If you want lighting to be the sole determinant of the color of a plot, use the Appearance page options in the 3D Plot Format dialog box to fill the plot with solid white.

To enable lighting:

1. Double-click the plot to open the tabbed dialog box.
2. Click the Lighting tab.
3. Check Enable Lighting in the Lighting section.
4. Click the options on tabs labeled Light 1, Light 2, etc. to enable a directed light and set its color and location. Mathcad lets you set up to eight directed lights.
5. Click the Ambient Light Color box to set the ambient light color. Note that black corresponds to no ambient light.

Online Help   For details on the options available on the Lighting page, click the Help button at the bottom of the dialog box. For additional information on lighting, see online Help.

Changing One 3D Plot to Another

Note   You can change almost any three-dimensional plot into another kind of three-dimensional plot by using the Display As options on the General tab in the 3D Plot Format dialog box. Simply select another available 3D plot type and click Apply or OK to change the plot instantaneously to another type. Figure 12-11 shows the same matrix displayed as three different plot types.

Note   Some three-dimensional plots cannot be converted to other forms. For example, you cannot convert a vector field plot into any other kind of plot. If a plot cannot be converted to another kind of plot, that plot type is grayed in the 3D Plot Format dialog box.

Annotations

To add a text annotation to a three-dimensional plot, just drag text or bitmaps directly onto the plot.

You can select the text annotation on your plot to reposition it. To edit a text annotation on a plot, select the text and drag it off the plot to your worksheet. You can now edit the text region. Then drag the text region back onto the plot.

Tip   To place a bitmap you created in another application onto a three-dimensional plot, copy the bitmap from the other application to the Clipboard, right click on the plot and choose **Paste Special** from the popup menu.

Modifying 3D QuickPlot Data

When you create a 3D QuickPlot you can change the range and step size of each independent variable by using the settings on the QuickPlot Data page of the 3D Plot Format dialog box.

To change the range of either independent variable:

1. Set the start and end values of either range using the text boxes for each range.
2. Click Apply to preview.

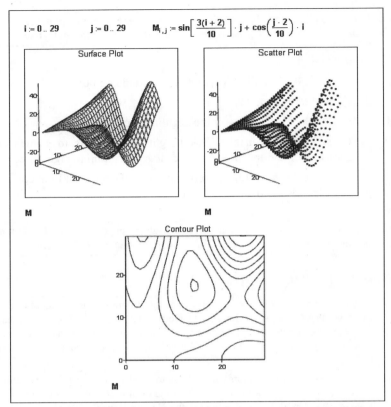

Figure 12-11: The same data displayed in several different 3D plots.

To change the step size, the number of grids generated along each variable's axis between the start and end values:

1. Use the arrows next to # of Grids for each range to increase or decrease the grid value. Alternatively, you can type in a value in the text box.

2. Click Apply to preview your changes.

The ranges you set for the independent variables in the QuickPlot Data page do not necessarily control the axis limits of the plot, unless you are plotting a single function of two variables in Cartesian coordinates. In all other cases, the axis limits are determined by the x-, y-, and z-data generated for the QuickPlot by your function(s).

To perform automatic coordinate system conversions on your QuickPlot data:

1. Click the radio button under the Coordinate System corresponding to the coordinate system of the function you are plotting.

2. Click Apply to preview your changes.

Rotating and Zooming on 3D Plots

You can resize a three-dimensional plot using the same methods you use to resize any graph region in Mathcad. Click on it and use the handles that appear along the edges to drag out the edges. Mathcad provides several additional options for manipulating the presentation of your 3D plot:

- You can rotate the plot to see it from a different perspective.
- You can set the plot in motion about an axis of rotation so that it spins continuously.
- You can zoom in or out on a portion of the plot.

Note When you rotate, spin, or zoom a three-dimensional plot, any visible axes move or resize themselves with the plot. Text or graphic annotations you add to the plot (see page 191) remain anchored at their original sizes and positions.

Rotating a Plot

You can rotate a plot interactively with the mouse or by specifying parameters in the 3D Plot Format dialog box.

To rotate a three-dimensional plot interactively by using the mouse:

1. Click in the plot, and hold the mouse button down.
2. Drag the mouse in the direction you want the plot to turn.
3. Release the mouse button when the plot is in the desired position.

To rotate a three-dimensional plot by using the 3D Plot Format dialog box:

1. Click once on the plot to select it and choose **Graph⇒3D Plot** from the **Format** menu.
2. Click the General tab.
3. Edit the settings for Rotation, Tilt, and Twist in the View options.
4. Click Apply to preview the plot.

Spinning a Plot

You can set a plot in motion so that it spins continuously about an axis of rotation:

1. Click in the plot, and hold the [**Shift**] key and the mouse button down.
2. Drag the mouse in the direction you want the plot to spin.
3. Release the mouse button to set the plot in motion.

The plot spins continuously until you click again inside the plot.

Note If you make changes to equations that affect a plot, the plot recomputes even when it is spinning!

Tip To create an AVI file of a spinning plot, see "Animation" on page 121.

Zooming a Plot

You can zoom in or out of a plot interactively or by specifying a zoom factor in the 3D Plot Format dialog box.

To zoom in on a three-dimensional plot by using the mouse:

1. Click in the plot, and hold the [**Ctrl**] key and the mouse button down.
2. Drag the mouse toward the top of the plot to zoom out, or drag the mouse toward the bottom to zoom in.
3. Release the mouse button when the plot is at the desired zoom factor.

Tip   If you use an IntelliMouse-compatible mouse with a center wheel, you can rotate the wheel to zoom in or out of a three-dimensional plot.

To zoom in or out of a three-dimensional plot by using the 3D Plot Format dialog box:

1. Click once on the plot to select it and choose **Graph⇒3D Plot** from the **Format** menu.
2. Click the General tab.
3. Edit the Zoom setting in the View options.
4. Click Apply to preview the plot.

Chapter 13
Symbolic Calculation

◆ Overview of Symbolic Math

◆ Live Symbolic Evaluation

◆ Using the Symbolics Menu

◆ Examples of Symbolic Calculation

◆ Symbolic Optimization

Overview of Symbolic Math

Whenever you evaluate an expression *numerically*, Mathcad returns one or more *numbers,* as shown at the top of Figure 13-1. When Mathcad calculates *symbolically*, however, the result of evaluating an expression is generally another expression, as shown in the bottom of Figure 13-1.

A numerical calculation gives nothing but numbers:

$$F(x) := \sum_{k=0}^{3} \frac{3!}{k! \cdot (3-k)!} \cdot x^k \cdot 2^{3-k}$$

$$F(2) = 64$$

$$F(-5) = -27$$

But a symbolic transformation can yield insight into the underlying expression:

$$F(x) \rightarrow 8 + 12 \cdot x + 6 \cdot x^2 + x^3$$

Figure 13-1: A numeric and symbolic evaluation of the same expression.

There are three ways to perform a symbolic transformation on an expression.

- You can use the symbolic equal sign as described in "Live Symbolic Evaluation" on page 196. This method feels very much as if you're engaging in numeric math. If you need more control over the symbolic transformation, you can use *keywords* with the symbolic equal sign.

- You can use commands from the **Symbolics** menu. See "Using the Symbolics Menu" on page 201.

- You can make the numeric and symbolic processors work together, the latter simplifying an expression behind the scenes so that the former can work with it more efficiently. This is discussed in "Symbolic Optimization" on page 212.

> **Note** For a computer, symbolic operations are, in general, much more difficult than the corresponding numeric operations. In fact, many complicated functions and deceptively simple-looking functions have no closed-forms as integrals or roots.

Live Symbolic Evaluation

The symbolic equal sign provides a way to extend Mathcad's live document interface beyond the numeric evaluation of expressions. You can think of it as being analogous to the equal sign "=." Unlike the equal sign, which always gives a numeric result on the right-hand side, the symbolic equal sign is capable of returning *expressions*. You can use it to symbolically evaluate expressions, variables, functions, or programs.

To use the symbolic equal sign:

Make sure that **Calculate⇒Automatic Calculation** on the **Tools** menu has a check beside it. If it doesn't, choose it from the menu.

1. Enter the expression you want to evaluate.

    $$\frac{d}{dx}(x^3 - 2 \cdot y \cdot x)|$$

2. Click ![→] on the Symbolic toolbar or press **[Ctrl]**. (the Control key followed by a period). Mathcad displays a symbolic equal sign, "→"

    $$\frac{d}{dx}(x^3 - 2 \cdot y \cdot x) \rightarrow$$

3. Click outside the expression. Mathcad displays a simplified version of the original expression. If an expression cannot be simplified further, Mathcad simply repeats it to the right of the symbolic equal sign.

    $$\frac{d}{dx}(x^3 - 2 \cdot y \cdot x) \rightarrow 3 \cdot x^2 - 2 \cdot y$$

The symbolic equal sign is a live operator just like any Mathcad operator. When you make a change anywhere above or to the left of it, Mathcad updates the result. The symbolic equal sign "knows" about previously defined functions and variables and uses them wherever appropriate. You can force the symbolic equal sign to ignore prior definitions of functions and variables by defining them recursively just before you evaluate them, as shown in Figure 13-6 on page 201.

Figure 13-2 shows some examples of how to use the symbolic equal sign, "→"

> **Note** The symbolic equal sign, "→," applies to an entire expression. You cannot use the symbolic equal sign to transform only part of an expression.

> **Tip** Figure 13-2 also illustrates the fact that the symbolic processor treats numbers containing a decimal point differently from numbers without a decimal point. When you send numbers with decimal points to the symbolic processor, any numeric results you get back are decimal approximations to the exact answer. Otherwise, any numeric results you get back are expressed without decimal points whenever possible.

Press [Ctrl][Period] to get the symbolic equal sign.

$$\int_{a}^{b} x^2 \, dx \rightarrow \frac{1}{3} \cdot b^3 - \frac{1}{3} \cdot a^3$$

The symbolic equal sign uses previous definitions:

$$x := 8$$

$$y + 2 \cdot x \rightarrow y + 16$$

If the expression cannot be simplified further, the symbolic equal sign does nothing.

$$y^2 \rightarrow y^2$$

This is analogous to the equal sign you use for numerical evaluation:

$$2 = 2$$

When decimals are used, the symbolic equal sign returns decimal approximation

$$\sqrt{17} \rightarrow \sqrt{17} \qquad \sqrt{17.0} \rightarrow 4.1231056256176605498$$

Figure 13-2: Using the symbolic equal sign.

Using Keywords

The "→" takes the left-hand side and places a simplified version of it on the right-hand side. Of course, exactly what "simplify" means is a matter of opinion. You can, to a limited extent, control how the "→" transforms the expression by using one of the *symbolic keywords*.

To do so:

1. Enter the expression you want to evaluate.

$(x + y)^3$

2. Click 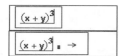 on the Symbolic toolbar or press [Ctrl] [Shift]. (Press the Control and Shift keys and type a period.) Mathcad displays a placeholder to the left of the symbolic equal sign, "→."

$(x + y)^3 \blacksquare \rightarrow$

3. Click on the placeholder to the left of the symbolic equal sign and type any of the keywords from the following table. If the keyword requires any additional arguments, separate the arguments from the keyword with commas.

$(x + y)^3 \text{ expand} \rightarrow$

4. Press [Enter] to see the result.

$(x + y)^3 \text{ expand} \rightarrow x^3 + 3 \cdot x^2 \cdot y + 3 \cdot x \cdot y^2 + y^3$

Tip   Another way to use a keyword is to enter the expression you want to evaluate and click on a keyword button from the Symbolic toolbar. This inserts the keyword, placeholders for any additional arguments, and the symbolic equal sign, "→." Just press [Enter] to see the result.

Chapter 18, "Symbolic Keywords," lists and describes all the symbolic keywords accessible from the Symbolics and Modifier toolbars.

Many of the keywords take at least one additional argument, typically the name of a variable with respect to which you are performing the symbolic operation. Some of the arguments are optional. See Figure 13-3 and Figure 13-4 for examples.

By itself, the symbolic equal sign simply evaluates the expression to the left of it and places it on the right:

$$\frac{d}{dx}(x + y)^3 \rightarrow 3 \cdot (x + y)^2$$

But when preceded by an appropriate keyword, the symbolic equal can change its meaning:

$$(x + y)^3 \text{ expand } \rightarrow x^3 + 3 \cdot x^2 \cdot y + 3 \cdot x \cdot y^2 + y^3$$

The keyword "float" makes the result display as a floating point number whenever possible:

$$x \cdot acos(0) \rightarrow \frac{1}{2} \cdot x \cdot \pi \qquad x \cdot acos(0) \text{ float, 4} \rightarrow 1.571 \cdot x$$

The keyword "laplace" returns the Laplace transform of a function:

$$exp(-a \cdot t) \text{ laplace, t } \rightarrow \frac{1}{(s + a)}$$

Figure 13-3: Using keywords with a symbolic evaluation sign.

Symbolic evaluation   **Complex evaluation**

$$\int_0^\infty e^{-x^2} dx \rightarrow \frac{1}{2} \cdot \pi^{\frac{1}{2}} \qquad e^{i \cdot n \cdot \theta} \text{ complex } \rightarrow \cos(n \cdot \theta) + i \cdot \sin(n \cdot \theta)$$

Floating point evaluation

$$\int_0^\infty e^{-x^2} dx \text{ float, 10} \rightarrow .8862269255$$

Constrained evaluation

$$x \cdot \int_0^\infty e^{-\alpha \cdot t} dt \text{ assume, } \alpha > 1 \rightarrow \frac{x}{\alpha} \qquad \begin{array}{l} \text{("}\alpha\text{" is constrained to be} \\ \text{greater than 1)} \end{array}$$

Figure 13-4: Evaluating expressions symbolically.

Note Keywords are case sensitive and must therefore be typed exactly as shown. Unlike variables, however, they are not font sensitive.

Keyword modifiers

Some keywords take additional modifiers that specify the kind of symbolic evaluation even further.

To use a modifier, separate it from its keyword with a comma. For example, to use the "assume=real" modifier with the **simplify** keyword on an expression:

1. Enter the expression to simplify.

2. Click [■→] on the Symbolic toolbar or press [**Ctrl**] [**Shift**]. (hold down the Control and Shift keys and type a period). Mathcad displays a placeholder to the left of the symbolic equal sign, "→."

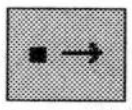

3. Enter **simplify,assume=real** into the placeholder (press [**Ctrl**]= for the equal sign).

4. Press [**Enter**] to see the result.

The Modifiers keyword button corresponds to symbolic modifiers. Modifiers for "assume" are detailed on page 422, and modifiers for "simplify" are described on page 428.

Figure 13-5 shows some examples using the **simplify** keyword with and without additional modifiers.

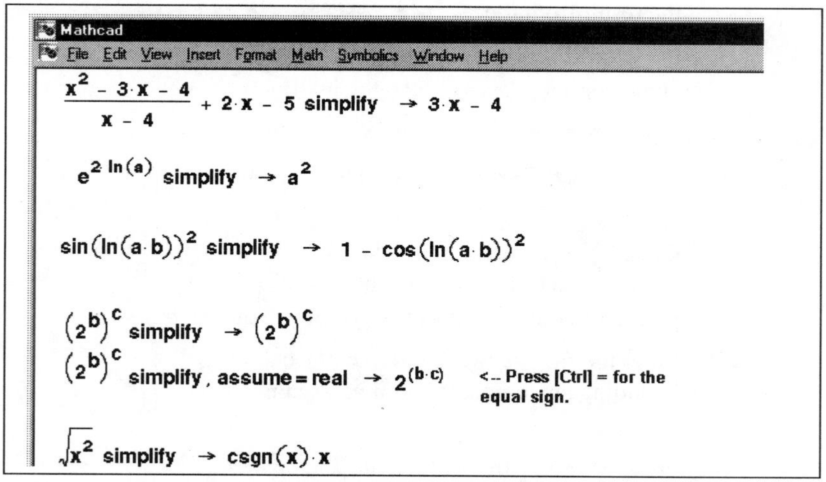

Figure 13-5: Modifiers such as "assume=real" allow you to control simplification.

Using More Than One Keyword

In some cases, you may want to perform two or more types of symbolic evaluation consecutively on an expression. Mathcad allows you to apply several symbolic keywords to a single expression. There are two ways of applying multiple keywords. The method you choose depends on whether you want to see the results from each keyword or only the final result.

To apply several keywords and see the results from each:

1. Enter the expression you want to evaluate.

   $e^{x}|$

2. Press [■ →] on the Symbolic toolbar or type
   [**Ctrl**] [**Shift**]. (Hold down the Control and
   Shift keys and type a period.) Mathcad displays a placeholder to the left of the
   symbolic equal sign, "→."

   $e^{x} \ \blacksquare \ \rightarrow$

3. Enter the first keyword into the placeholder to
   the left of the symbolic equal sign, including
   any comma-delimited arguments the keyword
   takes.

   $e^{x} \ \text{series}, x, 3| \ \rightarrow$

4. Press [**Enter**] to see the result from the first
   keyword.

   $e^{x} \ \text{series}, x, 3 \ \rightarrow \ 1 + x + \frac{1}{2} \cdot x^{2}$

5. Click on the result and press [**Ctrl**] [**Shift**].
   again. The first result disappears temporarily.
   Enter a second keyword and any modifiers into
   the placeholder.

   $e^{x} \ \text{series}, x, 3 \ \rightarrow \text{float}, 1| \rightarrow$

6. Press [**Enter**] to see
   the result from the
   second keyword.

   $e^{x} \ \text{series}, x, 3 \ \rightarrow \ 1 + x + \frac{1}{2} \cdot x^{2} \ \text{float}, 1 \ \rightarrow \ 1. + x + .5 \cdot x^{2}$

Continue applying keywords to the intermediate results in this manner.

To apply several keywords and see only the final result:

1. Enter the expression you want to evaluate.

   $e^{x}|$

2. Click [■ →] on the Symbolic toolbar or press
   [**Ctrl**] [**Shift**]. so that Mathcad displays a
   placeholder to the left of the symbolic equal sign, "→."

   $e^{x} \ \blacksquare \ \rightarrow$

3. Enter the first keyword into the placeholder,
   including any comma-delimited arguments it
   takes.

   $e^{x} \ \text{series}, x, 3| \ \rightarrow$

4. Press [**Ctrl**] [**Shift**]. again and enter a
   second keyword into the placeholder. The
   second keyword is placed immediately below
   the first keyword.

   $e^{x} \ \begin{vmatrix} \text{series}, x, 3 \\ \text{float}, 1| \end{vmatrix} \ \rightarrow$

5. Continue adding keywords by pressing [**Ctrl**]
   [**Shift**]. after each one. Press [**Enter**] to see
   the final result.

   $e^{x} \ \begin{vmatrix} \text{series}, x, 3 \\ \text{float}, 1 \end{vmatrix} \ \rightarrow \ 1. + x + .5 \cdot x^{2}$

Ignoring Previous Definitions

When you use the symbolic equal sign to evaluate an expression, Mathcad checks all the variables and functions making up that expression to see if they've been defined earlier in the worksheet. If Mathcad does find a definition, it uses it. Any other variables and functions are evaluated symbolically.

There are two exceptions to this. In evaluating an expression made up of previously defined variables and functions, Mathcad *ignores* prior definitions when the variable has been defined recursively.

This exception is illustrated in Figure 13-6.

```
x := 3

(x + 1)·(z − 1) expand  → 4·z − 4          Mathcad substitutes the value of
                                            3 for x before evaluating this
                                            expression.

x := x      recursive definition            Although x is defined to be 3,
                                            Mathcad ignores that definition for
                                            symbolic evaluation because of the
(x + 1)·(x + 1) expand  → x² + 2·x + 1      recursive definition.
```

Figure 13-6: Defining a variable in terms of itself makes the symbolic processor ignore previous definitions of that variable.

Using the Symbolics Menu

One advantage to using the symbolic equal sign, sometimes together with keywords and modifiers as discussed in the last section, is that it is "live," just like the numeric processing in Mathcad. That is, Mathcad checks all the variables and functions making up the expression being evaluated to see if they've been defined earlier in the worksheet. If Mathcad does find a definition, it uses it. Any other variables and functions are evaluated symbolically. Later on, whenever you make a change to the worksheet, the results automatically update. This is useful when the symbolic and numeric equations in the worksheet are tied together.

There may be times, however, when a symbolic calculation is quite separate from the rest of your worksheet and does not need to be tied to any previous definitions. In these cases, you can use commands from the **Symbolics** menu. These commands are not live: you apply them on a case by case basis to selected expressions, they do not "know" about previous definitions, and they do not automatically update.

The commands on the **Symbolics** menu perform the same manipulations as many of the keywords listed on page 421. For example, the **Symbolics** menu command **Polynomial Coefficients** evaluates an expression just as the keyword **coeffs** does. The only differences are that the menu command does not recognize previous definitions and does not automatically update.

The basic steps for using the **Symbolics** menu are the same for all the menu commands:

1. Place whatever math expression you want to evaluate *between the two editing lines*. You can drag-select a part of the expression to place it between the editing lines.

2. Choose the appropriate command from the **Symbolics** menu. Mathcad then places the evaluated expression into your document.

For example, to evaluate an expression symbolically using the **Symbolics** menu, follow these steps:

1. Enter the expression you want to evaluate.

$$\frac{d}{dx}\left(x^3 - 2\cdot y\cdot x\right)$$

2. Surround the expression with the editing lines.

$$\frac{d}{dx}\left(x^3 - 2\cdot y\cdot x\right)$$

3. Choose **Evaluate⇒Symbolically** from the **Symbolics** menu. Mathcad places the evaluated expression into your worksheet. The location of the result in relation to the original expression depends on the Evaluation Style you've selected (see "Displaying Symbolic Results" on page 202).

$$3\cdot x^2 - 2\cdot y$$

Some commands on the **Symbolics** menu require that you click on or select the variable of interest rather than select the entire expression. If a menu command is unavailable, try selecting a single variable rather than an entire expression.

Tip   Since the commands on the **Symbolics** menu operate only on the part of the expression currently selected by the editing lines, they are useful when you want to address parts of an expression. For example, if evaluating or simplifying the entire expression doesn't give the answer you want, try selecting a subexpression and choose a command from the **Symbolics** menu.

Long Results

Symbolic calculations can easily produce results so long that they don't fit conveniently in your window. If you obtain a symbolic result consisting of several terms by using commands on the **Symbolics** menu, you can reformat such a result by using Mathcad's "Addition with line break" operator (see "Operators" on page 391).

Sometimes, a symbolic result is so long that you can't conveniently display it in your worksheet. When this happens, Mathcad asks if you want the result placed in the Clipboard. If you click "OK," Mathcad places a string representing the result on the Clipboard. When you examine the contents of the clipboard, you'll see a result written in a Fortran-like syntax. See the topic "Special functions and syntax used in Symbolic results" in the online Help for more information on this syntax.

Displaying Symbolic Results

If you're using the symbolic equal sign, "→," the result of a symbolic transformation always goes to the right of the "→." However, when you use the **Symbolics** menu, you can tell Mathcad to place the symbolic results in one of the following ways:

• The symbolic result can go below the original expression.

• The symbolic result can go to the right of the original expression.

• The symbolic result can simply replace the original expression.

In addition, you can choose whether you want Mathcad to generate text describing what had to be done to get from the original expression to the symbolic result. This text goes between the original expression and the symbolic result, creating a narrative for the symbolic evaluation. These text regions are referred to as "evaluation comments."

To control both the placement of the symbolic result and the presence of narrative text, choose **Evaluation Style** from the **Symbolics** menu to bring up the "Evaluation Style" dialog box.

Examples of Symbolic Calculation

Just as you can carry out a variety of numeric calculations in Mathcad, you can carry out all kinds of symbolic calculations. As a general rule, any expression involving variables, functions, and operators can be evaluated symbolically using either the symbolic equal sign or the menu commands, as described earlier in this chapter.

Tip When deciding whether to use the symbolic equal sign or menu commands from the **Symbolics** menu, remember that unlike the keyword-modified expressions, expressions modified by commands from the **Symbolics** menu do not update automatically.

Note Functions and variables you define yourself are recognized by the symbolic processor when you use the symbolic equal sign. They are not, however, recognized when you use the **Symbolics** menu commands. Figure 13-7 shows the difference.

Mathcad's symbolic processor recognizes many of its built-in math functions and constants:

$$e^{\ln(x)} \to x \qquad \sin\left(\frac{\pi}{4}\right) \to \frac{1}{2} \cdot 2^{\frac{1}{2}}$$

but not the ones that don't have a commonly accepted meaning:

$$rnd(x) \to rnd(x)$$

Functions and variables you define yourself are recognized where you use the symbolic equal sign:

$$F(x) := \frac{\ln(x)}{2} \qquad a := 3$$

$$e^{F(x)} \to x^{\frac{1}{2}} \qquad a^2 \cdot \sin(a) \to 9 \cdot \sin(3)$$

but not when you use commands from the Symbolics menu:

$$e^{F(x)} \qquad\qquad a^2 \cdot \sin(a)$$

simplifies to   simplifies to

$$\exp(F(x)) \qquad\qquad a^2 \cdot \sin(a)$$

Figure 13-7: The symbolic processor recognizes certain built-in functions. Functions and variables you define yourself are only recognized when you use the symbolic equal sign.

Derivatives

To evaluate a derivative symbolically, you can use Mathcad's derivative operator and the live symbolic equal sign as shown in Figure 13-8:

Some integrals evaluated symbolically using the symbolic equal sign ([Ctrl] + Period)

$$\int_1^c x^3 \, dx \rightarrow \frac{1}{4} \cdot c^4 - \frac{1}{4} \qquad \leftarrow \text{Press \& for definite integral}$$

$$\int_0^\infty e^{-x^2} \, dx \rightarrow \frac{1}{2} \cdot \pi^{\left(\frac{1}{2}\right)} \qquad \leftarrow \text{Press [Ctrl][Shift]Z for "∞" in upper limit}$$

$$\int a \cdot x^2 \, dx \rightarrow \frac{1}{3} \cdot a \cdot x^3 \qquad \leftarrow \text{Press [Ctrl]i for indefinite integral}$$

A second derivative:

$$\frac{d^2}{dz^2} z \cdot \text{atan}(z) \rightarrow \frac{2}{\left(1 + z^2\right)} - 2 \cdot \frac{z^2}{\left(1 + z^2\right)^2} \qquad \begin{array}{l} \leftarrow \text{Press [Ctrl] ? to} \\ \text{get the nth derivative} \\ \text{operator.} \end{array}$$

Figure 13-8: Evaluating integrals and derivatives symbolically.

1. Click $\boxed{\frac{d}{dx}}$ on the Calculus toolbar or type **?** to insert the derivative operator. Alternatively, click $\boxed{\frac{d^n}{dx^n}}$ on the Calculus toolbar or type **[Ctrl]?** to insert the *n*th order derivative operator.

2. Enter the expression you want to differentiate and the variable with respect to which you are differentiating in the placeholders.

3. Click $\boxed{\rightarrow}$ on the Symbolic toolbar or press **[Ctrl].** (the Control key followed by a period). Mathcad displays a symbolic equal sign, "→."

4. Press **[Enter]** to see the result.

Figure 13-9 shows you how to differentiate an expression without using the derivative operator. The **Symbolics** menu command **Variable⇒Differentiate** differentiates an expression with respect to a selected variable. For example, to differentiate $2 \cdot x^2 + y$ with respect to x:

1. Enter the expression.

2. Click on the x to select it.

3. Choose **Variable⇒Differentiate** from the **Symbolics** menu. Mathcad displays the derivative, $4 \cdot x$. Note that y is treated as a constant.

If the expression in which you've selected a variable is one element of an array, Mathcad differentiates only that array element. To differentiate an entire array, differentiate each element individually: select a variable in that element and choose **Variable⇒Differentiate** from the **Symbolics** menu.

Click on "x" and choose Variable ⇒ Differentiate from the Symbolics menu.

$2 \cdot x^2 + y$ by differentiation, yields $4 \cdot x$

⇒

$$\frac{x}{\cosh(x)}$$ by differentiation, yields $\frac{1}{\cosh(x)} - \frac{x}{\cosh(x)^2} \cdot \sinh(x)$

Click on "x" and choose Variable ⇒ Integrate from the Symbolics menu.

$x^2 \cdot e^x$ by integration, yields $x^2 \cdot \exp(x) - 2 \cdot x \cdot \exp(x) + 2 \cdot \exp(x)$

$$\frac{x + a}{x^2 + b}$$ by integration, yields $\frac{1}{2} \cdot \ln(x^2 + b) + \frac{a}{b^{\left(\frac{1}{2}\right)}} \cdot \operatorname{atan}\left[\frac{x}{b^{\left(\frac{1}{2}\right)}}\right]$

Figure 13-9: Differentiating and integrating with menu commands.

Tip   Be sure to select a variable in an expression before choosing from the **Symbolics** menu. Otherwise, the **Variable⇒Differentiate** menu command is not available.

Integrals

To symbolically evaluate a definite or indefinite integral:

1. Click ⌠⌡ or ∫ on the Calculus toolbar to insert the definite or indefinite integral operator.

2. Fill in the placeholder for the integrand and, if applicable, the placeholders for the limits of integration.

3. Place the integration variable in the placeholder next to the "*d*." This can be any variable name.

4. Click → on the Symbolic toolbar or press [**Ctrl**]. (the Control key followed by a period). Mathcad displays a symbolic equal sign, "→."

5. Press [**Enter**] to see the result.

See Figure 13-8 for examples of integrals evaluated symbolically.

When evaluating a definite integral, the symbolic processor attempts to find an indefinite integral of your integrand before substituting the limits you specified. If the symbolic integration succeeds and the limits of integration are integers, fractions, or exact constants like π, you get an exact value for your integral. If the symbolic processor can't find a closed form for the integral, you'll see an appropriate error message.

Another way to integrate an expression indefinitely is to enter the expression and click on the variable of integration. Then choose **Variable⇒Integrate** from the **Symbolics** menu. See Figure 13-9 for an example.

Tip When you apply the **Variable⇒Integrate** command on the **Symbolics** menu, the expression you select should not usually include the integral operator. You should select only an expression to integrate. If you include the integral operator in the selected expression, you are taking a double integral.

Limits

Mathcad provides three limit operators. These can only be evaluated symbolically. To use the limit operators:

1. Click [lim →a] on the Calculus toolbar or press **[Ctrl]L** to insert the limit operator. To insert the operator for a limit from the left or right, click [lim →a⁻], or [lim →a⁺] on the Calculus toolbar or press **[Ctrl][Shift]B** or **[Ctrl][Shift]A**.

2. Enter the expression in the placeholder to the right of the "lim."

3. Enter the limiting variable in the left-hand placeholder below the "lim."

4. Enter the limiting value in the right-hand placeholder below the "lim."

5. Click [→] on the Symbolic toolbar or press **[Ctrl].** (the Control key followed by a period). Mathcad displays a symbolic equal sign, "→."

6. Press **[Enter]** to see the result.

Mathcad returns a result for the limit. If the limit does not exist, Mathcad returns an error message. Figure 13-10 shows some examples of evaluating limits.

Using the limit operators and the live symbolics equal sign ([Ctrl] + Period)

$$\lim_{x \to \infty} \frac{\sqrt{x^2 + 2}}{3 \cdot x + 6} \to \frac{1}{3}$$ <-- Press [Ctrl] [Shift] Z for ∞

A limit from the right:

$$\lim_{x \to a^+} \frac{3 \cdot x + b}{x^2} \to \frac{(3 \cdot a + b)}{a^2}$$

A limit from the left:

$$\lim_{x \to 0^-} \frac{\sin(x)}{x} \to 1$$

Figure 13-10: Evaluating limits.

Solving an Equation for a Variable

To solve an equation symbolically for a variable, use the keyword **solve**:

1. Type the equation. Make sure you click [=] on the Boolean toolbar or type **[Ctrl]=** to create the bold equal sign.

Note When solving for the root of an expression, there is no need to set the expression equal to zero. See Figure 13-11 for an example.

2. Click ![icon] on the Symbolic toolbar or type **[Ctrl] [Shift].** (hold down the Control and Shift keys and type a period). Mathcad displays a placeholder to the left of the symbolic equal sign, "→."

3. Type **solve** in the placeholder, followed by a comma and the variable for which to solve.

4. Press **[Enter]** to see the result.

Mathcad solves for the variable and inserts the result to the right of the "→." Note that if the variable was squared in the original equation, you may get *two* results back when you solve. Mathcad displays these in a vector. Figure 13-11 shows an example.

$$A1 = \frac{L}{r^2} + 2 \cdot C \; solve, r \; \rightarrow \left[\begin{array}{c} \frac{1}{(-A1 + 2 \cdot C)} \cdot [-(-A1 + 2 \cdot C) \cdot L]^{\frac{1}{2}} \\ \frac{-1}{(-A1 + 2 \cdot C)} \cdot [-(-A1 + 2 \cdot C) \cdot L]^{\frac{1}{2}} \end{array} \right]$$

$a := 34$

$\frac{1}{2} \cdot x + x = -2 + a \; solve, x \; \rightarrow \frac{64}{3}$ Use [Ctrl]= for equal sign

$x^3 - 5 \cdot x^2 - 4 \cdot x + 20 > 0 \; solve, x \; \rightarrow \left[\begin{array}{c} (-2 < x) \cdot (x < 2) \\ 5 < x \end{array} \right]$

$e^t + 1 \; solve, t \; \rightarrow i \cdot \pi$ You don't need = 0 when finding roots.

Figure 13-11: Solving equations, solving inequalities, and finding roots.

Tip Another way to solve for a variable is to enter the equation, click on the variable you want to solve for in the equation, and choose **Variable⇒Solve** from the **Symbolics** menu.

Solving a System of Equations Symbolically: "Solve" Keyword

One way to symbolically solve a system of equations is to use the same **solve** keyword used to solve one equation in one unknown. To solve a system of *n* equations for *n* unknowns:

1. Press ![icon] on the Matrix toolbar or type **[Ctrl]M** to insert a vector having *n* rows and 1 column.

2. Fill in each placeholder of the vector with one of the *n* equations making up the system. Make sure you click ![icon] on the Boolean toolbar or type **[Ctrl]=** to enter the bold equal sign.

3. Press ▪→ on the Symbolic toolbar or type **[Ctrl] [Shift].** (hold down the Control and Shift keys and type a period). Mathcad displays a placeholder to the left of the symbolic equal sign, "→."

4. Type **solve** followed by a comma in the placeholder.

5. Type **[Ctrl]M** or press ⊞ on the Matrix toolbar to create a vector having *n* rows and 1 column. Then enter the variables you are solving for.

6. Press **[Enter]** to see the result.

Mathcad displays the *n* solutions to the system of equations to the right of the symbolic equal sign. Figure 13-12 shows an example.

Use the **solve** keyword by pressing [Ctrl][Shift][.] (period)

$$\begin{pmatrix} x + 2 \cdot \pi \cdot y = a \\ 4 \cdot x + y = b \end{pmatrix} \text{solve}, \begin{pmatrix} x \\ y \end{pmatrix} \rightarrow \left[\frac{-(-2 \cdot \pi \cdot b + a)}{(-1 + 8 \cdot \pi)} \quad \frac{(4 \cdot a - b)}{(-1 + 8 \cdot \pi)} \right]$$

Using a solve block:

Given

$$x + 2\pi \cdot y = a \qquad \text{Use [Ctrl] = to type the equal signs}$$
$$4 \cdot x + y = b$$

$$\text{Find}(x, y) \rightarrow \left[\begin{array}{c} \dfrac{(2 \cdot \pi \cdot b - a)}{(-1 + 8 \cdot \pi)} \\ \dfrac{(4 \cdot a - b)}{(-1 + 8 \cdot \pi)} \end{array} \right] \qquad +$$

Figure 13-12: Two methods for solving a system of equations symbolically.

Solving a System of Equations Symbolically: Solve Block

Another way to solve a system of equations symbolically is to use a solve block, similar to the numeric solve blocks described in "Solving and Optimization Functions" on page 125:

1. Type the word *Given*. This tells Mathcad that what follows is a system of equations. You can type *Given* in any combination of upper- and lowercase letters and in any font. Just be sure you don't type it while in a text region.

2. Now enter the equations in any order below the word *Given*. Make sure that for every equation you click ▬ on the Boolean toolbar or type **[Ctrl]=** to insert the bold equal sign for each equation.

3. Enter the *Find* function with arguments appropriate for your system of equations. This function is described in "Linear/Nonlinear System Solving and Optimization" on page 127.

4. Click → on the Symbolic toolbar or press **[Ctrl].** (the Control key followed by a period). Mathcad displays the symbolic equal sign.

5. Click outside the *Find* function or press [**Enter**].

Mathcad displays the solutions to the system of equations to the right of the symbolic equal sign. Figure 13-12 shows an example.

Most of the guidelines for solve blocks described in "Linear/Nonlinear System Solving and Optimization" on page 127 apply to the symbolic solution of systems of equations. The main difference is that when you solve equations symbolically, you do not enter guess values for the solutions.

Symbolic Matrix Manipulation

You can use Mathcad to find the symbolic transpose, inverse, or determinant of a matrix using a built-in operator and the symbolic equal sign. To find the transpose of a matrix, for example:

1. Place the entire matrix between the two editing lines by clicking [**Space**] one or more times.

2. Click $\boxed{M^T}$ on the Matrix toolbar or press [**Ctrl**] | to insert the matrix transpose operator.

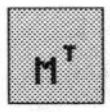

3. Click $\boxed{\rightarrow}$ on the Symbolic toolbar or press [**Ctrl**]. (the Control key followed by a period). Mathcad displays the symbolic equal sign, "→."

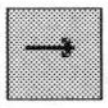

4. Press [**Enter**] to see the result.

Mathcad returns the result to the right of the "→." Figure 13-13 shows some examples.

Figure 13-13: Symbolic matrix operations.

Another way to find the transpose, inverse, or determinant of a matrix is to use the **Matrix** commands on the **Symbolics** menu. For example, to find the transpose of a matrix:

1. Place the entire matrix between the two editing lines by pressing [**Space**] one or more times.

2. Choose **Matrix⟹Transpose** from the **Symbolics** menu.

Unlike matrices evaluated with the symbolic equal sign, matrices modified by commands from the **Symbolics** menu do not update automatically, as described in the section "Using the Symbolics Menu" on page 201.

Transformations

You can use symbolic keywords to evaluate the Fourier, Laplace, or *z*- transform of a expression and to evaluate the inverse transform. For example, to evaluate the Fourier transform of an expression:

1. Enter the expression you want to transform.

2. Click ▪→ on the Symbolic toolbar or type [**Ctrl**] [**Shift**]. (hold down the Control and Shift keys and type a period). Mathcad displays a placeholder to the left of the symbolic equal sign, "→."

3. Type **fourier** in the placeholder, followed by a comma and the name of the transform variable.

4. Press [**Enter**] to see the result.

Note   Mathcad returns a function in a variable commonly used for the transform you perform. If the expression you are transforming already contains this variable, Mathcad avoids ambiguity by returning a function of a double variable. For example, Mathcad returns a function in the variable ω when you perform a Fourier transform. If the expression you are transforming already contains an ω, Mathcad returns a function of the variable ωω instead.

The Fourier transform result is a function of ω given by:

$$\int_{-\infty}^{+\infty} f(t)e^{-i\omega t}dt$$

Use the keyword **invfourier** to return the inverse Fourier transform as a function given by:

$$\frac{1}{2\pi}\int_{-\infty}^{+\infty} F(\omega)e^{i\omega t}d\omega$$

where $f(t)$ and $F(\omega)$ are the expressions to be transformed.

Use the keywords **laplace**, **invlaplace**, **ztrans**, and **invztrans** to perform a Laplace or *z*-transform or their inverses.

The Laplace transform result is a function of *s* given by:

$$\int_{0}^{+\infty} f(t)e^{-st}dt$$

Its inverse is given by:

$$\frac{1}{2\pi} \int_{\sigma - i\infty}^{\sigma + i\infty} F(s) e^{st} \, dt$$

where $f(t)$ and $F(s)$ are the expressions to be transformed. All singularities of $F(s)$ are to the left of the line $\text{Re}(s) = \sigma$.

The z-transform result is a function of z given by:

$$\sum_{n = 0}^{+\infty} f(n) z^{-n}$$

Its inverse is given by:

$$\frac{1}{2\pi i} \int_C F(z) z^{n - 1} \, dz$$

where $f(n)$ and $F(z)$ are the expressions to be transformed and C is a contour enclosing all singularities of the integrand.

Tip You can substitute a different variable for the one Mathcad returns from a transform or its inverse by using the **substitute** keyword.

Another way to evaluate the Fourier, Laplace, or z- transform or their inverses on an expression is to use commands on the **Symbolics** menu. For example, to find the Laplace transform of an expression:

- Enter the expression.

- Click on the transform variable.

- Choose **Transform⇒Laplace** from the **Symbolics** menu.

Keep in mind that, unlike keyword-modified expressions, expressions modified by commands from the **Symbolics** menu do not update automatically, as described in the section "Using the Symbolics Menu" on page 201.

Note Results from symbolic transformations may contain functions that are recognized by Mathcad's symbolic processor but not by its numeric processor. An example is the function *Dirac* shown in the middle of Figure 13-14. You'll find numeric definitions for this and other such functions in "Appendix A: Special Functions" on page 432, as well as in the QuickSheet titled "Special Functions."

$$\text{Dirac}\,(t)\;\text{fourier}\,,\,t\;\;\to\;1$$

Press [Ctrl] [Shift] . to insert a transform keyword.

$$\frac{3}{1+x^2}\;\text{invfourier}\,,\,x\;\;\to\;\frac{3}{2}\cdot\exp(-t)\cdot\Phi(t)\;+\;\frac{3}{2}\cdot\exp(t)\cdot\Phi(-t)$$

$$\exp(-a\cdot t)\;\text{laplace}\,,\,t\;\;\to\;\frac{1}{(s+a)}$$

$$\frac{s}{s+a}\;\text{invlaplace}\,,\,s\;\;\to\;\Delta\,(t)\;-\;a\cdot\exp(-a\cdot t)$$

← Δ (t) is an impulse at t=0. Although not numerically defined. Mathcad's symbolic processor recognizes this function. Δ (t) is also known as the Dirac function.

$$\sin\!\left(\frac{\pi}{2}\cdot t\right)\;\text{ztrans}\,,\,t\;\;\to\;\frac{z}{\left(1+z^2\right)}$$

$$\frac{z}{z-2}\;\text{invztrans}\,,\,z\;\;\to\;2^n$$

Figure 13-14: Performing symbolic transforms.

Symbolic Optimization

In general, Mathcad's symbolic and numeric processors don't communicate with one another. You can, however, make the numeric processor ask the symbolic processor for advice before starting what could be a needlessly complicated calculation.

For example, if you were to evaluate an expression such as:

$$\int_0^u \int_0^v \int_0^w x^2 + y^2 + z^2 \, dx \, dy \, dz$$

Mathcad would undertake the task of evaluating a numeric approximation of the triple integral even though one could arrive at an exact solution by first performing a few elementary calculus operations.

This happens because by itself, Mathcad's numeric processor does not simplify before plunging ahead into the calculation. Although Mathcad's symbolic processor knows all about simplifying complicated expressions, these two processors do not consult with each other, although for certain definitions, it would be helpful. To make these two processors talk to each other for a particular definition click on a definition with the right mouse button and choose **Optimize** from the popup menu.

Once you've done this, Mathcad's live symbolic processor simplifies the expression to the right of a ":=" *before* the numeric processor begins its calculations. This helps Mathcad's numeric processor evaluate the expression more quickly. It can also avoid any computational issues inherent in the numeric calculation.

If Mathcad finds a simpler form for the expression, it responds by doing the following:

• It marks the region with a red asterisk.

• It *internally* replaces what you've typed with a simplified form.

- The equivalent expression is evaluated instead of the expression you specified. To see this equivalent expression, double-click the red asterisk beside the region.

If Mathcad is unable to find a simpler form for the expression, it places a *blue* asterisk next to it.

In the previous example, the symbolic processor would examine the triple integral and return the equivalent, but much simpler expression:

$$\frac{1}{3}(w^3vu + wv^3u + wvu^3)$$

Then it uses any definitions that exist in your worksheet and simplifies the expression further. To see this expression in a popup window, click the red asterisk with the right mouse button and choose **Show Popup** from the popup menu (see Figure 13-15).

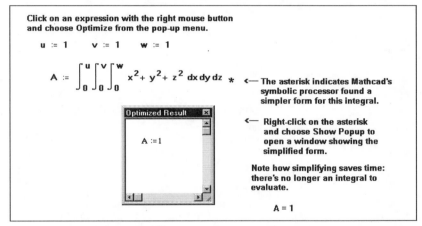

Figure 13-15: A popup window showing the equivalent expression that Mathcad actually evaluates.

To enable optimization for an entire worksheet, choose **Optimize⇒Worksheet** from the **Tools** menu. To disable optimization for an expression, right click it and uncheck **Optimize** on the popup menu. Mathcad evaluates the expression exactly as you typed it.

To disable optimization for all expressions, remove the check from **Optimize⇒Worksheet** on the **Tools** menu.

Chapter 14
Importing and Exporting Data

♦ Overview

♦ Functions for Reading and Writing Files

♦ Exchanging Data with Other Applications

♦ Data Input and Output Components

♦ Application Components

Overview

In this chapter, you will learn how to extend Mathcad's functionality by bringing the feature sets and data of other applications into your Mathcad worksheet. Likewise, you can expand the usefulness of other programs by interfacing them with Mathcad. In both cases, you take advantage of Mathcad's Object Linking and Embedding (OLE) capabilities.

Functions for Reading and Writing Files

Mathcad comes with a set of built-in functions for reading and writing files in various formats. While the File Input/Output and Data Table components discussed later in this chapter are fairly flexible in allowing you to access data files, you will need to use these command line functions in program, for reading images and WAVs, and when reading a file with global definitions.

Mathcad's built-in file access functions can be broken down into four categories:

- **ASCII Data File** functions, which allow you to create, modify, and access structured data files. Mathcad contains three built-in functions for accessing ASCII data files: READPRN, WRITEPRN, and APPENDPRN.

- **Binary Data File** functions, which allow you to create and access binary data files. Mathcad contains two built-in functions for accessing binary data files: READBIN and WRITEBIN.

- **Image** functions, which allow you to create and access file formats designed to store image data. Mathcad contains eighteen built-in functions specifically for accessing image files. See "Image Processing Functions" on page 253 for a complete list.

- **WAV** functions, which allow you to create and edit pulse-code-modulated files stored in Microsoft's WAV format. Mathcad contains three built-in functions specifically for accessing WAV files: READWAV, WRITEWAV, and GETWAVINFO.

See Chapter 16, "Functions," and on-line Help for more information.

Exchanging Data with Other Applications

Mathcad *components* are specialized OLE objects in your Mathcad worksheet. They allow you to exchange data with other applications or sources. *Application components* allow you to access functions and data from other computational applications such as Excel, SmartSketch, and MATLAB. Unlike other kinds of OLE objects described in the section "Inserting Objects" in Chapter 10, a component can receive data from Mathcad, return data to Mathcad, or do both, dynamically linking the object to your Mathcad computations.

Components that connect Mathcad to other applications include:

- File Input and Output components for reading and writing data files.
- Axum, for creating highly customizable Axum graphs
- Excel, for accessing cells and formulas in a Microsoft Excel spreadsheet.
- MATLAB, for accessing the programming environment of MATLAB.
- ODBC Input for retrieving data from an ODBC-compliant database that supports SQL.
- SmartSketch, for creating 2D drawings and designs.
- S-PLUS Graph, for creating S-PLUS graphs.
- S-PLUS Script, for accessing the programming environment of S-PLUS.

Note To use an application component, you must have the application for that component installed, but not necessarily running, on your system.

Other built-in components that may be customized using scripting:

- Data Acquisition, for sending data to or getting data from a measurement device
- Mathsoft Controls, for creating custom forms controls such as buttons and text boxes

For linking dynamically to an object for which Mathcad does not have a dedicated component, see "Scripting Custom OLE Automation Objects" on page 243.

Tip See "Using Mathcad with Other Applications" in **QuickSheets** under the **Help** menu for a variety of example files.

How to Use Components

In general, components receive *input* from one or more Mathcad variables, perform operations on the data you specify, and return *output* to other Mathcad variables. An "input variable" is a scalar, vector, matrix, or, in some cases, a string, that you have already defined in your Mathcad worksheet. It contains the data that is passed into a component. Output from a component (again, either a scalar, vector, matrix, or string) is then assigned to a Mathcad variable. This variable is referred to as an "output variable."

The basic steps for using a component are as follows:

1. Insert the component.
2. Specify the input variable(s) and output variable(s).
3. Configure the component to handle inputs from and return outputs to Mathcad.

Since some components only take input or only send output, these steps differ slightly for each component. The ideas presented in the steps that follow provide an overview of the process.

Note   You cannot insert a component into an existing variable definition. You must click in a blank area of the worksheet, insert the component, then fill in the variable name after the component is created.

Step 1: Inserting a component

To insert a component into a Mathcad worksheet:

1. Click in a blank area of your Mathcad worksheet. Click below or to the right of definitions for any variables that will become inputs to the component.
2. Choose **Data**, **Controls**, or **Component** from the **Insert** menu. This launches the Component Wizard for the component type you are trying to insert.
3. Choose a component from the list and click "Next" or "Finish," depending on the component you choose. You may see additional dialog boxes that let you specify properties of the component before it is inserted. When you click "Finish," the component is inserted into your worksheet.

If you don't see a Wizard when you choose one of the components from the Insert Component dialog box, you'll immediately see the component inserted into your worksheet with some default properties.

Each component has its own particular appearance, but all components have one or more placeholders to the left of the :=, if it returns data to Mathcad, and/or at the bottom of the component, if it receives data from Mathcad. For example, the Excel component (with one input and two outputs) looks like this when inserted into your worksheet:

The placeholder(s) at the bottom of the component are for the names of previously defined input variables. The placeholder(s) you see to the left of the := are for the output variables.

After you fill in the placeholders for the input and output variables, you can hide the variables by clicking with the right mouse button on the component and choosing **Hide Arguments** from the pop up menu.

When you insert an application component, you see a small window on that application's environment embedded in your Mathcad worksheet. When you *double-click* the component, the component is *in-place activated,* and Mathcad's menus and toolbars change to those of the other application. This gives you access to the features of that application without leaving the Mathcad environment.

Step 2: Configuring a component

Once you've inserted a component, you can configure its properties so that the component knows how to handle any inputs it receives from Mathcad and what to send as output. To configure the properties for a component:

1. Click on the component once to select it.

2. Right click on the component to see a pop up menu.

3. Choose **Properties** from the pop up menu.

The settings in the Properties dialog box differ for each component. For example, the Properties dialog box for the Excel component lets you specify the starting cells in which the input values are stored and the cell range from which the output is sent.

To add an input or output variable, right click on the component and choose **Add Input Variable** or **Add Output Variable** from the pop up menu. To eliminate an input or output, choose **Remove Input Variable** or **Remove Output Variable** from the menu. Some components limit you to a finite number of inputs and outputs in which case Add Input Variable or Add Output Variable is grayed out on the pop up menu.

Tip   You can hide the input and output variables for a component by right clicking on the component and choosing **Hide Arguments** from the pop up menu.

Note   Some components require you to use certain variables within the component itself in order to exchange data with Mathcad

Step 3: Exchanging data

Once you've configured the component, click outside it elsewhere in the worksheet. At that point, the region recalculates and data exchange takes place: data passes from the input variable(s) into the component, the component processes the data, and the output variable(s) receive output from the component. This exchange happens whenever:

- You click on the component and press [**F9**] to recalculate the region.

- The input variables change and Automatic Calculation is turned on.

- You choose **Calculate**⇒**Calculate Worksheet** from the **Tools** menu.

Tip   Some components allow you to save the file with which the component exchanges data as a separate file. Click on a component with the right mouse button and choose **Save As...** from the pop up menu.

Data Input and Output Components

File Input and File Output

File Input, File Output, and Data Tables can be found under **Data** in the **Insert** menu. Use File Input/Output to link a particular data file dynamically to a Mathcad worksheet. For File Input, when the data source is updated, so are calculations dependent on it in the worksheet. For File Output, the data file is updated whenever calculations in the worksheet change. Use Data Tables to copy data from the clipboard or a data file or to enter data by hand into a table in your worksheet.

Tip   Mathcad also provides a number of built-in functions for importing ASCII data files, binary files, and image files. These are useful inside program loops and in global assignments, where components cannot be used. See "File Access Functions" on page 250.

When you use File Input or File Output from the **Insert ⇒ Data** menu pick, you'll see an icon and the path to the data file with an assignment operator (:=) and an empty placeholder. Enter the name of a Mathcad variable in the placeholder. When you

click outside this new equation region, the data file is read, and the data is assigned to the Mathcad array variable entered in the placeholder. The data can now be used like any other Mathcad array or matrix.

Mathcad File Input and Output components can import and export real numbers, complex numbers, numbers with exponential notation, and strings from the various file formats. File Input and File Output also accept a variety of delimeters between data fields in text files, including tabs, semicolons, spaces, and commas. The delimeter must be consistent throughout the file. Mathcad tries to determine if data entries are strings automatically by comparing against various standard number formats.

Note   If a data file has alphabetic characters in some cells, or a space between characters when spaces are not the data delimeter, then data are imported as a string variable, and display in quotes. Empty cells are imported as 0.

Each time you calculate the worksheet, Mathcad re-reads the data from the file you have specified. Figure 14-1 shows an example. If you want to import data from a file just once into Mathcad using a Data Table, see "Importing Once from a Data File" on page 220.

To read in a different data file or a different type of data file:

1. Right click on the component and select **Properties** from the component pop up menu.

2. On the File Options tab, select your file type from the dropdown list, and browse or type the name of the file you'd like to open.

3. If desired, click the "Data Range" tab and select a subset of the rows, columns or cells in your data file.

4. On the File Options tab, click "Open."

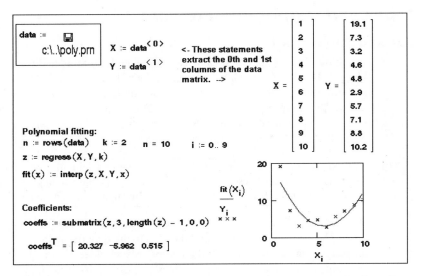

Figure 14-1: Reading in data from a data file. Whenever you calculate the worksheet, the data file is read in.

Tip   All file reading and writing components described in this section can be created using buttons on the **Standard** toolbar in Mathcad. To add these buttons to your toolbar, right click on the toolbar and add the desired buttons to the list.

Importing Once from a Data File

File Input and Output components read the contents of their associated data file every time their regions are calculated. You can use a Data Table component to import a data file only once.

1. Insert an Data Table by selecting **Data⇒Table** from the **Insert** menu.
2. In the placeholder that appears to the left of the table, enter the name of the Mathcad variable to which this data will be assigned.
3. Click on the table to select it. Then right click on the table and choose **Import** from the popup menu.
4. The Read from File dialog box appears. In the "Files of type" dropdown list, choose the type of file you'd like to import. If desired, click the data range tab and select a subset of the rows, columns or cells in your data file. Use the dialog box to browse to the data file and click "Open."

The data from the data file appears in your worksheet in the table.

ODBC Input

The Open Database Connectivity (ODBC) Input component allows you to retrieve information from a database that supports SQL in its ODBC driver, like Microsoft Access or FoxPro. There are some programs that have SQL support within their application, but do not support SQL in their ODBC driver, such as Microsoft Excel.

In order to establish a link to a database on your system or network, in **Start⇒Settings** open **Administrative Tools⇒Data Sources (ODBC)** control panel (Windows 2000 or XP) or ODBC Data Sources control in Windows 98 and NT. For more information about ODBC and SQL support, check the documentation that comes with your database application.

Inserting an ODBC Input component

When you insert an ODBC Input component, the Component Wizard presents you with the following options:

- **Select ODBC Data Source**. Specifies the data source to access with the component.
- **Username/Password**. If the data source you are attempting to access is password-protected, you will need to enter a username and password. If the data source is not password protected, these fields must be left blank.
- **Select Table**. Selects the table to access. You can only access one table per ODBC Input component.
- **Select Fields**. Selects the fields to access and pass to Mathcad. By default, only field types supported by Mathcad are shown.
- **Show fields with unsupported data types**. Displays those fields Mathcad cannot read.

Once a link to a particular database has been established, you may want to change the data source, the table, or the columns of data to be imported to your Mathcad worksheet.

To change the data imported from an ODBC Input component:

1. Right click the component and select **Properties** from the pop up menu.
2. On the Data Source tab, change the database, table, and columns of data as necessary. If required, specify a valid username and password.
3. Click "OK" to close the dialog box and update your worksheet.

Note You can change the order in which the fields of your database are stored in the columns of the output matrix in Mathcad. To do so, right click the ODBC Input component and choose **Properties** from the pop up menu. Navigate to the Advanced tab, and rearrange the order of the fields in the columns of the matrix using the "move up" and "move down" buttons.

To filter your data before bringing it into a Mathcad output variable, you can query your database directly through the ODBC Input component using a SQL "where" statement.

To filter your data through the ODBC Input component:

1. Right click the component and select **Properties** from the pop up menu.
2. On the Advanced tab, check "Select data rows using a SQL 'where' clause" and type a "where" statement in the text box.
3. Click "OK" to close the dialog box and update your worksheet.

Figure 14-2 shows the use of a SQL "where" statement.

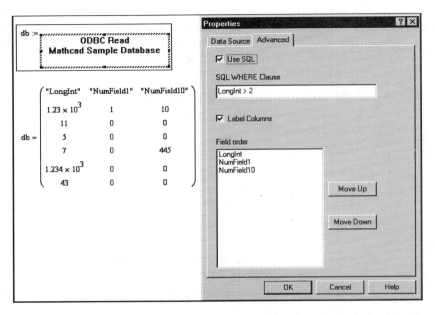

Figure 14-2: Using a SQL "where" statement to filter data through the ODBC component.

Tip Checking the "Show fields with unsupported data types" option in the ODBC Input component Wizard or on the Data Source page of the **Properties** dialog box displays all data fields, even those not supported by Mathcad variables. For example, Mathcad does not support any time data types, but you can select and display time indices from your database in a Mathcad output variable.

Application Components

Application components allow you to exchange data between Mathcad and another application via an ActiveX control. When you insert an application component, a document object for the application is created in your worksheet. If the component wizard allows you to create this object from an existing file, a copy of the file is inserted into your worksheet. Changing the document will not change the original file. If you want your component to access and update a file on your system, use the **File Input/ Output** components discussed previously in the section "Data Input and Output Components" on page 219.

Excel Component

The Excel component allows you to exchange data with and access the functions of Microsoft Excel (version 7 or higher), if it is installed on your system.

Note The Excel component accepts scalars, vectors, two-dimensional matrices, and strings as input and output.

Tip If you only need to import or export a static data file in Excel format, use File Input and Output described above.

Inserting an Excel component

When you insert an Excel component, the Component Wizard offers you the following options:

- **Create an empty Excel Worksheet**. Creates your component using a blank file based on the Excel worksheet template.

- **Create from file**. Creates your component using a specific Excel worksheet. If you already have an Excel worksheet and want to supply input data to it from Mathcad, or want to use its results in your Mathcad worksheet, use this option.

- **Display as Icon**. Inserts your Excel component in icon form. This is particularly useful if your worksheet is fairly large, or if viewing the results in Excel is not important.

- **The number of input and output variables**. Controls the number of multiple input and output variables your component is inserted with. The number of input and output variables you can pass between Mathcad and Excel is only limited by the memory and speed of your computer. There is no set limit.

- **Input ranges**. Specifies the cells in which the values of each input variable from Mathcad will be stored. Enter the starting cell, which is the cell that will hold the element in the upper left corner of an input array. For example, for an input variable containing a 3×3 matrix of values, you can specify A1 as the starting cell, and the values will be placed in cells A1 through C3.

- **Output ranges**. Specifies the cells whose values you want to pass back to Mathcad. For example, enter C2:L11 to extract the values in cells C2 through L11 and create a 10×10 matrix.

Tip You can specify a particular Excel worksheet and cell range using standard Excel notation such as Sheet2!B2:C2. You can also specify named cells and cell ranges.

When you finish using the Wizard, the Excel component appears in your worksheet with placeholders for the input and output variables. Enter the names of input variables in the bottom placeholders. Enter the names of the output variables into the placeholders to the left of the :=. When you click outside the component, input variables are sent to Excel from Mathcad and a range of cells are returned to Mathcad.

Figure 14-3 shows an example of an Excel component in a Mathcad worksheet.

Note By default, the Excel component displays only some of the rows and columns of the underlying spreadsheet object. To see more or fewer rows and columns, click the component so that you see handles along its sides. Resize the component by dragging a handle. To see different rows or columns than the ones shown in the view, double-click the component and use the scroll bars to find the rows or columns of interest.

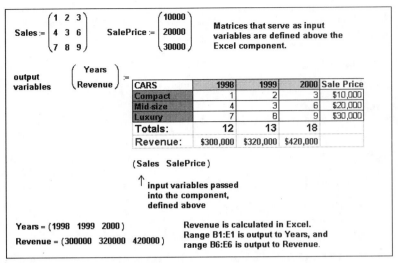

$$Sales := \begin{pmatrix} 1 & 2 & 3 \\ 4 & 3 & 6 \\ 7 & 8 & 9 \end{pmatrix} \qquad SalePrice := \begin{pmatrix} 10000 \\ 20000 \\ 30000 \end{pmatrix}$$

Matrices that serve as input variables are defined above the Excel component.

output variables $\begin{pmatrix} Years \\ Revenue \end{pmatrix} :=$

CARS	1998	1999	2000	Sale Price
Compact	1	2	3	$10,000
Mid size	4	3	6	$20,000
Luxury	7	8	9	$30,000
Totals:	12	13	18	
Revenue:	$300,000	$320,000	$420,000	

(Sales   SalePrice)

↑ **input variables passed into the component, defined above**

Years = (1998   1999   2000)

Revenue = (300000   320000   420000)

Revenue is calculated in Excel. Range B1:E1 is output to Years, and range B6:E6 is output to Revenue.

Figure 14-3: An Excel spreadsheet object in a Mathcad worksheet.

Changing the inputs and outputs

If you add input or output variables, you will need to specify which cells in the component will store the new input and which will provide the new output. You can do so in the Excel component's Properties dialog on either the Inputs or Outputs tab. From here, you can also change the cell ranges for inputs and outputs initially specified in the Setup Wizard.

Axum/S-PLUS Graph and Script Components

The Axum/S-PLUS Graph and Script components allow you to access the advanced charting capabilities of Insightful's Axum and S-PLUS programs. You must have Axum 5 or higher, or S-PLUS 4.5 or higher installed on your system in order to insert an Axum/S-PLUS Graph component.

Inserting an Axum or S-PLUS Graph component

The Component Wizard offers you the following options:

- **Axis and Plot Type**. Allows you to customize the graph displayed.

- **The number of input variables**. Controls the number of input variables to insert the component. The maximum number of input variables for Axum and S-PLUS components is four.

- **Use Last Input for Conditioning Variables**. Defines a conditioning variable for creating a Trellis graph.

When you click outside the component, input variables from Mathcad are sent to Axum/S-PLUS and the graph updates.

Note If you want to create an Axum graph component with two independent traces, define *x*- and *y*-vectors for each plot. Then, choose the plot type "Scatter Plots of XY Pairs" from the Axum Graph dialog and specify the input variables corresponding to your vectors of data. Enter the vector names in the placeholders in *xy*-pairs, i.e., (x1 y1 x2 y2).

If you change the vectors of data upon which your Axum graph component is dependent, your graph updates automatically. Figure 14-4 shows an Axum graph that has been customized with axes labels, a title, and text and graphic annotations.

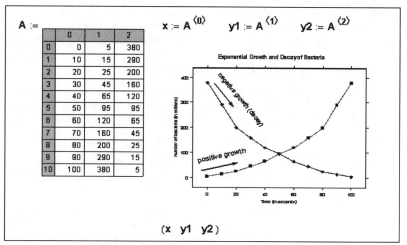

Figure 14-4: An Axum graph in a Mathcad worksheet.

Inserting an Axum or S-PLUS Script Component

When you insert an Axum or S-PLUS Script component in your worksheet, the Component Wizard offers you the following options:

- **S-PLUS Script Text.** You can enter your S-PLUS Script into the component wizard. If you have an S-PLUS script (*.ssc) file, you can leave this blank.

- **The number of input and output variables.** Controls the number of input and output variables your component is inserted with. The Axum/S-PLUS Script component is limited to four inputs and four outputs.

Tip To import an S-PLUS script file into your component, right click the component and choose **Edit Script...** from the popup menu to access the script editor. In the script editor, import your script by choosing **Import** from the **File** menu.

When you click outside the component, input variables from Mathcad are sent to Axum/S-PLUS and values from Axum/S-PLUS are assigned to output variables in Mathcad.

By default, the Mathcad input variables will be sent into the component as variables named **in0**, **in1**, **in2**, and **in3**. The Axum/S-PLUS variables **out0**, **out1**, **out2**, and **out3** will define the output variables to be created in Mathcad. You can change these names on the Input Variable Names and Output Variable Names tabs of the component's Properties dialog.

MATLAB Component

The MATLAB component allows you to exchange data with and access the programming environment of The MathWorks' MATLAB Professional 4.2c or higher, if it is installed on your system.

Tip If you only need to import or export a static data file in MATLAB format, use the File Input/Output component as described previously under "Data Input and Output Components" on page 219.

Note Some versions of MATLAB support multidimensional arrays and other complex data structures. While you may use these structures within the MATLAB component, you may pass only scalars, vectors, and two-dimensional arrays from Mathcad to the MATLAB component and vice versa.

Inserting a MATLAB component

Inserting a MATLAB component from the Component Wizard places the component into your worksheet with no options. However, before you can actually use your MATLAB component, you must first edit the component's script.

To use the MATLAB component to perform calculations in MATLAB:

1. Right click the MATLAB component in your Mathcad worksheet and select **Edit Script** from the pop up menu. This action opens a text window for entering MATLAB commands.

2. Edit the MATLAB script to your liking. Be sure to use appropriate MATLAB variable names to take input from Mathcad and provide output. If you have a MATLAB .m file, you can import it into the component as well, by choosing **Import** from the **File** menu in the Script Editor window.

When you click outside the component, input variables from Mathcad are sent to MATLAB, and arrays from MATLAB are assigned to output variables in Mathcad.

By default, the data in the Mathcad input variables are sent into MATLAB variables named **in0**, **in1**, **in2**, and **in3**. The MATLAB variables **out0**, **out1**, **out2**, and **out3** define the data to be passed to the Mathcad output variables. To change these names, choose **Properties** from the component's pop up menu and type in new names in the Inputs and Outputs tabs.

SmartSketch

SmartSketch is a 2D drawing and design tool developed by Intergraph. The SmartSketch component allows you to create in a Mathcad worksheet SmartSketch drawings whose dimensions are computationally linked to your Mathcad calculations. For example, your Mathcad equations can drive the size of drawing objects.

The SmartSketch component makes Mathcad the ideal platform for creating technical illustrations and specification-driven designs. You can use the SmartSketch component if you have SmartSketch 3 or higher, Imagination Engineer, or Imagineer Technical 2.

Inserting a SmartSketch drawing

When you insert a SmartSketch component, the Component Wizard offers you the following options:

- **New SmartSketch Document**. Creates your component with a blank SmartSketch drawing file.

- **From Existing File**. Creates your component using a specific SmartSketch drawing file. If you already have a drawing file and want to supply input data to it from Mathcad or want to use its results in your Mathcad worksheet, use this option.

- **The number of input and output variables**. Controls the number of input and output variables your component is inserted with. The number of input and output variables you can pass between Mathcad and SmartSketch is only limited by the memory and speed of your computer. There is no set limit.

- **Input and Output Variable names**. If you are creating your component with an existing drawing file, specify the SmartSketch variable corresponding to each input or output variable.

When you click "Finish," the SmartSketch component appears in your worksheet with placeholders for the input and output variables. Enter the names of Mathcad input variables in the bottom placeholders. Enter the output variables in the placeholders to the left of the :=.

Next, you need to bind variables, dimensions, or symbols in your drawing to the inputs or outputs. Each SmartSketch drawing contains a Variable Table where you can define variables and edit dimensions. The SmartSketch component binds these entries to your worksheet inputs and outputs. Right click on the component in Mathcad and choose Properties from the pop up menu, where you can specify:

- **Input names.** The dimension, symbol, or variable names used in the SmartSketch drawing that are controlled by the inputs to the SmartSketch component. Choose a dimension or variable name from the drop-down list.

- **Output names.** The dimension, symbol, or variable names used in the SmartSketch drawing that define the output variables in Mathcad. Choose a dimension or variable name from the drop-down list.

When you click outside the component, input values are sent to the SmartSketch drawing from Mathcad and values are returned to Mathcad as output.

Note Input values that do not have units attached are passed in SI units. For example, if you send 2.0 as input for a length, it is assumed to be 2.0 meters. SmartSketch, by default, converts this to the display units (inches by default) and creates the drawing.

Tip If the drawing is so large that it extends beyond the component window, right click on the component, choose **Properties** from the pop up menu, and click the box next to Automatic Resizing.

Figure 14-5 shows a SmartSketch drawing inserted into a Mathcad worksheet. The values from the variables *RadiusA*, *RadiusB*, and *Distance* are sent to SmartSketch as input and used to create the drawing. The variables *WrapB*, *BLength*, and *Beta1* are output variables.

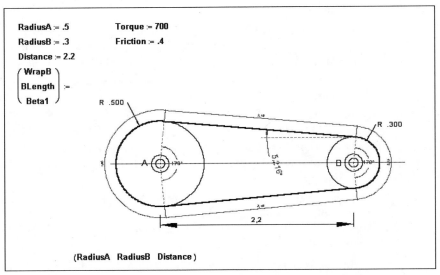

Figure 14-5: Integrating a SmartSketch drawing into a Mathcad worksheet

Changing the inputs and outputs

If you add input or output variables, you will need to specify which variables in your drawing will store the new input and which will provide the new output. You can do so in the component's Properties dialog, on either the Inputs or Outputs tab. You can also change the variables mapped to inputs and outputs initially specified in the Setup Wizard.

Note   In order for the dimensions in a drawing to resize relative to any changes to the dimensions, check the box next to **Maintain Relationships** under the **Tools** menu in SmartSketch. To verify this setting, double-click on the component and choose **Tools** from the menu bar.

For more information on SmartSketch, refer to the tutorials and documentation available from the **Help** menu in SmartSketch. Example Mathcad files containing SmartSketch components can be found in "Using Mathcad with Other Applications" in **QuickSheets** under the **Help** menu.

The Data Acquisition Control

The Data Acquisition Control (DAC) allows you to read data directly from or send data directly to a measurement device installed in your system. The DAC eliminates the step of saving data to an external file before importing your data into Mathcad for display and analysis, and to some degree allows for "real time" data logging and analysis. The current version of the DAC supports National Instruments E-series and Measurement Computing (formerly Computerboards) data acquisition cards and boards. A complete list of supported devices is available in the online **Developer's Reference**.

Note   If you are using the DAC control to bring analog waveform data into Mathcad for "real time" analysis, be sure that Automatic Calculation, under the **Tools** menu, is turned on. The degree to which "real time" data logging and analysis is possible depends on the size of the data being transferred, the complexity of the calculations being performed, and the speed of your computer. If at some point Mathcad is unable to keep up with the data transfer or calculations, real-time analysis is no longer possible.

Tip   You can simulate a waveform in Mathcad and use the DAC to send it out to a test device, and then have the results returned to Mathcad via another DAC.

Note   The DAC is not a native component, but rather is embedded in a scriptable object component. As such, some scripting may be necessary for your DAC to work as desired. If you plan to use the DAC in your worksheet, you should first read the section on "Scripting Custom OLE Automation Objects" on page 243.

Inserting a Data Acquisition control

Inserting a DAC from the Component Wizard places the component into your Mathcad worksheet with no options.

Note   The Data Acquisition component is only visible in the Components Wizard dialog box when you have a supported data device attached.

The DAC is inserted into the worksheet with default properties, namely, one output and single point analog data collection. These properties are easily modified, however, using either the object's Properties dialog box, the Script Editor, or the user interface for the control, shown in Figure 14-6.

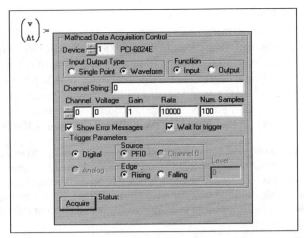

Figure 14-6: User Interface of the Data Acquisition Control (DAC).

Customizing a Data Acquisition Control

Once you've inserted a DAC, you can modify it in several ways:

- **The DAC User Interface**. The DAC is inserted with a visible user interface, where you can tailor the data stream to or from the attached measurement device.

- **Adding or Removing Inputs and Outputs**. The DAC supports up to four inputs and four outputs. The number of inputs and outputs can be specified by right clicking on the DAC and selecting **Add or Remove Input Variable** or **Output Variable** from the pop up menu or by selecting **Properties** from the pop up menu.

- **The DAC Script**. In addition to changing the DAC's user interface, you can also change its functionality programmatically. The function of the DAC is driven by a Visual Basic script, which you can edit by right clicking on the DAC and choosing **Edit Script** from the pop up menu.

Note For more information about the properties and methods associated with the DAC and other Scriptable Object components, see the **Developer's Reference** under the **Help** menu.

Example worksheets under "Using Mathcad with Other Applications" in the **QuickSheets** under the **Help** menu show usage of the DAC for single point and analog waveform input and output. Context sensitive help is available for all methods, properties, and events associated with the Mathcad Data Acquisition control. You can access context sensitive help by looking at the AnalogIO object in the Visual Basic object browser and clicking on the help button.

Chapter 15
Extending and Automating Mathcad

- ♦ Overview
- ♦ Programming within Mathcad
- ♦ Building Function DLLs
- ♦ Creating Your Own Components
- ♦ Accessing Mathcad from Within Another Application

Overview

Mathcad comes with functions and operators spanning mathematical disciplines from simple arithmetic to trigonometry to calculus and beyond. Even so, you may find that the basic functionality is not enough to meet your needs. With that in mind, Mathcad can be extended in several ways, outlined in this section.

Programming within Mathcad

A Mathcad program is a special kind of expression made up of a sequence of statements created using *programming operators*, available on the Programming toolbar. You can open the **Programming** toolbar from the **View** menu.

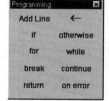

You can think of a program as a compound expression that involves potentially many programming operators. Like any expression, a program returns a value — a scalar, vector, array, nested array, or string — when evaluated either numerically or symbolically. Just as you can define a variable or function in terms of an expression, you can also define them in terms of a program.

Note   The symbolic processor treats any units it encounters in a program as undefined variables. To avoid problems — especially with unit conversions — make sure any program you evaluate symbolically does not involve units.

Defining a Program

The following example shows how to make a simple program to define the function:

$$f(x, w) = \log\left(\frac{x}{w}\right)$$

Although the example chosen is simple enough not to require programming, it illustrates how to separate the statements that make up a program and how to use the local assignment operator, "←."

Note A program can have any number of statements. To add a statement, click [Add Line] on the Programming toolbar or press **[**. Mathcad inserts a placeholder below whatever statement you've selected. To delete the placeholder, click on it and press **[Bksp]**.

Tip You can use the **Add Line** operator in any placeholder in a program, including those associated with other programming operators such as **if**, **for**, and **while**.

1. Type the left side of the function definition, followed by a "**:=**". Make sure the placeholder is selected.

    $$f(x,w) := \blacksquare$$

2. Click [Add Line] on the Programming toolbar or press **]**. You'll see a vertical bar with two placeholders, which will hold the statements that comprise your program.

    $$f(x,w) := \begin{array}{|l} \blacksquare \\ \blacksquare \end{array}$$

3. Click in the top placeholder and type **z**. Click [←] on the Programming toolbar. Alternatively, press **{** to insert a "←," the local definition symbol.

    $$f(x,w) := \begin{array}{|l} z \leftarrow \blacksquare \\ \blacksquare \end{array}$$

4. Type **x/w** in the placeholder to the right of the local definition symbol. Press **[Tab]** to move to the bottom placeholder.

    $$f(x,w) := \begin{array}{|l} z \leftarrow \dfrac{x}{w} \\ \blacksquare \end{array}$$

5. Enter the value to be returned by the program, in this case **log(z)**.

    $$f(x,w) := \begin{array}{|l} z \leftarrow \dfrac{x}{w} \\ \log(z) \end{array}$$

    You can now use this function just as you would any other function in your worksheet.

Note You cannot use Mathcad's usual assignment operator, "**:=**," inside a program. You must use the local assignment operator, represented by "**←**," instead. Variables defined inside a program with the local assignment operator, such as z in the example above, are local to the program and are undefined elsewhere in the worksheet. However, within a program, you can refer to Mathcad variables and functions defined previously in the worksheet.

Note Certain operators on the **Programming** toolbar insert with visible text. When inserting a **for**, **while**, **if**, **otherwise**, **break**, **continue**, **return**, or **on error** operator, you must use the toolbar button or keystroke. Typing in the word "break," for example, is not the same as inserting the **break** operator.

Figure 15-1 shows a more complex example involving the quadratic formula. Although you can define the quadratic formula with a single statement as shown in the top half of the figure, you may find it easier to define it with a series of simple statements as shown in the bottom half.

As with any expression, a Mathcad program must have a value. This value is simply the value of the last statement executed by the program. It can be a string expression, a single number, or an array of numbers. It can even be an array of arrays (see "Nested Arrays" on page 63).

$$q(a,b,c) := \frac{-b + \sqrt{b^2 - 4 \cdot a \cdot c}}{2 \cdot a}$$

Although you can define complicated functions all on one line...

$$r(a,b,c) := \begin{vmatrix} \text{discr} \leftarrow b^2 - 4 \cdot a \cdot c \\ \text{num} \leftarrow -b + \sqrt{\text{discr}} \\ \text{denom} \leftarrow 2 \cdot a \\ \frac{\text{num}}{\text{denom}} \end{vmatrix}$$

...it's sometimes easier to break them up into simpler steps anyway.

Figure 15-1: A more complex function defined in terms of both an expression and a program.

You can also write a Mathcad program to return a *symbolic* expression. When you evaluate a program using the symbolic equal sign, "→," described in Chapter 13, "Symbolic Calculation," Mathcad passes the expression to its symbolic processor and, when possible, returns a simplified symbolic expression. You can use Mathcad's ability to evaluate programs symbolically to generate complicated symbolic expressions, polynomials, and matrices. Figure 15-2 shows a function that, when evaluated symbolically, generates symbolic polynomials.

A function to generate a polynomial.

$$f(n) := \begin{vmatrix} a \leftarrow 0 \\ i \leftarrow 0 \\ \text{while} \quad i \leq n \\ \quad \begin{vmatrix} a \leftarrow [a + (1 + x)^i] \\ i \leftarrow i + 1 \end{vmatrix} \\ a \end{vmatrix}$$

<-- Mathcad can evaluate the program symbolically even though x is undefined.

Evaluate symbolically . . .

$$f(3) \text{ expand} \rightarrow 4 + 6 \cdot x + 4 \cdot x^2 + x^3$$

<-- Expand symbolic keyword expands the result. Press [Ctrl][Shift][period] for the symbolic keyword operator.

Figure 15-2: Using a Mathcad program to generate a symbolic expression.

Note Programs that include the **return** and **on error** statements, described on page 238 and page 239, cannot be evaluated symbolically since the symbolic processor does not recognize these operators.

Online Help The "Programming" section in the **QuickSheets** under the **Help** menu provides examples you can modify. You can also download the module "Programming in Mathcad" from www.mathcad.com for more detailed examples and explanations.

Conditional Statements

In general, Mathcad evaluates each statement in your program from the top down. There may be times, however, when you want Mathcad to evaluate a statement only when a particular condition is met. You can do this by including an **if** operator.

For example, suppose you want to define a function that forms a semicircle around the origin but is otherwise constant. To do this:

1. Type the left side of the function definition, followed by a ": =". Make sure the placeholder is selected.

2. Click Add Line on the Programming toolbar. Alternatively, press]. You'll see a vertical bar with two placeholders. These placeholders will hold the statements making up your program.

3. Click if on the Programming toolbar in the top placeholder. Alternatively, press }. Do not type "if."

4. Enter a Boolean expression in the right placeholder using one of the relational operators on the Boolean toolbar. In the left placeholder, type the value you want the program to return whenever the expression in the right placeholder is true. If necessary, add more placeholders by clicking Add Line.

5. Select the remaining placeholder and click otherwise on the Programming toolbar or press [Ctrl] 3.

6. Type the value you want the program to return if the condition in the first statement is false.

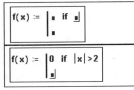

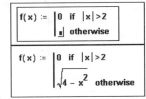

Figure 15-3 shows a plot of this function.

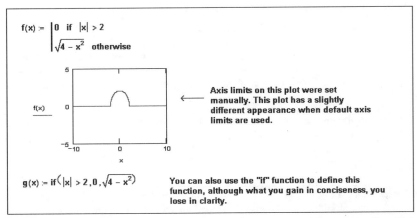

$$f(x) := \begin{array}{|ll} 0 & \text{if } |x| > 2 \\ \sqrt{4 - x^2} & \text{otherwise} \end{array}$$

Axis limits on this plot were set manually. This plot has a slightly different appearance when default axis limits are used.

$$g(x) := \text{if}\left(|x| > 2, 0, \sqrt{4 - x^2}\right)$$

You can also use the "if" function to define this function, although what you gain in conciseness, you lose in clarity.

*Figure 15-3: Using the **if** operator to define a piecewise continuous function.*

Note   The **if** operator in a Mathcad program is not the same as the *if* function (see "Piecewise Continuous Functions" on page 254). Although it is not hard to define a simple program using the *if* function, as shown in Figure 15-3, the *if* function can become unwieldy when the number of branches exceeds two.

Note   When using a block of conditional statements in a program, you should always end the block with an **otherwise** operator. Failing to do so may cause an error when your program is evaluated.

Looping

One of the greatest strengths of programmability is the ability to execute a sequence of statements repeatedly in a loop. Mathcad provides two loop structures. The choice of which loop to use depends on how you plan to tell the loop to stop executing.

- If you know exactly how many times you want a loop to execute, use a **for** loop.

- If you want the loop to stop when a condition has been met, but you don't know how many loops will be required, use a **while** loop.

Tip   See "Controlling Program Execution" on page 237 for methods to interrupt calculation within the body of a loop.

For Loops

A **for** loop terminates after a predetermined number of iterations. Iteration is controlled by an *iteration variable* defined at the top of the loop. The definition of the iteration variable is local to the program.

To create a **for** loop:

1. Click ▭ **for** ▭ on the Programming toolbar or press [**Ctrl**] ". Do not type the word "for."

2. Type the name of the iteration variable in the placeholder to the left of the "∈."

3. Enter the range of values the iteration variable should take in the placeholder to the right of the "∈." You usually specify this range the same way you would for a range variable (see page 103).

4. Type the expression you want to evaluate in the remaining placeholder. This expression generally involves the iteration variable. If necessary, add placeholders by clicking ▭ Add Line ▭ on the Programming toolbar.

The upper half of Figure 15-4 shows this **for** loop being used to add a sequence of integers.

Note   Although the expression to the right of the ▮ for ▮ is usually a range, it can also be a vector or a list of scalars, ranges, and vectors separated by commas. The lower half of Figure 15-4 shows an example in which the iteration variable is defined as the elements of two vectors.

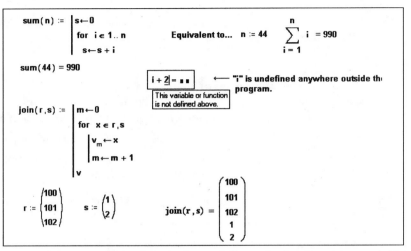

Figure 15-4: Using a **for** *loop with two different kinds of iteration variables.*

While Loops

A **while** loop is driven by the truth of some condition. Because of this, you don't need to know in advance how many times the loop will execute. It is important, however, to have a statement somewhere, within the loop, that eventually makes the condition *false*. Otherwise, the loop executes indefinitely.

To create a **while** loop:

1. Click ▮ while ▮ on the Programming toolbar or press [**Ctrl**] **]** . Do not type the word "while."

2. Click in the top placeholder and type a condition. This is typically a Boolean expression like the one shown.

3. Type the expression you want evaluated in the remaining placeholder. If necessary, add placeholders by clicking ▮ Add Line ▮ on the Programming toolbar.

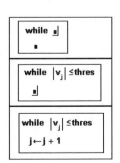

Figure 15-5 shows a larger program incorporating the above loop.

Upon encountering a **while** loop, Mathcad checks the condition. If the condition is true, Mathcad executes the body of the loop and checks the condition again. If the condition is false, Mathcad exits the loop.

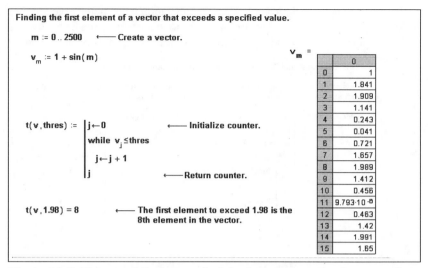

Figure 15-5: Using a **while** *loop to find the first occurrence of a particular number in a matrix.*

Controlling Program Execution

The Programming toolbar in Mathcad includes three **operators** for controlling program execution:

- **Break**. Used within a **for** or **while** loop to interrupt the loop when a condition occurs and move execution to the next statement outside the loop.

- **Continue**: Used within a **for** or **while** loop to interrupt the current iteration and force program execution to continue with the next iteration of the loop.

- **Return**: Stops a program and returns a particular value from within the program rather than from the last statement evaluated.

Break and Continue

It is often useful to ignore iterations of a loop upon the occurrence of some condition. Mathcad offers two programming operators for this purpose: **break**, if you want to exit the loop completely, thereby ignoring all further iterations; and **continue** if you want to ignore the current iteration and proceed to the next one. To insert the **break** operator, click on a placeholder inside a loop and click ▊break▊ on the Programming toolbar or press [**Ctrl**] {. Do not type the word "break." You typically insert **break** into the left-hand placeholder of an **if** operator. The **break** is evaluated only when the right-hand side of the **if** is *true*.

To insert the **continue** operator, click on a placeholder inside a loop and click ▊continue▊ on the Programming toolbar or press [**Ctrl**] [. Do not type the word "continue." As with **break**, you typically insert **continue** into the left-hand placeholder of an **if** operator. The **continue** statement is evaluated only when the right-hand side of the **if** is *true*.

In Figure 15-6, **break** is used to stop a loop when a negative number is encountered in an input vector and return the result to that point, while **continue** is used to ignore non-positive numbers in an input vector, returning a vector of all positive numbers in v.

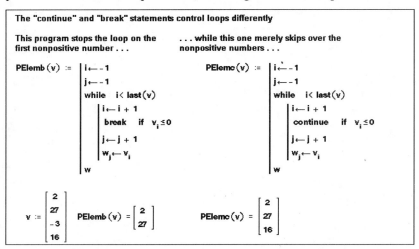

*Figure 15-6: Using **break** statement halts the loop. Program execution resumes on the next iteration when **continue** is used instead.*

Return

A Mathcad program returns the value of the last expression evaluated in the program. In simple programs, the last expression evaluated is in the last line of the program. As you create more complicated programs, you may need more flexibility. **Return** allows you to interrupt the program and return particular values other than the default value.

A **return** statement can be used anywhere in a program, even within a deeply nested loop, to force program termination and the return of a scalar, vector, array, or string. As with **break** and **continue**, you typically use **return** on the left-hand side of an **if** operator, and the **return** statement is evaluated only when the right-hand side is *true*.

The following program fragment shows how a **return** statement is used to return a string upon the occurrence of a particular condition:

1. Click ▓▓ **if** ▓▓ on the Programming toolbar.

   ┌──────────────────────────┐
   │ ■ if ■   │
   └──────────────────────────┘

2. Now click ▓ return ▓ on the Programming toolbar or press [**Ctrl**]|. Do not type "return."

   ┌──────────────────────────┐
   │ return ▪| if ■   │
   └──────────────────────────┘

3. Create a string by typing the double-quote key (**"**) on the placeholder to the right of **return**. Then type the string to be returned by the program. Mathcad displays the string between a pair of quotes.

   ┌──────────────────────────┐
   │ return "int" if ■   │
   └──────────────────────────┘

4. Type a condition in the right placeholder of **if**. This is typically a Boolean expression like the one shown. (Type [**Ctrl**]= for the bold equal sign.)

   ┌──────────────────────────┐
   │ return "int" if floor(x) = x │
   └──────────────────────────┘

In this example, the program returns the string "int" when the expression $floor(x) = x$ is true.

Tip   You can add more lines to the expression to the right of **return** by clicking [Add Line] on the Programming toolbar.

Error Handling

Errors may occur during program execution, causing Mathcad to stop calculating the program. For example, because of a particular input, a program may attempt to divide by 0 in an expression and therefore encounter a singularity. In these cases Mathcad treats the program as it does any math expression: it marks the offending expression with an error message and highlights the offending name or operator in a different color, as described in Chapter 8, "Calculating in Mathcad."

Mathcad gives you two features to improve error handling in programs:

- The **on error** operator on the Programming toolbar allows you to trap a numerical error that would otherwise force Mathcad to stop calculating the program.

- The *error* function gives you access to Mathcad's error tip mechanism and lets you customize error messages issued by your program.

On Error

In some cases you may be able to anticipate program inputs that lead to a numerical error (such as a singularity, an overflow, or a failure to converge) that would force Mathcad to stop calculating the program. In more complicated cases, especially when your programs rely heavily on Mathcad's numerical operators or built-in function set, you may not be able to anticipate all of the possible numerical errors that can occur in a program. The **on error** statement is designed as a general-purpose error trap to compute an alternative expression a program encounters a numerical error that would otherwise stop calculation.

To use **on error**, click [on error] on the Programming toolbar or type [**Ctrl**] `. Do not type "on error." In the placeholder to the right of **on error**, enter the program statement(s) you ordinarily expect to evaluate but in which you wish to trap any numerical errors. In the placeholder to the left of **on error**, enter the program statement(s) you want to evaluate should the default expression on the right-hand side fail. Figure 15-7 shows **on error** operating in a program to find a root of an expression.

Issuing Error Messages

Just as Mathcad automatically stops further evaluation and produces an appropriate "error tip" on an expression that generates an error (see the bottom of Figure 15-7 for an example), you can use the *error* function to stop evaluation and create customized error tips that appear when your programs or other expressions are used improperly or cannot return answers.

Typically you use the *error* function in the placeholder on the left-hand side of an **if** or **on error** operator so that an error tip is generated when a particular condition is encountered. Figure 15-8 shows how custom errors can be used even in a small program.

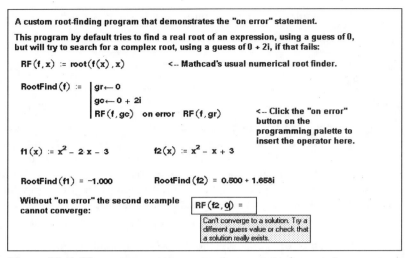

Figure 15-7: The **on error** *statement traps numerical errors in a program.*

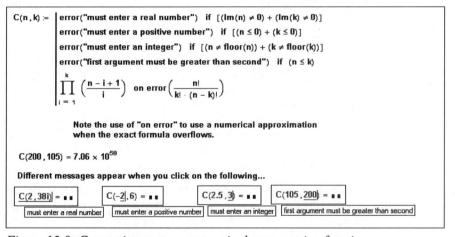

Figure 15-8: Generating custom errors via the error *string function.*

Tip   For more information on the error function, see "String Functions" on page 256.

Note   Some error strings are automatically translated to a Mathcad error message that is similar to the error string. For example "must be real" is translated to "This value must be real. Its imaginary part must be zero."

Programs Within Programs

The examples in previous sections have been chosen more for illustrative purposes rather than their power. This section shows examples of more sophisticated programs.

Much of the flexibility inherent in programming arises from the ability to embed programming structures inside one another. In Mathcad, you can do this in the following ways:

- You can make one of the statements in a program be another program, or you can define a program elsewhere and call it from within another program as if it were a *subroutine*.

- You can define a function *recursively*.

Subroutines

In Figure 15-9 both programs contain a statement, which itself is a program. In principle, there is no limit to how deeply you can nest a program.

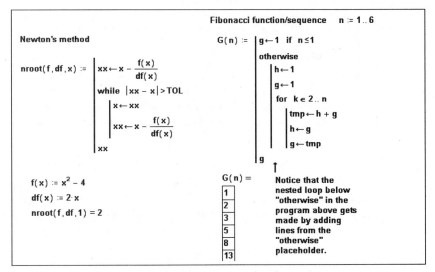

Figure 15-9: Programs in which statements are themselves programs.

One way many programmers avoid overly complicated programs is to bury the complexity in *subroutines*. Figure 15-10 shows an example of this technique.

Tip   Breaking up long programs with subroutines is good programming practice. Long programs, especially those containing deeply nested statements can become difficult for other users to understand at a glance. They are also more cumbersome to edit and debug.

In Figure 15-10, the function *adapt* carries out an adaptive quadrature or integration routine by using *intsimp* to approximate the area in each subinterval. By defining *intsimp* elsewhere and using it within *adapt*, the program used to define *adapt* becomes considerably simpler.

INTEGRATION IN WHICH WIDTHS OF INTERVALS ARE CHOSEN ADAPTIVELY

$$\text{intsimp}(f,a,b,N) := \begin{vmatrix} s \leftarrow 0 \\ w \leftarrow \dfrac{b-a}{N} \\ \text{for } i \in 1..N \\ \qquad s \leftarrow s + w \cdot \dfrac{\left[f(a+(i-1)\cdot w)+4\cdot f\left(a-\dfrac{w}{2}+i\cdot w\right)\right]+f(a+i\cdot w)}{6} \\ s \end{vmatrix}$$

$$\text{adapt}(f,a,b) := \begin{vmatrix} x \leftarrow \text{intsimp}(f,a,b,10) \\ x \quad \text{if } |x - \text{intsimp}(f,a,b,5)| \leq \text{TOL} \\ \text{adapt}\left(f,a,\dfrac{a+b}{2}\right) + \text{adapt}\left(f,\dfrac{a+b}{2},b\right) \quad \text{otherwise} \end{vmatrix}$$

$$\text{adapt}(\log,10^{-15},1) = -0.434958018397141$$

Figure 15-10: Using a subroutine to manage complexity.

Recursion

Recursion is a powerful programming technique where a function is defined in terms of itself, as was done with the definition of adapt in Figure 15-10. Recursion is similar to mathematical induction: if you can determine $f(n + 1)$ from $f(n)$, and you know $f(0)$, then you know all there is to know about f. Recursive definitions have two parts:

- A definition, written in terms of a previous evaluation of the function.

- An initial condition, which prevents the recursion from continuing forever.

Some mathematical examples of a recursive function are the *factorial,* where the factorial of n is n times the factorial of $n–1$, and the compounding of interest. Mathcad implementations of these examples as recursive programs are shown in Figure 15-11.

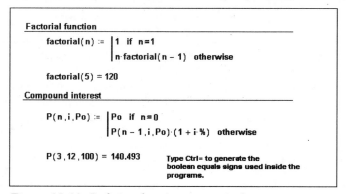

Figure 15-11: Defining functions recursively.

Tip   Recursive function definitions, while appearing elegant and concise, are not always computationally efficient. You may find that an equivalent definition using one of the iterative loops evaluates more quickly.

Building Function DLLs

If your program is complex enough, you may benefit by implementing it as a DLL. The UserEFI interface allows you to access a function you compile as if it were built into Mathcad. Compiling a function into DLL form will speed up its execution and allow for greater reusability between worksheets. The UserEFI directory of your Mathcad installation contains header and library files necessary for creating your own DLLs and instructions for creating Mathcad DLLs with several different C++ compilers. Check the environment information in your compiler's documentation before attempting to compile your own DLLs.

Mathcad's UserEFI interface allows you to pass scalars, vectors, two-dimensional arrays, and strings to and from any DLL you create. Nested matrices are not supported by the UserEFI interface.

Once you create your DLL, you can add it to Mathcad's **Insert Function** dialog by creating a function entry in the file USER.XML, located in the **Doc\Funcdoc** directory of your Mathcad installation. USER.XML contains a template you can copy and fill out with the pertinent information for your function.

Tip   For more information on creating your own DLLs, please consult the "Creating a User DLL" section of the **Developer's Reference,** available from the **Help.**

Creating Your Own Components

Scripting Custom OLE Automation Objects

As described in the previous chapter, Mathcad has several specialized components for accessing the functionality of other applications within your Mathcad worksheet. However, it is possible to dynamically exchange data between a Mathcad worksheet and any other application that supports OLE Automation, even if Mathcad does not have a specific component for that application. To do so, you must use the *Scriptable Object component* (SOC).

In addition to programming the SOC to interface with other OLE applications, you can build customized *Controls* that respond to user input in the worksheet, such as buttons and text boxes. Also, you can use the SOC to retrieve data from measurement devices attached to your system. Scripted objects to perform these tasks come pre-installed with Mathcad. Brief descriptions of their use appear under "Customizing and Redistributing Components" on page 247 and "The Data Acquisition Control" on page 229. These components appear in the Insert Component list, but they may need to be customized through modifications to their scripts in your worksheet.

How to Use Scriptable Object Components

In general, you can create a custom scriptable object from any object you can insert into a Mathcad worksheet as well as any ActiveX controls installed on your computer.

To create a Scriptable Object component, you must:

1. Be proficient in a supported scripting language installed on your system, such as Microsoft VBScript or JScript.

2. Be familiar with the Object Model of the application you are scripting.

3. Have the application or control installed on your system.

Scripting Languages

To use a Scriptable Object component, you must have a supported scripting language installed on your system. Two scripting languages are supported by Mathcad: Microsoft VBScript (Visual Basic Scripting Edition) and Microsoft JScript (an implementation of JavaScript). Other languages may be available on your system and usable for scripting; however, Mathcad will not automatically generate an appropriate script template for your component, and there is no assurance that a component scripted with another scripting language will work properly.

VBScript and JScript are included with Microsoft Internet Explorer, which can be installed from the Mathcad CD. These scripting languages can also be downloaded at no charge as part of the Microsoft Windows Script package. at:

http://msdn.microsoft.com/scripting

For more information on scripting languages and syntax associated with their usage, see the **Developer's Reference** under the Mathcad **Help** menu.

Inserting a Scriptable Object

When you select the Scriptable Object component in the Component Wizard, Mathcad, launches the Scripting Wizard. The "Object to Script" scrolling list shows the available server applications on your system. Choose an application that supports the OLE 2 automation interface (consult documentation for the application for details).

You must specify:

• Whether the component is a new file or whether you will insert an existing file.

• Whether you will see the actual file or an icon in your Mathcad worksheet.

In the remaining pages of the Wizard you specify: the type of object you want to script, the scripting language you are using, the name of the object, and the number of inputs and outputs the object will accept and provide.

A Scriptable Object component appears in your worksheet with placeholders for the input and output variables. Enter the input variables in the bottom placeholders. Enter the output variables into the placeholders to the left of the :=.

Tip   If you want to set a Mathcad variable using multiple controls, you can use a Frame Object as a container object. For more information, consult the **Developer's Reference**.

Note There are two Properties dialog boxes for any customized Scripted Object component, one for the *object* and one for the *embedded control*. Access the one for the object by right clicking on the object and choosing **Properties** from the popup menu. This dialog box allows you to specify the number of inputs and outputs and the name of the object. Access the one for the underlying control by right clicking on the object and choosing **[Control Name] Object⇒Properties**. This dialog box allows you to modify the settings for the embedded control. For example, in the Data Acquisition Control (see page 229), you use it to change the data collection mode from single point to waveform.

Mathsoft Controls

The Mathsoft Controls allow you to insert buttons, text boxes, list boxes, and sliders into your Mathcad worksheet. These components operate in a fashion similar to Microsoft Forms Controls, which you can insert as Scripted Object components.

Mathsoft Controls provide you, as an author, a means of entering information into a worksheet other than the standard variable mechanism. This is particularly useful if the end user is a novice user of Mathcad, or if you want to streamline an oft-repeated process. These controls are also useful for expanding the degree to which worksheets can be used as templates for processes. For example, a set of controls can allow the user to specify quickly and easily various parameters used to compute a series of calculations. In this way, controls further facilitate your design of a solution rather than just a worksheet.

Note For more information about the properties and methods associated with Mathsoft Controls and other Scriptable Object components, see the **Developer's Reference** under the **Help** menu in Mathcad.

Inserting a Mathsoft Control

To insert a Mathsoft Control into a Mathcad worksheet:

1. Click in a blank spot in your worksheet. If you want to send values to the component from a Mathcad variable, click below or to the right of the variable definition.

2. Choose **Control** from the **Insert** menu or the **Controls** toolbar. Select the control you want from the submenu.

3. In the placeholder that appears to the left of the component, enter the name of the Mathcad variable to be defined.

To add input or output variables to your component, right click the embedded control (i.e., the button, list box, text box, etc.) and select **Add Input Variable** or **Add Output Variable** from the popup menu. If you add or remove input or output variables from the component, you must make changes to the script. To edit the script, right click the embedded control and select **Edit Script...** from the popup menu.

You are allowed a maximum of four inputs and four outputs for any Mathsoft Control. For information on inputs, outputs, and scripting a control see the **Developer's Reference** under **Help** in Mathcad.

Tip For most Mathsoft Controls, you specify outputs only. For example, for a TextBox control you will get 0 inputs and 1 output, the output being based on the text entered in the text box.

To change the appearance of a Mathsoft Control:

1. Right click on the component and select **Mathsoft [Control] Object⇒Properties** from the popup menu.

2. In the **Properties** dialog box you will see various options that let you change the appearance of the control. For example, you can change the Button control from a checkbox to a push button within this dialog box. Make your selections.

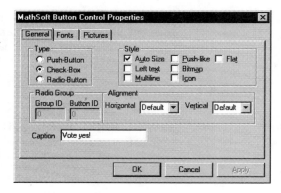

3. Click "Apply" to keep the Properties dialog box open and preview the changes in your worksheet. Click "OK" to close the dialog box and return to the worksheet.

Tip To customize a button quickly with a specific graphic image, create an image and copy it into your clipboard. Right click on the button and select **Mathsoft [Control] Object⇒Paste Bitmap** from the popup menu. Alternatively, you can browse for a bitmap or icon file through the Pictures tab in the Properties dialog box.

Note The properties of a control are not preserved if you change them through the control's interface — only if they are changed programmatically, in the script associated with the control. For example, if you want a checkbox to be checked by default when you open your worksheet, you should set the checked state in the script, rather than by clicking on the checkbox, and saving the worksheet.

To edit the script of a Mathsoft Control:

1. Right click on the component and select **Mathsoft [Control] Object⇒Edit Script...** from the popup menu.

2. Make your changes and close the Script Editor.

3. To update the component in your Mathcad worksheet, select **Calculate⇒Calculate Worksheet** from the **Tools** menu or click on the component and press **[F9]**.

Note You cannot send a string as input to any Mathsoft Control component. The only types of input variables allowed are scalars, vectors, and matrices. However, you can define an output variable as a string in a Mathsoft Control component. See CONTROLS.MCD in the QSHEET\SAMPLES\CONTROLS directory for examples of Mathsoft Controls.

Customizing and Redistributing Components

Once you have scripted a scripted object or control to your liking, you can save it as a customized Scripted Object component for future use. This creates an ActiveX object on your system that you can insert into your worksheet from the **Insert Component** dialog box. You can also redistribute your component to other users of Mathcad (version 2001 or later), so that they can use it as well. For example, you could create components to set various Mathcad built-in variables (TOL, ORIGIN, etc.) within a worksheet you distribute to others, rather than relying on them to know Mathcad interface well enough to change the variables on their own.

To export a Scripted Object as a component:

1. Right click on the customized control or control that you wish to save. Choose **Export as Component** from the popup menu.

2. In the dialog, specify the name of your component, as it will appear in the **Insert Component** dialog box, (e.g., My Listbox) and where you would like to save it. Click "Next."

3. If you want to protect the script and settings of your component, specify and verify a password. Otherwise, leave these fields blank. Click "Finish."

The component will be saved as an MCM file and registered, making it appear in the **Insert Component** dialog box and ready to use.

If you want to share your component with another Mathcad user, you need only supply them with a copy of the MCM file. To use a component you have received:

1. Copy the MCM file to the MCM folder of your Mathcad installation.

2. Double-click the MCM file to register the component.

3. Start Mathcad. The component will be available in the **Insert Component** dialog.

Deleting an Exported Component

To remove an MCM file from your system, perform the following steps:

1. Open the **Start** menu in Windows, and click Run.

2. Click the Browse button. Navigate to your Mathcad program directory, and select the file mcmreg.exe and click "OK."

3. In the Run dialog, add the following command-line arguments: /u mcm\control.mcm, where control.mcm is the MCM file you want to delete; for example, it is located in the MCM directory of your Mathcad installation. The "/u" removes information on the MCM file from the Windows Registry.

4. Once you have unregistered the component, it will no longer appear in the Component Wizard and you can delete the MCM file from your system.

These steps will only work for components exported as MCMfiles, and not for components shipped with Mathcad.

Opening a Worksheet Containing a Scripted Component

Mathcad can protect you from potentially damaging code within certain types of scriptable components. By default, Mathcad will prompt you to enable or disable evaluation of scriptable components upon opening a worksheet containing them. If you elect to disable evaluation of a scriptable component when opening the worksheet, you may re-enable evaluation by right clicking on the component and choosing **Enable Evaluation**.

You can adjust the level of security for Mathcad on the **Security** tab in the **Preferences** dialog under the **Tools** menu. There are three settings:

- **High Security**. All scripted components are disabled when you open a worksheet.
- **Medium Security** *(default setting)*. You are notified of the presence of one or more scripted components when opening your worksheet and given the choice to disable them or not.
- **Low Security**. No precautions are taken when opening a worksheet containing scripted components.

Script Security affects the Scriptable Object component, the Mathsoft Controls, and any scripted components you export as MCM files.

Accessing Mathcad from Within Another Application

The previous sections have described how to extend the functionality of Mathcad. Mathcad's OLE automation interface grants the complementary ability to extend the functionality of other Windows applications by allowing them to access the computational features of Mathcad. Using Mathcad's OLE automation interface, you can send data dynamically to Mathcad from another application, use Mathcad to perform calculations or other data manipulations, and send results back to the original application

Mathcad Add-ins

There are several applications for which specialized Mathcad Add-ins have been created. An Add-in allows you to insert a Mathcad object into another application. Visit the Download area of the Mathcad web site at **http://www.mathcad.com/** for a complete list of available Mathcad Add-ins and information about how to download them for use.

Note The OLE automation interface is supported in Mathcad 7.02 and higher and supersedes the DDE interface supported in Mathcad 5 and 6. For information on the interface, see the **Developer's Reference** under the **Help** menu in Mathcad. For specific examples, see TRAJECTORY.XLS in the QSHEET\SAMPLES\EXCEL and DOUGHNUT.EXE in the QSHEET\SAMPLES\VBASIC in your Mathcad installation.

Chapter 16
Functions

Built-in Functions

Mathcad provides a set of built-in functions, which you can expand by installing additional Extension Packs or writing your own built-in functions. The core set of Mathcad functions is accessible by choosing **Function** from the **Insert** menu.

Mathcad Extension Packs

An Extension Pack consists of advanced functions geared to a particular area of application. Available Extension Packs include *Signal Processing, Image Processing, Wavelets, Communications System Design,* and *Solving and Optimization.* To find out more about Mathcad Extension Packs, contact Mathsoft or your local distributor, or visit Mathsoft's Web site at:

http://www.mathcad.com/

After you install an Extension Pack, the additional functions will appear in the Insert Function dialog box.

Built-in functions you write yourself in C

If you have a supported 32-bit C/C++ compiler, you can write your own built-in functions for Mathcad. For details see the **Developer's Reference** under **Help**.

Function Categories

Bessel Functions

$Ai(z)$	$bei(n, x)$	$ber(n, x)$	$Bi(z)$
$H(m, x)$	$H1.sc(m, x)$	$H2(m, x)$	$H2.sc(m, x)$
$I0(z)$	$I0.sc(x)$	$I1(z)$	$I1.sc(x)$
$In(m, z)$	$In.sc(m, x)$	$J0(z)$	$J0.sc(x)$
$J1(z)$	$J1.sc(x)$	$Jn(m, z)$	$Jn.sc(m, x)$
$js(n, z)$	$K0(z)$	$K0.sc(x)$	$K1(z)$
$Y0(z)$	$Y1(z)$		
$Yn(m, z)$	$ys(n, z)$		$Kn(m, z)$
$KI.sc(x)$	$Kn.sc(m, x)$	$Y0.sc(x)$	$Y1.sc(x)$
$Yn.sc(m, x)$			

The sc versions are scaled.

Complex Numbers Functions

$arg(z)$	$csgn(z)$	$Im(z)$	$Re(z)$
$signum(z)$			

Curve Fitting and Smoothing Functions

expfit(**vx**, **vy**, [vg])	genfit(**vx**, **vy**, **vg**, **F**)	intercept(**vx**, **vy**)
ksmooth(**vx**,**vy**, *b*)	lgsfit(**vx**, **vy**, **vg**)	line(**vx**, **vy**)
linfit(**vx**, **vy**, **F**)	lnfit(**vx**, **vy**)	loess(**vx**, **vy**, *span*)
logfit(**vx**, **vy**, **vg**)	medfit(**vx**, **vy**)	medsmooth(**vy**, *n*)
pwrfit(**vx**, **vy**, **vg**)	regress(**vx**, **vy**, *n*)	sinfit(**vx**, **vy**, **vg**)
slope(**vx**, **vy**)	stderr(**vx**, **vy**)	supsmooth(**vx**,**vy**)

See Chapter 9, "Solving and Data Analysis," and online **Tutorials** on Data Analysis under the **Help** menu.

Differential Equation Solving Functions

Bulstoer(y, *x1*, *x2*, *npoints*, D)   bulstoer(**y**, *x1*, *x2*, *acc*, **D**, *kmax*, *save*)

bvalfit(**v1**, **v2**, *x1*, *x2*, *xf*, **D**, **load1**, **load2**, **score**)   multigrid(**M**, *ncycle*)

numol(x_endpts, xpts, t_endpts, tpts, num_pde, num_pae, pde_func, pinit, bc_codes, bc_func)

Odesolve(**vf**, *x*, *b*, [*step*])

Pdesolve(u, x, x-range, t, trange, [xpts], [tpts])

Radau(**y**, *x1*, *x2*, *npoints*, D)   radau(**y**, *x1*, *x2*, *acc*, **D**, *kmax*, *save*)

relax(**a**, **b**, **c**, **d**, **e**, **f**, **u**, *rjac*)   Rkadapt(y, *x1*, *x2*, *npoints*, D)

rkadapt(**y**, *x1*, *x2*, *acc*, **D**, *kmax*, *save*)   rkfixed(**y**, x1, x2, npoints, **D**)

sbval(**v**, *x1*, *x2*, **D**, **load**, **score**)   Stiffb(y, *x1*, *x2*, *npoints*, D, J)

stiffb(**y**, *x1*, *x2*, *acc*, **D**, **J**, *kmax*, *save*)   Stiffr(y, *x1*, *x2*, *npoints*, D, J)

stiffr(**y**, *x1*, *x2*, *acc*, **D**, **J**, *kmax*, *save*)

See Chapter 9, "Solving and Data Analysis," for more information on differential equation solving in Mathcad.

Expression Type Functions

These functions identify if an expression is a matrix or vector, real or complex, string, or units of x. They are most useful inside programs.

IsArray(*x*)	IsScalar(*x*)	IsString(*x*)	UnitsOf(*x*)

File Access Functions

The file argument you supply to a Mathcad file access function is a *string*—or a variable to which a string is assigned—that corresponds either to:

- The name of a data or image file in the folder of the Mathcad worksheet you're currently working on.

- The name of a colormap file (see page 308) in the CMAP subfolder of your Mathcad installation folder.

- A full or relative path to a data, image, or colormap file located elsewhere on a local or network file system.

Reading and writing ASCII data files

APPENDPRN(*file*)	WRITEPRN(*file*)	READPRN(*file*)

Files in plain ASCII format consist only of numbers separated by commas, spaces, or carriage returns. The numbers in the data files can be integers like **3** or **−1**, floating-point numbers like **2.54**, or E-format numbers like **4.51E-4** (for $4.51 \cdot 10^{-4}$).

Tip These ASCII data file access functions are provided mainly for compatibility with worksheets created in earlier versions of Mathcad. The Data Table and File Input/Output components provide more general methods of importing and exporting data in a variety of formats. See Chapter 14, "Importing and Exporting Data."

Reading and writing WAV files

GETWAVINFO(*file*)   READWAV(*file*)   WRITEWAV(*file*, *r*, *b*)

Reading and writing binary (BIN) files

READBIN(*file*, *type*, [[*endian*], [*cols*], [*skip*], [*maxrows*]])
WRITEBIN(*file*, *type*, *endian*)

Loading and saving colormaps

LoadColormap(*file*)   SaveColormap(*file*, **M**)

Reading and Writing Image Files

See "Image Processing Functions" on page 253.

Finance Functions

cnper(*rate*, *pv*, *fv*)   crate(*nper*, *pv*, *fv*)

cumint(*rate*, *nper*, *pv*, *start*, *end*, [*type*])   cumprn(*rate*, *nper*, *pv*, *start*, *end*, [*type*])

eff(*rate*, *nper*)   fv(*rate*, *nper*, *pmt*, [[*pv*], [*type*]])

fvadj(*prin*, **v**)   fvc(*rate*, **v**)

ipmt(*rate*, *per*, *nper*, *pv*, [[*fv*], [*type*]])   irr(**v**, [*guess*])

mirr(**v**, *fin_rate*, *rein_rate*)   nom(*rate*, *nper*)

nper(*rate*, *pmt*, *pv*, [[*fv*], [*type*]])   npv(*rate*, **v**)

pmt(*rate*, *nper*, *pv*, [[*fv*], [*type*]])   ppmt(*rate*, *per*, *nper*, *pv*, [[*fv*], [*type*]])

pv(*rate*, *nper*, *pmt*, [[*fv*] [*type*]])   rate(*nper*, *pmt*, *pv*, [[*fv*], [*type*], [*guess*]])

All finance functions take only real values. Payments made must be entered as negative numbers. Cash received must be entered as positive numbers. If you want to specify the timing of a payment, use the optional timing variable, *type*, which can be equal to 0 for the end of the period and 1 for the beginning. If omitted, *type* is 0.

Note When using functions that require information about rates and periods, use the same unit of time for each. For example, if you make monthly payments on a four-year loan at an annual interest rate of 12%, use 1% as the interest rate per period (one month) and 48 months as the number of periods.

Fourier Transforms on Real and Complex Data

CFFT(**A**)   cfft(**A**)   FFT(**v**)   fft(**v**)

ICFFT(**A**)   icfft(**A**)   IFFT(**v**)   ifft(**v**)

All Fourier transform functions require vectors as arguments.

The monthly payment for a $10,000 loan that accrues interest at
an annual rate of 8% and that you must pay off in 10 months:

$$rate := \frac{8\%}{12} \quad nper := 10 \quad pv := 10000 \quad per := 5$$

pmt(rate, nper, pv) = −1037.03

The portion of the 5th payment that is interest:

ipmt(rate, per, nper, pv) = −40.53

The portion of the 5th payment that is principal:

ppmt(rate, per, nper, pv) = −996.50

Figure 16-1: Using the pmt, ipmt, *and* ppmt *functions.*

Note When you define a vector **v** for use with Fourier or wavelet transforms, Mathcad indexes the vector beginning at 0, by default, unless you have set the value of the built-in variable ORIGIN to a value other than 0 (see page 100). If you do not define v_0, Mathcad automatically sets it to zero. This can distort the results of the transform functions.

Mathcad comes with two types of Fourier transform pairs: *fft / ifft* (or the alternative *FFT / IFFT*) and *cfft / icfft* (or the alternative *CFFT / ICFFT*). These functions are discrete: they apply to and return vectors and matrices only. You cannot use them with other functions.

Use the *fft* and *ifft* (or *FFT / IFFT*) functions if:

- the data values in the time domain are real, and
- the data vector has 2^m elements.

Use the *cfft* and *icfft* (or *CFFT / ICFFT*) functions in all other cases.

Be sure to use these functions in pairs. For example, if you used *CFFT* to go from the time domain to the frequency domain, you must use *ICFFT* to transform back to the time domain. See Figure 16-2 for an example.

Note Different sources use different conventions concerning the initial factor of the Fourier transform and whether to conjugate the results of either the transform or the inverse transform. The functions *fft*, *ifft*, *cfft*, and *icfft* use $1 / \sqrt{N}$ as a normalizing factor and a positive exponent in going from the time to the frequency domain. The functions *FFT*, *IFFT*, *CFFT*, and *ICFFT* use $1 / N$ as a normalizing factor and a negative exponent in going from the time to the frequency domain.

Graph

CreateMesh(F, s0, s1, t0, t1, sgrid, tgrid, fmap)
CreateSpace(F, t0, t1, tgrid, fmap)
Polyhedron(S)   PolyLookup(n)

Hyperbolic Functions

acosh(z)	acoth(z)	acsch(z)	asech(z)
asinh(z)	atanh(z)	cosh(z)	coth(z)
csch(z)	sech(z)	sinh(z)	tanh(z)

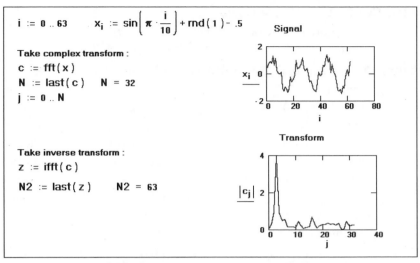

$$i := 0 \ldots 63 \qquad x_i := \sin\left(\pi \cdot \frac{i}{10}\right) + \text{rnd}(1) - .5$$

Take complex transform :
$$c := \text{fft}(x)$$
$$N := \text{last}(c) \qquad N = 32$$
$$j := 0 \ldots N$$

Take inverse transform :
$$z := \text{ifft}(c)$$
$$N2 := \text{last}(z) \qquad N2 = 63$$

Figure 16-2: Use of fast Fourier transforms in Mathcad. Since the random number generator gives different numbers every time, you may not be able to recreate this example exactly as you see it.

Image Processing Functions

READ_BLUE(*file*)	READBMP(*file*)	READ_GREEN(*file*)
READ_HLS(*file*)	READ_HLS_HUE(*file*)	READ_HLS_LIGHT(*file*)
READ_HLS_SAT(*file*)	READ_HSV(*file*)	READ_HSV_HUE(*file*)
READ_HSV_SAT(*file*)	READ_HSV_VALUE(*file*)	READ_IMAGE(*file*)
READ_RED(*file*)	READRGB(*file*)	WRITEBMP(*file*)
WRITE_HLS(*file*)	WRITE_HSV(*file*)	WRITERGB(*file*)

Interpolation and Prediction Functions

bspline(**vx**, **vy**, **u**, n)	cspline(**vx**, **vy**)	interp(**vs**, **vx**, **vy**, x)
linterp(**vx**, **vy**, x)	lspline(**vx**, **vy**)	predict(**v**, m, n)
pspline(**vx**, **vy**)		

Log and Exponential Functions

$\exp(z)$ $\qquad$ $\ln(z)$ $\qquad$ $\text{lnGamma}(z)$ $\qquad$ $\log(z, b)$

Mathcad's exponential and logarithmic functions can accept and return complex arguments. *ln* returns the *principal branch* of the natural log function.

Lookup Functions

hlookup(z, **A**, r) $\qquad$ lookup(z, **A**, **B**) $\qquad$ match(z, **A**) $\qquad$ vlookup(z, **A**, r)

Number Theory/Combinatorics

combin(n, k)	gcd(**A**, **B**, **C**, ...)	lcm(**A**, **B**, **C**, ...)
mod(x, y)	permut(n, k)	

Piecewise Continuous Functions

ε antisymmetric tensor(i, j, k)	if(*cond, tvl, fvl*)	δ Kronecker delta(*m, n*)
$\varepsilon(i, j, k)$	Φ heaviside step(x)	sign(x)

Probability Densities and Probability Distributions

cnorm(x)	dbeta(x, s_1, s_2)	dbinom(k, n, p)
dcauchy(x, l, s)	dchisq(x, d)	dexp(x, r)
dF(x, d_1, d_2)	dgamma(x, s)	dgeom(k, p)
dhypergeom(M, a, b, n)	dlnorm(x, μ, σ)	dlogis(x, l, s)
dnbinom(k, n, p)	dnorm(x, μ, σ)	dpois(k, λ)
dt(x, d)	dunif(x, a, b)	dweibull(x, s)
pbeta(x, s_1, s_2)	pbinom(k, n, p)	pcauchy(x, l, s)
pchisq(x, d)	pexp(x, r)	pF(x, d_1, d_2)
pgamma(x, s)	pgeom(k, p)	phypergeom(M, a, b, n)
plnorm(x, μ, σ)	plogis(x, l, s)	pnbinom(k, n, p)
pnorm(x, μ, σ)	ppois(k, λ)	pt(x, d)
punif(x, a, b)	pweibull(x, s)	qbeta(p, s_1, s_2)
qbinom(p, n, r)	qcauchy(p, l, s)	qchisq(p, d)
qexp(p, r)	qF(p, d_1, d_2)	qgamma(p, s)
qgeom(p, r)	qhypergeom(p, a, b, n)	qlnorm(p, μ, σ)
qlogis(p, l, s)	qnbinom(p, n, r)	qnorm(p, μ, σ)
qpois(p, λ)	qt(p, d)	qunif(p, a, b)
qweibull(p, s)		

Mathcad includes functions for working with several common probability densities. These functions fall into four classes:

- **Probability densities,** beginning with the letter "**d**," give the likelihood that a random variable will take on a particular value.

- **Cumulative probability distributions,** beginning with the letter "**p**," give the probability that a random variable will take on a value *less than or equal to* a specified value. These are obtained by simply integrating (or summing when appropriate) the corresponding probability density from $-\infty$ to a specified value.

- **Inverse cumulative probability distributions**, beginning with the letter "**q**," take a probability p between 0 and 1 as an argument and return a value such that the probability that a random variable will be *less than or equal to* that value is p.

- **Random number generators,** beginning with the letter "**r**," return a vector of m elements drawn from the corresponding probability distribution. Each time you recalculate an equation containing one of these functions, Mathcad generates new random numbers.

Tip   Two additional functions that are useful for common probability calculations are *rnd*(x), which is equivalent to *runif*(1, 0, x), and *cnorm*(x), which is equivalent to *pnorm*(x, 0, 1).

> **Tip** Mathcad's random number generators have a "seed value" associated with them. A given seed value always generates the same sequence of random numbers, and choosing **Calculate** from the **Tools** menu advances Mathcad along this random number sequence. Changing the seed value, however, advances Mathcad along a different random number sequence. To change the seed value, choose **Worksheet Options** from the **Tools** menu and enter a value on the Built-in Variables tab.

Random Numbers

rbeta(m, s_1, s_2)	rbinom(m, n, p)	rcauchy(m, l, s)
rchisq(m, d)	rexp(m, r)	rF(m, d_1, d_2)
rgamma(m, s)	rgeom(m, p)	rhypergeom(M, a, b, n)
rlnorm(m, μ, σ)	rlogis(m, l, s)	rnbinom(m, n, p)
rnd(x)	rnorm(m, μ, σ)	rpois(m, λ)
rt(m, d)	runif(m, a, b)	rweibull(m, s)

Solving Functions

Finding Roots

polyroots(**v**)	root(f(var), var, [a, b])	root($f(z)$, z, a, b)

Solve Blocks

find(var1, var2, ...)	maximize(f, var1, var2, ...)
minerr(var1, var2, ...)	minimize(f, var1, var2, ...)

Solving a Linear System of Equations

lsolve(**M**, **v**)

Sorting Functions

csort(**A**, n)	reverse(**A**)	rsort(**A**, n)	sort(**v**)

> **Tip** Unless you change the value of ORIGIN, matrices are numbered by default starting with row zero and column zero. To sort on the first column of a matrix, for example, use *csort*(**A**, 0).

Special Functions

erf(x)	erfc(x)	fhyper(a, b, c, x)	$\Gamma(z)$
$\Gamma(x, y)$	Her(n, x)	ibeta(a, x, y)	Jac(n, a, b, x)
Lag(n, x)	Leg(n, x)	lnGamma(z)	
mhyper(a, b, x)	Tcheb(n, x)	zUcheb(n, x)	

Statistical Functions

corr(**A**, **B**)	cvar(**A**, **B**)	gmean(**A**, **B**, **C**, ...)
hist(**int**, **A**)	histogram(**int**, **A**)	hmean(**A**, **B**, **C**, ...)
kurt(**A**, **B**, **C**, ...)	mean(**A**, **B**, **C**, ...)	median(**A**, **B**, **C**, ...)
mode(**A**, **B**, **C**, ...)	skew(**A**, **B**, **C**, ...)	stderr(vx, vy)
Stdev(**A**, **B**, **C**, ...)	stdev(**A**, **B**, **C**, ...)	Var(**A**, **B**, **C**, ...)
var(**A**, **B**, **C**, ...)		

If you are interested in graphing the result of a frequency analysis in a 2D bar plot showing the distribution of data across the bins, use the function *histogram* rather than *hist*, and plot the first column of the result against the second column of the result.

String Functions

concat(*S1, S2, S3, ...*)	error(*S*)	IsString(*x*)
num2str(*z*)	search(*S, S1, m*)	str2num(*S*)
str2vec(*S*)	strlen(*S*)	substr(*S, m, n*)
vec2str(**v**)		

The strings used and returned by most of these functions are typed in a math placeholder by pressing the double-quote key (") and entering any combination of letters, numbers, or other ASCII characters. Mathcad automatically places double quotes around the string expression and displays quotes around a string returned as a result.

Trigonometric Functions

acos(*z*)	acot(*z*)	acsc(*z*)	angle(*x, y*)
asec(*z*)	asin(*z*)	atan(*z*)	atan2(*x, y*)
cos(*z*)	cot(*z*)	csc(*z*)	sec(*z*)
sin(*z*)	sinc(*z*)	tan(*z*)	

Mathcad's trig functions and their inverses accept any scalar argument: real, complex, or imaginary. They also return complex numbers wherever appropriate.

Trigonometric functions expect their arguments in *radians*. To pass an argument in degrees, use the built-in unit *deg*. For example, to evaluate the sine of 45 degrees, type **sin(45*deg)**. Likewise, to convert a result into degrees, either divide the result by the built-in unit *deg* or type **deg** in the units placeholder.

In Mathcad you enter powers of trig functions such as $\sin^2(x)$ as $\sin(x)^2$. Alternatively, you can use the prefix operator described in "Defining a Custom Operator" on page 392. For example, to type $\sin^2(x)$, click $\boxed{f\ x}$ on the Evaluation toolbar, enter $\mathbf{sin^2}$ in the left-hand placeholder and enter **(x)** in the right-hand placeholder.

Truncation and Round-off Functions

Ceil(*x, y*)	ceil(*x*)	Floor(*x, y*)	floor(*x*)
Round(*x, y*)	round(*x, n*)	Trunc(*x, y*)	trunc(*x*)

User-defined Functions

kronecker(m, n)	Psi(z)

Vector and Matrix Functions

Definition

IsArray(x)	IsScalar(x)

Forming New Matrices

augment(**A**, **B**, **C**, ...)

CreateMesh(**F**, [[*s0*], [*s1*], [*t0*], [*t1*], [*sgrid*], [*tgrid*], [**fmap**]])

CreateSpace(**F**,[[*t0*], [*t1*], [*tgrid*], [**fmap**]])

matrix(*m*, *n*, *f*)   stack(**A**, **B**, **C**, ...)   submatrix(**A**, *ir*, *jr*, *ic*, *jc*)

Size and Scope of an Array

cols(**A**)   last(**v**)   length(**v**)   max(**A**, **B**, **C**, ...)

min(**A**, **B**, **C**, ...)   rows(**A**)

Solving a Linear System of Equations

lsolve(m, v)

Special Characteristics of a Matrix

cond1(**M**)   cond2(**M**)   conde(**M**)   condi(**M**)

norm1(**M**)   norm2(**M**)   norme(**M**)   normi(**M**)

rank(**A**)   tr(**M**)

Special Types of Matrices

diag(**v**)   geninv(**A**)   identity(*n*)   rref(**A**)

Note that functions that expect vectors always expect column vectors rather than row vectors. To change a row vector into a column vector, use the transpose operator (click M^T on the **Matrix** toolbar).

$$
v := \begin{bmatrix} 2 \\ 8 \\ 9 \\ 7 \end{bmatrix} \qquad diag(v) = \begin{bmatrix} 2 & 0 & 0 & 0 \\ 0 & 8 & 0 & 0 \\ 0 & 0 & 9 & 0 \\ 0 & 0 & 0 & 7 \end{bmatrix}
$$

← A diagonal matrix formed from a vector. (Mathcad Professional)

$$
A := \begin{pmatrix} 2 & 4 & 6 \\ 4 & 5 & 6 \\ 2 & 7 & 12 \end{pmatrix} \qquad rref(A) = \begin{pmatrix} 1 & 0 & -1 \\ 0 & 1 & 2 \\ 0 & 0 & 0 \end{pmatrix}
$$

← The reduced-row echelon form of a matrix.

$$
B := \begin{bmatrix} 5 + 2i \\ 2.54 - 3i \\ 3 + (4 + .8) \cdot i \end{bmatrix} \qquad Im(B) = \begin{pmatrix} 2 \\ -3 \\ 4.8 \end{pmatrix}
$$

← The imaginary part of a matrix.

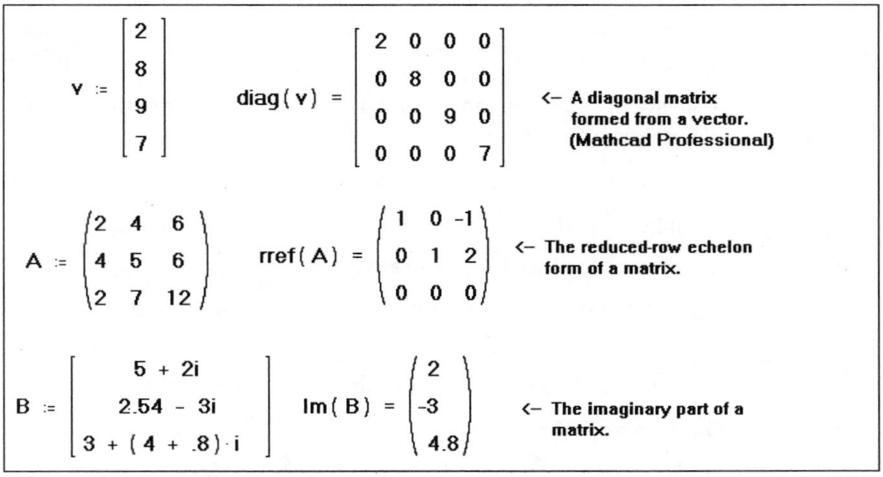

Figure 16-3: Functions for transforming arrays.

Note For the functions *CreateMesh* and *CreateSpace*, instead of using a vector-valued function, **F**, you can use three functions, **f1**, **f2**, and **f3**, representing the x-, y-, and z-coordinates of the parametric surface or space curve. Your call to one of these functions might look something like this: $CreateMesh(f1, f2, f3)$. Alternatively, for **CreateMesh**, you can use a single function of two variables such as $F(x, y) = \dfrac{\sin(x) + \cos(y)}{2}$.

Figure 16-4 shows examples of using *stack* and *augment*.

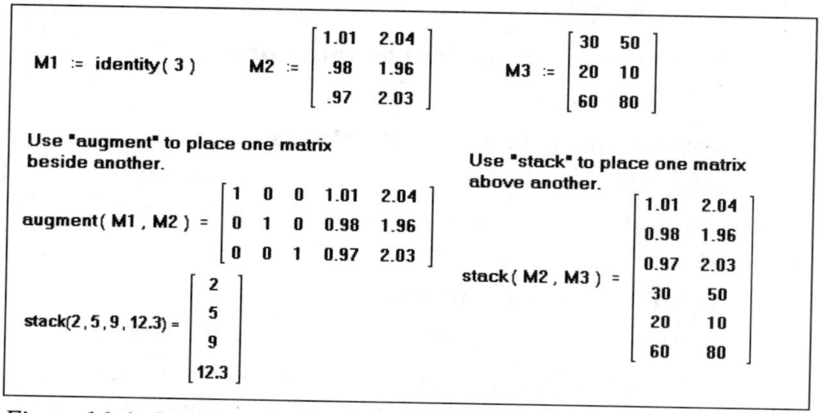

Figure 16-4: Joining matrices with the augment *and* stack *functions.*

Mapping Functions

cyl2xyz(r, θ, z)   pol2xy(r, θ)   sph2xyz(r, θ, φ)

xy2pol(x, y)   xyz2cyl(x, y, z)   xyz2sph(x, y, z)

Use any of the 3D mapping functions as the fmap argument for the CreateSpace and CreateMesh functions.

Lookup Functions

lookup(z, **A**, **B**)   hlookup(z, **A**, r)   vlookup(z, **A**, r)   match(z, **A**)

Eigenvalues and Eigenvectors

eigenvals(**M**)   eigenvec(**M**, z)   eigenvecs(**M**)   genvals(**M**, **N**)

genvecs(**M**, **N**)

Figure 16-5 shows how some of these functions are used.

Decomposition

cholesky(**M**)   lu(**M**)   qr(**A**)   svd(**A**)

svds(**A**)

Wavelet Transforms

wave(**v**)   iwave(**v**)

Finding eigenvalues and eigenvectors of a real matrix . .

$$A := \begin{pmatrix} 1 & -2 & 6 \\ 3 & 0 & 10 \\ 2 & 5 & -1 \end{pmatrix} \qquad c := \text{eigenvals}(A) \qquad c = \begin{pmatrix} 0.105 \\ 7.497 \\ -7.602 \end{pmatrix}$$

To find **all** the corresponding eigenvectors at once:

$$v := \text{eigenvecs}(A) \qquad v = \begin{pmatrix} 0.873 & 0.244 & -0.554 \\ -0.408 & 0.81 & -0.574 \\ -0.266 & 0.534 & 0.603 \end{pmatrix}$$

The first column of v is the eigenvector corresponding to 0.105, the first element of c. Similarly, the second column of v is the eigenvector corresponding to 7.497, the second element of c.

Figure 16-5: Eigenvalues and eigenvectors in Mathcad.

Mathcad Functions Listed Alphabetically

Notes on the Function Listings

Many functions described as accepting scalar arguments will, in fact, accept vector arguments. For example, while the input z for the acos function is specified as a "real or complex number," acos will in fact evaluate correctly at each of a vector input of real or complex numbers.

Other functions may possess optional arguments, for example, cumint or fv. For such functions f and g, the notation $f(x,[y])$ means that y can be omitted, while the notation $g(x,[[y],[z]])$ means that both y and z can be omitted (but not just y or just z).

Some functions don't accept input arguments with units. For such a function, f, an error message "must be dimensionless" will arise when evaluating $f(x)$, if x has units.

About the References

References are provided in the Appendices for you to learn more about the numerical algorithm underlying a given Mathcad function or operator. References are not intended to give a description of the actual underlying source code. The references are cited for background information only.

Functions

acos		Trigonometric

Syntax   acos(z)

Description   Returns the inverse cosine of z (in radians). The result is between 0 and π if $-1 \le z \le 1$. For complex z, the result is the principal value.

Arguments
z   real or complex number

acosh		Hyperbolic

Syntax   acosh(z)

Description   Returns the inverse hyperbolic cosine of z. The result is the principal value for complex z.

Arguments
z   real or complex number

acot		Trigonometric

Syntax   acot(z)

Description   Returns the inverse cotangent of z (in radians). The result is between 0 and π if z is real. For complex z, the result is the principal value.

Arguments
z   real or complex number

acoth
Hyperbolic

Syntax   acoth(z)

Description   Returns the inverse hyperbolic cotangent of z. The result is the principal value for complex z.

Arguments
z real or complex number

acsc
Trigonometric

Syntax   acsc(z)

Description   Returns the inverse cosecant of z (in radians). The result is the principal value for complex z.

Arguments
z real or complex number

acsch
Hyperbolic

Syntax   acsch(z)

Description   Returns the inverse hyperbolic cosecant of z. The result is the principal value for complex z.

Arguments
z real or complex number

Ai
Bessel

Syntax   Ai(x)

Description   Returns the value of the Airy function of the first kind.

Arguments
x real number

Example

Comments   This function is a solution of the differential equation: $\dfrac{d^2}{dx^2}y - x \cdot y = 0$.

Algorithm   Asymptotic expansion (Abramowitz and Stegun, 1972)

See also   Bi

angle
Trigonometric

Syntax	angle(x, y)
Description	Returns the angle (in radians) from positive x-axis to point (x, y) in x-y plane. The result is between 0 and 2π.
Arguments	
x, y	real numbers
See also	arg, atan, atan2

APPENDPRN
File Access

Syntax	APPENDPRN(*file*) := **A**
Description	Appends a matrix **A** to an existing structured ASCII data file. Each row in the matrix becomes a new line in the data file. Existing data must have as many columns as **A**. The function must appear alone on the left side of a definition.
Arguments	
file	string variable corresponding to structured ASCII data filename or path
See also	WRITEPRN for more details

arg
Complex Numbers

Syntax	arg(z)
Description	Returns the angle (in radians) from the positive real axis to point z in the complex plane. The result is between $-\pi$ and π. Returns the same value as that of θ when z is written as $r \cdot e^{i \cdot \theta}$.
Arguments	
z	real or complex number
See also	angle, atan, atan2

asec
Trigonometric

Syntax	asec(z)
Description	Returns the inverse secant of z (in radians). The result is the principal value for complex z.
Arguments	
z	real or complex number

asech
Hyperbolic

Syntax	asech(z)
Description	Returns the inverse hyperbolic secant of z. The result is the principal value for complex z.
Arguments	
z	real or complex number

asin
Trigonometric

Syntax   asin(z)

Description   Returns the inverse sine of z (in radians). The result is between $-\pi/2$ and $\pi/2$ if $-1 \leq z \leq 1$. For complex z, the result is the principal value.

Arguments
z real or complex number

asinh
Hyperbolic

Syntax   asinh(z)

Description   Returns the inverse hyperbolic sine of z. The result is the principal value for complex z.

Arguments
z real or complex number

atan
Trigonometric

Syntax   atan(z)

Description   Returns the inverse tangent of z (in radians). The result is between $-\pi/2$ and $\pi/2$ if z is real. For complex z, the result is the principal value.

Arguments
z real or complex number

See also   angle, arg, atan2

atan2
Trigonometric

Syntax   atan2(x, y)

Description   Returns the angle (in radians) from positive x-axis to point (x, y) in x-y plane. The result is between $-\pi$ and π.

Arguments
x, y real numbers

See also   angle, arg, atan

atanh
Hyperbolic

Syntax   atanh(z)

Description   Returns the inverse hyperbolic tangent of z. The result is the principal value for complex z.

Arguments
z real or complex number

augment
Vector and Matrix

Syntax   augment(**A**, **B**, **C**, ...)

Description   Returns a matrix formed by placing the matrices **A**, **B**, **C**, ... left to right.

Arguments
A, B, C, ...   at least two matrices or vectors; **A, B, C, ...** must have the same number of rows

Example

$$A := \begin{bmatrix} \sqrt{2} \\ e \\ \pi \end{bmatrix} \qquad B := \textbf{identity}(3) \qquad B = \begin{bmatrix} 1 & 0 & 0 \\ 0 & 1 & 0 \\ 0 & 0 & 1 \end{bmatrix} \qquad \textbf{augment}(3,5,7) = (3\ \ 5\ \ 7)$$

$$\textbf{augment}(A,B) = \begin{bmatrix} 1.41421 & 1 & 0 & 0 \\ 2.71828 & 0 & 1 & 0 \\ 3.14159 & 0 & 0 & 1 \end{bmatrix} \qquad \textbf{stack}\left(A^T, B\right) = \begin{bmatrix} 1.41421 & 2.71828 & 3.14159 \\ 1 & 0 & 0 \\ 0 & 1 & 0 \\ 0 & 0 & 1 \end{bmatrix}$$

See also   stack

bei
Bessel

Syntax   bei(n, x)

Description   Returns the value of the imaginary Bessel Kelvin function of order n.

Arguments

n integer, $n \geq 0$

x real number

Comments   The function $\text{ber}(n, x) + i \cdot \text{bei}(n, x)$ is a solution of the differential equation:

$$x^2 \frac{d^2}{dx^2} y + x \cdot \frac{d}{dx} y - (i \cdot x^2 + n^2) \cdot y = 0.$$

Algorithm   Series expansion (Abramowitz and Stegun, 1972)

See also   ber

ber
Bessel

Syntax   ber(n, x)

Description   Returns the value of the real Bessel Kelvin function of order n.

Arguments

n integer, $n \geq 0$

x real number

Comments   The function $\text{ber}(n, x) + i \cdot \text{bei}(n, x)$ is a solution of the differential equation:

$$x^2 \frac{d^2}{dx^2} y + x \cdot \frac{d}{dx} y - (i \cdot x^2 + n^2) \cdot y = 0.$$

Algorithm   Series expansion (Abramowitz and Stegun, 1972)

See also   bei

Bi
Bessel

Syntax   Bi(x)

Description   Returns the value of the Airy function of the second kind.

Arguments

x real number

Comments This function is a solution of the differential equation:

$$\frac{d^2}{dx^2}y - x \cdot y = 0 .$$

Algorithm Asymptotic expansion (Abramowitz and Stegun, 1972)

See also Ai for example

---

bspline
Interpolation and Prediction

Syntax bspline(**vx**, **vy**, **u**, n)

Description Returns the vector of coefficients of a B-spline of degree n, given the knot locations indicated by the values in **u**. The output vector becomes the first argument of the interp function.

Arguments

vx, vy real vectors of the same size; elements of **vx** must be in ascending order

u real vector with $n - 1$ fewer elements than **vx**; elements of **u** must be in ascending order; first element of **vx** is $\geq$ first element of **u**; last element of **vx** is $\leq$ last element of **u**

n integer equal to 1, 2, or 3; represents the degree of the individual piecewise linear, quadratic, or cubic polynomial fits

Comments The knots, those values where the pieces fit together, are contained in the input vector **u**. This is unlike traditional splines (lspline, cspline, and pspline) where the knots are forced to be the values contained in the vector **vx**. The fact that knots are chosen or modified by the user gives bspline more flexibility than the other splines.

See also lspline for more details

---

bulstoer
Differential Equation Solving

Syntax bulstoer(**y**, $x1$, $x2$, acc, **D**, $kmax$, $save$)

Description Solves a differential equation using the smooth Bulirsch-Stoer method. Provides DE solution estimate at $x2$.

Arguments Several arguments for this function are the same as described for rkfixed.

y real vector of initial values

$x1, x2$ real endpoints of the solution interval

acc real $acc > 0$ controls the accuracy of the solution; a small value of acc forces the algorithm to take smaller steps along the trajectory, thereby increasing the accuracy of the solution. Values of acc around 0.001 will generally yield accurate solutions.

D(x, y) real vector-valued function containing the derivatives of the unknown functions

$kmax$ integer $kmax > 0$ specifies maximum number of intermediate points at which the solution is approximated; places an upper bound on the number of rows of the matrix returned by these functions

$save$ real $save > 0$ specifies the smallest allowable spacing between values at which the solutions are approximated; places a lower bound on the difference between any two numbers in the first column of the matrix returned by the function

Comments	The specialized DE solvers Bulstoer, Rkadapt, Radau, Stiffb, and Stiffr provide the solution $y(x)$ over a number of uniformly spaced x-values in the integration interval bounded by $x1$ and $x2$. When you want the value of the solution at only the endpoint, $y(x2)$, use bulstoer, rkadapt, radau, stiffb, and stiffr instead.
Algorithm	Adaptive step Bulirsch-Stoer method (Press *et al.*, 1992)
See also	rkfixed, a more general differential equation solver, for information on output and arguments.

Bulstoer   Differential Equation Solving

Syntax	Bulstoer($\mathbf{y}$, $x1$, $x2$, *npts*, $\mathbf{D}$)
Description	Solves a differential equation using the smooth Bulirsch-Stoer method. Provides DE solution at equally spaced x-values by repeated calls to bulstoer.
Arguments	All arguments for this function are the same as described for rkfixed.
$\mathbf{y}$	real vector of initial values
$x1$, $x2$	real endpoints of the solution interval
npts	integer *npts* > 0 specifies the number of points beyond initial point at which the solution is to be approximated; controls the number of rows in the matrix output
$\mathbf{D}(x,y)$	real vector-valued function containing the derivatives of the unknown functions
Comments	When you know the solution is smooth, use the Bulstoer function instead of rkfixed. The Bulstoer function uses the Bulirsch-Stoer method which is slightly more accurate under these circumstances than the Runge-Kutta method used by rkfixed.
Algorithm	Fixed step Bulirsch-Stoer method with adaptive intermediate steps (Press *et al.*, 1992)
See also	rkfixed, a more general differential equation solver, for information on output and arguments.

bvalfit   Differential Equation Solving

Syntax	bvalfit($\mathbf{v1}$, $\mathbf{v2}$, $x1$, $x2$, xf, $\mathbf{D}$, $\mathbf{load1}$, $\mathbf{load2}$, $\mathbf{score}$)
Description	Converts a boundary value differential equation to initial/terminal value problems. Useful when derivatives have a single discontinuity at an intermediate point xf.
Arguments	
$\mathbf{v1}$	real vector containing guesses for initial values left unspecified at $x1$
$\mathbf{v2}$	real vector containing guesses for initial values left unspecified at $x2$
$x1$, $x2$	real endpoints of the interval on which the solution to the DEs are evaluated
xf	point between $x1$ and $x2$ at which the trajectories of the solutions beginning at $x1$ and those beginning at $x2$ are constrained to be equal
$\mathbf{D}(x, y)$	real n-element vector-valued function containing the derivatives of the unknown functions
$\mathbf{load1}(x1, \mathbf{v1})$	real vector-valued function whose n elements correspond to the values of the n unknown functions at $x1$. Some of these values are constants specified by your initial conditions. If a value is unknown, you should use the corresponding guess value from $\mathbf{v1}$
$\mathbf{load2}(x2, \mathbf{v2})$	analogous to $\mathbf{load1}$ but for values taken by the n unknown functions at $x2$
$\mathbf{score}(xf, \mathbf{y})$	real n-element vector-valued function used to specify how you want the solutions to match at xf. One usually defines score(xf, $\mathbf{y}$) := $\mathbf{y}$ to make the solutions to all unknown functions match up at xf

Example

$$\text{Solve} \quad y'' = \begin{pmatrix} y \\ -y \end{pmatrix} \quad \begin{matrix} \text{for } x < 0 \\ \text{for } x \geq 0 \end{matrix} \quad \text{where } y(-1)=1 \text{ and } y(1)=2$$

$$D(x, y) := \begin{bmatrix} y_1 \\ (x < 0) \cdot y_0 + (x \geq 0) \cdot -y_0 \end{bmatrix}$$

$v1_0 := 1$ ← guess value for y'(-1)

$v2_0 := 1$ ← guess value for y'(1) $xf := 0$ ← point of discontinuity

$$\text{load1}(x1, v1) := \begin{pmatrix} 1 \\ v1_0 \end{pmatrix} \begin{matrix} \text{← y(-1)} \\ \text{← guess value for y'(-1)} \end{matrix}$$

$$\text{load2}(x2, v2) := \begin{pmatrix} 2 \\ v2_0 \end{pmatrix} \begin{matrix} \text{← y(1)} \\ \text{← guess value for y'(1)} \end{matrix}$$

$\text{score}(xf, y) := y$ ← tells Mathcad to match the two halves of the solution at x=xf

$S := \text{bvalfit}(v1, v2, -1, 1, 0, D, \text{load1}, \text{load2}, \text{score})$

$S = (\ 0.092\ \ -0.678\ )$ ← contains (y'(-1)   y'(1))

Comments

If you have information at the initial and terminal points, use sbval. If you know something about the solution and its first $n-1$ derivatives at some intermediate value xf, use bvalfit.

bvalfit solves a two-point boundary value problem of this type by shooting from the endpoints and matching the trajectories of the solution and its derivatives at the intermediate point. bvalfit is especially useful when a derivative has a discontinuity somewhere in the integration interval, as the above example illustrates. bvalfit does not return a solution to a differential equation. It merely computes the initial values the solution must have in order for the solution to match the final values you specify. You must then take the initial values returned by bvalfit and solve the resulting initial value problem using rkfixed or any of the other more specialized DE solvers.

Algorithm

Shooting method with 4th order Runge-Kutta method (Press *et al.*, 1992)

See also

rkfixed, for more information on output and arguments.

ceil
Truncation and Round-off

Syntax   ceil(z)

Description   Returns the least integer $\geq z$.

Arguments

z complex number

Comments   ceil no longer takes arguments with units.

Ceil(x, y) Returns the smallest multiple of y greater than or equal to x. y must be real and nonzero. Ceil scales by the threshold before performing the truncation, then rescales after truncation.

See also   floor for more details, round, trunc

cfft
Fourier Transform

Syntax   cfft(**A**)

Description   Returns the fast discrete Fourier transform of complex data (representing measurements at regular intervals in the time domain). Returns an array of the same size as its argument.

Arguments

A   real or complex matrix or vector

Example

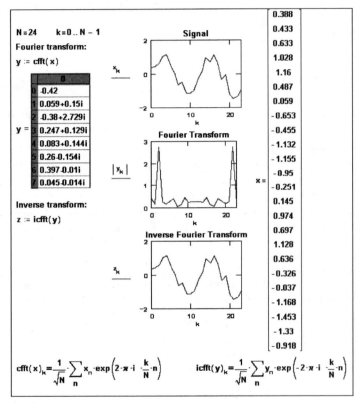

Comments   There are two reasons why you may not be able to use the fft/ifft Fourier transform pair:

- The data may be complex-valued, hence Mathcad can no longer exploit the symmetry present in the real-valued case.
- The data vector might not have exactly 2^n data points in it, hence Mathcad cannot take advantage of the efficient FFT algorithm used by the fft/ifft pair.

Although the cfft/icfft pair works on arrays of any size, the functions work significantly faster when the number of rows and columns contains many smaller factors. Vectors with length 2^n fall into this category, as do vectors having lengths like 100 or 120. Conversely, a vector whose length is a large prime number slows down the Fourier transform algorithm.

Algorithm   Singleton method (Singleton, 1986)

See also   fft for more details

CFFT
Fourier Transform

Syntax   CFFT($\mathbf{A}$)

Description   Returns the fast discrete Fourier transform of complex data (representing measurements at regular intervals in the time domain). Returns an array of the same size as its argument.

Identical to cfft($\mathbf{A}$), except uses a different normalizing factor and sign convention (see example).

Arguments
$\mathbf{A}$ real or complex matrix or vector

Example

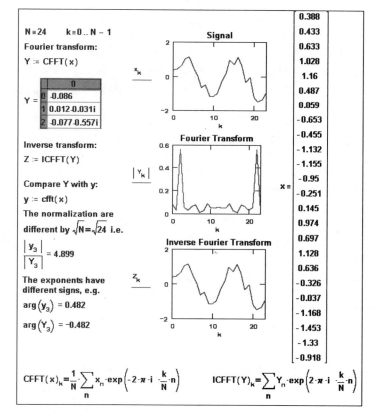

$$CFFT(x)_k = \frac{1}{N} \sum_n x_n \cdot \exp\left(-2 \cdot \pi \cdot i \cdot \frac{k}{N} \cdot n\right) \qquad ICFFT(Y)_k = \sum_n Y_n \cdot \exp\left(2 \cdot \pi \cdot i \cdot \frac{k}{N} \cdot n\right)$$

Algorithm   Singleton method (Singleton, 1986)

See also   fft for more details

cholesky
Vector and Matrix

Syntax   cholesky($\mathbf{M}$)

Description   Returns a lower triangular matrix $\mathbf{L}$ satisfying the equation $\mathbf{L} \cdot \mathbf{L}^T = \mathbf{M}$.

Arguments
$\mathbf{M}$ real, symmetric, positive definite, square matrix

Comments   cholesky takes $\mathbf{M}$ to be symmetric, in the sense that it uses only the upper triangular part of $\mathbf{M}$ and assumes it to match the lower triangular part.

cnorm

Syntax	cnorm(x)
Description	Returns the cumulative standard normal distribution. Same as pnorm(x, 0, 1).
Arguments	
x	real number
Comments	cnorm is provided mainly for compatibility with documents created in earlier versions of Mathcad.

cnper

Syntax	cnper(*rate*, *pv*, *fv*)
Description	Returns the number of compounding periods required for an investment to yield a specified future value, *fv*, given a present value, *pv*, and an interest rate period, *rate*.
Arguments	
rate	real rate, *rate* > -1
pv	real present value, *pv* > 0
fv	real future value, *fv* > 0
Comments	If you know the annual interest rate for the investment, *ann_rate*, you must calculate the interest rate per period as *rate* = *ann_rate*/*nper*.
See also	crate, nper

cols

Syntax	cols(**A**)
Description	Returns the number of columns in array **A**.
Arguments	
A	matrix or vector
Example	

Matrix M . . .

$$M := \begin{pmatrix} 0 & 1 \\ 5 & 3 \\ 6 & -2 \end{pmatrix} \quad \begin{array}{l} \text{cols}(M) = 2 \\ \text{rows}(M) = 3 \end{array} \quad \begin{array}{l} \leftarrow \text{Return no. of rows and} \\ \quad \text{columns in M} \end{array}$$

See also	rows

combin

Syntax	combin(n, k)
Description	Returns the number of subsets each of size k that can be formed from n objects.
Arguments	
n, k	integers, $0 \le k \le n$
Comments	Each such subset is known as a combination. The number of combinations is $C^n_k = \dfrac{n!}{k! \cdot (n-k)!}$.
See also	permut

concat
String

Syntax	concat(*S1*, *S2*, *S3*, ...)
Description	Appends string *S2* to the end of string *S1*, string *S3* to the end of string *S2*, and so on.
Arguments *S1*, *S2*, *S3*, ...	string expressions

cond1
Vector and Matrix

Syntax	cond1(**M**)
Description	Returns the condition number of the matrix **M** based on the L_1 norm.
Arguments **M**	real or complex square matrix

cond2
Vector and Matrix

Syntax	cond2(**M**)
Description	Returns the condition number of the matrix **M** based on the L_2 norm.
Arguments **M**	real or complex square matrix
Algorithm	Singular value computation (Wilkinson and Reinsch, 1971)

conde
Vector and Matrix

Syntax	conde(**M**)
Description	Returns the condition number of the matrix **M** based on the Euclidean norm.
Arguments **M**	real or complex square matrix

condi
Vector and Matrix

Syntax	condi(**M**)
Description	Returns the condition number of the matrix **M** based on the infinity norm.
Arguments **M**	real or complex square matrix

corr
Statistics

Syntax	corr(**A**, **B**)
Description	Returns the Pearson correlation coefficient for the elements in two $m \times n$ arrays **A** and **B**:

$$\text{corr}(\mathbf{A}, \mathbf{B}) = \frac{\text{cvar}(\mathbf{A}, \mathbf{B})}{\text{stdev}(\mathbf{A}) \cdot \text{stdev}(\mathbf{B})}$$

Arguments **A, B**	real or complex $m \times n$ matrices or vectors of the same size
See also	cvar

cos
Trigonometric

Syntax	$\cos(z)$, for z in radians; $\cos(z\ \text{deg})$, for z in degrees
Description	Returns the cosine of z.
Arguments	
z	real or complex number

cosh
Hyperbolic

Syntax	$\cosh(z)$
Description	Returns the hyperbolic cosine of z.
Arguments	
z	real or complex number

cot
Trigonometric

Syntax	$\cot(z)$, for z in radians; $\cot(z\ \text{deg})$, for z in degrees
Description	Returns the cotangent of z.
Arguments	
z	real or complex number; z is not a multiple of π

coth
Hyperbolic

Syntax	$\coth(z)$
Description	Returns the hyperbolic cotangent of z.
Arguments	
z	real or complex number

crate
Finance

Syntax	$\text{crate}(nper, pv, fv)$
Description	Returns the fixed interest rate required for an investment at present value, pv, to yield a specified future value, fv, over a given number of compounding periods, $nper$.
Arguments	
$nper$	integer number of compounding periods, $nper \geq 1$
pv	real present value, $pv > 0$
fv	real future value, $fv > 0$
See also	cnper, rate

CreateMesh
Vector and Matrix

Syntax	CreateMesh($\mathbf{F}$, *s0*, *s1*, *t0*, *t1*, *sgrid*, *tgrid*, **fmap**)
Description	Returns a nested array containing points on the parametric surface in 3D space defined by $\mathbf{F}$.
Arguments	
$\mathbf{F}$	real three-dimensional vector-valued function of two variables *s* and *t*; defines a parametric surface in (u,v,w)-space
s0, *s1*	(optional) real endpoints for the domain for *s*, $s0 < s1$
t0, *t1*	(optional) real endpoints for the domain for *t*, $t0 < t1$
sgrid	(optional) integer number of gridpoints in *s*, $sgrid > 0$
tgrid	(optional) integer number of gridpoints in *t*, $tgrid > 0$
fmap	(optional) real three-dimensional vector-valued function of three variables *u*, *v* and *w*; defines Cartesian coordinates (x,y,z) in terms of (u,v,w)

Comments   CreateMesh is used internally by Mathcad when making 3D QuickPlots of surfaces. The default value for *s0* and *t0* is -5, for *s1* and *t1* it is 5, for *sgrid* and *tgrid* it is 20, and for **fmap** it is the identity mapping. If *s0* and *s1* are explicitly specified, then *t0* and *t1* must also be specified. The number of cells in the grid determined by *sgrid* and *tgrid* is $(sgrid-1)(tgrid-1)$.

There is flexibility in specifying the function $\mathbf{F}$. Calls to CreateMesh might look like CreateMesh($\mathbf{G}$), where $\mathbf{G}$ is a real scalar-valued function of *u* and *v* (and $w=\mathbf{G}(u,v)$); or CreateMesh($h1,h2,h3$), where $h1$, $h2$, and $h3$ are real scalar-valued functions of *s* and *t* (and $u=h1(s,t)$, $v=h2(s,t)$, $w=h3(s,t)$).

Also, the mapping **fmap** may be defined to be sph2xyz, a Mathcad built-in function which converts spherical coordinates (r,θ,ϕ) to Cartesian coordinates (x,y,z):

$$x = u \sin(w) \cos(v) = r \sin(\phi) \cos(\theta)$$

$$y = u \sin(w) \sin(v) = r \sin(\phi) \sin(\theta)$$

$$z = u \cos(w) = r \cos(\phi)$$

or cyl2xyz, which converts cylindrical coordinates (r,θ,z) to (x,y,z) :

$$x = u \cos(v) = r \cos(\theta)$$

$$y = u \sin(v) = r \sin(\theta)$$

$$z = w = z.$$

CreateSpace
Vector and Matrix

Syntax	CreateSpace($\mathbf{F}$, *t0*, *t1*, *tgrid*, **fmap**)
Description	Returns a nested array containing points on the parametric curve in 3D space defined by $\mathbf{F}$.
Arguments	
$\mathbf{F}$	real three-dimensional vector-valued function of one variable *t*; defines a parametric curve in (u,v,w)-space
t0, *t1*	(optional) real endpoints for the domain for *t*, $t0 < t1$
tgrid	(optional) integer number of gridpoints in *t*, $tgrid > 0$
fmap	(optional) real three-dimensional vector-valued function of three variables *u*, *v* and *w*; defines Cartesian coordinates (x,y,z) in terms of (u,v,w)

Comments   CreateSpace is used internally by Mathcad when making 3D QuickPlots of curves. The default value for *t0* is -5, for *t1* it is 5, for *tgrid* it is 20, and for **fmap** it is the identity mapping. The number of cells in the grid determined by *tgrid* is $tgrid-1$.

There is flexibility in specifying the function **F**. Calls to CreateSpace might look like CreateSpace(*g1,g2,g3*), where *g1*, *g2*, and *g3* are real scalar-valued functions of *t* and $u=g1(t)$, $v=g2(t)$, $w=g3(t)$.

See also	CreateMesh for information about the mapping **fmap**.

---

csc

Trigonometric

Syntax	csc(*z*), for *z* in radians; csc(*z* deg), for *z* in degrees
Description	Returns the cosecant of *z*.
Arguments	
z	real or complex number; *z* is not a multiple of π

---

csch

Hyperbolic

Syntax	csch(*z*)
Description	Returns the hyperbolic cosecant of *z*.
Arguments	
z	real or complex number

---

csgn

Complex Numbers

Syntax	csgn(*z*)
Description	Returns 0 if $z=0$, 1 if $\mathrm{Re}(z)>0$ or ($\mathrm{Re}(z)=0$ and $\mathrm{Im}(z)>0$), -1 otherwise.
Arguments	
z	real or complex number
See also	sign, signum

---

csort

Sorting

Syntax	csort(**A**, *j*)
Description	Sorts the rows of the matrix **A** by placing the elements in column *j* in ascending order. The result is the same size as **A**.
Arguments	
A	$m \times n$ matrix or vector
j	integer, $0 \leq j \leq n-1$
Algorithm	Heap sort (Press *et al.*, 1992)
See also	sort for more details, rsort

---

cspline

Interpolation and Prediction

One-dimensional Case

Syntax	cspline(**vx**, **vy**)
Description	Returns the vector of coefficients of a cubic spline with cubic ends. This vector becomes the first argument of the interp function.
Arguments	
vx, vy	real vectors of the same size; elements of **vx** must be in ascending order

Two-dimensional Case

Syntax   cspline(**Mxy**, **Mz**)

Description   Returns the vector of coefficients of a two-dimensional cubic spline, constrained to be cubic at region boundaries spanned by **Mxy**. This vector becomes the first argument of interp.

Arguments
Mxy $n \times 2$ matrix whose elements, $Mxy_{i, 0}$ and $Mxy_{i, 1}$, specify the x- and y-coordinates along the *diagonal* of a rectangular grid. This matrix plays exactly the same role as **vx** in the one-dimensional case described above. Since these points describe a diagonal, the elements in each column of **Mxy** must be in ascending order ($Mxy_{i, k} < Mxy_{j, k}$ whenever $i < j$).

Mz $n \times n$ matrix whose ijth element is the z-coordinate corresponding to the point $x = Mxy_{i, 0}$ and $y = Mxy_{j, 1}$. **Mz** plays exactly the same role as **vy** does in the one-dimensional case above.

Algorithm   Tridiagonal system solving (Press *et al.*, 1992; Lorczak)

See also   lspline for more details

---

cumint

Syntax   cumint(*rate*, *nper*, *pv*, *start*, *end*, [*type*])

Description   Returns the cumulative interest paid on a loan between a starting period, *start*, and an ending period, *end*, given a fixed interest rate, *rate*, the total number of compounding periods, *nper*, and the present value of the loan, *pv*.

Arguments
rate   real rate, $rate \geq 0$

nper   integer number of compounding periods, $nper \geq 1$

pv   real present value

start   integer starting period of the accumulation, $start \geq 1$

end   integer ending period of the accumulation, $end \geq 1$, $start \leq end$, $end \leq nper$

type   (optional) indicator payment timing, 0 for payment made at the end of the period, 1 for payment made at the beginning, default is $type = 0$

Comments   If you know the annual interest rate for the loan, *ann_rate*, you must calculate the interest rate per period as $rate = ann\_rate/nper$.

A home mortgage has the following terms:

Interest rate:	9%	(annually)	Term:	30yrs	
Present value:	$125,000				

Calculate the total (cumulative) interest paid in the
10th year of payments (payments 121 through 132):

$rate := \dfrac{9\%}{12}$ $nper := 30 \cdot 12$ $pv := 125000$

$start := 120$ $end := 132$

cumint(rate, nper, pv, start, end) = −10815.54

Figure 16-6: Using the cumint *function.*

See also   cumprn, ipmt, pmt

cumprn
Finance

Syntax	cumprn(*rate*, *nper*, *pv*, *start*, *end*, [*type*])
Description	Returns the cumulative principal paid on a loan between a starting period, *start*, and an ending period, *end*, given a fixed interest rate, *rate*, the total number of compounding periods, *nper*, and the present value of the loan, *pv*.

Arguments	
rate	real rate, $rate \geq 0$
nper	integer number of compounding periods, $nper \geq 1$
pv	real present value
start	integer starting period of the accumulation, $start \geq 1$
end	integer ending period of the accumulation, $end \geq 1$, $start \leq end$, $end \leq nper$
type	(optional) indicator payment timing, 0 for payment made at the end of the period, 1 for payment made at the beginning, default is $type = 0$

Comments	If you know the annual interest rate for the loan, *ann_rate*, you must calculate the interest rate per period as $rate = ann\_rate/nper$.
See also	cumint, pmt, ppmt

cvar
Statistics

Syntax	cvar(**A**, **B**)
Description	Returns the covariance of the elements in two $m \times n$ arrays **A** and **B**:

$$\text{cvar}(\mathbf{A}, \mathbf{B}) = \frac{1}{mn} \sum_{i=0}^{m-1} \sum_{j=0}^{n-1} [A_{i,j} - \text{mean}(\mathbf{A})] \overline{[B_{i,j} - \text{mean}(\mathbf{B})]}, \text{ where the bar indicates}$$

complex conjugation.

Arguments	
A, B	real or complex $m \times n$ matrices or vectors
See also	corr

cyl2xyz
Vector and Matrix

Syntax	cyl2xyz(*r*, θ, *z*) or cyl2xyz(*v*)
Description	Converts the cylindrical coordinates of a point in 3D space to rectangular coordinates.

Arguments	
r, θ, *z*	real numbers
Comments	$x = r \cos(\theta)$, $y = r \sin(\theta)$, $z = z$, $v = \begin{bmatrix} r \\ \theta \\ z \end{bmatrix}$
See also	xyz2cyl

dbeta
Probability Density

Syntax	dbeta(*x*, *s1*, *s2*)
Description	Returns the probability density for a beta distribution: $\dfrac{\Gamma(s_1 + s_2)}{\Gamma(s_1) \cdot \Gamma(s_2)} \cdot x^{s_1 - 1} \cdot (1 - x)^{s_2 - 1}$.

Arguments	
x	real number, $0 < x < 1$
s_1, s_2	real shape parameters, $s_1 > 0$, $s_2 > 0$

dbinom
Probability Density

Syntax	dbinom(k, n, p)
Description	Returns $\Pr(X = k)$ when the random variable X has the binomial distribution: $\dfrac{n!}{k!(n-k)!}p^k(1-p)^{n-k}$.
Arguments	
k, n	integers, $0 \leq k \leq n$
p	real number, $0 \leq p \leq 1$

dcauchy
Probability Density

Syntax	dcauchy(x, l, s)
Description	Returns the probability density for the Cauchy distribution: $(\pi s(1 + ((x-l)/s)^2))^{-1}$.
Arguments	
x	real number
l	real location parameter
s	real scale parameter, $s > 0$

dchisq
Probability Density

Syntax	dchisq(x, d)
Description	Returns the probability density for the chi-squared distribution: $\dfrac{e^{-x/2}}{2\Gamma(d/2)}\left(\dfrac{x}{2}\right)^{(d/2-1)}$.
Arguments	
x	real number, $x \geq 0$
d	integer degrees of freedom, $d > 0$

dexp
Probability Density

Syntax	dexp(x, r)
Description	Returns the probability density for the exponential distribution: re^{-rx} .
Arguments	
x	real number, $x \geq 0$
r	real rate, $r > 0$

dF
Probability Density

Syntax	dF($x, d1, d2$)
Description	Returns the probability density for the F distribution:

$$\frac{d_1^{d_1/2} d_2^{d_2/2} \Gamma((d_1 + d_2)/2)}{\Gamma(d_1/2)\Gamma(d_2/2)} \cdot \frac{x^{(d_1-2)/2}}{(d_2 + d_1 x)^{(d_1+d_2)/2}} .$$

Arguments	
x	real number, $x \geq 0$
d_1, d_2	integer degrees of freedom, $d_1 > 0, d_2 > 0$

dgamma

Probability Density

Syntax dgamma(x, s)

Description Returns the probability density for the gamma distribution: $\dfrac{x^{s-1}e^{-x}}{\Gamma(s)}$.

Arguments

x real number, $x \geq 0$

s real shape parameter, $s > 0$

dgeom

Probability Density

Syntax dgeom(k, p)

Description Returns $\Pr(X = k)$ when the random variable X has the geometric distribution: $p(1-p)^k$.

Arguments

k integer, $k \geq 0$

p real number, $0 < p \leq 1$

dhypergeom

Probability Density

Syntax dhypergeom(m, a, b, n)

Description Returns $\Pr(X = m)$ when the random variable X has the hypergeometric distribution:

$$\binom{a}{m} \cdot \binom{b}{n-m} \Big/ \binom{a+b}{n} \quad \text{where } max\{0, n-b\} \leq m \leq min\{n, a\} ; 0 \text{ for } m \text{ elsewhere.}$$

Arguments

m, a, b, n integers, $0 \leq m \leq a$, $0 \leq n - m \leq b$, $0 \leq n \leq a + b$

diag

Vector and Matrix

Syntax diag($\mathbf{v}$)

Description Returns a diagonal matrix containing, on its diagonal, the elements of $\mathbf{v}$.

Arguments

$\mathbf{v}$ real or complex vector

dlnorm

Probability Density

Syntax dlnorm(x, μ, σ)

Description Returns the probability density for the lognormal distribution: $\dfrac{1}{\sqrt{2\pi}\sigma x}\exp\left(-\dfrac{1}{2\sigma^2}(\ln(x)-\mu)^2\right)$.

Arguments

x real number, $x \geq 0$

μ real logmean

σ real logdeviation, $\sigma > 0$

dlogis

Probability Density

Syntax dlogis(x, l, s)

Description Returns the probability density for the logistic distribution: $\dfrac{\exp(-(x-l)/s)}{s(1 + \exp(-(x-l)/s))^2}$.

Arguments

x real number

l real location parameter

s real scale parameter, $s > 0$

dnbinom
Probability Density

Syntax   dnbinom(k, n, p)

Description   Returns Pr($X = k$) when the random variable X has the negative binomial distribution:

$$\binom{n+k-1}{k} p^n(1-p)^k$$

Arguments

k, n integers, $n > 0$ and $k \ge 0$

p real number, $0 < p \le 1$

dnorm
Probability Density

Syntax   dnorm(x, μ, σ)

Description   Returns the probability density for the normal distribution: $\dfrac{1}{\sqrt{2\pi}\sigma} \exp\!\left(-\dfrac{1}{2\sigma^2}(x-\mu)^2\right)$.

Arguments

x real number

μ real mean

σ real standard deviation, $\sigma > 0$

Example

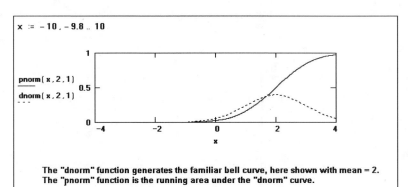

```
x := -10, -9.8 .. 10
```

The "dnorm" function generates the familiar bell curve, here shown with mean = 2.
The "pnorm" function is the running area under the "dnorm" curve.

dpois
Probability Density

Syntax   dpois(k, λ)

Description   Returns Pr($X = k$) when the random variable X has the Poisson distribution: $\dfrac{\lambda^k}{k!}e^{-\lambda}$.

Arguments

k integer, $k \ge 0$

λ real mean, $\lambda > 0$.

dt
Probability Density

Syntax   dt(x, d)

Description   Returns the probability density for Student's t distribution: $\dfrac{\Gamma((d+1)/2)}{\Gamma(d/2)\sqrt{\pi d}}\left(1+\dfrac{x^2}{d}\right)^{-(d+1)/2}$.

Arguments

x real number

d integer degrees of freedom, $d > 0$.

dunif
Probability Density

Syntax	dunif(x, a, b)
Description	Returns the probability density for the uniform distribution: $\dfrac{1}{b-a}$.
Arguments	
x	real number, $a \le x \le b$
a, b	real numbers, $a < b$

dweibull
Probability Density

Syntax	dweibull(x, s)
Description	Returns the probability density for the Weibull distribution: $sx^{s-1}\exp(-x^s)$.
Arguments	
x	real number, $x \ge 0$
s	real shape parameter, $s > 0$

eff
Finance

Syntax	eff(*rate*, *nper*)
Description	Returns the effective annual interest rate given the nominal interest rate, *rate*, and the number of compounding periods per year, *nper*.
Arguments	
rate	real rate
nper	real number of compounding periods, *nper* ≥ 1
Comments	Effective annual interest rate is also known as annual percentage rate (APR).
See also	nom

eigenvals
Vector and Matrix

Syntax	eigenvals(**M**)
Description	Returns a vector of eigenvalues for the matrix **M**.
Arguments	
M	real or complex square matrix

Example

$$A := \begin{pmatrix} 1 & -7 & 6 \\ 3 & 0 & 10 \\ 2 & 5 & -1 \end{pmatrix} \qquad c := \mathbf{eigenvals}(A) \qquad c = \begin{pmatrix} 3.805 + 1.194i \\ 3.805 - 1.194i \\ -7.609 \end{pmatrix}$$

Algorithm	Reduction to Hessenberg form coupled with QR decomposition (Press *et al.*, 1992)
See also	eigenvec, eigenvecs

eigenvec
Vector and Matrix

Syntax	eigenvec($\mathbf{M}$, z)
Description	Returns a vector containing the normalized eigenvector corresponding to the eigenvalue z of the square matrix $\mathbf{M}$.
Arguments	
$\mathbf{M}$	real or complex square matrix
z	real or complex number
Algorithm	Inverse iteration (Press *et al.*, 1992; Lorczak)
See also	eigenvals, eigenvecs

eigenvecs
Vector and Matrix

Syntax	eigenvecs($\mathbf{M}$)
Description	Returns a matrix containing the normalized eigenvectors corresponding to the eigenvalues of the matrix $\mathbf{M}$. The nth column of the matrix is the eigenvector corresponding to the nth eigenvalue returned by eigenvals.
Arguments	
$\mathbf{M}$	real or complex square matrix
Algorithm	Reduction to Hessenberg form coupled with QR decomposition (Press *et al.*, 1992)
See also	eigenvals, eigenvec
Example	

Finding eigenvalues and eigenvectors of a real matrix . .

$$A := \begin{pmatrix} 1 & -2 & 6 \\ 3 & 0 & 10 \\ 2 & 5 & -1 \end{pmatrix} \qquad c := \text{eigenvals}(A) \qquad c = \begin{pmatrix} 0.105 \\ 7.497 \\ -7.602 \end{pmatrix}$$

To find **all** the corresponding eigenvectors at once
(Mathcad Professional)

$$v := \text{eigenvecs}(A) \qquad v = \begin{pmatrix} 0.873 & 0.244 & -0.554 \\ -0.408 & 0.81 & -0.574 \\ -0.266 & 0.534 & 0.603 \end{pmatrix}$$

The first column of v is the eigenvector corresponding to 0.105, the first element of c. Similarly, the second column of v is the eigenvector corresponding to 7.497, the second element of c.

---

erf
Special

Syntax	erf(z)
Description	Returns the error function $\text{erf}(x) = \int_0^x \frac{2}{\sqrt{\pi}} e^{-t^2} dt$.
Arguments	
z	real or complex number
Algorithm	Continued fraction expansion (Abramowitz and Stegun, 1972; Lorczak)
See also	erfc

erfc
Special

Syntax	erfc(z)
Description	Returns the complementary error function $\mathrm{erfc}(x) := 1 - \mathrm{erf}(x)$.
Arguments	
z	complex or negative number
Algorithm	Continued fraction expansion (Abramowitz and Stegun, 1972; Lorczak)
See also	erf

error
String

Syntax	error(S)
Description	Returns the string S as an error message.
Arguments	
S	string
Example	

$$f(x) := \mathrm{if}\left(x<5, x \cdot \frac{2}{\pi}, \mathrm{error}(\text{"x should be less than 5"})\right)$$

$f(7) = \blacksquare \ \mathrm{d}$

x should be less than 5

Comments

Mathcad's built-in error messages appear as "error tips" when a built-in function is used incorrectly or could not return a result.

Use the string function error to define specialized error messages that will appear when your user-defined functions are used improperly or cannot return answers. This function is especially useful for trapping erroneous inputs to Mathcad programs you write.

When Mathcad encounters the error function in an expression, it highlights the expression in red. When you click on the expression, the error message appears in a tooltip that hovers over the expression. The text of the message is the string argument you supply to the error function.

exp
Log and Exponential

Syntax	exp(z)
Description	Returns the value of the exponential function e^z.
Arguments	
z	real or complex number

expfit
Curve Fitting and Smoothing

Syntax	expfit(**vx**, **vy**, [**vg**])
Description	Returns a vector containing the parameters (a, b, c) that make the function $a \cdot e^{b \cdot x} + c$ best approximate the data in **vx** and **vy**.
Arguments	
vx, **vy**	real vectors of the same size
vg	real vector of guess values for (a, b, c) (optional)

Comments   This is a special case of the genfit function. A vector of guess values may be used for initialization. If no guess values are provided, the function will generate its own set. By decreasing the value of the built-in TOL variable, higher accuracy in expfit might be achieved.

See Also   line, linfit, genfit, logfit, lnfit, pwrfit, lgsfit, sinfit, medfit

---

fft   Fourier Transform

Syntax   fft(v)

Description Returns the fast discrete Fourier transform of real data. Returns a vector of size $2^{n-1}+1$.

Arguments
v   real vector with 2^n elements (representing measurements at regular intervals in the time domain), where n is an integer, $n > 0$.

Example

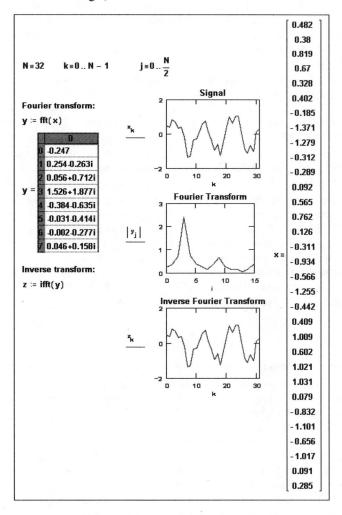

Comments   When you define a vector **v** for use with Fourier or wavelet transforms, be sure to start with v_0 (or change the value of ORIGIN). If you do not define v_0, Mathcad automatically sets it to zero. This can distort the results of the transform functions.

Mathcad comes with two types of Fourier transform pairs: fft/ifft and cfft/icfft. These functions can be applied only to discrete data (i.e., the inputs and outputs are vectors and matrices only). You cannot apply them to continuous data.

Use the fft and ifft functions if:

- the data values in the time domain are real, and
- the data vector has 2^n elements.

Use the cfft and icfft functions in all other cases.

The first condition is required because the fft/ifft pair takes advantage of the fact that, for real data, the second half of the transform is just the conjugate of the first. Mathcad discards the second half of the result vector to save time and memory. The cfft/icfft pair does not assume symmetry in the transform; therefore you *must* use this pair for complex valued data. Because the real numbers are just a subset of the complex numbers, you can use the cfft/icfft pair for real numbers as well.

The second condition is required because the fft/ifft transform pair uses a highly efficient fast Fourier transform algorithm. In order to do so, the vector you use with fft must have 2^n elements. The cfft/icfft Fourier transform pair uses an algorithm that permits vectors as well as matrices of arbitrary size. When you use this transform pair with a matrix, you get back a two-dimensional Fourier transform.

If you used fft to get to the frequency domain, you *must* use ifft to get back to the time domain. Similarly, if you used cfft to get to the frequency domain, you *must* use icfft to get back to the time domain.

Different sources use different conventions concerning the initial factor of the Fourier transform and whether to conjugate the results of either the transform or the inverse transform. The functions fft, ifft, cfft, and icfft use as a normalizing factor and a positive exponent in going from the time to the frequency domain. The functions FFT, IFFT, CFFT, and ICFFT use $1/n$ as a normalizing factor and a negative exponent in going from the time to the frequency domain. Be sure to use these functions in pairs. For example, if you used CFFT to go from the time domain to the frequency domain, you *must* use ICFFT to transform back to the time domain.

The elements of the vector returned by fft satisfy the following equation:

$$c_j = \frac{1}{\sqrt{n}} \sum_{k=0}^{n-1} v_k e^{2\pi i (j/n)k}$$

In this formula, n is the number of elements in **v** and i is the imaginary unit.

The elements in the vector returned by the fft function correspond to different frequencies. To recover the actual frequency, you must know the sampling frequency of the original signal. If **v** is an n-element vector passed to the fft function, and the sampling frequency is f_s, the frequency corresponding to c_k is

$$f_k = \frac{k}{n} \cdot f_s$$

Therefore, it is impossible to detect frequencies above the sampling frequency. This is a limitation not of Mathcad, but of the underlying mathematics itself. In order to correctly recover a signal from the Fourier transform of its samples, you must sample the signal with a frequency of at least twice its bandwidth. A thorough discussion of this phenomenon is outside the scope of this manual but within that of any textbook on digital signal processing.

Algorithm   Cooley-Tukey (Press *et al.*, 1992)

FFT

Fourier Transform

Syntax   FFT($\mathbf{v}$)

Description   Identical to fft($\mathbf{v}$), except uses a different normalizing factor and sign convention. Returns a vector of size $2^{n-1} + 1$.

Arguments
$\mathbf{v}$ real vector with 2^n elements (representing measurements at regular intervals in the time domain), where n is an integer, $n > 0$.

Comments   The definitions for the Fourier transform discussed in the fft entry are not the only ones used. For example, the following definitions for the discrete Fourier transform and its inverse appear in Ronald Bracewell's *The Fourier Transform and Its Applications* (McGraw-Hill, 1986):

$$F(\upsilon) = \frac{1}{n} \sum_{\tau = 1}^{n} f(\tau) e^{-2\pi i (\upsilon/n)\tau} \quad f(\tau) = \sum_{\upsilon = 1}^{n} F(\upsilon) e^{2\pi i (\tau/n)\upsilon}$$

These definitions are very common in engineering literature. To use these definitions rather than those presented in the last section, use the functions FFT, IFFT, CFFT, and ICFFT. These differ from those discussed in the last section as follows:

- Instead of a factor of $1/\sqrt{n}$ in front of both forms, there is a factor of $1/n$ in front of the transform and no factor in front of the inverse.
- The minus sign appears in the exponent of the transform instead of in its inverse.

The functions FFT, IFFT, CFFT, and ICFFT are used in exactly the same way as the functions fft, ifft, cfft, and icfft.

Algorithm   Cooley-Tukey (Press *et al.*, 1992)

See also   fft for more details

fhyper

Special

Syntax   fhyper(a, b, c, x)

Description   Returns the value of the Gauss hypergeometric function $_2F_1(a, b;c;x)$.

Arguments
a, b, c, x real numbers, $-1 < x < 1$

Comments   The hypergeometric function is a solution of the differential equation

$$x \cdot (1 - x) \cdot \frac{d^2}{dx^2} y + (c - (a + b + 1) \cdot x) \cdot \frac{d}{dx} y - a \cdot b \cdot y = 0 .$$

Many functions are special cases of the hypergeometric function, e.g., elementary ones like

$$\ln(1 + x) = x \cdot \text{fhyper}(1, 1, 2, -x) , \quad \text{asin}(x) = x \cdot \text{fhyper}\left(\frac{1}{2}, \frac{1}{2}, \frac{3}{2}, x^2\right)$$

and more complicated ones like Legendre functions.

Algorithm   Series expansion (Abramowitz and Stegun, 1972)

Find

Syntax	Find(*var1*, *var2*, ...)
Description	Returns values of *var1*, *var2*, ... which solve a prescribed system of equations, subject to prescribed inequalities. The number of arguments matches the number of unknowns. Output is a scalar if only one argument; otherwise it is a vector of answers.
Arguments *var1*, *var2*, ...	real or complex variables; *var1*, *var2*,.. must be assigned guess values before using Find.
Examples	

```
Intersection of Circle and line:

Guess values:    x := 1
                 y := 1

Given            x² + y² = 6        Circle
                 x + y = 2          Line
                 x ≤ 1
                 y > 2              Inequality
                                    constraints

                 (xval)
                 (yval) := Find(x, y)

Results:         xval = -0.414
                 yval = 2.414

Check that point is an actual solution:

     xval² + yval² = 6              xval + yval = 2
```

A solve block with both equations and inequalities.

Comments
Mathcad lets you numerically solve a system of up to 200 simultaneous equations in 200 unknowns. If you aren't sure that a given system possesses a solution but need an approximate answer which minimizes error, use Minerr instead. To solve an equation symbolically, that is, to find an exact answer in terms of elementary functions, choose **Variable ⇒ Solve** from the **Symbolics** menu or use the solve keyword.

There are four steps to solving a system of simultaneous equations:

1. Provide initial guesses for all the unknowns you intend to solve for. These give Mathcad a place to start searching for solutions. Use complex guess values if you anticipate complex solutions; use real guess values if you anticipate real solutions.

2. Type the word Given. This tells Mathcad that what follows is a system of equality or inequality constraints. You can type Given or given in any style. Just don't type it while in a text region.

3. Type the equations and inequalities in any order below the word Given. Use [Ctrl]= to type "=."

4. Finally, type the Find function with your list of unknowns. You can't put numerical values in the list of unknowns: for example, Find(2) in Example 1 isn't permitted. Like given, you can type Find or find in any style.

The word Given, the equations and inequalities that follow, and the Find function form a *solve block*.

The types of allowable constraints are $z=w$, $x>y$, $x<y$, $x \geq y$ and $x \leq y$. Mathcad does not allow the following inside a solve block:

- Constraints with "$\neq$"
- Range variables or expressions involving range variables of any kind
- Any kind of assignment statement (statements like **x:=1**)

The popup menu (right mouse click) associated with Find contains the following options:

- **AutoSelect**
- **Linear**—applies the linear Simplex method; guess values for *var1*, *var2*,... are not required.
- **Nonlinear**—applies one of the following to the problem: the conjugate gradient solver; if that fails to converge, the Levenberg-Marquardt solver; if that fails, the quasi-Newton solver; guess values for *var1*, *var2*,... markedly affect the solution
- **Quadratic**—applies a quadratic simplex method; guess values for *var1*, *var2*,... are not required
- **Advanced options**—applies only to the nonlinear conjugate gradient and the quasi-Newton solvers

You may also adjust the values of the built-in variables CTOL and TOL. The *constraint tolerance* CTOL controls how closely a constraint must be met for a solution to be acceptable; TOL is the *convergence tolerance* . The default value for CTOL is 10^{-3}.

For more information and examples, see Chapter 9, "Solving and Data Analysis."

Algorithm   For the non-linear case: Levenberg-Marquardt, Quasi-Newton, Conjugate Gradient. For the linear case: simplex method with branch/bound techniques (Press *et al.*, 1992; Polak, 1997; Winston, 1994)

See also   Minerr, Maximize, Minimize

---

floor
Truncation and Round-off

Syntax   floor(z)

Description   Returns the greatest integer $\leq z$.

Arguments
z complex number

Example

```
ceil( 3.25 ) = 4          floor( 3.25 ) = 3

mantissa( x ) := x - floor( x )

       mantissa( 3.45 ) = 0.45
```

Comments   Can be used to define the positive fractional part of a number: mantissa(x) := x - floor(x). When a complex number is used as the argument, floor returns *floor(Re) + floor(Im)*.

floor no longer takes arguments with units.

Floor(x, y) Returns the greatest multiple of y less than or equal to x. y must be real and nonzero. Floor scales by the threshold before performing the truncation, then rescales after truncation.

See also   ceil, round, trunc

fv
Finance

Syntax	fv(*rate*, *nper*, *pmt*, [[*pv*], [*type*]])
Description	Returns the future value of an investment or loan over a specified number of compounding periods, *nper*, given a periodic, constant payment, *pmt*, and a fixed interest rate, *rate*.

Arguments

rate	real rate
nper	integer number of compounding periods, $nper \geq 1$
pmt	real payment
pv	(optional) real present value, default is $pv = 0$
type	(optional) indicator payment timing, 0 for payment made at the end of the period, 1 for payment made at the beginning, default is $type = 0$

Comments	If you know the annual interest rate, *ann_rate*, you must calculate the interest rate per period as $rate = ann\_rate/nper$.
	Payments you make, such as deposits into a savings account or payments toward a loan, must be entered as negative numbers. Cash you receive, such as dividend checks, must be entered as positive numbers.
See also	fvadj, fvc, nper, pmt, pv, rate

fvadj
Finance

Syntax	fvadj(*prin*, **v**)
Description	Returns the future value of an initial principal, *prin*, after applying a series of compound interest rates stored in a vector, **v**.

Arguments

prin	real principal
v	real vector of interest rates

Comments	Use fvadj to calculate the future value of an investment with a variable or adjustable interest rate.
See also	fv, fvc

fvc
Finance

Syntax	fvc(*rate*, **v**)
Description	Returns the future value of a list of cash flows occurring at regular intervals, **v**, earning a specified interest rate, *rate*.

Arguments

rate	real rate
v	real vector of cash flows

Comments	In **v**, payments must be entered as negative numbers and income must be entered as positive numbers.
	fvc assumes that the payment is made at the end of the period.
See also	fv, fvadj

gcd

Syntax	gcd(**A**)
Description	Returns the largest positive integer that is a divisor of all the values in the array **A**. This integer is known as the greatest common divisor of the elements in **A**.
Arguments	
A	integer matrix or vector; all elements of **A** are greater than zero
Comments	gcd(**A, B, C, ...**) is also permissible and returns the greatest common divisor of the elements of **A, B, C, ...**
Algorithm	Euclid's algorithm (Niven and Zuckerman, 1972)
See also	lcm

genfit

Syntax	genfit(**vx, vy, vg, F**)
Description	Returns a vector containing the parameters that make a function f of x and n parameters $u_0, u_1, ..., u_{n-1}$ best approximate the data in **vx** and **vy**.
Arguments	
vx, vy	real vectors of the same size
vg	real vector of guess values for the n parameters
F	a function that returns an $n+1$ element vector containing f and its partial derivatives with respect to its n parameters

Example

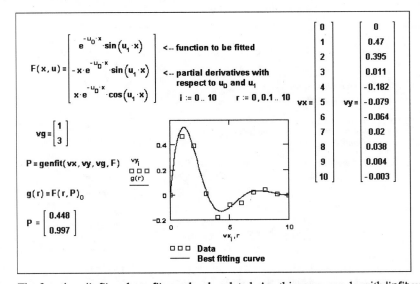

Comments   The functions linfit and genfit are closely related. Anything you can do with linfit you can also do, albeit less conveniently, with genfit. The difference between these two functions is analogous to the difference between solving a system of linear equations and solving a system of nonlinear equations. The former is easily done using the methods of linear algebra. The latter is far more difficult and generally must be solved by iteration. This explains why genfit needs a vector of guess values as an argument and linfit does not.

The example above uses genfit to find the exponent that best fits a set of data. By decreasing the value of the built-in TOL variable, higher accuracy in genfit might be achieved.

Algorithm	Levenberg-Marquardt (Press *et al.*, 1992)
See also	line, linfit, expfit, logfit, lnfit, pwrfit, lgsfit, sinfit, medfit

---

geninv
Vector and Matrix

Syntax	geninv($\mathbf{A}$)
Description	Returns the left inverse of a matrix $\mathbf{A}$.
Arguments	
$\mathbf{A}$	real $m \times n$ matrix, where $m \geq n$.
Comments	If $\mathbf{L}$ denotes the left inverse, then $\mathbf{L} \cdot \mathbf{A} = \mathbf{I}$ where $\mathbf{I}$ is the identity matrix with cols($\mathbf{I}$)=cols($\mathbf{A}$).
Algorithm	SVD-based construction (Nash, 1979)

---

genvals
Vector and Matrix

Syntax	genvals($\mathbf{M}$, $\mathbf{N}$)
Description	Returns a vector $\mathbf{v}$ of eigenvalues each of which satisfies the generalized eigenvalue equation $\mathbf{M} \cdot \mathbf{x} = v_j \cdot \mathbf{N} \cdot \mathbf{x}$ for nonzero eigenvectors $\mathbf{x}$.
Arguments	
$\mathbf{M}$, $\mathbf{N}$	real square matrices of the same size
Example	

$$\mathbf{M} := \begin{bmatrix} -3 & 6 & 0 \\ 3 & 0 & -4 \\ 6 & 6 & -5 \end{bmatrix} \qquad \mathbf{N} := \begin{bmatrix} -5 & 9 & -1 \\ 0 & 4 & -7 \\ -3 & 10 & 4 \end{bmatrix}$$

Vector of generalized eigenvalues:

$$\mathbf{v} := \text{genvals}(\mathbf{M}, \mathbf{N}) \qquad \mathbf{v} = \begin{bmatrix} 2.177 \\ 0.803 \\ 0.285 \end{bmatrix}$$

Matrix of generalized eigenvectors which correspond to the generalized eigenvalues in vector v:

$$\mathbf{x} := \text{genvecs}(\mathbf{M}, \mathbf{N}) \qquad \mathbf{x} = \begin{bmatrix} 0.839 & 0.562 & -0.597 \\ 0.515 & 0.725 & -0.21 \\ 0.175 & 0.397 & -0.774 \end{bmatrix}$$

x0 := submatrix($\mathbf{x}$,0,2,0,0)
x1 := submatrix($\mathbf{x}$,0,2,1,1)
x2 := submatrix($\mathbf{x}$,0,2,2,2)

Compare:

$$\mathbf{M} \cdot \mathbf{x0} = \begin{bmatrix} 0.571 \\ 1.818 \\ 7.25 \end{bmatrix} \qquad \mathbf{M} \cdot \mathbf{x1} = \begin{bmatrix} 2.666 \\ 0.1 \\ 5.744 \end{bmatrix} \qquad \mathbf{M} \cdot \mathbf{x2} = \begin{bmatrix} 0.534 \\ 1.306 \\ -0.969 \end{bmatrix}$$

$$\mathbf{v}_0 \cdot (\mathbf{N} \cdot \mathbf{x0}) = \begin{bmatrix} 0.571 \\ 1.818 \\ 7.25 \end{bmatrix} \quad \mathbf{v}_1 \cdot (\mathbf{N} \cdot \mathbf{x1}) = \begin{bmatrix} 2.666 \\ 0.1 \\ 5.744 \end{bmatrix} \quad \mathbf{v}_2 \cdot (\mathbf{N} \cdot \mathbf{x2}) = \begin{bmatrix} 0.534 \\ 1.306 \\ -0.969 \end{bmatrix}$$

Comments	To compute the eigenvectors, use genvecs.
Algorithm	Stable QZ method (Golub and Van Loan, 1989)

genvecs
Vector and Matrix

Syntax	genvecs($\mathbf{M}$, $\mathbf{N}$)
Description	Returns a matrix of normalized eigenvectors corresponding to the eigenvalues in $\mathbf{v}$, the vector returned by genvals. The jth column of this matrix is the eigenvector $\mathbf{x}$ satisfying the generalized eigenvalue problem $\mathbf{M} \cdot \mathbf{x} = v_j \cdot \mathbf{N} \cdot \mathbf{x}$.
Arguments $\mathbf{M}, \mathbf{N}$	real square matrices of the same size
Algorithm	Stable QZ method (Golub and Van Loan, 1989)
See also	genvals for example

GETWAVINFO
File Access

Syntax	GETWAVINFO(*file*)
Description	Creates a vector with four elements containing information about *file*. The elements corresponds to the number of channels, the sample rate, the number of bits per sample (resolution), and average number of bytes per second, respectively.
Arguments *file*	string variable corresponding to pulse code modulated (PCM) Microsoft WAV filename or path
Comments	Data from a WAV file is not scaled.
See also	READWAV and WRITEWAV

gmean
Statistics

Syntax	gmean($\mathbf{A}$)
Description	Returns the geometric mean of the elements of $\mathbf{A}$: $\text{gmean}(\mathbf{A}) = \left(\prod_{i=0}^{m-1} \prod_{j=0}^{n-1} \mathbf{A}_{i,j} \right)^{1/(mn)}$.
Arguments $\mathbf{A}$	real $m \times n$ matrix or vector with all elements greater than zero
Comments	gmean($\mathbf{A}$, $\mathbf{B}$, $\mathbf{C}$, ...) is also permissible and returns the geometric mean of the elements of $\mathbf{A}$, $\mathbf{B}$, $\mathbf{C}$, ...
See also	hmean, mean, median, mode

H1
Bessel

Syntax	H1(m, z)
Description	Returns the value of the Hankel function $H1(z)$ of the first kind.
Arguments m	non-negative real number
z	real or complex number
Comments	Hankel functions are Bessel functions of the third kind. $H1(m,z) = J_n(m,z) + iY_n(m,z)$. H1.sc($z$), where sc means scaled and is a literal subscript, gives $exp(-zi)H1(z)$. Scaled functions are useful for calculating large arguments without overflow.
Algorithm	AMOSLIB; ACM TOMS 12 (1986) 265-273.
See also	Jn, Yn, H2

H2
Bessel

Syntax	H2(m, z)
Description	Returns the value of the Hankel function $H2(z)$ of the second kind.
Arguments	
m	non-negative real number
z	real or complex number
Comments	Hankel functions are Bessel functions of the third kind. $H2(m,z) = J_n(m,z) - iY_n(m,z)$. H2.sc($z$), where sc means scaled and is a literal subscript, gives $exp(zi)$H2(z). Scaled functions are useful for calculating large arguments without overflow.
Algorithm	AMOSLIB; ACM TOMS 12 (1986) 265-273.
See also	Jn, Yn, H1

Her
Special

Syntax	Her(n, x)
Description	Returns the value of the Hermite polynomial of degree n at x.
Arguments	
n	integer, $n \geq 0$
x	real number
Comments	The nth degree Hermite polynomial is a solution of the differential equation:

$$x \cdot \frac{d^2}{dx^2}y - 2 \cdot x \cdot \frac{d}{dx}y + 2 \cdot n \cdot y = 0 .$$

Algorithm	Recurrence relation (Abramowitz and Stegun, 1972)

hist
Statistics

Uniform Bin Case

Syntax	hist(n, **A**)
Description	Returns a vector containing the frequencies with which values in **A** fall in n subintervals of the range $\min(\mathbf{A}) \leq \text{value} \leq \max(\mathbf{A})$ of equal length. The resulting histogram vector has n elements.
Arguments	
n	integer, $n > 0$
A	real matrix
Comments	This is identical to hist(**intervals**, **A**) with $intervals_i = \min(\mathbf{A}) + \frac{\max(\mathbf{A}) - \min(\mathbf{A})}{n} \cdot i$ and $0 \leq i \leq n$ (see below).

Non-uniform Bin Case

Syntax	hist(**intervals**, **A**)
Description	Returns a vector containing the frequencies with which values in **A** fall in the intervals represented by the **intervals** vector. The resulting histogram vector is one element shorter than **intervals**.

Arguments

intervals	real vector with elements in ascending order
A	real matrix

Example

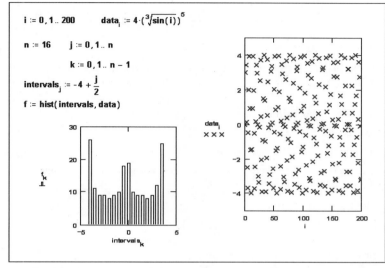

Comments The **intervals** vector contains the endpoints of subintervals constituting a partition of the data. The result of the hist function is a vector **f**, in which f_i is the number of values in **A** satisfying the condition $intervals_i \leq value < intervals_{i+1}$.

Mathcad ignores data points less than the first value in **intervals** or greater than the last value in **intervals**.

See also histogram

histogram

Statistics

Uniform Bin Case

Syntax histogram(n, **A**)

Description Returns a matrix with two columns. The first column contains midpoints of the n subintervals of the range $\min(\mathbf{A}) \leq value \leq \max(\mathbf{A})$ of equal length. The second column is identical to hist(n, **A**), and hence the resulting matrix has n rows.

Arguments

n	integer, $n > 0$
A	real matrix

Comments Using histogram rather than hist saves you the additional step of defining horizontal axis data when plotting.

Non-uniform Bin Case

Syntax histogram(**intervals**, **A**)

Description Returns a matrix with two columns. The first column contains midpoints of the intervals represented by the **intervals** vector. The second column is identical to hist(**intervals**, **A**), and hence the resulting matrix has one less row than **intervals**.

Arguments

intervals | real vector with elements in ascending order
A | real matrix

See also | hist

---

hlookup Vector and Matrix

Syntax | hlookup(z, **A**, r)

Description | Looks in the first row of a matrix, **A**, for a given value, z, and returns the value(s) in the same column(s) in the row specified, r. When multiple values are returned, they appear in a vector.

Arguments

z | real or complex number, or string
A | real, complex or string $m \times n$ matrix
r | integer, $ORIGIN \le r \le ORIGIN + m - 1$

Comments | The degree of precision to which the comparison adheres is determined by the TOL setting of the worksheet.

See Also | lookup, vlookup, match

---

hmean Statistics

Syntax | hmean(**A**)

Description | Returns the harmonic mean of the elements of **A**: $\text{hmean}(\mathbf{A}) = \left(\frac{1}{mn} \sum_{i=0}^{m-1} \sum_{j=0}^{n-1} \frac{1}{\mathbf{A}_{i,j}} \right)^{-1}$.

Arguments

A | real $m \times n$ matrix or vector with all elements greater than zero

Comments | hmean(**A**, **B**, **C**, ...) is also permissible and returns the harmonic mean of the elements of **A**, **B**, **C**, ...

See also | gmean, mean, median, mode

I0 Bessel

Syntax | I0(z)

Description | Returns the value of the modified Bessel function $I_0(z)$ of the first kind. Same as In(0, z).

Arguments

z | real or complex number

Comments | I0.sc(z), where sc means scaled and is a literal subscript, gives $exp(-|Re(z)|)I0(z)$. Scaled functions are useful for calculating large arguments without overflow.

Algorithm | Small order approximation (Abramowitz and Stegun, 1972)

See also | In

I1   Bessel

Syntax	$I1(z)$
Description	Returns the value of the modified Bessel function $I_1(z)$ of the first kind. Same as $In(1, z)$.
Arguments	
z	real or complex number
Comments	$I1.sc(z)$, where sc means scaled and is a literal subscript, gives $exp(-|Re(z)|)I1(z)$. Scaled functions are useful for calculating large arguments without overflow.
Algorithm	Small order approximation (Abramowitz and Stegun, 1972)

ibeta   Special

Syntax	$ibeta(a, x, y)$
Description	Returns the value of the incomplete beta function with parameter a, at (x, y).
Arguments	
a	real number, $0 \le a \le 1$
x, y	real numbers, $x > 0, y > 0$
Comments	The incomplete beta function often arises in probabilistic applications. It is defined by the following formula:

$$ibeta(a, x, y) = \frac{\Gamma(x+y)}{\Gamma(x) \cdot \Gamma(y)} \cdot \int_0^a t^{x-1} \cdot (1-t)^{y-1} dt.$$

Algorithm	Continued fraction expansion (Abramowitz and Stegun, 1972)

icfft   Fourier Transform

Syntax	$icfft(A)$
Description	Returns the inverse Fourier transform corresponding to cfft. Returns an array of the same size as its argument.
Arguments	
A	real or complex matrix or vector
Comments	The cfft and icfft functions are exact inverses; $icfft(cfft(A)) = A$.
Algorithm	Singleton method (Singleton, 1986)
See also	fft for more details and cfft for example

ICFFT   Fourier Transform

Syntax	$ICFFT(A)$
Description	Returns the inverse Fourier transform corresponding to CFFT. Returns an array of the same size as its argument.
Arguments	
A	real or complex matrix or vector
Comments	The CFFT and ICFFT functions are exact inverses; $ICFFT(CFFT(A)) = A$.
Algorithm	Singleton method (Singleton, 1986)
See also	fft for more details and CFFT for example

identity

Vector and Matrix

Syntax   identity(*n*)

Description   Returns the $n \times n$ identity matrix.

Arguments

n integer, $n > 0$

if

Piecewise Continuous

Syntax   if(*cond*, *x*, *y*)

Description   Returns x or y depending on the value of *cond*.
If *cond* is true (non-zero), returns x. If *cond* is false (zero), returns y.

Arguments

cond   arbitrary expression (usually a Boolean expression)

x, y   arbitrary real or complex numbers, arrays, or strings

Example

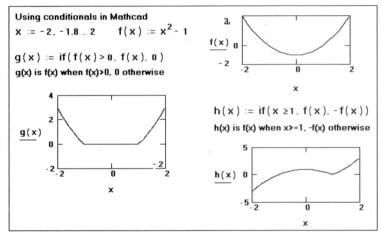

Comments   Use if to define a function that behaves one way below a certain number and a different way above that number. That point of discontinuity is specified by its first argument, *cond*. The remaining two arguments let you specify the behavior of the function on either side of that discontinuity. The argument *cond* is usually a Boolean expression that relates two math expressions with a Boolean operator from the Boolean toolbar ($=, >, <, \geq, \leq, \neq, \wedge, \vee, \oplus,$ or $\neg$). (See "Boolean Operators" on page 415.)

To save time, Mathcad evaluates only the necessary arguments. For example, if *cond* is false, there is no need to evaluate x because it will not be returned anyway. Therefore, errors in the unevaluated argument can escape detection. For example, Mathcad will never detect the fact that $\ln(0)$ is undefined in the expression if($|z| < 0$, $\ln(0)$, $\ln(z)$).

You can combine Boolean operators to create more complicated conditions. For example, the condition $(x < 1) \wedge (x > 0)$ acts like an "and" gate, returning 1 if and only if x is between 0 and 1. Similarly, the expression $(x < 1) \vee (x > 0)$ acts like an "or" gate, returning a 1 if and only if $x > 1$ or $x < 0$.

ifft

Syntax	ifft(**v**)
Description	Returns the inverse Fourier transform corresponding to fft. Returns a real vector of size 2^n.
Arguments	
v	real or complex vector of size $1 + 2^{n-1}$, where n is an integer.
Comments	The argument **v** is a vector similar to those generated by the fft function. To compute the result, Mathcad first creates a new vector **w** by taking the conjugates of the elements of **v** and appending them to the vector **v**. Then Mathcad computes a vector **d** whose elements satisfy this formula:

$$d_j = \frac{1}{\sqrt{n}} \sum_{k=0}^{n-1} w_k e^{-2\pi i(j/n)k} .$$

	This is the same formula as the fft formula, except for the minus sign in the exponent. The fft and ifft functions are exact inverses. For all real **v**, $\text{ifft}(\text{fft}(\mathbf{v})) = \mathbf{v}$.
Algorithm	Cooley-Tukey (Press *et al.*, 1992)
See also	fft for more details

IFFT

Syntax	IFFT(**v**)
Description	Returns the inverse transform corresponding to FFT. Returns a real vector of size 2^n.
Arguments	
v	real or complex vector of size $1 + 2^{n-1}$, where n is an integer.
Algorithm	Cooley-Tukey (Press *et al.*, 1992)
See also	fft for more details

Im

Syntax	Im(z)
Description	Returns the imaginary part of z.
Arguments	
z	real or complex number
See also	Re

In

Syntax	In(m, z)
Description	Returns the value of the modified Bessel function $I_m(z)$ of the first kind.
Arguments	
m	real number, $-100 \le m \le 100$
z	complex number
Comments	Solution of the differential equation $x^2 \cdot \dfrac{d^2}{dx^2}y + x \cdot \dfrac{d}{dx}y - (x^2 + m^2) \cdot y = 0$. In.sc($m,z$), where sc means scaled and is a literal subscript, gives $exp(-|Re(z)|)\text{In}(m,z)$. Scaled functions are useful for calculating large arguments without overflow.
Algorithm	AMOSLIB; ACM TOMS 12 (1986) 265-273.
See also	Kn

intercept

Syntax	intercept(**vx, vy**)
Description	Returns the y-intercept of the least-squares regression line.
Arguments	
vx, vy	real vectors of the same size
See also	slope for more details, line, stderr, medfit

interp

One-dimensional Case

Syntax	interp(**vs, vx, vy**, x)
Description	Interpolates the value from spline coefficients or regression coefficients. Takes three vector arguments **vx, vy** (of the same size) and **vs**. Returns the interpolated y value corresponding to the point x.
Arguments	
vs	real vector output from interpolation routine bspline, cspline, lspline, or pspline or regression routine regress or loess
vx, vy	real vectors of the same size
x	real number
Comments	Let us first discuss interp on the output of cubic spline routines. To find the interpolated value for a particular x, Mathcad finds the two points which x falls between. It then returns the y value on the cubic section enclosed by these two points. For x values less than the smallest point in **vx**, Mathcad extrapolates the cubic section connecting the smallest two points of **vx**. Similarly, for x values greater than the largest point in **vx**, Mathcad extrapolates the cubic section connecting the largest two points of **vx**.
	For best results, do not use the interp function on values of x far from the fitted points. Splines are intended for interpolation, not extrapolation. Consequently, computed values for such x values are unlikely to be useful. See predict for an alternative.
	In the regress case, interp simply computes the value of the regression polynomial; for loess, interp uses the local least-squares polynomial on the interval.

Two-dimensional Case

Syntax	interp(**vs**, **Mxy**, **Mz**, **v**)
Description	Interpolates the value from spline coefficients or regression coefficients. Takes two matrix arguments **Mxy** and **Mz** (with the same number of rows) and one vector argument **vs**. Returns the interpolated z value corresponding to the point $x = v_0$ and $y = v_1$.

Arguments

vs	real vector output from interpolation routine bspline, cspline, lspline, or pspline or regression routine regress or loess
Mxy, Mz	real matrices (with the same number of rows)
v	real two-dimensional vector

Comments	For best results, do not use the interp function on values of x and y far from the grid points. Splines are intended for interpolation, not extrapolation. Consequently, computed values for such x and y values are unlikely to be useful. See predict for an alternative.
See also	lspline for example, bspline, cspline, pspline, regress, loess

ipmt
Finance

Syntax	ipmt(*rate*, *per*, *nper*, *pv*, [[*fv*], [*type*]])
Description	Returns the interest payment of an investment or loan for a given period, *per*, based on periodic constant payments over a given number of compounding periods, *nper*, using a fixed interest rate, *rate*, and a specified present value, *pv*.

Arguments

rate	real rate
per	integer period number, $per \geq 1$
nper	integer number of compounding periods, $1 \leq per \leq nper$
pv	real present value
fv	(optional) real future value, default is $fv = 0$
type	(optional) indicator payment timing, 0 for payment made at the end of the period, 1 for payment made at the beginning, default is $type = 0$

Comments	If you know the annual interest rate, *ann_rate*, you must calculate the interest rate per period as $rate = ann\_rate/nper$.
	Payments you make, such as deposits into a savings account or payments toward a loan, must be entered as negative numbers. Cash you receive, such as dividend checks, must be entered as positive numbers.
See also	cumint, pmt, ppmt

irr
Finance

Syntax	irr(**v**, [*guess*])
Description	Returns the internal rate of return for a series of cash flows, **v**, occurring at regular intervals.

Arguments

v	real vector of cash flows
guess	(optional) real guess value, default is $guess = 0.1$ (10%)

Comments	In **v**, payments must be entered as negative numbers and income must be entered as positive numbers. There must be at least one negative value and one positive value in **v**.

If irr cannot find a result that is accurate to within $1 \cdot 10^{-5}$ percent after 20 iterations, it returns an error. In such a case, a different guess value should be tried, although it will not guarantee a solution. In most cases *irr* converges if *guess* is between 0 and 1.

Note	*irr* and *npv* are related functions. The internal rate of return (*irr*) is the rate for which the net present value (*npv*) is zero.
See also	mirr, npv

IsArray
Expression Type

Syntax	IsArray(x)
Description	Returns 1 if x is a matrix or vector; 0 otherwise.
Arguments	
x	arbitrary real or complex number, array, or string

IsScalar
Expression Type

Syntax	IsScalar(x)
Description	Returns 1 if x is a real or complex number; 0 otherwise.
Arguments	
x	arbitrary real or complex number, array, or string

IsString
Expression Type

Syntax	IsString(x)
Description	Returns 1 if x is a string; 0 otherwise.
Arguments	
x	arbitrary real or complex number, array, or string

iwave
Wavelet Transform

Syntax	iwave($\mathbf{v}$)
Description	Returns the inverse wavelet transform corresponding to wave.
Arguments	
$\mathbf{v}$	real vector of 2^n elements, where n is an integer, $n > 0$.
Algorithm	Pyramidal Daubechies 4-coefficient wavelet filter (Press *et al.*, 1992)
See also	wave for example

J0
Bessel

Syntax	J0(z)
Description	Returns the value of the Bessel function $J_0(z)$ of the first kind. Same as Jn(0, z).
Arguments	
z	real or complex number
Comments	J0.sc(z), where sc means scaled and is a literal subscript, gives J0(z) multiplied by exp(-|Im(z)|). Scaled functions are useful for calculating large arguments without overflow.
Algorithm	SLATEC Common Mathematical Library; ACM TOMS 21 (1995) 388-393

J1
Bessel

Syntax	J1(z)
Description	Returns the value of the Bessel function $J_1(z)$ of the first kind. Same as Jn(1, z).
Arguments	
z	real or complex number
Comments	J1.sc(z), where sc means scaled and is a literal subscript, gives J1(z) multiplied by exp(-|Im(z)|). Scaled functions are useful for calculating large arguments without overflow.
Algorithm	SLATEC Common Mathematical Library; ACM TOMS 21 (1995) 388-393

Jac
Special

Syntax	Jac(n, a, b, x)
Description	Returns the value of the Jacobi polynomial of degree n with parameters a and b, at x.
Arguments	
n	integer, $n \geq 0$
a, b	real numbers, $a > -1$, $b > -1$
x	real number
Comments	The Jacobi polynomials are solutions of the differential equation:

$$(1 - x^2) \cdot \frac{d^2}{dx^2} y + (b - a - (a + b + 2) \cdot x) \cdot \frac{d}{dx} y + n \cdot (n + a + b + 1) \cdot y = 0$$

and include the Chebyshev and Legendre polynomials as special cases.

Algorithm	Recurrence relation (Abramowitz and Stegun, 1972)

Jn
Bessel

Syntax	Jn(m, z)
Description	Returns the value of the Bessel function $J_m(z)$ of the first kind.
Arguments	
m	real number, $-100 \leq m \leq 100$
z	real or complex number
Comments	Solution of the differential equation $x^2 \cdot \frac{d^2}{dx^2} y + x \cdot \frac{d}{dx} y + (x^2 - m^2) \cdot y = 0$.
	Jn.sc(m, z), where sc means scaled and is a literal subscript, gives J0(m,z) multiplied by exp(-|Im(z)|). Scaled functions are useful for calculating large arguments without overflow.
Algorithm	AMOSLIB; ACM TOMS 12 (1986) 265-273.
See also	Yn, H1, H2

js
Bessel

Syntax	js(n, x)
Description	Returns the value of the spherical Bessel function of the first kind, of order n, at x.
Arguments	
n	integer, $-200 \leq n$
x	real number, $x > 0$; $x = 0$ is permitted for js if $n \geq 0$
Comments	Solution of the differential equation: $x^2 \cdot \dfrac{d^2}{dx^2}y + 2x \cdot \dfrac{d}{dx}y + (x^2 - n \cdot (n + 1))y = 0$.
Algorithm	Small order approximation, upward recurrence relation (Abramowitz and Stegun, 1972; Press *et al.*, 1992)
See also	ys

K0
Bessel

Syntax	K0(z)
Description	Returns the value of the modified Bessel function $K_0(x)$ of the second kind. Same as Kn(0, x).
Arguments	
z	real or complex number
Comments	K0.sc(z), where sc means scaled and is a literal subscript, gives K0(z) multiplied by exp(z). Scaled functions are useful for calculating large arguments with adequate resolution.
Algorithm	AMOSLIB; ACM TOMS 12 (1986) 265-273.

K1
Bessel

Syntax	K1(z)
Description	Returns the value of the modified Bessel function $K_1(x)$ of the second kind. Same as Kn(1, x).
Arguments	
z	real or complex number
Comments	K1.sc(z), where sc means scaled and is a literal subscript, gives K1(z) multiplied by exp(z). Scaled functions are useful for calculating large arguments with adequate resolution.
Algorithm	AMOSLIB; ACM TOMS 12 (1986) 265-273.

Kn
Bessel

Syntax	Kn(m, z)
Description	Returns the value of the modified Bessel function $K_m(x)$ of the second kind.
Arguments	
m	real number
z	real or complex number
Comments	Solution of the differential equation $x^2 \cdot \dfrac{d^2}{dx^2}y + x \cdot \dfrac{d}{dx}y - (x^2 + m^2) \cdot y = 0$. Kn.sc($z$), where sc means scaled and is a literal subscript, gives Kn(m, z) multiplied by exp(z). Scaled functions are useful for calculating large arguments with adequate resolution.
See also	In
Algorithm	AMOSLIB; ACM TOMS 12 (1986) 265-273.

ksmooth
Curve Fitting and Smoothing

Syntax   ksmooth(**vx**, **vy**, b)

Description   Creates a new vector, of the same size as **vy**, by using a Gaussian kernel to return weighted averages of **vy**.

Arguments

vx, vy   real vectors of the same size; elements of **vx** must be in ascending order

b real bandwidth $b > 0$; controls the smoothing window and should be set to a few times the spacing between your data points on the x-axis, depending on how big of a window you want to use when smoothing

Comments   The ksmooth function uses a Gaussian kernel to compute local weighted averages of the input vector **vy**. This smoother is most useful when your data lies along a band of relatively constant width. If your data lies scattered along a band whose width fluctuates considerably, you should use an adaptive smoother like supsmooth.

For each vy_i in the n-element vector **vy**, the ksmooth function returns a new vy'_i given by:

$$vy'_i = \frac{\sum_{j=1}^{n} K\left(\frac{vx_i - vx_j}{b}\right) vy_j}{\sum_{j=1}^{n} K\left(\frac{vx_i - vx_j}{b}\right)} \quad \text{where: } K(t) = \frac{1}{\sqrt{2\pi} \cdot (0.37)} \cdot \exp\left(-\frac{t^2}{2 \cdot (0.37)^2}\right)$$

and b is a bandwidth which you supply to the ksmooth function. The bandwidth is usually set to a few times the spacing between data points on the x axis, depending on how big a window you want to use when smoothing.

Algorithm   Moving window Gaussian kernel smoothing (Lorczak)

See also   "medsmooth" on page 318 for more details, "supsmooth" on page 378.

kurt
Statistics

Syntax   kurt(**A**)

Description   Returns the kurtosis of the elements of **A**:

$$\text{kurt}(\mathbf{A}) = \left(\frac{mn(mn+1)}{(mn-1)(mn-2)(mn-3)} \sum_{i=0}^{m-1} \sum_{j=0}^{n-1} \left(\frac{A_{i,j} - \text{mean}(\mathbf{A})}{\text{Stdev}(\mathbf{A})}\right)^4\right) - \frac{3(mn-1)^2}{(mn-2)(mn-3)}$$

Arguments

A   real or complex $m \times n$ matrix or vector; $m \cdot n \geq 4$

Comments   kurt(**A**, **B**, **C**, ...) is also permissible and returns the kurtosis of the elements of **A**, **B**, **C**, ...

Lag
Special

Syntax   Lag(n, x)

Description   Returns the value of the Laguerre polynomial of degree n at x.

Arguments

n integer, $n \geq 0$

x real number

Comments	The Laguerre polynomials are solutions of the differential equation

$$x \cdot \frac{d^2}{dx^2}y + (1-x) \cdot \frac{d}{dx}y + n \cdot y = 0 \,.$$

Algorithm	Recurrence relation (Abramowitz and Stegun, 1972)

last
Vector and Matrix

Syntax	last(v)
Description	Returns the index of the last element in vector **v**.
Arguments	
v	vector
Comments	last(v) = length(v) – 1 + ORIGIN
See also	rows

lcm
Number Theory/Combinatorics

Syntax	lcm(A)
Description	Returns the smallest positive integer that is a multiple of all the values in the array **A**. This integer is known as the least common multiple of the elements in **A**.
Arguments	
A	integer matrix or vector; all elements of **A** are greater than zero
Comments	lcm(**A, B, C, ...**) is also permissible and returns the least common multiple of the elements of **A**, **B, C, ...**
Algorithm	Euclid's algorithm (Niven and Zuckerman, 1972)
See also	gcd

Leg
Special

Syntax	Leg(n, x)
Description	Returns the value of the Legendre polynomial of degree n at x.
Arguments	
n	integer, $n \geq 0$
x	real number
Comments	The Legendre polynomials are solution of the differential equation

$$(1-x^2) \cdot \frac{d^2}{dx^2}y - 2 \cdot x \cdot \frac{d}{dx}y + n \cdot (n+1) \cdot y = 0 \,.$$

Algorithm	Recurrence relation (Abramowitz and Stegun, 1972)

length
Vector and Matrix

Syntax	length(v)
Description	Returns the number of elements in vector **v**.
Arguments	
v	vector
Comments	Same as rows(**v**)

lgsfit

Syntax	lgsfit(**vx**, **vy**, **vg**)
Description	Returns a vector containing the parameters (a, b, c) that make the function $a \cdot (1 + b\exp(-cx))^{-1}$ best approximate the data in **vx** and **vy**.
Arguments	
vx, **vy**	real vectors of the same size
vg	real vector of guess values for (a, b, c)
Comments	This is a special case of the genfit function. A vector of guess values is needed for initialization. By decreasing the value of the built-in TOL variable, higher accuracy in lgsfit might be achieved.
See Also	line, linfit, genfit, expfit, logfit, lnfit, pwrfit, sinfit, medfit

line

Syntax	line(**vx**, **vy**)
Description	Returns a vector containing the y-intercept and the slope of the least-squares regression line.
Arguments	
vx, **vy**	real vectors of the same size
See Also	slope for more details, intercept, stderr, medfit

linfit

Syntax	linfit(**vx**, **vy**, **F**)
Description	Returns a vector containing the coefficients used to create a linear combination of the functions in **F** which best approximates the data in **vx** and **vy**. See genfit for a more general technique.
Arguments	
vx, **vy**	real vectors of the same size; elements of **vx** should be in ascending order
F	a function of a single variable that returns a vector of functions

Example

$$vx := \begin{bmatrix} 0 \\ .2 \\ .4 \\ .6 \\ .8 \\ 1 \end{bmatrix} \qquad vy := \begin{bmatrix} .43 \\ .22 \\ .8 \\ .1 \\ 1 \\ 2 \end{bmatrix} \qquad F(x) := \begin{bmatrix} x^2 \\ x \\ 1 \\ \dfrac{1}{x+1} \end{bmatrix} \qquad \begin{array}{l} j := 0 .. 5 \\ S := \text{linfit}(vx, vy, F) \\ r := 0, .025 .. 1 \end{array}$$

$$g(t) := F(t) \cdot S$$

$$S = \begin{pmatrix} 3.087 \\ -1.475 \\ 0.515 \end{pmatrix}$$

Best fit is given by $3.087x^2 - 1.475 x + 0.515 \dfrac{1}{x+1}$

Comments   Not all data sets can be modeled by lines or polynomials. There are times when you need to model your data with a linear combination of arbitrary functions, none of which represent terms of a polynomial. For example, in a Fourier series you try to approximate data using a linear combination of complex exponentials. Or you may believe your data can be modeled by a weighted combination of Legendre polynomials, but you just don't know what weights to assign.

The linfit function is designed to solve these kinds of problems. If you believe your data could be modeled by a linear combination of arbitrary functions:
$y = a_0 \cdot f_0(x) + a_1 \cdot f_1(x) + \ldots + a_n \cdot f_n(x)$, you should use linfit to evaluate the a_i. The example above shows a linear combination of three functions x, x^2, and $(x+1)^{-1}$ to model some data.

There are times however when the flexibility of linfit is still not enough. Your data may have to be modeled not by a linear combination of data but by some function whose parameters must be chosen. For example, if your data can be modeled by the sum: $f(x) = a_1 \cdot \sin(2x) + a_2 \cdot \tanh(3x)$ and all you need to do is solve for the unknown weights a_1 and a_2, then the linfit function is sufficient. By contrast, if instead your data is to be modeled by the sum: $f(x) = 2 \cdot \sin(a_1 x) + 3 \cdot \tanh(a_2 x)$ and you now have to solve for the unknown parameters a_1 and a_2, you should use the genfit function.

Algorithm   SVD-based least squares minimization (Press *et al.*, 1992)

See also   line, genfit

linterp   Interpolation and Prediction

Syntax   linterp(**vx**, **vy**, x)

Description   Returns a linearly interpolated value at x.

Arguments

vx, vy   real vectors of the same size; elements of **vx** should be in ascending order

x real number at which to interpolate

Example

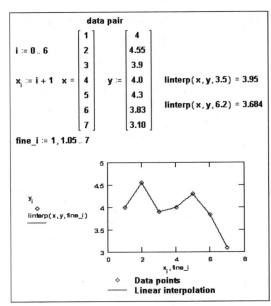

Comments   Interpolation involves using existing data points to predict values between these data points. Mathcad allows you to either connect the data points with straight lines (linear interpolation, as with linterp) or to connect them with sections of a cubic polynomial (cubic spline interpolation, as with lspline, pspline, cspline, bspline and interp).

Unlike the regression functions discussed elsewhere, these interpolation functions return a curve which must pass through the points you specify. Therefore, the resulting function is very sensitive to spurious data points. If your data is noisy, you should consider using the regression functions instead.

Be sure that every element in the **vx** and **vy** arrays contains a data value. Because every element in an array must have a value, Mathcad assigns 0 to any elements you have not explicitly assigned.

To find the interpolated value for a particular x, linterp finds the two points between which the value falls and returns the corresponding y value on the straight line between the two points.

For x values before the first point in **vx**, linterp extrapolates the straight line between the first two data points. For x values beyond the last point in **vx**, linterp extrapolates the straight line between the last two data points.

For best results, the value of x should be between the largest and smallest values in the vector **vx**. The linterp function is intended for interpolation, not extrapolation. Consequently, computed values for x outside this range are unlikely to be useful. See predict for an alternative.

---

ln

Log and Exponential

Syntax   ln(z)

Description   Returns the natural logarithm of nonzero z (to base e). It is the principal value (imaginary part between π and $-\pi$) for complex z.

Arguments

z real or complex nonzero number

Example

```
ln( 2 ) = 0.693      <——>    e^.693 = 2

ln( -2 ) = 0.693 + 3.142i  <— Log of a negative number is always
                              log of the magnitude plus πi

ln( 0 ) =       <— Since anything raised to the 0 is 1,
                   you can never have a log of zero.
domain error

ln( 1 ) = 0    <—>    e^0 = 1
```

Comments   In general, a complex argument to the natural log function returns:

$$\ln(x + i \cdot y) = \ln|x + i \cdot y| + \operatorname{atan}(y/x) \cdot i + 2 \cdot n \cdot \pi \cdot i$$

Mathcad's ln function returns the value corresponding to $n = 0$, namely: $\ln(x + i \cdot y) = \ln|x + i \cdot y| + \operatorname{atan}(y/x) \cdot i$ (principal branch of the natural log function).

See also   log

lnfit

Syntax	lnfit(**vx**, **vy**)
Description	Returns a vector containing the parameters (a, b) that make the function $a \cdot \ln(x) + b$ best approximate the data in **vx** and **vy**.
Arguments	
vx, vy	real vectors of the same size
Comments	This is a two-parameter alternative to the three-parameter logfit function. It uses linear regression to perform the curve fit (by taking the logarithm of y-values), hence there is no need for a guess values vector.
See Also	line, linfit, genfit, expfit, pwrfit, logfit, lgsfit, sinfit, medfit

LoadColormap

Syntax	LoadColormap(*file*)
Description	Returns an array containing the values in the colormap *file*.
Arguments	
file	string variable corresponding to CMP filename
Comments	The file *file* is the name of a colormap located in the CMAPS subdirectory of your Mathcad directory. The function LoadColormap is useful when you want to edit a colormap or use it to create a new colormap. See online Help for more information.
See also	SaveColormap

loess

One-dimensional Case

Syntax	loess(**vx**, **vy**, *span*)
Description	Returns the vector required by the interp function to find the set of second order polynomials that best fit particular neighborhoods of data points specified in arrays **vx** and **vy**.
Arguments	
vx, vy	real vectors of the same size
span	real *span* > 0 specifies how large a neighborhood loess will consider in performing this local regression

Example

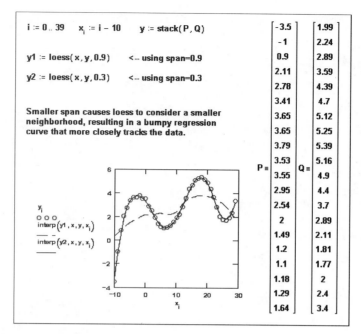

$$i := 0 .. 39 \quad x_i := i - 10 \quad y := stack(P, Q)$$

$$y1 := loess(x, y, 0.9) \qquad \text{<-- using span=0.9}$$

$$y2 := loess(x, y, 0.3) \qquad \text{<-- using span=0.3}$$

Smaller span causes loess to consider a smaller neighborhood, resulting in a bumpy regression curve that more closely tracks the data.

$$P = \begin{bmatrix} -3.5 \\ -1 \\ 0.9 \\ 2.11 \\ 2.78 \\ 3.41 \\ 3.65 \\ 3.65 \\ 3.79 \\ 3.53 \\ 3.55 \\ 2.95 \\ 2.54 \\ 2 \\ 1.49 \\ 1.2 \\ 1.1 \\ 1.18 \\ 1.29 \\ 1.64 \end{bmatrix} \quad Q = \begin{bmatrix} 1.99 \\ 2.24 \\ 2.89 \\ 3.59 \\ 4.39 \\ 4.7 \\ 5.12 \\ 5.25 \\ 5.39 \\ 5.16 \\ 4.9 \\ 4.4 \\ 3.7 \\ 2.89 \\ 2.11 \\ 1.81 \\ 1.77 \\ 2 \\ 2.4 \\ 3.4 \end{bmatrix}$$

Comments Instead of generating a single polynomial the way regress does, loess generates a different second order polynomial depending on where you are on the curve. It does this by examining the data in a small neighborhood of the point you're interested in. The argument *span* controls the size of this neighborhood. As *span* gets larger, loess becomes equivalent to regress with $n = 2$. A good default value is $span = 0.75$.

The example above shows how *span* affects the fit generated by the loess function. A smaller value of *span* makes the fitted curve track fluctuations in data more effectively. A larger value of *span* tends to smear out fluctuations in data and thereby generates a smoother fit.

Two-dimensional Case

Syntax loess(**Mxy**, **vz**, *span*)

Description Returns the vector required by the interp function to find the set of second order polynomials that best fit particular neighborhoods of data points specified in arrays **Mxy** and **vz**.

Arguments

Mxy real $m \times 2$ matrix containing *x-y* coordinates of the *m* data points

vz real *m*-element vector containing the *z* coordinates corresponding to the points specified in **Mxy**

span real *span* > 0 specifies how large a neighborhood loess will consider in performing this local regression

Comments Can be extended naturally to the three- and four-dimensional cases (that is, up to four independent variables).

Algorithm Local polynomial estimation (Cleveland and Devlin, 1988)

See also "regress" on page 354 for more details.

log

Classical Definition

Syntax	log(z)
Description	Returns the common logarithm of nonzero z to base 10. The result is the principal value (imaginary part between π and $-\pi$) for complex z.
Arguments	
z	real or complex nonzero number

Extended Definition

Syntax	log(z, b)
Description	Returns the logarithm of nonzero z to base b. The result is the principal value (imaginary part between π and $-\pi$) for complex z.
Arguments	
z	real or complex nonzero number
b	real number, $b > 0$, $b \neq 1$
See also	ln

logfit

Syntax	logfit(**vx**, **vy**, **vg**)
Description	Returns a vector containing the parameters (a, b, c) that make the function $a \cdot \ln(x + b) + c$ best approximate the data in **vx** and **vy**.
Arguments	
vx, **vy**	real vectors of the same size
vg	real vector of guess values for (a, b, c)
Comments	This is a special case of the genfit function. A vector of guess values is needed for initialization. By decreasing the value of the built-in TOL variable, higher accuracy in logfit might be achieved.
See Also	line, linfit, genfit, expfit, pwrfit, lnfit, lgsfit, sinfit, medfit

lookup

Syntax	lookup(z, **A**, **B**)
Description	Looks in a vector or matrix, **A**, for a given value, z, and returns the value(s) in the same position(s) (i.e., with the same row and column numbers) in another matrix, **B**. When multiple values are returned, they appear in a vector in row-wise order, starting with the top left corner of **B** and sweeping to the right.
Arguments	
z	real or complex number, or string
A, **B**	real, complex or string $m \times n$ matrices or vectors
Comments	The degree of precision to which the comparison adheres is determined by the TOL setting of the worksheet.
See Also	hlookup, vlookup, match

Isolve

Syntax	Isolve(**M**, **v**)
Description	Returns a solution vector **x** such that $\mathbf{M} \cdot \mathbf{x} = \mathbf{v}$.
Arguments	
M	real or complex square matrix that is neither singular nor nearly singular
v	real or complex vector

Example

$3 \cdot x + 6 \cdot y = 9$ ← System of equations to be solved.
$2 \cdot x + .54 \cdot y = 4$

$M := \begin{pmatrix} 3 & 6 \\ 2 & .54 \end{pmatrix}$ $V := \begin{pmatrix} 9 \\ 4 \end{pmatrix}$ ← Create your matrix and vector.

$\text{Isolve}(M, v) = \begin{pmatrix} 1.844 \\ 0.578 \end{pmatrix}$ ← Value for x satisfying the system of equations.
                          ← Value for y satisfying the system of equations.

Note: The "Isolve" function is only available with Mathcad Professional.

Comments	A matrix is singular if its determinant is zero; it is nearly singular if it has a high condition number. Alternatively, you can solve a system of linear equations by using matrix inversion, via numeric or symbolic solve blocks.
Algorithm	LU decomposition and forward/backward substitution (Press *et al.*, 1992)

Ispline

One-dimensional Case

Syntax	Ispline(**vx**, **vy**)
Description	Returns the vector of coefficients of a cubic spline with linear ends. This vector becomes the first argument of the interp function.
Arguments	
vx, vy	real vectors of the same size; elements of **vx** must be in ascending order

Example

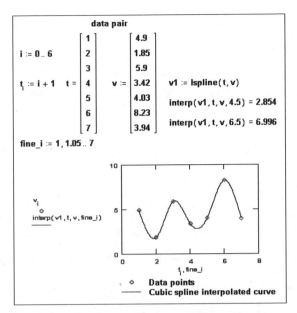

Comments Cubic spline interpolation lets you pass a curve through a set of points so that the first and second derivatives of the curve are continuous across each point. This curve is assembled by taking three adjacent points and constructing a cubic polynomial passing through those points. These cubic polynomials are then strung together to form the completed curve.

To fit a cubic spline curve through a set of points:

1. Create the vectors **vx** and **vy** containing the x and y coordinates through which you want the cubic spline to pass. The elements of **vx** should be in ascending order. (Although we use the names **vx**, **vy**, and **vs**, there is nothing special about these variable names; you can use whatever names you prefer.)

2. Generate the vector **vs** := lspline(**vx**, **vy**). The vector **vs** is a vector of intermediate results designed to be used with interp. It contains, among other things, the second derivatives for the spline curve used to fit the points in **vx** and **vy**.

3. To evaluate the cubic spline at an arbitrary point, say $x0$, evaluate interp(**vs**, **vx**, **vy**, $x0$) here **vs**, **vx**, and **vy** are the vectors described earlier. You could have accomplished the same task by evaluating: interp(lspline(**vx**, **vy**), **vx**, **vy**, $x0$) . As a practical matter, though, you'll probably be evaluating interp for many different points.

The call to lspline can be time-consuming and the result won't change from one point to the next, so it makes sense to do it just once and store the outcome in the **vs** array.

Be sure that every element in the input arrays contains a data value. Because every element in a array must have a value, Mathcad assigns 0 to any elements you have not explicitly assigned.

In addition to lspline, Mathcad comes with three other cubic spline functions: pspline, cspline, and bspline. The pspline function generates a spline curve that approaches a parabola at the endpoints, while the cspline function generates a spline curve that can be fully cubic at the endpoints. bspline, on the other hand, allows the interpolation knots to be chosen by the user.

For lspline, the first three components of the output vector **vs** are $\mathbf{vs}_0=0$ (a code telling interp that **vs** is the output of a spline function as opposed to a regression function), $\mathbf{vs}_1=3$ (the index within **vs** where the second derivative coefficients begin) and $\mathbf{vs}_2=0$ (a code denoting lspline). The first three components for pspline and cspline are identical except $\mathbf{vs}_2=1$ (the code denoting pspline) and $\mathbf{vs}_2=2$ (the code denoting cspline), respectively.

Two-dimensional Case

Syntax   lspline(**Mxy, Mz**)

Description   Returns the vector of coefficients of a two-dimensional cubic spline, constrained to be linear at region boundaries spanned by **Mxy**. This vector becomes the first argument of the interp function.

Arguments

Mxy $n \times 2$ matrix whose elements, $Mxy_{i,0}$ and $Mxy_{i,1}$, specify the x- and y-coordinates along the *diagonal* of a rectangular grid. This matrix plays exactly the same role as **vx** in the one-dimensional case described earlier. Since these points describe a diagonal, the elements in each column of **Mxy** must be in ascending order ($Mxy_{i,k} < Mxy_{j,k}$ whenever $i < j$).

Mz $n \times n$ matrix whose ijth element is the z-coordinate corresponding to the point $x = Mxy_{i,0}$ and $y = Mxy_{j,1}$. **Mz** plays exactly the same role as **vy** does in the one-dimensional case above.

Comments   Mathcad handles two-dimensional cubic spline interpolation in much the same way as the one-dimensional case. Instead of passing a curve through a set of points so that the first and second derivatives of the curve are continuous across each point, Mathcad passes a surface through a grid of points. This surface corresponds to a cubic polynomial in x and y in which the first and second partial derivatives are continuous in the corresponding direction across each grid point.

The first step in two-dimensional spline interpolation is exactly the same as that in the one-dimensional case: specify the points through which the surface is to pass. The procedure, however, is more complicated because you now have to specify a grid of points.

To perform two-dimensional spline interpolation, follow these steps:

1. Create **Mxy**.

2. Create **Mz**.

3. Generate the vector $\mathbf{vs} := \text{lspline}(\mathbf{Mxy}, \mathbf{Mz})$. The vector **vs** is a vector of intermediate results designed to be used with interp.
   To evaluate the cubic spline at an arbitrary point, say $(x0, y0)$, evaluate

   $$\text{interp}\left(\mathbf{vs}, \mathbf{Mxy}, \mathbf{Mz}, \begin{bmatrix} x0 \\ y0 \end{bmatrix}\right),$$ where **vs**, **Mxy**, and **Mz** are as described earlier.

   The result is the value of the interpolating surface corresponding to the arbitrary point $(x0, y0)$. You could have accomplished exactly the same task by evaluating:

   $$\text{interp}\left(\text{lspline}(\mathbf{Mxy}, \mathbf{Mz}), \mathbf{Mxy}, \mathbf{Mz}, \begin{bmatrix} x0 \\ y0 \end{bmatrix}\right).$$

As a practical matter though, you'll probably be evaluating interp for many different points. The call to lspline can be time-consuming, and the result won't change from one point to the next, so do it just once and store the outcome in the **vs** array.

In addition to lspline, Mathcad comes with two other cubic spline functions for the two-dimensional case: pspline and cspline. The pspline function generates a spline curve that approaches a second degree polynomial in x and y along the edges. The cspline function generates a spline curve that approaches a third degree polynomial in x and y along the edges.

Algorithm	Tridiagonal system solving (Press *et al.*, 1992; Lorczak)

lu
Vector and Matrix

Syntax	lu(**M**)
Description	Returns an $n \times (3 \cdot n)$ matrix whose first n columns contain an $n \times n$ permutation matrix **P**, whose next n columns contain an $n \times n$ lower triangular matrix **L**, and whose remaining n columns contain an $n \times n$ upper triangular matrix **U**. These matrices satisfy the equation $\mathbf{P} \cdot \mathbf{M} = \mathbf{L} \cdot \mathbf{U}$.
Arguments	
M	real or complex $n \times n$ matrix
Comments	This is known as the LU decomposition (or factorization) of the matrix **M**, permuted by **P**.
Algorithm	Crout's method with partial pivoting (Press *et al.*, 1992; Golub and Van Loan, 1989)

match
Vector and Matrix

Syntax	match(z, **A**)
Description	Looks in a vector or matrix, **A**, for a given value, z, and returns the index (indices) of its positions in **A**. When multiple values are returned, they appear in a nested array in row-wise order, starting with the top left corner of **A** and sweeping to the right.
Arguments	
z	real or complex number, or string
A	real, complex or string $m \times n$ matrix or vector
Comments	The degree of precision to which the comparison adheres is determined by the TOL setting of the worksheet.
See Also	lookup, hlookup, vlookup

matrix
Vector and Matrix

Syntax	matrix(m, n, f)
Description	Creates a matrix in which the ijth element is the value $f(i, j)$, where $i = 0, 1, ..., m - 1$ and $j = 0, 1, ..., n - 1$.
Arguments	
m, n	integers
f	scalar-valued function

max
Vector and Matrix

Syntax	max(**A**)
Description	Returns the largest element in **A**. If **A** is complex, returns max(Re(**A**)) + i max(Im(**A**)).
Arguments	
A	real or complex $m \times n$ matrix or vector, or string
Comments	max(**A**, **B**, **C**, ...) is also permissible and returns the largest element in **A**, **B**, **C**, ...
See also	min

Maximize
Solving

Syntax	Maximize(*f*, *var1*, *var2*,...)
Description	Returns values of *var1*, *var2*,... which solve a prescribed system of equations, subject to prescribed inequalities, and which make the function *f* take on its largest value. The number of arguments matches the number of unknowns, plus one. Output is a scalar if only one unknown; otherwise it is a vector of answers.
Arguments	
f	real-valued objective function
var1, *var2*, ...	real or complex variables; *var1*, *var2*, ... must be assigned guess values before using Maximize
Examples	

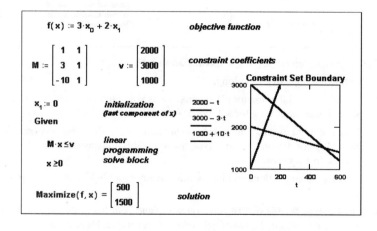

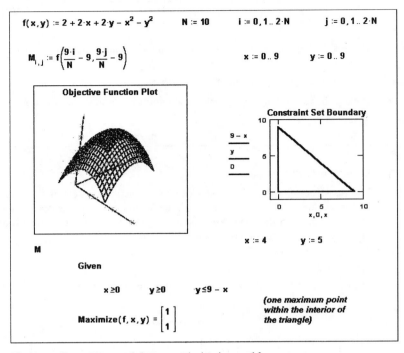

$$f(x, y) := 2 + 2 \cdot x + 2 \cdot y - x^2 - y^2 \qquad N := 10 \qquad i := 0, 1 .. 2 \cdot N \qquad j := 0, 1 .. 2 \cdot N$$

$$M_{i,j} := f\left(\frac{9 \cdot i}{N} - 9, \frac{9 \cdot j}{N} - 9\right) \qquad\qquad x := 0 .. 9 \qquad y := 0 .. 9$$

Objective Function Plot

M

Constraint Set Boundary

$\frac{9 - x}{y}$
0

$x, 0, x$

$$x := 4 \qquad y := 5$$

Given

$$x \geq 0 \qquad y \geq 0 \qquad y \leq 9 - x$$

$$\text{Maximize}(f, x, y) = \begin{bmatrix} 1 \\ 1 \end{bmatrix}$$

(one maximum point within the interior of the triangle)

Comments   There are five steps to solving a maximization problem:

1. Define the objective function f.

2. Provide an initial guess for all the unknowns you intend to solve for. This gives Mathcad a place to start searching for solutions.

3. Type the word given. This tells Mathcad that what follows is a system of equality or inequality constraints. You can type given or Given in any style. Just be sure you don't type it while in a text region.

4. Now type the equations and inequalities in any order below the word given. Use [Ctrl]= to type "=."

5. Finally, type the Maximize function with f and your list of unknowns. You can't put numerical values in the list of unknowns; for example, Maximize(f, 2) isn't permitted. Like given, you can type maximize or Maximize in any style.

The Maximize function returns values as follows:

*   If there is one unknown, Maximize returns a scalar value that optimizes f.
*   If there is more than one unknown, Maximize returns a vector of answers; for example, Maximize(f, *var1*, *var2*) returns a vector containing values of *var1* and *var2* that satisfy the constraints and optimize f.

The word Given, the equations and inequalities that follow, and the Maximize function form a *solve block*.

By default, Mathcad examines your objective function and the constraints, and solves using an appropriate method. If you want to try different algorithms for testing and comparison, you can choose options from the popup menu associated with Maximize (available via right mouse click), which include:

- AutoSelect—chooses an appropriate algorithm for you
- Linear option—indicates that the problem is linear (and thus applies linear programming methods to the problem) – guess values for *var1*, *var2*,... are immaterial (can all be zero)
- Nonlinear option—indicates that the problem is nonlinear (and thus applies these general methods to the problem: the conjugate gradient solver; if that fails to converge, the quasi-Newton solver)—guess values for *var1*, *var2*,... greatly affect the solution
- Quadratic option—indicates that the problem is quadratic (and thus applies quadratic programming methods to the problem)—guess values for *var1*, *var2*,... are immaterial (can all be zero)
- Advanced options—applies only to the nonlinear conjugate gradient and the quasi-Newton solvers

These options provide more control for you to try different algorithms for testing and comparison. You may also adjust the values of the built-in variables CTOL and TOL. The *constraint tolerance* CTOL controls how closely a constraint must be met for a solution to be acceptable, e.g., if CTOL were 0.001, then a constraint such as x < 2 would be considered satisfied if the value of x satisfied x < 2.001. This can be defined or changed in the same way as the *convergence tolerance* TOL, which is discussed further in connection with the Find function. Since Maximize can be used without constraints, the value of CTOL will sometimes be irrelevant. Its default value is 10^{-3}.

For an unconstrained maximization problem, the word Given and constraints are unnecessary.

| Algorithm | For the non-linear case: quasi-Newton, conjugate gradient |
| | For the linear case: simplex method with branch/bound techniques (Press *et al.*, 1992; Polak, 1997; Winston, 1994) |

| See also | Find for more details about solve blocks; Minerr, Minimize |

mean Statistics

Syntax	mean(**A**)
Description	Returns the arithmetic mean of the elements of **A**: $\text{mean}(\mathbf{A}) = \dfrac{1}{mn}\sum_{i=0}^{m-1}\sum_{j=0}^{n-1} A_{i,j}$.
Arguments	
A	real or complex $m \times n$ matrix or vector
Comments	mean(**A**, **B**, **C**, ...) is also permissible and returns the arithmetic mean of the elements of **A**, **B**, **C**, ...
See also	gmean, hmean, median, mode

medfit Curve Fitting and Smoothing

Syntax	medfit(**vx**, **vy**)
Description	Returns a vector containing the *y*-intercept and the slope of the median-median regression line.
Arguments	
vx, vy	real vectors of the same size
Comments	medfit provides a linear fit which is more robust (less sensitive to data outliers) than line. The data is divided into three sets, the median of the first and last subsets are calculated, and the intercept and slope of the line connecting those two medians comprises the fit.
See Also	line, linfit, genfit, expfit, logfit, lnfit, pwrfit, lgsfit, sinfit

median

Syntax	median(**A**)
Description	Returns the median of the elements of **A**. The median is the value above and below which there are an equal number of values. If **A** has an even number of elements, median is the arithmetic mean of the two central values.
Arguments	
A	real $m \times n$ matrix or vector
Comments	median(**A**, **B**, **C**, *...)* is also permissible and returns the median of the elements of **A**, **B**, **C**, ...
See also	gmean, mean, median, mode

medsmooth

Syntax	medsmooth(**vy**, *n)*
Description	Creates a new vector, of the same size as **vy**, by smoothing **vy** with running medians.
Arguments	
vy	real vector
n	odd integer, $n > 0$, the size of smoothing window
Example	

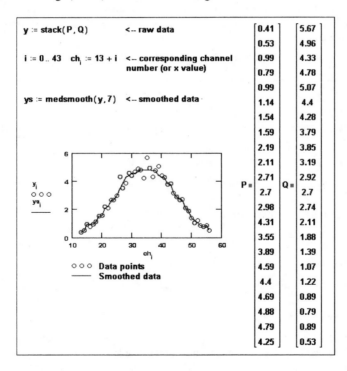

y := stack(P, Q)   <-- raw data

i := 0 .. 43   ch_i := 13 + i   <-- corresponding channel
number (or x value)

ys := medsmooth(y, 7)   <-- smoothed data

○ ○ ○ Data points
——— Smoothed data

$$P \equiv \begin{bmatrix} 0.41 \\ 0.53 \\ 0.99 \\ 0.79 \\ 0.99 \\ 1.14 \\ 1.54 \\ 1.59 \\ 2.19 \\ 2.11 \\ 2.71 \\ 2.7 \\ 2.98 \\ 4.31 \\ 3.55 \\ 3.89 \\ 4.59 \\ 4.4 \\ 4.69 \\ 4.88 \\ 4.79 \\ 4.25 \end{bmatrix} \quad Q \equiv \begin{bmatrix} 5.67 \\ 4.96 \\ 4.33 \\ 4.78 \\ 5.07 \\ 4.4 \\ 4.28 \\ 3.79 \\ 3.85 \\ 3.19 \\ 2.92 \\ 2.7 \\ 2.74 \\ 2.11 \\ 1.88 \\ 1.39 \\ 1.07 \\ 1.22 \\ 0.89 \\ 0.79 \\ 0.89 \\ 0.53 \end{bmatrix}$$

Comments   Smoothing involves taking a set of y (and possibly x) values and returning a new set of y values that is smoother than the original set. Unlike the interpolation functions lspline, pspline, cspline or bspline or regression functions **regress** or **loess**, smoothing results in a new set of y values, not a function that can be evaluated between the data points you specify. If you are interested in y values *between* the y values you specify, use an interpolation or regression function.

Whenever you use vectors in any of the functions described in this section, be sure that every element in the vector contains a data value. Because every element in a vector must have a value, Mathcad assigns 0 to any elements you have not explicitly assigned.

The medsmooth function is the most robust of Mathcad's three smoothing functions because it is least likely to be affected by spurious data points. This function uses a running median smoother, computes the residuals, smooths the residuals the same way, and adds these two smoothed vectors together.

medsmooth performs these steps:

1. Finds the running medians of the input vector **vy**. We'll call this **vy'** . The ith element is given by: $vy'_i = \text{median}(vy_{i-(n-1/2)}, \ldots, vy_i, \ldots, vy_{i+(n-1/2)})$.
2. Evaluates the residuals: **vr** $= $ **vy** $-$ **vy'** .
3. Smooths the residual vector, **vr**, using the same procedure described in step 1, to create a smoothed residual vector, **vr'** .
4. Returns the sum of these two smoothed vectors: medsmooth(**vy**, n) $= $ **vy'** $+ $ **vr'** .

medsmooth will leave the first and last $(n-1)/2$ points unchanged. In practice, the length of the smoothing window, n, should be small compared to the length of the data set.

Algorithm   Moving window median method (Lorczak)

See also   ksmooth and supsmooth

mhyper   Special

Syntax   mhyper(a, b, x)

Description   Returns the value of the confluent hypergeometric function, $_1F_1(a;b;x)$ or $M(a;b;x)$.

Arguments
a, b, x real numbers

Comments   The confluent hypergeometric function is a solution of the differential equation:

$$x \cdot \frac{d^2}{dx^2}y + (b-x) \cdot \frac{d}{dx}y - a \cdot y = 0$$ and is also known as the Kummer function.

Many functions are special cases of this, e.g., elementary ones like

$\exp(x) = \text{mhyper}(1, 1, x)$ $\exp(x) \cdot \sinh(x) = x \cdot \text{mhyper}(1, 2, 2 \cdot x)$

and more complicated ones like Hermite functions.

Algorithm   Series expansion, asymptotic approximations (Abramowitz and Stegun, 1972)

min
Vector and Matrix

Syntax	min(**A**)
Description	Returns the smallest element in **A**. If **A** is complex, returns $\min(\mathrm{Re}(\mathbf{A})) + i\,\min(\mathrm{Im}(\mathbf{A}))$.
Arguments	
A	real or complex $m \times n$ matrix or vector, or string
Comments	min(**A**, **B**, **C**, **...**) is also permissible and returns the smallest element in **A**, **B**, **C**, ...
See also	max

Minerr
Solving

Syntax	Minerr(*var1, var2,...*)
Description	Returns values of *var1, var2, ...* which come closest to solving a prescribed system of equations, subject to prescribed inequalities. The number of arguments matches the number of unknowns. Output is a scalar if only one argument; otherwise it is a vector of answers.
Arguments	
var1, var2, ...	real or complex variables; *var1, var2, ...* must be assigned guess values before using Minerr
Example	

$n := \mathrm{length}(y) - 1$

$F(x,\alpha,\beta) := \alpha \cdot \beta \cdot x^{\beta-1} \cdot \exp\left(-\alpha \cdot x^{\beta}\right)$ **Fitting function F**

$i := 1 .. n \qquad SSE(\alpha,\beta) := \sum_{i}\left(y_i - F\left(x_i,\alpha,\beta\right)\right)^2$

$\alpha := 0.8 \qquad \beta := 1$ <------ **Initial guess for parameters**

Given $\qquad SSE(\alpha,\beta)=0$

$\begin{bmatrix} \alpha \\ \beta \end{bmatrix} := \mathrm{Minerr}(\alpha,\beta) \qquad \alpha = 0.507 \qquad \beta = 1.979$

$z := 0, 0.1 .. 4$

$\dfrac{SSE(\alpha,\beta)}{n-2} = 0.002$

Mean squared error (this would be zero if a true solution existed)

$$x = \begin{bmatrix} .132 \\ .322 \\ .511 \\ .701 \\ .891 \\ 1.081 \\ 1.27 \\ 1.46 \\ 1.65 \\ 1.839 \\ 2.029 \\ 2.219 \end{bmatrix} \qquad y = \begin{bmatrix} .1 \\ .258 \\ .543 \\ .506 \\ .606 \\ .622 \\ .569 \\ .453 \\ .438 \\ .316 \\ .29 \\ .195 \end{bmatrix}$$

x-y data and best Weibull fit

Comments	The Minerr function is very similar to Find and uses exactly the same algorithm. The difference is that even if a system has no solutions, Minerr will attempt to find values which come closest to solving the system. The Find function, on the other hand, will return an error message indicating that it could not find a solution. You use Minerr exactly the way you use Find.
	Like Find, type the Minerr function with your list of unknowns. You can't put numerical values in the list of unknowns; e.g., in the example above, Minerr(0.8, 1) isn't permitted. Like Find, you can type Minerr or minerr in any style.

Minerr usually returns an answer that minimizes the errors in the constraints. However, Minerr cannot verify that its answers represent an absolute minimum for the errors in the constraints.

If you use Minerr in a solve block, you should always include additional checks on the reasonableness of the results. The built-in variable ERR gives the size of the error vector for the approximate solution returned by Minerr. There is no built-in variable for determining the size of the error for individual solutions to the unknowns.

Minerr is particularly useful for solving certain nonlinear least-squares problems. In the example, Minerr is used to obtain the unknown parameters in a Weibull distribution. The function genfit is also useful for solving nonlinear least-squares problems.

The popup menu (available via right mouse click) associated with Minerr contains options that are further described in the entry on the Maximize function, as well as the built-in variables CTOL and TOL.

Algorithm
Levenberg-Marquardt, quasi-Newton, conjugate gradient

See also
Find for more details about solve blocks; Maximize, Minimize

Minimize
Solving

Syntax
Minimize(*f*, *var1*, *var2*,...)

Description
Returns values of *var1*, *var2*,... which solve a prescribed system of equations, subject to prescribed inequalities, and which make the function *f* take on its smallest value. The number of arguments matches the number of unknowns, plus one. Output is a scalar if only one unknown; otherwise it is a vector of answers.

Arguments
f
real-valued function

var1, *var2*, ...
real or complex variables; *var1*, *var2*, ... must be assigned guess values before using Minimize.

Examples

$$f(x) := 8 \cdot x_0 + 10 \cdot x_1 + 7 \cdot x_2 + 6 \cdot x_3 + 11 \cdot x_4 + 9 \cdot x_5 \qquad \text{objective function}$$

$$M := \begin{bmatrix} 12 & 9 & 25 & 20 & 17 & 13 \\ 35 & 42 & 18 & 31 & 56 & 49 \\ 37 & 53 & 28 & 24 & 29 & 20 \end{bmatrix} \qquad v := \begin{bmatrix} 60 \\ 150 \\ 125 \end{bmatrix} \qquad \text{constraint coefficients}$$

$$x_5 := 0 \qquad \text{initialization} \\ \text{(last component of x)}$$

Given

$$M \cdot x \geq v \qquad \text{linear programming} \\ x \leq 1 \qquad \text{solve block} \\ x \geq 0$$

$$\text{Minimize}(f, x) = \begin{bmatrix} 1 \\ 0.623 \\ 0.343 \\ 1 \\ 0.048 \\ 1 \end{bmatrix} \qquad \text{solution}$$

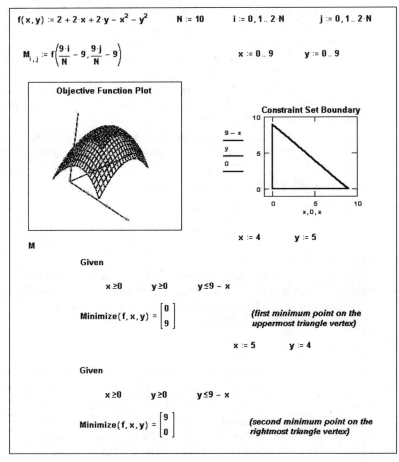

$$f(x,y) := 2 + 2 \cdot x + 2 \cdot y - x^2 - y^2 \qquad N := 10 \qquad i := 0, 1 .. 2 \cdot N \qquad j := 0, 1 .. 2 \cdot N$$

$$M_{i,j} := f\left(\frac{9 \cdot i}{N} - 9, \frac{9 \cdot j}{N} - 9\right) \qquad\qquad x := 0 .. 9 \qquad y := 0 .. 9$$

Objective Function Plot

M

Constraint Set Boundary

Given

$$x \geq 0 \qquad y \geq 0 \qquad y \leq 9 - x$$

$$\text{Minimize}(f, x, y) = \begin{bmatrix} 0 \\ 9 \end{bmatrix} \qquad \textit{(first minimum point on the uppermost triangle vertex)}$$

$$x := 5 \qquad y := 4$$

Given

$$x \geq 0 \qquad y \geq 0 \qquad y \leq 9 - x$$

$$\text{Minimize}(f, x, y) = \begin{bmatrix} 9 \\ 0 \end{bmatrix} \qquad \textit{(second minimum point on the rightmost triangle vertex)}$$

Comment   For information about the Minimize function, see the entry on the Maximize function.

See also   Find for more details about solve blocks; Maximize, Minerr

---

mirr
Finance

Syntax   mirr(v, *fin_rate*, *rein_rate*)

Description   Returns the modified internal rate of return for a series of cash flows occurring at regular intervals, **v**, given a finance rate payable on the cash flows you borrow, *fin_rate*, and a reinvestment rate earned on the cash flows as you reinvest them, *rein_rate*.

Arguments

v   real vector of cash flows

fin_rate   real finance rate

rein_rate   real reinvestment rate

Comments   In **v**, payments must be entered as negative numbers and income must be entered as positive numbers. There must be at least one positive value and one negative value in **v**.

See also   irr

mod

Number Theory/Combinatorics

Syntax	mod(n, k)
Description	Returns the remainder of n when divided by k. The result has the same sign as n.
Arguments	
n, k	integers, $k \neq 0$

mode

Statistics

Syntax	mode($\mathbf{A}$)
Description	Returns the value in $\mathbf{A}$ that occurs most often.
Arguments	
$\mathbf{A}$	real or complex $m \times n$ matrix or vector
Comments	mode($\mathbf{A}$, $\mathbf{B}$, $\mathbf{C}$, ...) is also permissible and returns the value in $\mathbf{A}$, $\mathbf{B}$, $\mathbf{C}$, ... that occurs most often.
See also	gmean, hmean, mean, median

multigrid

Differential Equation Solving

Syntax	multigrid($\mathbf{M}$, *ncycle*)
Description	Solves the Poisson partial differential equation over a planar square region. The $n \times n$ matrix $\mathbf{M}$ gives source function values, where $n - 1$ is a power of 2 and zero boundary conditions on all four edges are assumed. multigrid uses a different algorithm and is faster than relax, which is more general.
Arguments	
$\mathbf{M}$	$(1 + 2^k) \times (1 + 2^k)$ real square matrix containing the source term at each point in the region in which the solution is sought (for example, the right-hand side of equation below)
ncycle	positive integer specifying number of cycles at each level of the multigrid iteration; a value of 2 generally gives a good approximation of the solution
Example	

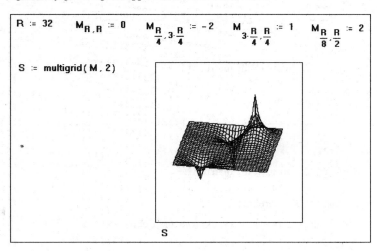

$$R := 32 \qquad M_{R,R} := 0 \qquad M_{\frac{R}{4}, 3 \cdot \frac{R}{4}} := -2 \qquad M_{3 \cdot \frac{R}{4}, \frac{R}{4}} := 1 \qquad M_{\frac{R}{8}, \frac{R}{2}} := 2$$

$$S := \text{multigrid}(M, 2)$$

S

Comments   Two partial differential equations that arise often in the analysis of physical systems are Poisson's equation:

$$\frac{\partial^2 u}{\partial x^2} + \frac{\partial^2 u}{\partial y^2} = \rho(x, y) \text{ and its homogeneous form, Laplace's equation.}$$

Mathcad has two functions for solving these equations over a square region, assuming the values taken by the unknown function $u(x, y)$ on all four sides of the boundary are known. The most general solver is the relax function. In the special case where $u(x, y)$ is known to be zero on all four sides of the boundary, you can use the multigrid function instead. This function often solves the problem faster than relax. If the boundary condition is the same on all four sides, you can simply transform the equation to an equivalent one in which the value is zero on all four sides.

The multigrid function returns a square matrix in which:

- an element's location in the matrix corresponds to its location within the square region, and
- its value approximates the value of the solution at that point.

Algorithm   Full multigrid algorithm (Press *et al.*, 1992)

See also   relax

---

nom
Finance

Syntax   nom(*rate*, *nper*)

Description   Returns the nominal interest rate given the effective annual interest rate, *rate*, and the number of compounding periods per year, *nper*.

Arguments
rate   real rate, $rate > -1$

nper   real number of compounding periods, $nper \geq 1$

Comments   Effective annual interest rate is also known as annual percentage rate (APR).

See also   eff

---

norm1
Vector and Matrix

Syntax   norm1(**M**)

Description   Returns the L_1 norm of the matrix **M**.

Arguments
M   real or complex square matrix

---

norm2
Vector and Matrix

Syntax   norm2(**M**)

Description   Returns the L_2 norm of the matrix **M**.

Arguments
M   real or complex square matrix

Algorithm   Singular value computation (Wilkinson and Reinsch, 1971)

norme
Vector and Matrix

Syntax   norme(**M**)

Description   Returns the Euclidean norm of the matrix **M**.

Arguments
M   real or complex square matrix

normi
Vector and Matrix

Syntax   normi(**M**)

Description   Returns the infinity norm of the matrix **M**.

Arguments
M   real or complex square matrix

nper
Finance

Syntax   nper(*rate*, *pmt*, *pv*, [[*fv*], [*type*]])

Description   Returns the number of compounding periods for an investment or loan based on periodic, constant payments, *pmt*, using a fixed interest rate, *rate*, and a specified present value, *pv*.

Arguments
rate   real rate

pmt   real payment

pv   real present value

fv   (optional) real future value, default is *fv* = 0

type   (optional) indicator payment timing, 0 for payment made at the end of the period, 1 for payment made at the beginning, default is *type* = 0

Comments   If you know the annual interest rate, *ann_rate*, you must calculate the interest rate per period as *rate* = *ann_rate*/*nper*.

Payments you make, such as deposits into a savings account or payments toward a loan, must be entered as negative numbers. Cash you receive, such as dividend checks, must be entered as positive numbers. Specific to *nper*, if *pmt* > 0, *rate* and *pv* must be opposite signs.

See also   cnper, fv, pmt, pv, rate

npv
Finance

Syntax   npv(*rate*, **v**)

Description   Returns the net present value of an investment given a discount rate, *rate*, and a series of cash flows occurring at regular intervals, **v**.

Arguments
rate   real rate
v   real vector of cash flows

Comments   *npv* assumes that the payment is made as the end of the period.

In **v**, payments must be entered as negative numbers and income must be entered as positive numbers.

The *npv* investment begins one period before the date of the first cash flow and ends with the last cash flow in the vector. If your first cash flow occurs at the beginning of the first period, the first value must be added to the *npv* result, not included in the vector of cash flows.

See also   irr, pv

num2str

String

Syntax	num2str(z)
Description	Returns the string whose characters correspond to the decimal value of z.
Arguments	
z	real or complex number
See also	str2num

numol

Differential Equation Solving

Syntax	numol(**x_endpts**, *xpts*, **t_endpts**, *tpts*, *num_pde*, *num_pae*, **pfunc**, **pinit_func**, **bc_func**)
Description	Solves a one-dimensional partial differential equation (PDE) or system of PDEs using the numerical method of lines at equally spaced x and t values.

Arguments	
x_endpts	real column vector ($x1$ $x2$) giving the endpoints of the integration interval in x.
xpts	integer *xpts* > 0 specifies the number of points between **x_endpts** at which the solution is to be approximated; controls the number of rows in the matrix output
t_endpts	real column vector ($t1$ $t2$) giving the endpoints of the integration interval in t.
tpts	integer *tpts* > 0 specifies the number of points between **t_endpts** at which the solution is to be approximated; controls the number of columns in the matrix output
num_pde	integer > 0 specifies the number of first-order, one-dimensional partial differential equations to solve
num_pae	integer $\geq$ 0 specifies the number of one-dimensional partial algebraic equations to solve
pfunc	real vector-valued function containing the right-hand-sides (rhs) of the PDEs and PAEs

- For single PDE, the vector degenerates to a scalar function
  $$rhs(x, t, u, ux, uxx) = au + bux + cuxx \quad .$$

- For a system of PDEs, the vector contains the rhs of each PDE and PAE, cast in terms of unknown solution vectors $\mathbf{u}$, $\mathbf{u_x}$, and $\mathbf{u_{xx}}$ (note the combination of literal and vector subscripts used here):

$$\text{rhs}\left(x, t, \mathbf{u}, \mathbf{u_x}, \mathbf{u_{xx}}\right) := \begin{pmatrix} A \cdot \mathbf{u}_0 + B \cdot \mathbf{u_x}_1 \\ C \cdot \mathbf{u}_1 + D \cdot \mathbf{u_{xx}}_0 \\ \cdot \\ \cdot \\ \cdot \\ X \cdot \mathbf{u}_n + Y \cdot \mathbf{u_{xx}}_n \end{pmatrix}$$

pinit_func	real vector-valued function containing the initial condition functions of the PDEs

- For single PDE, the vector degenerates to a scalar function, $pinit(x) = y(x)$.
- For a system of PDEs, the vector contains initial value functions for each equation, in terms of x.

bc_func	*num_pde x 3* matrix of boundary condition functions. If the PDE for a row contains 2nd-order spatial derivatives, specify the row

- *(left_cond(t) right_cond(t) "D")* (for Dirichlet), or
- *(left_cond(t) right_cond(t) "N")* (for Neumann).

If the PDE contains only first order spatial derivatives, use "NA" for either the right or left boundary condition. If no spatial derivatives are present, use "NA" for both BCs (the row will be ignored).

Comments	numol can be used to solve one-dimensional hyperbolic and parabolic partial differential equations, or systems of such equations. The left hand side is assumed to contain first order partial derivatives of time only. For a more complete discussion and examples, see Chapter 9, "Solving and Data Analysis."

For a single PDE , the output of numol is a *xpts* by *tpts* matrix in which each column contains the solution to the PDE at xpts for a single point in time. For a system of PDEs, *numol* returns an *xpts* by *tpts*(num_pde+num_pae)* matrix, placing each subsequent solution u_n side-by-side. The function numol the numerical method of lines, which allows it to solve hyperbolic and parabolic PDEs.

Algorithm	Numerical Method of Lines (*Schittkowski*, 2002)
See also	Mathcad QuickSheets and Differential Equations tutorial; also Pdesolve, for a solve block approach.

Odesolve
Differential Equation Solving

Case of a Single Differential Equation

Syntax	Odesolve(*x*, *b*, [*nstep*])
Description	Solves a single ordinary differential equation, subject to either initial value or boundary value constraints. The DE must be linear in the highest order derivative term, and the number of conditions must be equal to the order of the DE. The output is a function of *x*, interpolated from a table of values computed by fixed step, adaptive or stiff DE solvers.

Arguments

x	variable of integration, real
b	terminal point of integration interval, real
nstep	(optional) integer number of steps, *nstep* > 0

Example

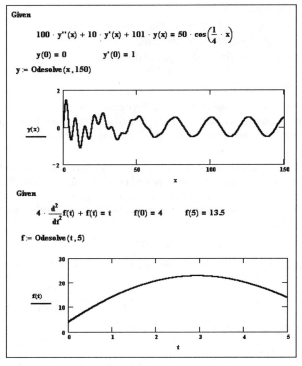

Given

$$100 \cdot y''(x) + 10 \cdot y'(x) + 101 \cdot y(x) = 50 \cdot \cos\left(\frac{1}{4} \cdot x\right)$$

$$y(0) = 0 \qquad y'(0) = 1$$

$$y := \text{Odesolve}(x, 150)$$

Given

$$4 \cdot \frac{d^2}{dt^2} f(t) + f(t) = t \qquad f(0) = 4 \qquad f(5) = 13.5$$

$$f := \text{Odesolve}(t, 5)$$

Comments   There are three steps to solving a DE using Odesolve:

1. Type the word Given. This tells Mathcad that what follows is a DE, along with initial value or boundary value constraints. You can type Given or given in any style. Just don't type it while in a text region.

2. Type the DE and constraints in any order below the word Given. Use [Ctrl]= to type "=" and [Ctrl]F7 to type a prime '. The DE can be written using the derivative operators d/dx, d^2/dx^2, d^3/dx^3, ... or using prime notation $y'(x)$, $y''(x)$, $y'''(x)$, ... Note that the independent variable x must be explicitly indicated throughout. A typical initial value constraint might be $y(a)=c$ or $y'(a)=d$; Mathcad does not allow more complicated constraints like $y(a)+y'(a)=e$.

3. Finally, type the Odesolve function. You can't put a numerical value in place of x: for example, Odesolve(2, 150) in the Example isn't permitted. Like given, you can type Odesolve or odesolve in any style.

The word Given, the equations that follow, and the Odesolve function form a *solve block*. This is similar to the solve block described with the Find function, except here no guess values are needed.

The following types of expressions and restrictions apply:

• Lower-order derivative terms can appear nonlinearly in the DE (e.g., they can be multiplied together or raised to powers), but the highest-order derivative term must appear linearly. I

• Inequality constraints are not allowed.

• There must be n independent equality constraints for an nth order DE. For an initial value problem, the values for $y(x)$ and its first $n-1$ derivatives at a single initial point a are required. For a boundary value problem, the n equality constraints should prescribe values for $y(x)$ and certain derivatives at exactly two points a and b. Mathcad will check for the correct type and number of conditions. Constraints on derivatives must be specified with prime [Ctrl-F7] notation.

- Algebraic constraints are allowed, e.g. $y(x) + z(x) = a$.

For initial value problems, the default routine employed by Odesolve is rkfixed. Fixed, adaptive, and stiff methods are available on the right click menu.

Internally, the output of each of these DE solvers is a table of values, which Mathcad interpolates using lspline followed by interp. Note in the Example that, although y and f are defined to be output of Odesolve (no independent variable is indicated), $y(x)$ and $f(t)$ are functions which can be plotted, etc., like any other function.

The default value for nsteps is ten times the length of the interval [a, b] (truncated to an integer).

Case of a System of Differential Equations

Syntax   Odesolve(**vf**, x, b, [$nstep$])

Description   Solves a system of ordinary differential equations, subject to initial value constraints (boundary values not allowed for systems). The DEs must each be linear in their highest order derivative terms, and the number of conditions must be equal to the sum of the orders of the DEs. The output is a vector of functions of x, interpolated from a table of values computed via either fixed step, adaptive or stiff DE solvers.

Arguments

vf   explicit vector of function names (with no variable names included) precisely as named in the solve block, real

x variable of integration, real

b terminal point of integration interval, real

$nstep$ (optional) integer number of steps, $nstep > 0$

The first argument **vf** is optional in the event of single ordinary differential equation (since ordering of the function solutions is an issue only if the numbers of DEs exceeds 1). For example, if the unknown functions are f, g, and h (as named in the solve block), then **vf** should be explicitly given in the Odesolve call as the column vector:

$$\begin{bmatrix} f \\ g \\ h \end{bmatrix}$$. Only the function names should appear; do not give the vector as: $$\begin{bmatrix} f(x) \\ g(x) \\ h(x) \end{bmatrix}$$.

Array subscripts may not be used when naming functions, but literal subscripts are fine. The comments for the single ODE case apply in the multiple ODEs case as well, suitably extended.

Odesolve can also solve differential algebraic equations (DAEs), for example, systems of ODEs involving unknown functions f, g, and h with the additional algebraic constraint that $f(x)^2 + g(x)^2 = h(x)$ for all x.

Example

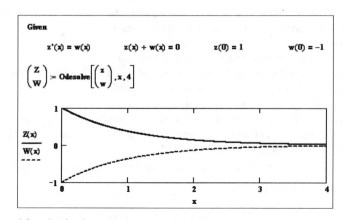

See also   rkfixed, Rkadapt, Radau, sbval, lspline, interp

---

pbeta   Probability Distribution

Syntax   pbeta(x, $s1$, $s2$)

Description   Returns the cumulative beta distribution with shape parameters $s1$ and $s2$.

Arguments

        x real number, $0 < x < 1$

     s_1, s_2 real shape parameters, $s_1 > 0$, $s_2 > 0$

Algorithm   Continued fraction expansion (Abramowitz and Stegun, 1972)

---

pbinom   Probability Distribution

Syntax   pbinom(k, n, p)

Description   Returns $\Pr(X \le k)$ when the random variable X has the binomial distribution with parameters n and p.

Arguments

     k, n integers, $0 \le k \le n$

        p real numbers, $0 \le p \le 1$

Algorithm   Continued fraction expansion (Abramowitz and Stegun, 1972)

---

pcauchy   Probability Distribution

Syntax   pcauchy(x, l, s)

Description   Returns the cumulative Cauchy distribution.

Arguments

        x real number

        l real location parameter

        s real scale parameter, $s > 0$

pchisq Probability Distribution

Syntax	pchisq(x, d)
Description	Returns the cumulative chi-squared distribution.
Arguments	
x	real number, $x \geq 0$
d	integer degrees of freedom, $d > 0$
Algorithm	Continued fraction and asymptotic expansions (Abramowitz and Stegun, 1972)

Pdesolve Differential Equation Solving

Case of a Single Partial Differential Equation

Syntax   Pdesolve(u, x, **xrange**, t, **trange**, [*xstep*, *tstep*])

Description   Solves a single 1-D hyperbolic or parabolic partial differential equation, or system of equations, subject to initial value and either Dirichlet or Neumann boundary value constraints. The PDE must be linear in the highest order derivative term, and the number of conditions must be equal to the order of the PDE. The output is a function of x and t, interpolated from a table of values computed by the method of lines.

Arguments

u	function of x and t, as specified in the PDE solve block	
x	spatial variable of integration, real	
xrange	$\begin{bmatrix} Lstart \\ Lend \end{bmatrix}$	two-element, real-valued column vector specifying the endpoints of the spatial integration range.
t	temporal variable of integration, real	
trange	$\begin{bmatrix} Tstart \\ Tend \end{bmatrix}$	two-element, real-valued column vector specifying the endpoints of the temporal integration range.
xstep, *tstep*	(optional) integer number of steps over each integration range, greater than 0.	

Example

Given

$$u_t(x,t) = \frac{1}{4} \cdot u_{xx}(x,t) - \frac{1}{2} \cdot u_x(x,t)$$

Initial condition:

$$u(x,0) = \sin\left(\pi \cdot \frac{x}{L}\right) + \frac{1}{2} \cdot \sin\left(3 \cdot \pi \cdot \frac{x}{L}\right)$$

Dirichlet bondary conditions:

$$u(0,t) = 0 \qquad\qquad u(L,t) = 0$$

$$u := \text{pdesolve}\left[u, x, \begin{pmatrix} 0 \\ L \end{pmatrix}, t, \begin{pmatrix} 0 \\ T \end{pmatrix}, 50, 30\right]$$

This creates a function u that can now be evaluated at any value of x and t in the specifed ranges. $u(.1,.2) = 0.08$

$$x := 0, .2 .. L \qquad t0 := 1.8 \qquad \text{Try changing the value of t0.}$$

Compare the exact solution with the numerical solver.

Using PDESolve for the 1-D heat equation with convection.

Comments

There are three steps to solving a PDE using Pdesolve:

1. Type the word **Given**. This tells Mathcad that what follows is a DE solve block, along with initial value or boundary value constraints. You must type Given as a math region, not a text region.

2. Type the PDE and constraints in any order below the word *Given*. Use the bold/symbolic equal sign [Ctrl] = for equality. Use subscript notation to indicate the partial derivative in either x or t, and explicitly specify the independent variables throughout, that is, use $y(x,t)$ or $y_{xx}(x,t)$, not just y or y_{xx}. Eeither Dirichlet ($y(0,t) = a$) or Neumann ($y_x(0,t) = a$) boundary conditions are accepted. Mathcad also allows algebraic constraints, such as $y(x,t) + z(x,t) = 2$.

3. Finally, type the *Pdesolve* function. The two-element column vectors **xrange** and **trange**, ranges over x and t, respectively, must agree with values assigned in the boundary conditions.

The word Given, the equations that follow, and the Odesolve function form a *solve block*. The following types of expressions and restrictions apply:

- Lower-order derivative terms can appear nonlinearly in the DE (e.g., they can be multiplied together or raised to powers), but the highest-order derivative term must appear linearly. I
- Inequality constraints are not allowed.
- There must be *n* independent boundary conditions, either Dirichlet or Neumann, for an *n*th order PDE, and there must always be an initial value value for $u(x,t)$. Mathcad will check for the correct type and number of conditions. Constraints on derivatives must be specified with prime [Ctrl-F7] notation.
- Algebraic constraints are allowed, e.g. $y(x,t) + z(x,t) = f(x,t)$.

Internally, the output of each of pdesolve is a table of values, which Mathcad interpolates using lspline followed by interp. Note in the Example that, although *u* is defined to be the output of the call to Pdesolve (no independent variable is indicated), $u(x, t)$ is a function which can be plotted, etc., like any other function.

In the case of a system of PDEs, the first argument of Pdesolve, **u,** is now a vector of functions used within the solve block, and will specify order of output, that is

$\begin{bmatrix} u \\ v \\ w \end{bmatrix}$. Only the function names should appear; do not give the vector as: $\begin{bmatrix} u(x) \\ v(x) \\ w(x) \end{bmatrix}$.

Array subscripts may not be used when naming functions, but literal subscripts are fine. Pdesolve can solve partial differential algebraic equations (DAEs), for example, systems of PDEs involving unknown functions u, v, and h with the additional algebraic constraint that $u(x,t)^2 + v(x,t)^2 = h(x)$ for all x.

Mathcad uses the numerical method of lines to compute PDEs. This method allows the solution of parabolic (heat), hyperbolic (wave), and mixed parabolic-hyperbolic equations. It does not accommodate elliptic equations, such as Poisson's equation. To solve other types of PDEs, try the *relax* function (page 356) and *multigrid* function (page 323).

See also   numol, relax, multigrid

---

permut   Number Theory/Combinatorics

Syntax   permut(n, k)

Description   Returns the number of ways of ordering n distinct objects taken k at a time.

Arguments
n, k integers, $0 \le k \le n$

Comments   Each such ordered arrangement is known as a permutation. The number of permutations is

$$P^n_k = \frac{n!}{(n-k)!}$$

See also   combin

---

pexp   Probability Distribution

Syntax   pexp(x, r)

Description   Returns the cumulative exponential distribution.

Arguments
x real number, $x \ge 0$
r real rate, $r > 0$

---

pF   Probability Distribution

Syntax   pF(x, $d1$, $d2$)

Description   Returns the cumulative F distribution.

Arguments
x real number, $x \ge 0$
d_1, d_2 integer degrees of freedom, $d_1 > 0$, $d_2 > 0$

Algorithm   Continued fraction expansion (Abramowitz and Stegun, 1972)

pgamma
Probability Distribution

Syntax	pgamma(x, s)
Description	Returns the cumulative gamma distribution.
Arguments	
x	real number, $x \geq 0$
s	real shape parameter, $s > 0$
Algorithm	Continued fraction and asymptotic expansion (Abramowitz and Stegun, 1972)

pgeom
Probability Distribution

Syntax	pgeom(k, p)
Description	Returns $\Pr(X \leq k)$ when the random variable X has the geometric distribution with parameter p.
Arguments	
k	integer, $k \geq 0$
p	real number, $0 < p \leq 1$

phypergeom
Probability Distribution

Syntax	phypergeom(m, a, b, n)
Description	Returns $\Pr(X \leq m)$ when the random variable X has the hypergeometric distribution with parameters a, b and n.
Arguments	
m, a, b, n	integers, $0 \leq m \leq a$, $0 \leq n - m \leq b$, $0 \leq n \leq a + b$

plnorm
Probability Distribution

Syntax	plnorm(x, μ, σ)
Description	Returns the cumulative lognormal distribution.
Arguments	
x	real number, $x \geq 0$
μ	real logmean
σ	real logdeviation, $\sigma > 0$

plogis
Probability Distribution

Syntax	plogis(x, l, s)
Description	Returns the cumulative logistic distribution.
Arguments	
x	real number
l	real location parameter
s	real scale parameter, $s > 0$

pmt
Finance

Syntax	pmt(*rate*, *nper*, *pv*, [[*fv*], [*type*]])
Description	Returns the payment for an investment or loan based on periodic, constant payments over a given number of compounding periods, *nper*, using a fixed interest rate, *rate*, and a specified present value, *pv*.

Arguments

rate	real rate
nper	integer number of compounding periods, *nper* ≥ 1
pv	real present value
fv	(optional) real future value, default is *fv* = 0
type	(optional) indicator payment timing, 0 for payment made at the end of the period, 1 for payment made at the beginning, default is *type* = 0

Comments	If you know the annual interest rate, *ann_rate*, you must calculate the interest rate per period as *rate* = *ann_rate*/*nper*.
	Payments you make, such as deposits into a savings account or payments toward a loan, must be entered as negative numbers. Cash you receive, such as dividend checks, must be entered as positive numbers.
See also	cumint, cumprn, fv, ipmt, nper, ppmt, pv, rate

pnbinom
Probability Distribution

Syntax	pnbinom(k, n, p)
Description	Returns the cumulative negative binomial distribution with parameters n and p.

Arguments

k, n	integers, $n > 0$ and $k \geq 0$
p	real number, $0 < p \leq 1$

Algorithm	Continued fraction expansion (Abramowitz and Stegun, 1972)

pnorm
Probability Distribution

Syntax	pnorm(x, μ, σ)
Description	Returns the cumulative normal distribution.

Arguments

x	real number
μ	real mean
σ	real standard deviation, $\sigma > 0$

Polyhedron
Vector and Matrix

Syntax	Polyhedron(S)
Description	Generates the uniform polyhedron whose name, number code, or Wythoff symbol is S.

Arguments

S	string expression containing the name of a polyhedron, its number code, or its Wythoff symbol

Example

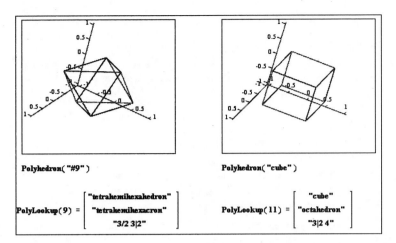

Polyhedron("#9")

$$\text{PolyLookup}(9) = \begin{bmatrix} \text{"tetrahemihexahedron"} \\ \text{"tetrahemihexacron"} \\ \text{"3/2 3|2"} \end{bmatrix}$$

Polyhedron("cube")

$$\text{PolyLookup}(11) = \begin{bmatrix} \text{"cube"} \\ \text{"octahedron"} \\ \text{"3|2 4"} \end{bmatrix}$$

Comments
The uniform polyhedron are regular polyhedra whose vertices are congruent. The Polyhedron function can construct 80 examples of these, and is used with the 3D surface plot tool as illustrated. Its argument is either a name ("cube"), the # symbol followed by a number ("#6"), or a Wythoff symbol ("3|2 4"). To look up these items use PolyLookup.

To graph a uniform polyhedron:

1. Click in a blank spot of your worksheet. Choose **Graph⇒Surface Plot** from the **Insert** menu.

2. In the placeholder, enter the *Polyhedron* function with an appropriate string argument.

3. Click outside the plot or press [**Enter**].

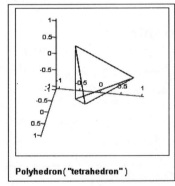

Polyhedron("tetrahedron")

PolyLookup
Vector and Matrix

Syntax
PolyLookup(*n*)

Description
Returns a vector containing the name, the dual name, and the Wythoff symbol for the polyhedron indicated by *n*.

Arguments

n
integer, is the code for a polyhedron; alternatively, a string expression containing the polyhedron's number code, name, or Wythoff symbol

See also
Polyhedron for example

polyroots

Syntax   polyroots(**v**)

Description   Returns the roots of an nth degree polynomial whose coefficients are in **v**. Output is a vector of length n.

Arguments

v   real or complex vector of length $n + 1$

Example

```
x³ - 10·x + 2          ←  Polynomial

      ⎡  2 ⎤
      ⎢ -10⎥             ←  A vector of the coefficients, begin
Y :=  ⎢  0 ⎥                with the constant term.  Be sure to
      ⎢  1 ⎥                include all coefficients, even if
      ⎣    ⎦                they are zero.

                  ⎡-3.258⎤
polyroots( v ) =  ⎢ 0.201⎥     ←  Returns all roots at once.
                  ⎣ 3.057⎦
```

Comments   To find the roots of an expression having the form: $v_n x^n + \ldots + v_2 x^2 + v_1 x + v_0$

you can use the polyroots function rather than the root function. Unlike root, polyroots does not require a guess value. Moreover, polyroots returns all roots at once, whether real or complex.

The polyroots function can solve only one polynomial equation in one unknown. See root for a more general equation solver. To solve several equations simultaneously, use solve blocks (Find or Minerr). To solve an equation symbolically—that is, to find an exact numerical answer in terms of elementary functions—choose **Solve for Variable** from the **Symbolics** menu or use the solve keyword.

Algorithm   Laguerre with deflation and polishing (Lorczak) is the default method; a companion matrix-based method (using Mathcad's eigenvals function) is available if you right click on the word polyroots and change the selection on a popup menu.

See also   See coeff keyword for a way to create the coefficient vector **v** immediately, given a polynomial.

pol2xy

Syntax   pol2xy(r, θ) or pol2xy(v)

Description   Converts the polar coordinates of a point in 2D space to rectangular coordinates.

Arguments

r, θ real numbers

Comments $x = r \cos(\theta)$, $y = r \sin(\theta)$, $v = \begin{bmatrix} r \\ \theta \end{bmatrix}$

See also   xy2pol

ppmt
Finance

Syntax	ppmt(*rate*, *per*, *nper*, *pv*, [[*fv*], [*type*]])
Description	Returns the payment on the principal, of an investment or loan, for a given period, *per*, based on periodic, constant payments over a given number of compounding periods, *nper*, using a fixed interest rate, *rate*, and a specified present value, *pv*.

Arguments

rate	real rate
per	integer period number, *per* ≥ 1
nper	integer number of compounding periods, $1 \leq per \leq nper$
pv	real present value
fv	(optional) real future value, default is *fv* = 0
type	(optional) indicator payment timing, 0 for payment made at the end of the period, 1 for payment made at the beginning, default is *type* = 0

Comments	If you know the annual interest rate, *ann_rate*, you must calculate the interest rate per period as *rate* = *ann_rate*/*nper*.
	Payments you make, such as deposits into a savings account or payments toward a loan, must be entered as negative numbers. Cash you receive, such as dividend checks, must be entered as positive numbers.
See also	cumprn, ipmt, pmt

ppois
Probability Distribution

Syntax	ppois(*k*, λ)
Description	Returns the cumulative Poisson distribution.

Arguments

k	integer, $k \geq 0$
λ	real mean, $\lambda > 0$

Algorithm	Continued fraction and asymptotic expansions (Abramowitz and Stegun, 1972)

predict
Interpolation and Prediction

Syntax	predict(**v**, *m*, *n*)
Description	Returns *n* predicted values based on *m* consecutive values from the data vector **v**. Elements in **v** should represent samples taken at equal intervals.

Arguments

v	real vector
m, *n*	integers, $m > 0$, $n > 0$

Example

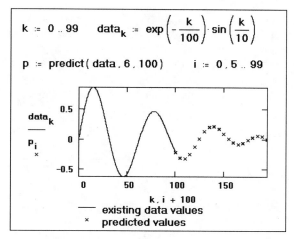

$$k := 0 .. 99 \qquad data_k := exp\left(-\frac{k}{100}\right) \cdot sin\left(\frac{k}{10}\right)$$

$$p := predict(\,data\,,\,6\,,\,100\,) \qquad i := 0\,,\,5 .. 99$$

$data_k$ ——
p_i ×

k , i + 100
—— existing data values
× predicted values

Comments

Interpolation functions such as cspline, lspline, or pspline, coupled with interp, allow you to find data points lying between existing data points. However, you may need to find data points that lie beyond your existing ones. Mathcad provides the function predict which uses some of your existing data to predict data points lying beyond existing ones. This function uses a linear prediction algorithm which is useful when your data is smooth and oscillatory, although not necessarily periodic. This algorithm can be seen as a kind of extrapolation method but should not be confused with linear or polynomial extrapolation.

The predict function uses the last m of the original data values to compute prediction coefficients. After it has these coefficients, it uses the last m points to predict the coordinates of the $(m+1)^{st}$ point, in effect creating a moving window that is m points wide.

Algorithm

Burg's method (Press *et al.*, 1992)

pspline

Interpolation and Prediction

One-dimensional Case

Syntax

pspline(**vx**, **vy**)

Description

Returns the vector of coefficients of a cubic spline with parabolic ends. This vector becomes the first argument of the interp function.

Arguments

vx, vy

real vectors of the same size; elements of **vx** must be in ascending order

Two-dimensional Case

Syntax

pspline(**Mxy**, **Mz**)

Description

Returns the vector of coefficients of a two-dimensional cubic spline, constrained to be parabolic at region boundaries spanned by **Mxy**. This vector becomes the first argument of the interp function.

Arguments	
Mxy	$n \times 2$ matrix whose elements, $Mxy_{i,\,0}$ and $Mxy_{i,\,1}$, specify the x- and y-coordinates along the *diagonal* of a rectangular grid. This matrix plays exactly the same role as **vx** in the one-dimensional case described earlier. Since these points describe a diagonal, the elements in each column of **Mxy** must be in ascending order ($Mxy_{i,\,k} < Mxy_{j,\,k}$ whenever $i < j$).
Mz	$n \times n$ matrix whose ijth element is the z-coordinate corresponding to the point $x = Mxy_{i,\,0}$ and $y = Mxy_{j,\,1}$. **Mz** plays exactly the same role as **vy** in the one-dimensional case above.
Algorithm	Tridiagonal system solving (Press *et al.*, 1992; Lorczak)
See also	lspline for more details

pt   Probability Distribution

Syntax	pt(x, d)
Description	Returns the cumulative Student's t distribution.
Arguments	
x	real number, $x \geq 0$
d	integer degrees of freedom, $d > 0$
Algorithm	Continued fraction expansion (Abramowitz and Stegun, 1972).

punif   Probability Distribution

Syntax	punif(x, a, b)
Description	Returns the cumulative uniform distribution.
Arguments	
x	real number
a, b	real numbers, $a < b$

pv   Finance

Syntax	pv(*rate*, *nper*, *pmt*, [[*fv*], [*type*]])
Description	Returns the present value of an investment or loan based on periodic, constant payments over a given number of compounding periods, *nper*, using a fixed interest rate, *rate*, and a specified payment, *pmt*.
Arguments	
rate	real rate
nper	integer number of compounding periods, *nper* ≥ 1
pmt	real payment
fv	(optional) real future value, default is *fv* = 0
type	(optional) indicator payment timing, 0 for payment made at the end of the period, 1 for payment made at the beginning, default is *type* = 0
Comments	If you know the annual interest rate, *ann_rate*, you must calculate the interest rate per period as *rate* = *ann_rate*/*nper*.
	Payments you make, such as deposits into a savings account or payments toward a loan, must be entered as negative numbers. Cash you receive, such as dividend checks, must be entered as positive numbers.
See also	fv, nper, pmt, rate

pweibull

Syntax	pweibull(x, s)
Description	Returns the cumulative Weibull distribution.
Arguments	
x	real number, $x \geq 0$
s	real shape parameter, $s > 0$

pwrfit

Syntax	pwrfit(**vx**, **vy**, **vg**)
Description	Returns a vector containing the parameters (a, b, c) that make the function $a \cdot x^b + c$ best approximate the data in **vx** and **vy**.
Arguments	
vx, vy	real vectors of the same size
vg	real vector of guess values for (a, b, c)
Comments	This is a special case of the genfit function. A vector of guess values is needed for initialization. By decreasing the value of the built-in TOL variable, higher accuracy in pwrfit might be achieved.
See Also	line, linfit, genfit, expfit, logfit, lnfit, lgsfit, sinfit, medfit

qbeta

Syntax	qbeta(p, $s1$, $s2$)
Description	Returns the inverse beta distribution with shape parameters $s1$ and $s2$.
Arguments	
p	real number, $0 \leq p \leq 1$
s_1, s_2	real shape parameters, $s_1 > 0, s_2 > 0$
Algorithm	Root finding (bisection and secant methods) (Press *et al.*, 1992)

qbinom

Syntax	qbinom(p, n, q)
Description	Returns the inverse binomial distribution function, that is, the smallest integer k so that pbinom(k, n, q) $\geq p$.
Arguments	
n	integer, $n > 0$
p, q	real numbers, $0 \leq p \leq 1$, $0 \leq q \leq 1$
Comments	k is approximately the integer for which $\Pr(X \leq k) = p$, when the random variable X has the binomial distribution with parameters n and q. This is the meaning of "inverse" binomial distribution function.
Algorithm	Discrete bisection method (Press *et al.*, 1992)

qcauchy
Probability Distribution

Syntax	qcauchy(p, l, s)
Description	Returns the inverse Cauchy distribution function.
Arguments	
p	real number, $0 < p < 1$
l	real location parameter
s	real scale parameter, $s > 0$

qchisq
Probability Distribution

Syntax	qchisq(p, d)
Description	Returns the inverse chi-squared distribution.
Arguments	
p	real number, $0 \leq p < 1$
d	integer degrees of freedom, $d > 0$
Algorithm	Root finding (bisection and secant methods) (Press *et al.*, 1992)
	Rational function approximations (Abramowitz and Stegun, 1972)

qexp
Probability Distribution

Syntax	qexp(p, r)
Description	Returns the inverse exponential distribution.
Arguments	
p	real number, $0 \leq p < 1$
r	real rate, $r > 0$

qF
Probability Distribution

Syntax	qF(p, $d1$, $d2$)
Description	Returns the inverse F distribution.
Arguments	
p	real number, $0 \leq p < 1$
d_1, d_2	integer degrees of freedom, $d_1 > 0$, $d_2 > 0$
Algorithm	Root finding (bisection and secant methods) (Press *et al.*, 1992)

qgamma
Probability Distribution

Syntax	qgamma(p, s)
Description	Returns the inverse gamma distribution.
Arguments	
p	real number, $0 \leq p < 1$
s	real shape parameter, $s > 0$
Algorithm	Root finding (bisection and secant methods) (Press *et al.*, 1992)
	Rational function approximations (Abramowitz and Stegun, 1972)

qgeom
Probability Distribution

Syntax   qgeom(p, q)

Description   Returns the inverse geometric distribution, that is, the smallest integer k so that pgeom(k, q) $\geq p$.

Arguments
p, q real numbers, $0 < p < 1$, $0 < q < 1$

Comments k is approximately the integer for which $\Pr(X \leq k) = p$, when the random variable X has the geometric distribution with parameter q. This is the meaning of "inverse" geometric distribution function.

qhypergeom
Probability Distribution

Syntax   qhypergeom(p, a, b, n)

Description   Returns the inverse hypergeometric distribution, that is, the smallest integer k so that phypergeom(k, a, b, n) $\geq p$.

Arguments
p real number, $0 \leq p \leq 1$

a, b, n integers, $0 \leq a$, $0 \leq b$, $0 \leq n \leq a + b$

Comments k is approximately the integer for which $\Pr(X \leq k) = p$, when the random variable X has the hypergeometric distribution with parameters a, b and n. This is the meaning of "inverse" hypergeometric distribution function.

Algorithm   Discrete bisection method (Press *et al.*, 1992)

qlnorm
Probability Distribution

Syntax   qlnorm(p, μ, σ)

Description   Returns the inverse log normal distribution.

Arguments
p real number; $0 \leq p < 1$

μ logmean

σ logdeviation; $\sigma > 0$

Algorithm   Root finding (bisection and secant methods) (Press *et al.*, 1992)

qlogis
Probability Distribution

Syntax   qlogis(p, l, s)

Description   Returns the inverse logistic distribution.

Arguments
p real number, $0 < p < 1$

l real location parameter

s real scale parameter, $s > 0$

qnbinom

Probability Distribution

Syntax	qnbinom(p, n, q)
Description	Returns the inverse negative binomial distribution function, that is, the smallest integer k so that pnbinom(k, n, q) $\geq p$.
Arguments	
n	integer, $n > 0$
p, q	real numbers, $0 < p < 1$, $0 < q < 1$
Comments	k is approximately the integer for which $\Pr(X \leq k) = p$, when the random variable X has the negative binomial distribution with parameters n and q. This is the meaning of "inverse" negative binomial distribution function.
Algorithm	Discrete bisection method (Press *et al.*, 1992)

qnorm

Probability Distribution

Syntax	qnorm(p, μ, σ)
Description	Returns the inverse normal distribution.
Arguments	
p	real number, $0 < p < 1$
m	real mean
s	standard deviation, $\sigma > 0$
Algorithm	Root finding (bisection and secant methods) (Press *et al.*, 1992)

qpois

Probability Distribution

Syntax	qpois(p, λ)
Description	Returns the inverse Poisson distribution, that is, the smallest integer k so that ppois(k, λ) $\geq p$.
Arguments	
p	real number,
λ	real mean, $\lambda > 0$
Comments	k is approximately the integer for which $\Pr(X \leq k) = p$, when the random variable X has the Poisson distribution with parameter λ. This is the meaning of "inverse" Poisson distribution function.
Algorithm	Discrete bisection method (Press *et al.*, 1992)

qr

Vector and Matrix

Syntax	qr($\mathbf{A}$)
Description	Returns an $m \times (m + n)$ matrix whose first m columns contain the $m \times m$ orthonormal matrix $\mathbf{Q}$, and whose remaining n columns contain the $m \times n$ upper triangular matrix $\mathbf{R}$. These satisfy the matrix equation $\mathbf{A} = \mathbf{Q} \cdot \mathbf{R}$.
Arguments	
$\mathbf{A}$	real $m \times n$ matrix

Example

$$
A := \begin{pmatrix} 1 & 2 & -1 \\ 2.3 & 4 & 4 \\ -2 & 5.1 & 1 \\ 0 & .8 & 6 \end{pmatrix} \qquad M := qr(A)
$$

$$
M = \begin{pmatrix} 0.312 & 0.279 & -0.411 & -0.81 & 3.208 & 0.312 & 1.933 \\ 0.717 & 0.553 & 0.117 & 0.407 & 0 & 6.823 & 3.415 \\ -0.623 & 0.776 & -0.072 & 0.064 & 0 & 0 & 6.213 \\ 0 & 0.117 & 0.901 & -0.417 & 0 & 0 & 0 \end{pmatrix}
$$

$$
Q := submatrix(M, 0, 3, 0, 3) \qquad R := submatrix(M, 0, 3, 4, 6)
$$

$$
Q \cdot Q^{T} = \begin{pmatrix} 1 & 0 & 0 & 0 \\ 0 & 1 & 0 & 0 \\ 0 & 0 & 1 & 0 \\ 0 & 0 & 0 & 1 \end{pmatrix} \qquad Q \cdot R = \begin{pmatrix} 1 & 2 & -1 \\ 2.3 & 4 & 4 \\ -2 & 5.1 & 1 \\ 0 & 0.8 & 6 \end{pmatrix}
$$

qt
Probability Distribution

Syntax	qt(p, d)
Description	Returns the inverse Student's t distribution.
Arguments	
p	real number, $0 < p < 1$
d	integer degrees of freedom, $d > 0$
Algorithm	Root finding (bisection and secant methods) (Press *et al.*, 1992).

qunif
Probability Distribution

Syntax	qunif(p, a, b)
Description	Returns the inverse uniform distribution.
Arguments	
p	real number, $0 \le p \le 1$
a, b	real numbers, $a < b$

qweibull
Probability Distribution

Syntax	qweibull(p, s)
Description	Returns the inverse Weibull distribution.
Arguments	
p	real number,
s	real shape parameter, $s > 0$

radau

Syntax	radau(y, *x1*, *x2*, *acc*, **D**, *kmax*, *save*)
Description	Solves a differential equation using a stiff RADAU5 method. Provides DE solution estimate at *x2*.
Arguments	*Several arguments for this function are the same as described for* rkfixed.
y	real vector of initial values
x1, *x2*	real endpoints of the solution interval
acc	real *acc* > 0 controls the accuracy of the solution; a small value of *acc* forces the algorithm to take smaller steps along the trajectory, thereby increasing the accuracy of the solution. Values of *acc* around 0.001 will generally yield accurate solutions.
D(*x*, **y**)	real vector-valued function containing the derivatives of the unknown functions
kmax	integer *kmax* > 0 specifies the maximum number of intermediate points at which the solution will be approximated. The value of *kmax* places an upper bound on the number of rows of the matrix returned by these functions.
save	real *save* > 0 specifies the smallest allowable spacing between the values at which the solutions are to be approximated. *save* places a lower bound on the difference between any two numbers in the first column of the matrix returned by the function.
Comments	The specialized DE solvers Bulstoer, Rkadapt, Radau, Stiffb, and Stiffr provide the solution *y(x)* over a number of uniformly spaced *x*-values in the integration interval bounded by *x1* and *x2*. When you want the value of the solution at only the endpoint, *y(x2)*, use bulstoer, rkadapt, radau, stiffb, and stiffr instead.
Algorithm	Implicit Runge-Kutta RADAU5 method (Hairer and Wanner, 1996)
See also	rkfixed, a more general differential equation solver, for information on output and arguments; Radau.

Radau

Syntax	Radau(**y**, *x1*, *x2*, *npts*, **D**)
Description	Solves a differential equation using a stiff RADAU5 method; provides DE solution at equally spaced *x* values by repeated calls to radau.
Arguments	*All arguments for this function are the same as described for* rkfixed.
y	real vector of initial values
x1, x2	real endpoints of the solution interval
npts	integer *npts* > 0 specifies the number of points beyond initial point at which the solution is to be approximated; controls the number of rows in the matrix output
D(x, **y**)	real vector-valued function containing the derivatives of the unknown functions
Comments	Radau and radau are especially intended for stiff ODEs. They have one advantage over Stiffb, Stiffr, stiffb and stiffr: the (symbolic) Jacobian matrix input J is not needed. (Of course, this is a disadvantage if J is readily available, because having J will tend to increase accuracy.)
	Radau takes the same arguments as rkfixed, and the matrix returned by Radau is identical in form to that returned by rkfixed.
Algorithm	Implicit Runge-Kutta RADAU5 method (Hairer and Wanner, 1996)
See also	rkfixed, a more general differential equation solver, for information on output and arguments; also Odesolve, for a solve block approach.

rank

Syntax	rank(**A**)
Description	Returns the rank of a matrix **A**, i.e., the maximum number of linearly independent columns in **A**.
Arguments	
A	real $m \times n$ matrix
Algorithm	Singular value computation (Wilkinson and Reinsch, 1971)

rate

Syntax	rate(*nper*, *pmt*, *pv*, [[*fv*], [*type*], [*guess*]])
Description	Returns the interest rate per period of an investment or loan over a specified number of compounding periods, *nper*, given a periodic, constant payment, *pmt*, and a specified present value, *pv*.
Arguments	
nper	integer number of compounding periods, *nper* ≥ 1
pmt	real payment
pv	real present value
fv	(optional) real future value, default is *fv* = 0
type	(optional) indicator payment timing, 0 for payment made at the end of the period, 1 for payment made at the beginning, default is *type* = 0
guess	(optional) real guess, default is *guess* = 0.1 (10%)

Comments	Payments made must be entered as negative numbers. Cash received must be entered as positive numbers.
	If rate cannot find a result that is accurate to within $1 \cdot 10^{-7}$ percent after 20 iterations, it returns an error. In such a case, a different guess value should be tried, but it will not guarantee a solution. In most cases *rate* converges if *guess* is between 0 and 1.
See also	crate, fv, nper, pmt, pv

rbeta   Random Numbers

Syntax	rbeta(*m*, *s1*, *s2*)
Description	Returns a vector of *m* random numbers having the beta distribution.
Arguments	
m	integer, $m > 0$
s_1, s_2	real shape parameters, $s_1 > 0$, $s_2 > 0$
Algorithm	Best's XG algorithm, Johnk's generator (Devroye, 1986)
See also	rnd

rbinom   Random Numbers

Syntax	rbinom(*m*, *n*, *p*)
Description	Returns a vector of *m* random numbers having the binomial distribution.
Arguments	
m, *n*	integers, $m > 0$, $n > 0$
p	real number, $0 \le p \le 1$
Algorithm	Waiting time and rejection algorithms (Devroye, 1986)
See also	rnd

rcauchy   Random Numbers

Syntax	rcauchy(*m*, *l*, *s*)
Description	Returns a vector of *m* random numbers having the Cauchy distribution.
Arguments	
m	integer, $m > 0$
l	real location parameter
s	real scale parameter, $s > 0$
Algorithm	Inverse cumulative density method (Press *et al.*, 1992)
See also	rnd

rchisq

Syntax	rchisq(*m*, *d*)
Description	Returns a vector of *m* random numbers having the chi-squared distribution.
Arguments	
m	integer, $m > 0$
d	integer degrees of freedom, $d > 0$
Algorithm	Best's XG algorithm, Johnk's generator (Devroye, 1986)
See also	rnd

Re

Syntax	Re(*z*)
Description	Returns the real part of *z*.
Arguments	
z	real or complex number
See also	Im

READBIN

Syntax	READBIN(*file*, *type*, [[*endian*], [*cols*], [*skip*], [*maxrows*]])
Description	Reads a file of binary data and returns a matrix. Used as follows: A := READBIN(*file*, *type*).
Arguments	
file	String variable corresponding to the binary data filename, including path. If no path is provided, the current working directory is assumed.
type	String argument specifying the data type used in the file. Must be one of the following: double (64 bit floating point), float (32 bit floating point), byte (8 bit unsigned integer), uint16 (16 bit unsigned integer), uint32 (32 bit unsigned integer), int16 (16 bit signed integer), or int32 (32 bit signed integer).
endian	(optional) Indicates whether data format is big-endian (high byte first) or little-endian (low byte first). Big-endian is represented by a 1, and little-endian by 0. Defaults to 0.
cols	(optional) Number of columns per row in the input file, $cols \geq 1$. Defaults to 1.
skip	(optional) Number of bytes to skip at the beginning of the file before reading data, $skip \geq 0$. Defaults to 0.
maxrows	(optional) Number of rows to limit input to, $maxrows \geq 0$. Defaults to 0.
See also	WRITEBIN

READ_BLUE

Syntax	READ_BLUE(*file*)
Description	Extracts only the blue component from *file* of a color image in BMP, JPG, GIF, TGA, and PCX format. The result is a matrix with one-third as many columns as the matrix returned by READRGB.
Arguments	
file	string variable corresponding to color image filename or path

READBMP

Syntax	READBMP(*file*)
Description	Creates a matrix containing a grayscale representation of the bitmap image in *file*. Each element in the matrix corresponds to a pixel. The value of a matrix element determines the shade of gray associated with the corresponding pixel. Each element is an integer between 0 (black) and 255 (white).
Arguments	
file	string variable corresponding to grayscale image BMP filename or path
Comments	Picture viewer will display the matrix.
	The function READ_IMAGE which reads not only BMP files but also JPG, GIF, TGA and PCX files.
See also	For color images, see READRGB.

READ_GREEN

Syntax	READ_GREEN(*file*)
Description	Extracts only the green component from *file* of a color image in BMP, JPG, GIF, TGA, and PCX format. The result is a matrix with one-third as many columns as the matrix returned by READRGB.
Arguments	
file	string variable corresponding to color image filename or path

READ_HLS

Syntax	READ_HLS(*file*)
Description	Creates a matrix in which the color information in *file* is represented by the appropriate values of hue, lightness, and saturation. *file* is in BMP, JPG, GIF, TGA, or PCX format.
Arguments	
file	string variable corresponding to color image filename or path
See also	See READRGB for an overview.

READ_HLS_HUE

Syntax	READ_HLS_HUE(*file*)
Description	Extracts only the hue component from *file* of a color image in BMP, JPG, GIF, TGA, or PCX format. The result is a matrix with one-third as many columns as the matrix returned by READ_HLS.
Arguments	
file	string variable corresponding to color image filename or path

READ_HLS_LIGHT

Syntax	READ_HLS_LIGHT(*file*)
Description	Extracts only the lightness component from *file* of a color image in BMP, JPG, GIF, TGA, or PCX format. The result is a matrix with one-third as many columns as the matrix returned by READ_HLS.
Arguments	
file	string variable corresponding to color image filename or path

READ_HLS_SAT

Syntax	READ_HLS_SAT(*file*)
Description	Extracts only the saturation component from *file* of a color image in BMP, JPG, GIF, TGA, or PCX format. The result is a matrix with one-third as many columns as the matrix returned by READ_HLS.
Arguments	
file	string variable corresponding to color image filename or path

READ_HSV

Syntax	READ_HSV(*file*)
Description	Creates a matrix in which the color information in *file* is represented by the appropriate values of hue, saturation and value. *file* is in BMP, JPG, GIF, TGA, or PCX format.
Arguments	
file	string variable corresponding to color image filename or path
See also	See READRGB for an overview of reading color data files.

READ_HSV_HUE

Syntax	READ_HSV_HUE(*file*)
Description	Extracts only the hue component from *file* of a color image in BMP, JPG, GIF, TGA, or PCX format. The result is a matrix with one-third as many columns as the matrix returned by READ_HSV.
Arguments	
file	string variable corresponding to color image filename or path

READ_HSV_SAT

Syntax	READ_HSV_SAT(*file*)
Description	Extracts only the saturation component from *file* of a color image in BMP, JPG, GIF, TGA, or PCX format. The result is a matrix with one-third as many columns as the matrix returned by READ_HSV.
Arguments	
file	string variable corresponding to color image filename or path

READ_HSV_VALUE

Syntax   READ_HSV_VALUE(*file*)

Description   Extracts only the value component from *file* of a color image in BMP, JPG, GIF, TGA, or PCX format. The result is a matrix with one-third as many columns as the matrix returned by READ_HSV.

Arguments
file   string variable corresponding to color image filename or path

READ_IMAGE

Syntax   READ_IMAGE(*file*)

Description   Creates a matrix containing a grayscale representation of the image in *file*. Each element in the matrix corresponds to a pixel. The value of a matrix element determines the shade of gray associated with the corresponding pixel. Each element is an integer between 0 (black) and 255 (white). *file* is in BMP, JPG, GIF, TGA, or PCX format.

Arguments
file   string variable corresponding to grayscale image filename or path

See also   For color images, see READRGB.

READPRN

Syntax   READPRN(*file*)

Description   Reads a structured ASCII data file and returns a matrix. Each line in the data file becomes a row in the matrix. The number of elements in each row must be the same. Used as follows: **A** := READPRN(*file*).

Arguments
file   string variable corresponding to structured ASCII data filename or path

Comments   The READPRN function reads an entire data file, determines the number of rows and columns, and creates a matrix out of the data.

When Mathcad reads data with the READPRN function:

- Each instance of the READPRN function reads an entire data file.
- All lines in the data file must have the same number of values. (Mathcad ignores lines with no values.) If the lines in the file have differing numbers of values, Mathcad marks the READPRN equation with an error message. Use a text editor to replace the missing values with zeros before you use READPRN.
- The READPRN function ignores text in the data file.
- The result of reading the data file is an *m*-by-*n* matrix **A**, where *m* is the number of lines containing data in the file and *n* is the number of values per line.

WRITEPRN and READPRN allow you to write out and read in *nested arrays* created in Mathcad.

READ_RED

Syntax   READ_RED(*file*)

Description   Extracts only the red component from *file* of a color image in BMP, JPG, GIF, TGA, or PCX format. The result is a matrix with one-third as many columns as the matrix returned by READRGB.

Arguments
file   string variable corresponding to color image filename or path

READRGB

Syntax   READRGB(*file*)

Description   Creates a matrix in which the color information in the BMP file *file* is represented by the appropriate values of red, green, and blue. This matrix consists of three submatrices, each with the same number of columns and rows. Three matrix elements, rather than one, correspond to each pixel. Each element is an integer between 0 and 255. The three corresponding elements, when taken together, establish the color of the pixel.

Arguments
file   string variable corresponding to color image filename or path

Example

```
color := "c:\images\monalisa.bmp"

gray := READBMP(color)
packed := READRGB(color)

r := rows( packed ) - 1        c := cols( packed )/3

red := submatrix( packed , 0 , r , 0 , c - 1)
green := submatrix( packed , 0 , r , c , 2·c - 1 )
blue := submatrix( packed , 0 , r , 2·c , 3·c - 1 )
```

Comments   To partition the matrix for a color image into its red, green, and blue components, use the submatrix function formulas shown in the example above. In this example, the color bitmap file **monalisa.bmp** is read into a grayscale matrix **gray**, as well as the packed RGB matrix **packed**, and then converted into three submatrices called **red**, **green**, and **blue**.

Picture viewer will display the matrix.

Mathcad includes several specialized functions for reading color images or image components, including functions for reading images in GIF, JPG, TGA and PCX formats.

Consult the following table to decide which function to use:

To separate a file into these components:	Use these functions:
red, green, and blue (RGB)	READ_RED, READ_GREEN, READ_BLUE
hue, lightness, and saturation (HLS)	READ_HLS, READ_HLS_HUE, READ_HLS_LIGHT, READ_HLS_SAT,
hue, saturation, and value (HSV)	READ_HSV, READ_HSV_HUE, READ_HSV_SAT, READ_HSV_VAL

Note	READ_HLS and READ_HSV work in exactly the same way as READRGB. All the others work in exactly the same way as READBMP.
See also	For grayscale images, see READBMP.

READWAV

File Access

Syntax	READWAV(*file*)
Description	Creates a matrix containing signal amplitudes in *file*. Each column represents a separate channel of data. Each row corresponds to a moment in time.
Arguments	
file	string variable corresponding to pulse code modulated (PCM) Microsoft WAV filename or path
Comments	Data from a WAV file is not scaled.
See also	WRITEWAV and GETWAVINFO

regress

Curve Fitting and Smoothing

One-dimensional Case

Syntax	regress(**vx**, **vy**, *n*)
Description	Returns the vector required by the interp function to find the *n*th order polynomial that best fits data arrays **vx** and **vy**.
Arguments	
vx, **vy**	real vectors of the same size
n	integer, $n > 0$
Example	

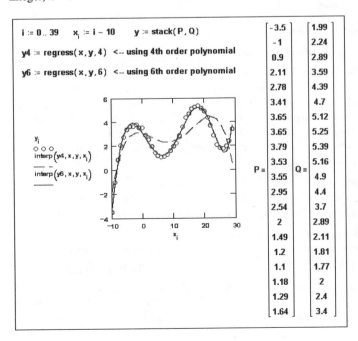

Comments

The regression functions regress and loess are useful when you have a set of measured y values corresponding to x values and you want to fit a polynomial of degree n through those y values. (For a simple linear fit, that is, n=1, you may as well use the line function.)

Use regress when you want to use a single polynomial to fit all your data values. The regress function lets you fit a polynomial of any order. However as a practical matter, you would rarely need to go beyond $n = 6$.

Since regress tries to accommodate all your data points using a single polynomial, it will not work well when your data does not behave like a single polynomial. For example, suppose you expect your y_i to be linear from x_1 to x_{10} and to behave like a cubic equation from x_{11} to x_{20}. If you use regress with $n = 3$ (a cubic), you may get a good fit for the second half but a poor fit for the first half.

The loess function alleviates these kinds of problems by performing a more localized regression.

For regress, the first three components of the output vector $\mathbf{vr} := \text{regress}(\mathbf{vx}, \mathbf{vy}, n)$ are $\mathbf{vr}_0$=3 (a code telling interp that $\mathbf{vr}$ is the output of regress as opposed to a spline function or loess), $\mathbf{vr}_1$=3 (the index within $\mathbf{vr}$ where the polynomial coefficients begin), and $\mathbf{vr}_2$=n (the order of the fit). The remaining $n + 1$ components are the coefficients of the fitting polynomial from the lowest degree term to the highest degree term.

Two-dimensional Case

Syntax

regress($\mathbf{Mxy}$, $\mathbf{vz}$, n)

Description

Returns the vector required by the interp function to find the nth order polynomial that best fits data arrays $\mathbf{Mxy}$ and $\mathbf{vz}$. $\mathbf{Mxy}$ is an $m \times 2$ matrix containing x-y coordinates. $\mathbf{vz}$ is an m-element vector containing the z coordinates corresponding to the m points specified in $\mathbf{Mxy}$.

Arguments

$\mathbf{Mxy}$ real $m \times 2$ matrix containing x-y coordinates of the m data points

$\mathbf{vz}$ real m-element vector containing the z coordinates corresponding to the points specified in $\mathbf{Mxy}$

n integer, $n > 0$

Comments

Assume, for example, that you have a set of measured z values corresponding to x and y values and you want to fit a polynomial surface through those z values. The meanings of the input arguments are more general than in the one-dimensional case:

- The argument $\mathbf{vx}$, which was an m-element vector of x values, becomes an $m \times 2$ matrix, $\mathbf{Mxy}$. Each row of $\mathbf{Mxy}$ contains an x in the first column and a corresponding y value in the second column.

- The argument x for the interp function becomes a 2-element vector $\mathbf{v}$ whose elements are the x and y values at which you want to evaluate the polynomial surface representing the best fit to the data points in $\mathbf{Mxy}$ and $\mathbf{vz}$.

This discussion can be extended naturally to higher dimensional cases. You can add independent variables by simply adding columns to the $\mathbf{Mxy}$ array. You would then add a corresponding number of rows to the vector $\mathbf{v}$ that you pass to the interp function. The regress function can have as many independent variables as you want. However, regress will calculate more slowly and require more memory when the number of independent variables and the degree are greater than four. The loess function is restricted to at most four independent variables.

Keep in mind that for regress, the number of data values, m must satisfy $m > \binom{n + k - 1}{n} \cdot \frac{n + k}{k}$, where k is the number of independent variables (hence the number of columns in **Mxy**), n is the degree of the desired polynomial, and m is the number of data values (hence the number of rows in **vz**). For example, if you have five explanatory variables and a fourth degree polynomial, you will need more than 126 observations.

The loess function works better than regress when your data does not behave like a single polynomial.

Algorithm   Normal equation solution through Gauss-Jordan elimination (Press *et al.*, 1992)

---

relax   Differential Equation Solving

Syntax   relax(**A, B, C, D, E, F, U**, *rjac*)

Description   Returns a matrix of solution values for a Poisson partial differential equation over a planar square region. More general than multigrid, which is faster.

Arguments

A, B, C, D, E   real square matrices all of the same size containing coefficients of the discretized Laplacian (for example, the left-hand side of equations below).

F   real square matrix containing the source term at each point in the region in which the solution is sought (for example, the right-hand side of equations below).

U   real square matrix containing boundary values along the edges of the region and initial guesses for the solution inside the region.

rjac   spectral radius of the Jacobi iteration, $0 < rjac < 1$, which controls the convergence of the relaxation algorithm. Its optimal value depends on the details of your problem.

Example

Comments   Two partial differential equations that arise often in the analysis of physical systems are Poisson's equation:

$$\frac{\partial^2 u}{\partial x^2} + \frac{\partial^2 u}{\partial y^2} = \rho(x, y)$$ and its homogeneous form, Laplace's equation.

Mathcad has two functions for solving these equations over a square region, assuming the values taken by the unknown function $u(x, y)$ on all four sides of the boundary are known. The most general solver is the relax function. In the special case when $u(x, y)$ is known to be zero on all four sides of the boundary, you can use the multigrid function instead. This function will often solve the problem faster than relax. If the boundary condition is the same on all four sides, you can simply transform the equation to an equivalent one in which the value is zero on all four sides.

The relax function returns a square matrix in which:

- an element's location in the matrix corresponds to its location within the square region, and
- its value approximates the value of the solution at that point.

This function uses the relaxation method to converge to the solution. Poisson's equation on a square domain is represented by:

$$a_{j,k}u_{j+1,k} + b_{j,k}u_{j-1,k} + c_{j,k}u_{j,k+1} + d_{j,k}u_{j,k-1} + e_{j,k}u_{j,k} = f_{j,k}.$$

Algorithm	Gauss-Seidel with successive overrelaxation (Press *et al.*, 1992)
See also	multigrid

---

reverse
Sorting

One-dimensional Case

Syntax	reverse(**v**)
Description	Reverses the order of the elements of vector **v**.
Arguments	
v	vector

Two-dimensional Case

Syntax	reverse(**A**)
Description	Reverses the order of the rows of matrix **A**.
Arguments	
A	matrix
See also	See sort for sample application.

---

rexp
Random Numbers

Syntax	rexp(*m*, *r*)
Description	Returns a vector of *m* random numbers having the exponential distribution.
Arguments	
m	integer, $m > 0$
r	real rate, $r > 0$
See also	rnd
Algorithm	Inverse cumulative density method (Press *et al.*, 1992)

---

rF
Random Numbers

Syntax	rF(*m*, *d1*, *d2*)
Description	Returns a vector of *m* random numbers having the F distribution.
Arguments	
m	integer, $m > 0$
d1, *d2*	integer degrees of freedom, $d1 > 0$, $d2 > 0$
Algorithm	Best's XG algorithm, Johnk's generator (Devroye, 1986)
See also	rnd

rgamma
Random Numbers

Syntax	rgamma(*m*, *s*)
Description	Returns a vector of *m* random numbers having the gamma distribution.
Arguments	
m	integer, $m > 0$
s	real shape parameter, $s > 0$
Algorithm	Best's XG algorithm, Johnk's generator (Devroye, 1986)
See also	rnd

rgeom
Random Numbers

Syntax	rgeom(*m*, *p*)
Description	Returns a vector of *m* random numbers having the geometric distribution.
Arguments	
m	integer, $m > 0$
p	real number, $0 < p < 1$
Algorithm	Inverse cumulative density method (Press *et al.*, 1992)
See also	rnd

rhypergeom
Random Numbers

Syntax	rhypergeom(*m*, *a*, *b*, *n*)
Description	Returns a vector of *m* random numbers having the hypergeometric distribution.
Arguments	
m	integer, $m > 0$
a, b, n	integers, $0 \leq a$, $0 \leq b$, $0 \leq n \leq a + b$
Algorithm	Uniform sampling methods (Devroye, 1986)
See also	rnd

rkadapt
Differential Equation Solving

Syntax	rkadapt(**y**, *x1*, *x2*, *acc*, **D**, *kmax*, *save*)
Description	Solves a differential equation using a slowly varying Runge-Kutta method. Provides DE solution estimate at *x2*.
Arguments	*Several arguments for this function are the same as described for* rkfixed.
y	real vector of initial values
x1, x2	real endpoints of the solution interval
acc	real *acc* > 0 controls the accuracy of the solution; a small value of *acc* forces the algorithm to take smaller steps along the trajectory, thereby increasing the accuracy of the solution. Values of *acc* around 0.001 will generally yield accurate solutions.
D(*x*, **y**)	real vector-valued function containing the derivatives of the unknown functions

kmax	integer *kmax* > 0 specifies the maximum number of intermediate points at which the solution will be approximated. The value of *kmax* places an upper bound on the number of rows of the matrix returned by these functions.
save	real *save* > 0 specifies the smallest allowable spacing between the values at which the solutions are to be approximated. *save* places a lower bound on the difference between any two numbers in the first column of the matrix returned by the function.
Comments	The specialized DE solvers Bulstoer, Rkadapt, Radau, Stiffb, and Stiffr provide the solution $y(x)$ over a number of uniformly spaced x-values in the integration interval bounded by $x1$ and $x2$. When you want the value of the solution at only the endpoint, $y(x2)$, use bulstoer, rkadapt, radau, stiffb, and stiffr instead.
Algorithm	Adaptive step 5th order Runge-Kutta method (Press *et al.*, 1992)
See also	rkfixed, a more general differential equation solver, for information on output and arguments; Rkadapt.

Rkadapt

Differential Equation Solving

Syntax	Rkadapt(**y**, *x1*, *x2*, *npts*, **D**)
Description	Solves a differential equation using a slowly varying Runge-Kutta method; provides DE solution at equally spaced x values by repeated calls to rkadapt.
Arguments	*All arguments for this function are the same as described for* rkfixed.
y	real vector of initial values
x1, x2	real endpoints of the solution interval
npts	integer *npts* > 0 specifies the number of points beyond initial point at which the solution is to be approximated; controls the number of rows in the matrix output
D(*x*, **y**)	real vector-valued function containing the derivatives of the unknown functions
Comments	Given a fixed number of points, you can approximate a function more accurately if you evaluate it frequently wherever it's changing fast, and infrequently wherever it's changing more slowly. If you know that the solution has this property, you may be better off using Rkadapt. Unlike rkfixed which evaluates a solution at equally spaced intervals, Rkadapt examines how fast the solution is changing and adapts its step size accordingly. This "adaptive step size control" enables Rkadapt to focus on those parts of the integration domain where the function is rapidly changing rather than wasting time on the parts where change is minimal.
	Although Rkadapt will use nonuniform step sizes internally when it solves the differential equation, it will nevertheless return the solution at equally spaced points.
	Rkadapt takes the same arguments as rkfixed, and the matrix returned by Rkadapt is identical in form to that returned by rkfixed.
Algorithm	Fixed step Runge-Kutta method with adaptive intermediate steps (5th order) (Press *et al.*, 1992)
See also	rkfixed, a more general differential equation solver, for information on output and arguments; also Odesolve, for a solve block approach.

rkfixed Differential Equation Solving

Syntax	rkfixed(**y0**, *x1*, *x2*, *npts*, **D**)
Description	Solves a differential equation using a standard Runge-Kutta method. Provides DE solution at equally spaced x values.

Arguments

y0   real vector of initial values whose length depends on the order of the DE or the size of the system of DEs.

- For a first order DE, the vector degenerates to one point, $y0 = y(x1)$.
- For higher order DEs, the vector has n elements for specifying initial conditions of y, $y', y'', ..., y^{(n-1)}$.
- For a first order system, the vector contains initial values for each unknown function.
- For higher order systems, the vector contains initial values for the $n - 1$ derivatives of each unknown function in addition to initial values for the functions themselves.

x1, x2   real endpoints of the interval on which the solution to the DEs will be evaluated; initial values in **y** are the values at *x1*

npts   integer *npts* > 0 specifies the number of points between the endpoints at which the solution is to be approximated; controls the number of rows in the matrix output

D*(x, y)*   real vector-valued function containing derivatives of the unknown functions.

- For a first order DE, the vector degenerates to a scalar function.
- For higher order DEs, the vector has n elements.
- For a first order system, the vector contains the first derivatives of each unknown function.
- For higher order systems, the vector contains expressions for the $n - 1$ derivatives of each unknown function in addition to nth derivatives.

$$\mathbf{D}(t, \mathbf{y}) = \begin{bmatrix} y'(t) \\ y''(t) \\ \cdot \\ \cdot \\ \cdot \\ y^{(n)}(t) \end{bmatrix}.$$

Examples   *rkfixed* can be used to solve linear, nonlinear, higher-order, and systems of equations. A few samples are shown here, but for a more complete discussion, see Chapter 9, "Solving and Data Analysis."

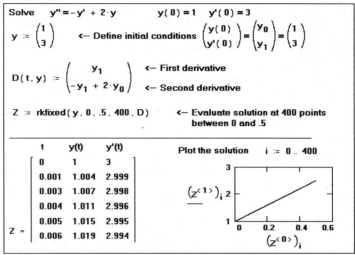

Example 1: Solving a second order differential equation.

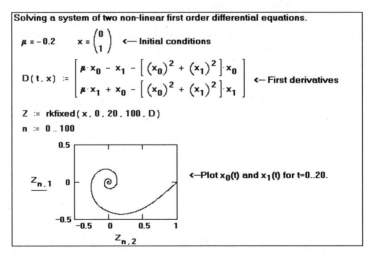

Example 2: Solving a system of first order linear equations.

Comments   For a first order DE , the output of rkfixed is a two-column matrix in which:

- The left-hand column contains the points at which the solution to the DE is evaluated.
- The right-hand column contains the corresponding values of the solution.

For higher order DEs, the output matrix contains n columns: the left-hand one for the t values and the remaining columns for values of $y(t)$, $y'(t)$, $y''(t)$, ..., $y^{(n-1)}(t)$.

For a first order system, the first column of the output matrix contains the points at which the solutions are evaluated and the remaining columns contain corresponding values of the solutions. For higher order systems:

- The first column contains the values at which the solutions and their derivatives are evaluated.
- The remaining columns contain corresponding values of the solutions and their derivatives. The order in which the solutions and their derivatives appear matches the order in which you put them into the vector of initial conditions.

The function rkfixed uses a fourth order Runge-Kutta method. Although it is not always the fastest method, the Runge-Kutta method nearly always succeeds. There are certain cases in which you may want to use one of Mathcad's more specialized DE solvers:

- Your system of DEs may have certain properties which are best exploited by functions other than rkfixed. The system may be stiff (Radau, Stiffb, Stiffr), smooth (Bulstoer), or slowly varying (Rkadapt).
- You may have a boundary value rather than an initial value problem (sbval and bvalfit).
- You may be interested in evaluating the solution only at one point (bulstoer, rkadapt, radau, stiffb and stiffr).

You may also want to try several methods on the same DE to see which one works the best.

Algorithm	Fixed step 4th order Runge-Kutta method (Press *et al.*, 1992)
See also	QuickSheets; Odesolve, for a solve block approach; "Differential Equation Solvers" on page 133; and the *Differential Equation Solve Blocks* E-book posted in the library on Mathcad.com

---

rlnorm Random Numbers

Syntax	rlnorm(m, μ, σ)
Description	Returns a vector of m random numbers having the lognormal distribution.
Arguments	
m	integer, $m > 0$
μ	real logmean
σ	real logdeviation, $\sigma > 0$
Algorithm	Ratio-of-uniforms method (Devroye, 1986)
See also	rnd

---

rlogis Random Numbers

Syntax	rlogis(m, l, s)
Description	Returns a vector of m random numbers having the logistic distribution.
Arguments	
m	integer, $m > 0$
l	real location parameter
s	real scale parameter, $s > 0$
Algorithm	Inverse cumulative density method (Press *et al.*, 1992)
See also	rnd

rnbinom
Random Numbers

Syntax	rnbinom(m, n, p)
Description	Returns a vector of m random numbers having the negative binomial distribution.
Arguments	
m, n	integers, $m > 0$, $n > 0$
p	real number, $0 < p \leq 1$
Algorithm	Based on rpois and rgamma (Devroye, 1986)
See also	rnd

rnd
Random Numbers

Syntax	rnd(x)
Description	Returns a random number between 0 and x. Identical to runif($1, 0, x$) if $x > 0$.
Arguments	
x	real number
Example	

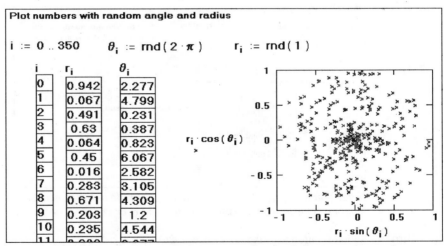

Note: You won't be able to recreate this example exactly because the random number generator gives different numbers every time.

Comments

Each time you recalculate an equation containing rnd or some other random variate built-in function, Mathcad generates new random numbers. Recalculation is performed by clicking on the equation and choosing **Calculate** from the **Worksheet Menu**.

These functions have a "seed value" associated with them. Each time you reset the seed, Mathcad generates new random numbers based on that seed. A given seed value will always generate the same sequence of random numbers. Choosing **Calculate** from the **Worksheet Menu** advances Mathcad along this random number sequence. Changing the seed value, however, advances Mathcad along a different random number sequence.

To change the seed value, choose **Options** from the **Worksheet Menu** and change the value of "seed" on the Built-In Variables tab, or use the Seed function. Be sure to supply an integer.

To reset Mathcad's random number generator without changing the seed value, choose **Options** from the **Worksheet** menu, click on the Built-In Variables tab, and click "OK" to accept the current seed. Then click on the equation containing the random number generating function and choose **Calculate** from the **Worksheet** menu. Since the randomizer has been reset, Mathcad generates the same random numbers it would generate if you restarted Mathcad.

There are many other random variate generators in Mathcad.

Algorithm   Linear congruence method (Knuth, 1997)

---

rnorm   Random Numbers

Syntax   rnorm(m, μ, σ)

Description   Returns a vector of m random numbers having the normal distribution.

Arguments
          m integer, $m > 0$
          μ   real mean
          σ   real standard deviation, σ > 0

Example

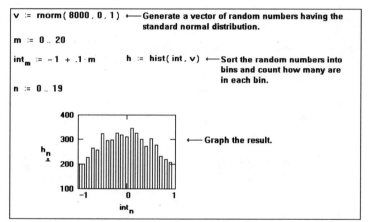

Note: You won't be able to recreate this example exactly because the random number generator gives different numbers every time.

Algorithm   Ratio-of-uniforms method (Devroye, 1986)

See also   rnd

---

root   Solving
Unbracketed Version

Syntax   root($f(var)$, var)

Description   Returns a value of var at which the expression $f(var)$ or function f is equal to 0.

Arguments
          var real or complex scalar; var must be assigned a guess value before using this version of root.
          f real or complex-valued function.

Example

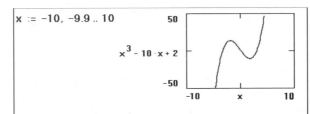

$$x := -10, -9.9 .. 10$$

$$x^3 - 10 \cdot x + 2$$

Now use three initial guesses to find three zeroes . . .

$$x := -2 \qquad \text{root}(x^3 - 10 \cdot x + 2, x) = -3.258$$

$$x := 0 \qquad \text{root}(x^3 - 10 \cdot x + 2, x) = 0.201$$

$$x := 3 \qquad \text{root}(x^3 - 10 \cdot x + 2, x) = 3.057$$

Comments   For expressions with several roots, your guess value determines which root Mathcad returns. The example shows a situation in which the root function returns several different values, each of which depends on the initial guess value.

You can't put numerical values in the list of unknowns; for example, root($f(x)$, -2) or root(14, −2) is not permitted in the example above.

Mathcad solves for complex roots as well as real roots. To find a complex root, you must start with a complex value for the initial guess.

See also polyroots for an efficient means to compute all roots of a polynomial at once. To change the accuracy of the root function, change the value of the built-in variable TOL.

Algorithm   Secant and Mueller methods (Press et al., 1992; Lorczak)

Bracketed Version

Syntax   root($f(var)$, *var*, *a*, *b*)

Description   Returns a value of *var* lying between *a* and *b* at which the expression $f(var)$ or function f is equal to 0.

Arguments
   var   real scalar
   f   real-valued function
   a, b   real numbers, $a < b$,

Comments   For expressions with several roots, your choice of interval endpoints *a* and *b* determines which root Mathcad returns. $f(a)$ and $f(b)$ must be of opposite signs. Observe that an initial guess for *var* is not required for the bracketed version of root to work.

If the optional arguments *a* and *b* are not included, then the unbracketed version of root is used. Note the restriction to real expressions and real variables in the bracketed case.

Mathcad evaluates the bracketed version of the root function using the *Ridder method*. If that method fails to find a root, then the *Brent method* is used.

The above comments concerning convergence and accuracy for the unbracketed version of root also apply to the bracketed version.

Algorithm   Ridder and Brent methods (Press *et al.*, 1992; Lorczak)

round
Truncation and Round-off

One-argument Version

Syntax	round(z)
Description	Rounds the real number z to the nearest integer. Same as round(x, 0).
Arguments	
z	complex number

Two-argument Version

Syntax	round(x, n)
Description	Rounds the real number x to n decimal places. If $n < 0$, x is rounded to the left of the decimal point.
Arguments	
x	real number
n	integer
Comments	round no longer takes arguments with units. Round(x, y) Rounds x to the closest multiple of y. y must be real and nonzero. Round takes a second threshold argument, scales by the threshold before performing the truncation, then rescales after truncation.
See also	ceil, floor, trunc

rows
Vector and Matrix

Syntax	rows(**A**)
Description	Returns the number of rows in array **A**.
Arguments	
A	matrix or vector
See also	cols for example

rpois
Random Numbers

Syntax	rpois(m, λ)
Description	Returns a vector of m random numbers having the Poisson distribution.
Arguments	
m	integer, $m > 0$
λ	real mean, $\lambda > 0$
Algorithm	Devroye, 1986
See also	rnd

rref
Vector and Matrix

Syntax	rref(**A**)
Description	Returns a matrix representing the row-reduced echelon form of **A**.
Arguments	
A	real $m \times n$ matrix
Algorithm	Elementary row reduction (Anton)

rsort
Sorting

Syntax	rsort($\mathbf{A}$, i)
Description	Sorts the columns of the matrix $\mathbf{A}$ by placing the elements in row i in ascending order. The result is the same size as $\mathbf{A}$.
Arguments	
$\mathbf{A}$	$m \times n$ matrix or vector
i	integer, $0 \le i \le m - 1$
Algorithm	Heap sort (Press *et al.*, 1992)
See also	sort for more details, csort

rt
Random Numbers

Syntax	rt(m, d)
Description	Returns a vector of m random numbers having Student's t distribution.
Arguments	
m	integer, $m > 0$
d	integer degrees of freedom, $d > 0$
Algorithm	Best's XG algorithm, Johnk's generator (Devroye, 1986)
See also	rnd

runif
Random Numbers

Syntax	runif(m, a, b)
Description	Returns a vector of m random numbers having the uniform distribution
Arguments	
m	integer, $m > 0$
a, b	real numbers, $a < b$
Algorithm	Linear congruence method (Knuth, 1997)
See also	rnd

rweibull
Random Numbers

Syntax	rweibull(m, s)
Description	Returns a vector of m random numbers having the Weibull distribution.
Arguments	
m	integer, $m > 0$
s	real shape parameter, $s > 0$
Algorithm	Inverse cumulative density method (Press *et al.*, 1992)
See also	rnd

SaveColormap   File Access

Syntax   SaveColormap(*file*, **M**)

Description   Creates a colormap *file* containing the values in the matrix **M**. Returns the number of rows written to *file*.

Arguments

file   string variable corresponding to CMP filename

M   integer matrix with three columns and whose elements $\mathbf{M}_{i,j}$ all satisfy $0 \le \mathbf{M}_{i,j} \le 255$.

Comments   The file *file* is the name of a colormap located in the CMAPS subdirectory of your Mathcad directory. After you use **SaveColormap**, the colormap is available on the Advanced tab in the 3D Plot Format dialog box. See online Help for more information.

See also   LoadColormap

---

sbval   Differential Equation Solving

Syntax   sbval(**v**, *x1*, *x2*, **D**, **load**, **score**)

Description   Converts a boundary value differential equation to an initial value problem. Useful when derivatives are continuous throughout.

Arguments

v   real vector containing guesses for missing initial values

x1, *x2*   real endpoints of the interval on which the solution to the DEs will be evaluated

D(*x*, **y**)   real *n*-element vector-valued function containing the derivatives of the unknown functions

load(*x1*, **v**)   real vector-valued function whose *n* elements correspond to the values of the *n* unknown functions at *x1*. Some of these values will be constants specified by your initial conditions. If a value is unknown, you should use the corresponding guess value from **v**.

score(*x2*, **y**)   real *n*-element vector-valued function which measures solution discrepancy at *x2*

Example

Comments	Initial value DE solvers like rkfixed assume that you know the value of the solution and its first $n - 1$ derivatives at the beginning of the interval of integration. Two-point boundary value DE solvers, like sbval and bvalfit, may be used if you lack this information about the solution at the beginning of the interval of integration, but you do know something about the solution elsewhere in the interval. In particular:

- You have an nth order differential equation.
- You know some but not all of the values of the solution and its first $n - 1$ derivatives at the beginning of the interval of integration, $x1$.
- You know some but not all of the values of the solution and its first $n - 1$ derivatives at the end of the interval of integration, $x2$.
- Between what you know about the solution at $x1$ and what you know about it at $x2$, you have n known values.

If there is a discontinuity at a point intermediate to $x1$ and $x2$, you should use bvalfit. If continuity holds throughout, then use sbval to evaluate those initial values left unspecified at $x1$. sbval does not actually return a solution to a differential equation; it merely computes the initial values the solution must have in order for the solution to match the final values you specify. You must then take the initial values returned by sbval and solve the resulting initial value problem using rkfixed or any of the other more specialized DE solvers.

Algorithm	Shooting method with 4th order Runge-Kutta method (Press *et al.*, 1992)
See also	rkfixed for more details; also Odesolve, for a solve block approach.

search
String

Syntax	search(S, $SubS$, m)
Description	Returns the starting position of the substring $SubS$ in S beginning from position m. Returns -1 if the substring is not found.
Arguments	
S	string expression; Mathcad assumes that the first character in S is at position 0
$SubS$	substring expression
m	integer, $m \geq 0$

sec
Trigonometric

Syntax	sec(z), for z in radians; sec(z deg), for z in degrees
Description	Returns the secant of z.
Arguments	
z	real or complex number; z is not an odd multiple of $\pi/2$

sech
Hyperbolic

Syntax	sech(z)
Description	Returns the hyperbolic secant of z.
Arguments	
z	real or complex number

Seed
Random Numbers

Syntax	Seed(x)
Description	Resets the seed for random number generation. Returns the value of the previous seed.
Arguments	
x	an integer
Comments	This function can be used instead of the **Worksheet Options...** dialog under **Tools** to set the value for the random number generator seed dynamically within a Mathcad worksheet. It may be used iteratively in programs. This function can also be used to check the current value of seed after a random number generation function has been called a number of times.
See Also	rnd

sign
Piecewise Continuous

Syntax	sign(x)
Description	Returns 0 if x=0, 1 if $x > 0$, and -1 otherwise.
Arguments	
x	real number
See also	csgn, signum

signum
Complex Numbers

Syntax	signum(z)
Description	Returns 1 if z=0 and $z/|z|$ otherwise.
Arguments	
z	real or complex number
See also	csgn, sign

sin
Trigonometric

Syntax	sin(z), for z in radians; sin(z deg), for z in degrees
Description	Returns the sine of z.
Arguments	
z	real or complex number
Comments	$sin(z)/z$ will behave correctly in the limit as z approaches 0 (that is, $sin(z)/z = 1$) for the case where z is a number. Abstracted cases, such as $f(z)/g(z)$, where $f(z) = sin(z)$, and $g(z) := z$, following Mathcad rules for the fraction 0/0.
See also	sinc

sinc
Trigonometric

Syntax sinc(z), for z in radians;
sinc(z deg), for z in degrees

Description Returns the sine of z divided by z.

Arguments
z real or complex number

Comments
returns the value 1in the case that z is 0.

See also sin

sinfit
Curve Fitting and Smoothing

Syntax sinfit(**vx**, **vy**, **vg**)

Description Returns a vector containing the parameters (a, b, c) that make the function $a \cdot \sin(x + b) + c$ best approximate the data in **vx** and **vy**.

Arguments
vx, vy real vectors of the same size

vg real vector of guess values for (a, b, c)

Comments This is a special case of the genfit function. A vector of guess values is needed for initialization. By decreasing the value of the built-in TOL variable, higher accuracy in sinfit might be achieved.

See Also line, linfit, genfit, expfit, logfit, lnfit, pwrfit, lgsfit, medfit

sinh
Hyperbolic

Syntax sinh(z)

Description Returns the hyperbolic sine of z.

Arguments
z real or complex number

skew
Statistics

Syntax skew(**A**)

Description Returns the skewness of the elements of **A**:

$$\text{skew}(\mathbf{A}) = \frac{mn}{(mn-1)(mn-2)} \sum_{i=0}^{m-1} \sum_{j=0}^{n-1} \left(\frac{\mathbf{A}_{i,j} - \text{mean}(\mathbf{A})}{\text{Stdev}(\mathbf{A})} \right)^3$$

Arguments
A real or complex $m \times n$ matrix or vector, $m \cdot n \geq 3$

Comments skew(**A, B, C, ...**) is also permissible and returns the skewness of the elements of **A, B, C**, ...

slope
Curve Fitting and Smoothing

Syntax slope(**vx**, **vy**)

Description Returns the slope of the least-squares regression line.

Arguments
vx, vy real vector arguments of the same size

Example

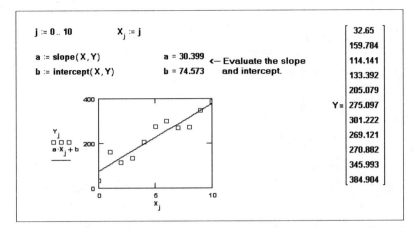

$$j := 0 .. 10 \qquad X_j := j$$

$$a := slope(X, Y) \qquad a = 30.399$$
$$b := intercept(X, Y) \qquad b = 74.573$$

← Evaluate the slope and intercept.

$$Y \equiv \begin{bmatrix} 32.65 \\ 159.784 \\ 114.141 \\ 133.392 \\ 205.079 \\ 275.097 \\ 301.222 \\ 269.121 \\ 270.882 \\ 345.993 \\ 384.904 \end{bmatrix}$$

Comments

The functions intercept and slope return the intercept and slope of the line which best fits the data in a least-squares sense: $y = intercept(\mathbf{vx}, \mathbf{vy}) + slope(\mathbf{vx}, \mathbf{vy}) \cdot x$. Alternatively, you may use the line function which returns both parameter estimates via one function call.

Be sure that every element in the **vx** and **vy** arrays contains a data value. Since every element in an array must have a value, Mathcad assigns 0 to any elements not explicitly assigned.

These functions are useful not only when the data is inherently linear, but also when it is exponential. If x and y are related by $y = Ae^{kx}$, you can apply these functions to the logarithm of the data values and make use of the fact that $\ln(y) = \ln(A) + kx$, hence $A = \exp(intercept(\mathbf{vx}, \ln(\mathbf{vy})))$ and $k = slope(\mathbf{vx}, \ln(\mathbf{vy}))$.

The resulting fit weighs the errors differently from a least-squares exponential fit (which the function expfit provides) but is usually a good approximation.

See also

intercept, line, stderr, medfit

sort
Sorting

Syntax

sort(**v**)

Description

Returns the elements of vector **v** sorted in ascending order.

Arguments

v   vector

Example

Comments
All of Mathcad's sorting functions accept matrices and vectors with complex elements. However in sorting them, Mathcad ignores the imaginary part.

To sort a vector or matrix in descending order, first sort in ascending order, then use reverse. For example, reverse(sort(v)) returns the elements of v sorted in descending order.

Unless you change the value of ORIGIN, matrices are numbered starting with row zero and column zero. If you forget this, it's easy to make the error of sorting a matrix on the wrong row or column by specifying an incorrect n argument for rsort and csort. To sort on the first column of a matrix, for example, you must use csort(**A**, 0).

Algorithm
Heap sort (Press *et al.*, 1992)

---

sph2xyz
Vector and Matrix

Syntax
sph2xyz(r, θ, ϕ) or sph2xyz(v)

Description
Converts the spherical coordinates of a point in 3D space to rectangular coordinates.

Arguments
r, θ, ϕ
real numbers

Comments
$x = r \sin(\phi) \cos(\theta)$, $y = r \sin(\phi) \sin(\theta)$, $z = r \cos(\phi)$, $v = \begin{bmatrix} r \\ \theta \\ \phi \end{bmatrix}$

See also
xyz2sph

---

stack
Vector and Matrix

Syntax
stack(**A**, **B**, **C**, ...)

Description
Returns a matrix formed by placing the matrices **A**, **B**, **C**, ... top to bottom.

Arguments
A, **B**, **C**, ...
at least two matrices or vectors; **A**, **B**, **C**, ... must have the same number of columns

See also
augment for example

stderr
Curve Fitting and Smoothing

Syntax   stderr(**vx**, **vy**)

Description   Returns the standard error associated with simple linear regression, measuring how closely data points are spread about the regression line.

$$\text{stderr}(\mathbf{vx}, \mathbf{vy}) = \sqrt{\frac{1}{n-2} \sum_{i=0}^{n-1} (\mathbf{vy}_i - (\text{intercept}(\mathbf{vx}, \mathbf{vy}) + \text{slope}(\mathbf{vx}, \mathbf{vy}) \cdot \mathbf{vx}_i))^2}.$$

Arguments

    vx, **vy**   real vector arguments of the same size

See also   slope, intercept

stdev
Statistics

Syntax   stdev(**A**)

Description   Returns the standard deviation of the elements of **A**, where mn (the sample size) is used in the denominator: $\text{stdev}(\mathbf{A}) = \sqrt{\text{var}(\mathbf{A})}$.

Arguments

    A   real or complex $m \times n$ matrix or vector

Comments   stdev(**A**, **B**, **C**, ...) is also permissible and returns the standard deviation of the elements of **A**, **B**, **C**, ...

See also   Stdev, var, Var

Stdev
Statistics

Syntax   Stdev(**A**)

Description   Returns the standard deviation of the elements of **A**, where $mn - 1$ (the sample size less one) is used in the denominator: $\text{Stdev}(\mathbf{A}) = \sqrt{\text{Var}(\mathbf{A})}$.

Arguments

    A   real or complex $m \times n$ matrix or vector

Comments   Stdev(**A**, **B**, **C**, ...) is also permissible and returns the standard deviation of the elements of **A**, **B**, **C**, ...

See also   stdev, var, Var

stiffb
Differential Equation Solving

Syntax   stiffb(**y**, *x1*, *x2*, *acc*, **D**, **J**, *kmax*, *save*)

Description   Solves a differential equation using the stiff Bulirsch-Stoer method. Provides DE solution estimate at *x2*.

Arguments   *Several arguments for this function are the same as described for* rkfixed.

    y   real vector of initial values.

    x1, x2   real endpoints of the solution interval.

    D(x, y)   real vector-valued function containing the derivatives of the unknown functions.

acc	real *acc* > 0 controls the accuracy of the solution; a small value of *acc* forces the algorithm to take smaller steps along the trajectory, thereby increasing the accuracy of the solution. Values of *acc* around 0.001 will generally yield accurate solutions.
J(*x*, **y**)	real vector-valued function which returns the $n \times (n + 1)$ matrix whose first column contains the derivatives $\partial \mathbf{D} / \partial x$ and whose remaining columns form the Jacobian matrix $(\partial \mathbf{D} / \partial y_k)$ for the system of DEs.
kmax	integer *kmax* > 0 specifies maximum number of intermediate points at which the solution will be approximated; places an upper bound on the number of rows of the matrix returned by these functions.
save	real *save* > 0 specifies the smallest allowable spacing between values at which the solutions are to be approximated; places a lower bound on the difference between any two numbers in the first column of the matrix returned by the function.
Comments	The specialized DE solvers Bulstoer, Rkadapt, Radau, Stiffb, and Stiffr provide the solution *y(x)* over a number of uniformly spaced *x*-values in the integration interval bounded by *x1* and *x2*. When you want the value of the solution at only the endpoint, *y(x2)*, use bulstoer, rkadapt, radau, stiffb, and stiffr instead.
Algorithm	Bulirsch-Stoer method with adaptive step size for stiff systems (Press *et al.*, 1992)
See also	rkfixed, a more general differential equation solver, for information on output and arguments; Stiffb.

Stiffb
Differential Equation Solving

Syntax	Stiffb(**y**, *x1*, *x2*, *npts*, **D**, **J**)
Description	Solves a differential equation using the stiff Bulirsch-Stoer method. Provides DE solution at equally spaced *x* values by repeated calls to stiffb.
Arguments	*Several arguments for this function are the same as described for* rkfixed.
y	real vector of initial values.
x1, *x2*	real endpoints of the solution interval.
D(*x*, **y**)	real vector-valued function containing the derivatives of the unknown functions.
npts	integer *npts* > 0 specifies the number of points beyond initial point at which the solution is to be approximated; controls the number of rows in the matrix output.
J(*x*, **y**)	real vector-valued function which returns the $n \times (n + 1)$ matrix whose first column contains the derivatives $\partial \mathbf{D} / \partial x$ and whose remaining columns form the Jacobian matrix $(\partial \mathbf{D} / \partial y_k)$ for the system of DEs. For example, if:

$$\mathbf{D}(x, \mathbf{y}) = \begin{bmatrix} x \cdot y_1 \\ -2 \cdot y_1 \cdot y_0 \end{bmatrix} \quad \text{then} \quad \mathbf{J}(x, \mathbf{y}) = \begin{bmatrix} y_1 & 0 & x \\ 0 & -2 \cdot y_1 & -2 \cdot y_0 \end{bmatrix}$$

Comments	A system of DEs expressed in the form $\mathbf{y} = \mathbf{A} \cdot \mathbf{x}$ is a stiff system if the matrix **A** is nearly singular. Under these conditions, the solution returned by rkfixed may oscillate or be unstable. When solving a stiff system, you should use one of the two DE solvers specifically designed for stiff systems: Stiffb and Stiffr. These use the Bulirsch-Stoer method and the Rosenbrock method, respectively, for stiff systems.
	The form of the matrix returned by these functions is identical to that returned by rkfixed. However, Stiffb and Stiffr require an extra argument **J**(*x*, **y**).

Algorithm	Fixed-step Bulirsch-Stoer method with adaptive intermediate step size for stiff systems (Press *et al.*, 1992)
See also	rkfixed, a more general differential equation solver, for information on output and arguments.

stiffr
Differential Equation Solving

Syntax	stiffr(y, *x1*, *x2*, *acc*, **D**, **J**, *kmax*, *save*)
Description	Solves a differential equation using the stiff Rosenbrock method. Provides DE solution estimate at *x2*.
Arguments	*Several arguments for this function the same as described for* rkfixed.
y	real vector of initial values.
x1, *x2*	real endpoints of the solution interval.
D(*x*, **y**)	real vector-valued function containing the derivatives of the unknown functions.
acc	real *acc* > 0 controls the accuracy of the solution; a small value of *acc* forces the algorithm to take smaller steps along the trajectory, thereby increasing the accuracy of the solution. Values of *acc* around 0.001 will generally yield accurate solutions.
J(*x*, **y**)	real vector-valued function that returns the $n \times (n + 1)$ matrix whose first column contains the the derivatives $\partial \mathbf{D} / \partial x$ and whose remaining columns form the Jacobian matrix $(\partial \mathbf{D} / \partial y_k)$ for the system of DEs.
kmax	integer *kmax* > 0 specifies maximum number of intermediate points at which the solution will be approximated; places an upper bound on the number of rows of the matrix returned by these functions.
save	real *save* > 0 specifies the smallest allowable spacing between values at which the solutions are to be approximated; places a lower bound on the difference between any two numbers in the first column of the matrix returned by the function.
Comments	The specialized DE solvers Bulstoer, Rkadapt, Radau, Stiffb, and Stiffr provide the solution *y(x)* over a number of uniformly spaced *x*-values in the integration interval bounded by *x1* and *x2*. When you want the value of the solution at only the endpoint, *y(x2)*, use bulstoer, rkadapt, radau, stiffb, and stiffr instead.
Algorithm	4th order Rosenbrock method with adaptive intermediate step size for stiff systems (Press *et al.*, 1992)
See also	rkfixed, a more general differential equation solver for information on output and arguments, and Stiffr

Stiffr
Differential Equation Solving

Syntax	Stiffb(**y**, *x1*, *x2*, *npts*, **D**, **J**)
Description	Solves a differential equation using the stiff Rosenbrock method. Provides DE solution at equally spaced *x* values by repeated calls to stiffr.
Arguments	*Several arguments for this function are the same as described for* rkfixed.
y	real vector of initial values.
x1, *x2*	real endpoints of the solution interval.
D(*x*, **y**)	real vector-valued function containing the derivatives of the unknown functions.
npts	integer *npts* > 0 specifies the number of points beyond initial point at which the solution is to be approximated; controls the number of rows in the matrix output.

$\mathbf{J}(x, y)$ real vector-valued function which returns the $n \times (n + 1)$ matrix whose first column contains the derivatives $\partial \mathbf{D} / \partial x$ and whose remaining columns form the Jacobian matrix ($\partial \mathbf{D} / \partial y_k$) for the system of DEs. For example, if:

$$\mathbf{D}(x, y) = \begin{bmatrix} x \cdot y_1 \\ -2 \cdot y_1 \cdot y_0 \end{bmatrix} \quad \text{then} \quad \mathbf{J}(x, y) = \begin{bmatrix} y_1 & 0 & x \\ 0 & -2 \cdot y_1 & -2 \cdot y_0 \end{bmatrix}$$

Comments   A system of DEs expressed in the form $y = \mathbf{A} \cdot \mathbf{x}$ is a stiff system if the matrix $\mathbf{A}$ is nearly singular. Under these conditions, the solution returned by rkfixed may oscillate or be unstable. When solving a stiff system, you should use one of the two DE solvers specifically designed for stiff systems: Stiffb and Stiffr. These use the Bulirsch-Stoer method and the Rosenbrock method, respectively, for stiff systems.

The form of the matrix returned by these functions is identical to that returned by rkfixed. However, Stiffb and Stiffr require an extra argument $\mathbf{J}(x, y)$.

Algorithm   Fixed-step 4th order Rosenbrock method with adaptive intermediate step size for stiff systems (Press *et al.*, 1992)

See also   rkfixed, a more general differential equation solver, for information on output and arguments.

---

str2num   String

Syntax   str2num(*S*)

Description   Returns the constant formed by converting the characters in *S* into a number. Characters in *S* must constitute an integer such as 17, a real floating-point number such as -16.5, a complex floating-point number such as $2.1+6i$ or $3.241 - 9.234j$, or an e-format number such as 4.51e-3 (for $4.51 \cdot 10^{-3}$). Mathcad ignores any spaces in the string.

Arguments
S   string expression

See also   num2str

---

str2vec   String

Syntax   str2vec(*S*)

Description   Returns the vector of ASCII codes corresponding to the characters in string *S*. For a list of ASCII codes, see the Appendix. For example, the ASCII code for letter "a" is 97, that for letter "b" is 98, and that for letter "c" is 99.

Arguments
S   string expression

See also   vec2str

---

strlen   String

Syntax   strlen(*S*)

Description   Returns the number of characters in *S*.

Arguments
S   string expression

submatrix

Vector and Matrix

Syntax   submatrix(**A**, *ir*, *jr*, *ic*, *jc*)

Description   Returns a submatrix of **A** consisting of all elements common to rows *ir* through *jr* and columns *ic* through *jc*. Make certain that $ir \leq jr$ and $ic \leq jc$, otherwise the order of rows and/or columns will be reversed.

Arguments

    A $m \times n$ matrix or vector

    ir, jr   integers, $0 \leq ir \leq jr \leq m$

    ic, jc   integers, $0 \leq ic \leq jc \leq n$

Example

$$M := \begin{bmatrix} 1 & 7 & 1 & 4 & 4 \\ -5 & -8 & -2 & 3 & 3 \\ -6 & -9 & -3 & 2 & 3 \\ 1 & 2 & 3 & 4 & 3 \\ 4 & 5 & 5 & 6 & 8 \end{bmatrix}$$

ORIGIN = 0

$$\text{submatrix}(M, 1, 2, 0, 2) = \begin{pmatrix} -5 & -8 & -2 \\ -6 & -9 & -3 \end{pmatrix}$$ ← Extracts all elements contained in both rows 1 and 2 and columns 0, 1 and 2.

$$\text{submatrix}(M, 1, 2, 2, 0) = \begin{pmatrix} -2 & -8 & -5 \\ -3 & -9 & -6 \end{pmatrix}$$ ← Swapping the last two arguments reverses the order of the columns.

$$\text{submatrix}(M, 2, 1, 2, 0) = \begin{pmatrix} -3 & -9 & -6 \\ -2 & -8 & -5 \end{pmatrix}$$ ← Swapping the first two arguments reverses the order of the rows.

substr

String

Syntax   substr(*S*, *m*, *n*)

Description   Returns a substring of *S* beginning with the character in the *m*th position and having at most *n* characters.

Arguments

    S   string expression. Mathcad assumes that the first character in *S* is at position 0.

    m, n   integers, $m \geq 0, n \geq 0$

supsmooth

Curve Fitting and Smoothing

Syntax   supsmooth(**vx**, **vy**)

Description   Creates a new vector, of the same size as **vy**, by piecewise use of a symmetric *k*-nearest neighbor linear least square fitting procedure in which *k* is adaptively chosen.

Arguments

    vx, vy   real vectors of the same size; elements of **vx** must be in ascending order

Example

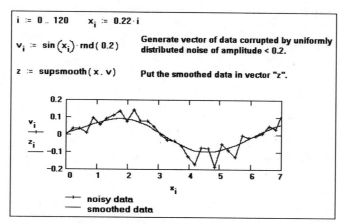

$i := 0 .. 120 \qquad x_i := 0.22 \cdot i$

$v_i := \sin(x_i) \cdot \text{rnd}(0.2)$ **Generate vector of data corrupted by uniformly distributed noise of amplitude < 0.2.**

$z := \text{supsmooth}(x, v)$ **Put the smoothed data in vector "z".**

Comments

The supsmooth function uses a symmetric k nearest neighbor linear least-squares fitting procedure to make a series of line segments through the data. Unlike ksmooth which uses a fixed bandwidth for all the data, supsmooth will adaptively choose different bandwidths for different portions of the data.

Algorithm

Variable span super-smoothing method (Friedman)

See also

medsmooth and ksmooth

---

svd
Vector and Matrix

Syntax   svd(A)

Description   Returns an $(m + n) \times n$ matrix whose first m rows contain the $m \times n$ orthonormal matrix **U**, and whose remaining n rows contain the $n \times n$ orthonormal matrix **V**. Matrices **U** and **V** satisfy the equation $\mathbf{A} = \mathbf{U} \cdot \text{diag}(\mathbf{s}) \cdot \mathbf{V}^T$, where **s** is the vector returned by svds(**A**).

Arguments

A $m \times n$ real matrix, where $m \geq n$

Example

The m x n matrix **A** to be decomposed is defined at the bottom.

st := svd(A)   <-- (m+n) x n matrix resulting from the
                     singular value decomposition

singval := svds(A)   <-- vector contains the singular values of A

$$singval = \begin{bmatrix} 133.214 \\ 40.406 \\ 21.404 \end{bmatrix}$$

m := rows(A)   m = 6   n := cols(A)   n = 3

U := submatrix(st, 0, m − 1, 0, n − 1)   <-- extract m x n orthonormal matrix U

V := submatrix(st, m, m + n − 1, 0, n − 1)   <-- extract n x n orthonormal matrix V

Compare A with $U \cdot diag(singval) \cdot V^T$:

$$A \equiv \begin{bmatrix} 20 & 32 & -4 \\ 4.5 & 100 & -4 \\ -5.8 & 68 & 15 \\ 1.5 & 10 & 26 \\ 7 & 30 & 18 \\ 4.2 & 28 & 25 \end{bmatrix} \quad U \cdot diag(singval) \cdot V^T = \begin{bmatrix} 20 & 32 & -4 \\ 4.5 & 100 & -4 \\ -5.8 & 68 & 15 \\ 1.5 & 10 & 26 \\ 7 & 30 & 18 \\ 4.2 & 28 & 25 \end{bmatrix}$$

$$U^T \cdot U = \begin{bmatrix} 1 & 0 & 0 \\ 0 & 1 & 0 \\ 0 & 0 & 1 \end{bmatrix}$$

$$V^T \cdot V = \begin{bmatrix} 1 & 0 & 0 \\ 0 & 1 & 0 \\ 0 & 0 & 1 \end{bmatrix}$$

Algorithm Householder reduction with QR transformation (Wilkinson and Reinsch, 1971)

See also svds

---

svds
Vector and Matrix

Syntax   svds(A)

Description   Returns a vector containing the singular values of **A**.

Arguments
A $m \times n$ real matrix, where $m \geq n$

Algorithm Householder reduction with QR transformation (Wilkinson and Reinsch, 1971)

See also svd

---

tan
Trigonometric

Syntax   tan(z) for z in radians;
               tan(z deg), for z in degrees

Description   Returns the tangent of z.

Arguments
z real or complex number

---

tanh
Hyperbolic

Syntax   tanh(z)

Description   Returns the hyperbolic tangent of z.

Arguments
z real or complex number

Tcheb
Special

Syntax	Tcheb(n, x)
Description	Returns the value of the Chebyshev polynomial of degree n of the first kind.
Arguments	
n	integer, $n \geq 0$
x	real number
Comments	Solution of the differential equation $(1 - x^2) \cdot \dfrac{d^2}{dx^2}y - x \cdot \dfrac{d}{dx}y + n^2 \cdot y = 0$.
Algorithm	Recurrence relation (Abramowitz and Stegun, 1972)
See also	Ucheb

tr
Vector and Matrix

Syntax	tr($\mathbf{M}$)
Description	Returns the trace of $\mathbf{M}$, the sum of diagonal elements.
Arguments	
$\mathbf{M}$	real or complex square matrix

trunc
Truncation and Round-off

Syntax	trunc(z)
Description	Returns the integer part of z. Same as floor(z) for $z > 0$ and ceil(z) for $z < 0$.
Arguments	
z	complex number
Comments	trunc no longer takes arguments with units.
	Trunc(x, y) Returns the value of trunc(x/y)*y. y must be real and nonzero. Round takes a second threshold argument, scales by the threshold before performing the truncation, then rescales after truncation.
See also	ceil, floor, round

Ucheb
Special

Syntax	Ucheb(n, x)
Description	Returns the value of the Chebyshev polynomial of degree n of the second kind.
Arguments	
n	integer, $n \geq 0$
x	real number
Comments	Solution of the differential equation $(1 - x^2) \cdot \dfrac{d^2}{dx^2}y - 3 \cdot x \cdot \dfrac{d}{dx}y + n \cdot (n + 2) \cdot y = 0$.
Algorithm	Recurrence relation (Abramowitz and Stegun, 1972)
See also	Tcheb

UnitsOf
Expression Type

Syntax	UnitsOf(x)
Description	Returns the units of x. Returns 1 if x has no units.
Arguments	
x	arbitrary real or complex number, or array
Comments	You can divide a value by the UnitsOf function to make it unitless. For example, some built-in functions, such as ln, require their arguments to be unitless. If an argument to ln has units, you can divide the argument by UnitsOf to remove them.

var
Statistics

Syntax	var(A)
Description	Returns the variance of the elements of A: $\text{var}(A) = \dfrac{1}{mn}\displaystyle\sum_{i=0}^{m-1}\sum_{j=0}^{n-1}\left|A_{i,j}-\text{mean}(A)\right|^2$.
	This expression is normalized by the sample size mn.
Arguments	
A	real or complex $m \times n$ matrix or array
Comments	var(A, B, C, ...) is also permissible and returns the variance of the elements of A, B, C, ...
See also	stdev, Stdev, Var

Var
Statistics

Syntax	Var(A)
Description	Returns the variance of the elements of A: $\text{var}(A) = \dfrac{1}{mn-1}\displaystyle\sum_{i=0}^{m-1}\sum_{j=0}^{n-1}\left|A_{i,j}-\text{mean}(A)\right|^2$.
	This expression is normalized by the sample size less one, $mn - 1$.
Arguments	
A	real or complex $m \times n$ matrix or array
Comments	Var(A, B, C, ...) is also permissible and returns the variance of the elements of A, B, C, ...
See also	stdev, Stdev, var

vec2str
String

Syntax	vec2str(v)
Description	Returns the string formed by converting a vector v of ASCII codes to characters. The elements of v must be integers between 0 and 255.
Arguments	
v	vector of ASCII codes
See also	str2vec

vlookup
Vector and Matrix

Syntax	vlookup(z, **A**, c)
Description	Looks in the first column of a matrix, **A**, for a given value, z, and returns the value(s) in the same row(s) in the column specified, c. When multiple values are returned, they appear in a vector.
Arguments	
z	real or complex number, or string
A	real, complex or string $m \times n$ matrix
c	integer, $ORIGIN \le c \le ORIGIN + n - 1$
Comments	The degree of precision to which the comparison adheres is determined by the *TOL* setting of the worksheet.
See Also	lookup, hlookup, match

wave
Wavelet Transform

Syntax	wave(**v**)
Description	Returns the discrete wavelet transform of real data using Daubechies four-coefficient wavelet filter.
Arguments	
v	real vector of 2^n elements, where $n > 0$ is an integer
Example	

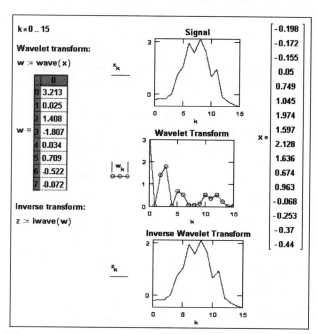

Comments	When you define a vector **v** for use with Fourier or wavelet transforms, be sure to start with v_0 (or change the value of ORIGIN). If you do not define v_0, Mathcad automatically sets it to zero. This can distort the results of the transform functions.
Algorithm	Pyramidal Daubechies 4-coefficient wavelet filter (Press *et al.*, 1992)
See also	iwave

WRITEBIN

Syntax	WRITEBIN(*file*, *type*)
Description	Writes out a matrix as a file of binary data. Used as follows: WRITEBIN(*file*, *type*) := A.
Arguments	
file	String variable corresponding to the binary data filename, including path
type	String argument specifying the data type used in the file. Must be one of the following: double (64 bit floating point), float (32 bit floating point), byte (8 bit unsigned integer), uint16 (16 bit unsigned integer), uint32 (32 bit unsigned integer), int16 (16 bit signed integer), or int32 (32 bit signed integer).
See also	READBIN

WRITEBMP

Syntax	WRITEBMP(*file*)
Description	Creates a grayscale BMP image file *file* out of a matrix. Used as follows: WRITEBMP(*file*) := **M**. The function must appear alone on the left side of a definition.
Arguments	
file	string variable corresponding to BMP filename or path
M	integer matrix, each element satisfying $0 \le \mathbf{M}_{i,j} \le 255$

WRITE_HLS

Syntax	WRITE_HLS(*file*)
Description	Creates a color BMP image file *file* out of a matrix formed by juxtaposing the three matrices giving the hue, lightness, and saturation components of an image.
Arguments	
file	string variable corresponding to BMP filename or path
M	integer matrix, each element satisfying $0 \le \mathbf{M}_{i,j} \le 255$
See also	See WRITERGB for an overview of creating color data files.

WRITE_HSV

Syntax	WRITE_HSV(*file*)
Description	Creates a color BMP image file *file* out of a matrix formed by juxtaposing the three matrices giving the hue, saturation, and value components of an image.
Arguments	
file	string variable corresponding to BMP filename or path
M	integer matrix, each element satisfying $0 \le \mathbf{M}_{i,j} \le 255$
See also	See WRITERGB for overview.

WRITEPRN

Syntax WRITEPRN(*file*) := **A**

Description Writes a matrix **A** into a structured ASCII data file *file*. Each row becomes a line in the file. The function must appear alone on the left side of a definition.

Arguments

file string variable corresponding to structured ASCII data filename or path

A matrix or vector

Comments The WRITEPRN and APPENDPRN functions write out data values neatly lined up in rows and columns. When you use these functions:

- Equations using WRITEPRN or APPENDPRN must be in a specified form. On the left should be WRITEPRN(*file*) or APPENDPRN(*file*). This is followed by a definition symbol (:=) and a matrix expression. Do not use range variables or subscripts on the matrix expression.

- Each new equation involving WRITEPRN writes a new file; if two equations write to the same file, the data written by the second equation will overwrite the data written by the first. Use APPENDPRN if you want to append values to a file rather than overwrite the file.

- The built-in variables *PRNCOLWIDTH* and *PRNPRECISION* determine the format of the data file that Mathcad creates. The value of *PRNCOLWIDTH* specifies the width of the columns (in characters). The value of *PRNPRECISION* specifies the number of significant digits used. By default, *PRNCOLWIDTH*=8 and *PRNPRECISION*=4. To change these values, choose **Options** from the **Worksheet Menu** and edit the numbers on the Built-In Variables tab, or enter definitions for these variables in your Mathcad document above the WRITEPRN function.

WRITEPRN and READPRN allow you to write out and read in *nested arrays* created in Mathcad.

If the array you are writing is either a nested array (an array whose elements are themselves arrays) or a complex array (an array whose elements are complex), then WRITEPRN will *not* create a simple ASCII file. Instead, WRITEPRN creates a file using a special format unlikely to be readable by other applications. This file can, however, be read by Mathcad's READPRN function.

By using the augment function, you can concatenate several variables and write them all using WRITEPRN to a data file.

See also APPENDPRN

WRITERGB

Syntax WRITERGB(*file*)

Description Creates a color BMP image file *file* out of a single matrix formed by juxtaposing the three matrices giving the red, green, and blue values of an image. Used as follows: WRITERGB(*file*) := **M**. The function must appear alone on the left side of a definition.

Arguments

file string variable corresponding to BMP filename or path

M integer matrix, each element satisfying $0 \le M_{i,j} \le 255$

Comments The function augment is helpful for combining submatrices prior to using WRITERGB.

Mathcad has functions for creating color BMP files out of matrices in which the image is stored in HLS or HSV format. These work in exactly the same way as WRITERGB.

See also WRITE_HLS and WRITE_HSV

WRITEWAV File Access

Syntax	WRITEWAV(*file, s, b*)
Description	Creates a WAVsignal file *file* out of a matrix. Used as follows: WRITEWAV(*file, s, b*) := **M**. The function must appear alone on the left side of a definition.
Arguments	
file	string variable corresponding to pulse code modulated (PCM) Microsoft WAV filename or path
s	integer sample rate
b	bit resolution
M	integer matrix
Comments	If the specified bit resolution is 1 – 8, the data is written to *file* as unsigned byte data. The limits on unsigned byte data are 0 to 256. If the bit resolution is 9 – 16, word data (two bytes) is written to *file*. The limits on word data are –32768 to 32767.
See also	GETWAVINFO and READWAV

xyz2cyl Vector and Matrix

Syntax	xyz2cyl(*x, y, z*) or xyz2cyl(*v*)
Description	Converts the rectangular coordinates of a point in 3D space to cylindrical coordinates.
Arguments	
x, y, z	real numbers
Comments	$x = r\cos(\theta)$, $y = r\sin(\theta)$, $z = z$, $v = \begin{bmatrix} x \\ y \\ z \end{bmatrix}$
See also	cyl2xyz

xy2pol Vector and Matrix

Syntax	xy2pol(*x, y*) or xy2pol(*v*)
Description	Converts the rectangular coordinates of a point in 2D space to polar coordinates.
Arguments	
x, y	real numbers
Comments	$x = r\cos(\theta)$, $y = r\sin(\theta)$, $v = \begin{bmatrix} x \\ y \end{bmatrix}$
See also	pol2xy

xyz2sph Vector and Matrix

Syntax	xyz2sph(*x, y, z*) or xyz2sph(*v*)
Description	Converts the rectangular coordinates of a point in 3D space to spherical coordinates.
Arguments	
x, y, z	real numbers
Comments	$x = r\sin(\phi)\cos(\theta)$, $y = r\sin(\phi)\sin(\theta)$, $z = r\cos(\phi)$, $v = \begin{bmatrix} x \\ y \\ z \end{bmatrix}$
See also	sph2xyz

Y0

Syntax	Y0(z)
Description	Returns the value of the Bessel function $Y_0(z)$ of the second kind. Same as Yn(0, z).
Arguments	
z	real or complex number
Comments	Y0.sc(z),where sc means scaled and is a literal subscript, gives Y0(z) multiplied by exp(-|Im(z)|). Scaled functions are useful for calculating large arguments without overflow.
Algorithm	AMOSLIB; ACM TOMS 12 (1986) 265-273.

Y1

Syntax	Y1(z)
Description	Returns the value of the Bessel function $Y_1(z)$ of the second kind. Same as Yn(1, z).
Arguments	
z	real or complex number
Comments	Y1.sc(z),where sc means scaled and is a literal subscript, gives Y1(z) multiplied by exp(-|Im(z)|). Scaled functions are useful for calculating large arguments without overflow.
Algorithm	AMOSLIB; ACM TOMS 12 (1986) 265-273.

Yn

Syntax	Yn(m, z)
Description	Returns the value of the Bessel function $Y_m(z)$ of the second kind.
Arguments	
m	real number
z	real or complex number
Comments	Solution of the differential equation $x^2 \cdot \frac{d^2}{dx^2}y + x \cdot \frac{d}{dx}y + (x^2 - m^2) \cdot y = 0$.
	Y1.sc(m, z),where sc means scaled and is a literal subscript, gives Yn(m, z) multiplied by exp(-|Im(z)|). Scaled functions are useful for calculating large arguments without overflow
Algorithm	AMOSLIB; ACM TOMS 12 (1986) 265-273.
See also	Jn

ys

Syntax	ys(n, z)
Description	Returns the value of the spherical Bessel function of the second kind, of order n, at x.
Arguments	
z	real or complex number
n	real number
Comments	Solution of the differential equation: $x^2 \cdot \frac{d^2}{dx^2}y + 2 \cdot x \cdot \frac{d}{dx}y + (x^2 - n \cdot (n+1))y = 0$.
Algorithm	Recurrence relation (Abramowitz and Stegun, 1972)
See also	js

δ   **Piecewise Continuous**

Syntax	$\delta(m, n)$
Description	Returns the value of the Kronecker delta function. Output is 1 if $m=n$ and 0 otherwise. (To type δ, press **d[Ctrl]G**).
Arguments m, n	integers

ε   **Piecewise Continuous**

Syntax	$\varepsilon(i, j, k)$
Description	Returns the value of a completely antisymmetric tensor of rank three. Output is 0 if any two arguments are the same, 1 if the three arguments are an even permutation of (0 1 2), and −1 if the arguments are an odd permutation of (0 1 2). (To type ε, press **e[Ctrl]g**).
Arguments i, j, k	integers between 0 and 2 inclusive (or between ORIGIN and ORIGIN+2 inclusive if ORIGIN$\neq$0)

Γ   **Special**

Classical Definition

Syntax	$\Gamma(z)$
Description	Returns the value of the classical Euler gamma function. (To type Γ, press **G[Ctrl]g**).
Arguments z	real or complex number; undefined for $z = 0, -1, -2, \ldots$
Description	For Re(z) > 0, $\Gamma(z) = \int_{0}^{\infty} t^{z-1}e^{-t}dt$. For Re($z$) < 0, function values analytically continue the above formula. Because $\Gamma(z + 1) = z!$, the gamma function extends the factorial function (traditionally defined only for positive integers).

Extended Definition

Syntax	$\Gamma(x, y)$
Description	Returns the value of the extended Euler gamma function. (To type Γ, press **G[Ctrl]g**).
Arguments x, y	real numbers, $x > 0, y \geq 0$
Description	Although restricted to real arguments, the function $\Gamma(x, y) = \int_{y}^{\infty} t^{x-1}e^{-t}dt$

extends the classical gamma function in the sense that the lower limit of integration y is free to vary. In the special case when $y=0$, the classical formulation applies and the first argument may assume complex values.

Φ

Syntax	$\Phi(x)$
Description	Returns the value of the Heaviside step function. Output is 1 if $x \geq 0$ and 0 otherwise. (To type Φ, press **F[Ctrl]g**).
Arguments	
x	real number
Example	

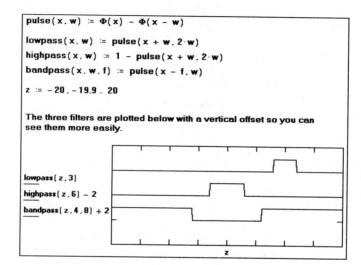

```
pulse ( x , w )  :=  Φ ( x )  -  Φ ( x  -  w )

lowpass ( x , w )  :=  pulse ( x + w , 2·w )
highpass ( x , w )  :=  1  -  pulse ( x + w , 2·w )
bandpass ( x , w , f )  :=  pulse ( x - f , w )

z  :=  - 20 , - 19.9 .. 20
```

The three filters are plotted below with a vertical offset so you can see them more easily.

lowpass (z , 3)

highpass (z , 6) - 2

bandpass (z , 4 , 8) + 2

z

Chapter 17
Operators

This chapter lists and describes Mathcad's built-in operators. The operators are listed according to the toolbar: Calculator, Graph, Matrix, Evaluation, Calculus, Boolean, Programming, Greek, Symbolic, and Modifier on which they appear.

Changing the Display of an Operator

When you insert an operator into a worksheet, it has a certain default appearance. For

example, when you type a colon **:** or click 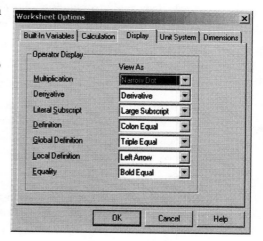 on the Calculator toolbar, Mathcad shows the colon as the definition symbol **:=**. This Mathcad symbol indicates a variable or function definition.

There may be times when you want to customize the appearance of operators. For example you may want the definition symbol to look like an ordinary equal sign. To change the way an operator is displayed throughout a worksheet:

1. Choose **Worksheet Options** from the **Tools** menu.

2. Click the Display tab.

3. Use the drop-down options next to each operator to select a display option.

To find the options available for each operator, click the Help button at the bottom of the Display tab.

To change the appearance of an operator in an individual expression, click on it with the right mouse button and use the popup menu. For example, to change the multiplication in an expression from a dot to an **x**:

1. Click on the multiplication with the right mouse button.

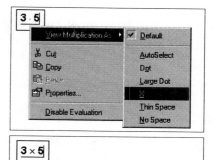

2. Choose **View Multiplication As... ⇒ X** from the popup menu.

Defining a Custom Operator

You define a custom operator just as you define a function:

1. Type the operator name followed by a pair of parentheses. Enter the operands (two at the most) between the parentheses.
2. Enter the definition symbol := by pressing the colon key.
3. Type an expression describing what you want the operator to do with its operands on the other side of the definition symbol.

Tip Mathcad provides a collection of math symbols to define custom operators. To access these symbols, open the **QuickSheets** from the **Help** menu and then choose "Extra Math Symbols." You can drag any of these symbols to your worksheet for use in creating a new operator name.

For example, suppose you want to define a new union operator using the symbol " $\cup$ ".

1. Drag the symbol into your worksheet from the "Extra Math Symbols" QuickSheet.

2. Type a left parenthesis followed by two names separated by a comma. Complete this argument list by typing a right parenthesis.

3. Press the colon (:) key. You see the definition symbol followed by a placeholder.

4. Type the function definition in the placeholder.

At this point, you've defined a function which behaves in every way like the user-defined functions described in Chapter 8, "Calculating in Mathcad." You could, if you wanted to, type " $\cup(1, 2)=$ " in your worksheet and see the result, a vector with the elements 1 and 2, on the other side of the equal sign.

Tip Once you've defined the new operator you can paste the definition into the QuickSheet. Choose *Annotate Book* from the **Book** menu, then *Save Section*. When you need to use this operator again, just open the QuickSheet and drag it into a new worksheet.

Using a Custom Operator

Once you've defined a new operator, you can use it in your calculations just as you would use any of Mathcad's built-in operators. The procedure for using a custom operator depends on whether the operator has one operand (like "−1 " or "5!") or two (like " 1 ÷ 2 ").

To use an operator having two operands:

1. Define any variables you want to use as arguments.

2. Click **xfy** on the **Evaluation** toolbar. You'll see three empty placeholders.

3. In the middle placeholder, insert the name of the operator. Or copy the name from the operator definition and paste it into the placeholder.

4. In the remaining two placeholders, enter the two operands.

$$\boxed{\;\mathbf{v} \cup \mathbf{u}\!\rfloor\;}$$

5. Press = to get the result.

$$\mathbf{v} \cup \mathbf{u} = \begin{pmatrix} 1 \\ 2 \\ 3 \\ 2 \\ 4 \\ 6 \end{pmatrix}$$

Tip Another way to display an operator having two operands is to click $\mathbf{x}^{\mathbf{f}}\mathbf{y}$ on the **Evaluation** toolbar. If you follow the preceding steps using this operator, you'll see a tree-shaped display.

To insert an operator having only one operand, decide first whether you want the operator to appear before the operand, as in "−1 ," or after the operand as in "5!." The former is called a *prefix* operator; the latter is a *postfix* operator. The example below shows how to use a postfix operator. The steps for creating a prefix operator are almost identical.

The following example shows how to define and use a new logical Not operator. First define an operator " ′(x)". To do so, follow the steps for defining $\cup(x, y)$ in the previous section, substituting the symbol " ′ " for "$\cup$" and using only one argument instead of two.

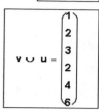

$$'(\mathbf{x}) := \neg\mathbf{x}$$

Then, to evaluate with the new operator:

1. Click $\mathbf{x}\,\mathbf{f}$ on the **Evaluation** toolbar to make a *postfix* operator.
   Otherwise, click $\mathbf{f}\,\mathbf{x}$. In either case, you see two empty placeholders.

   $$\boxed{\;\cdot\,\mathbf{\rfloor}\;}$$

2. If you clicked $\mathbf{x}\,\mathbf{f}$, put the operator name in the second placeholder. Otherwise put it in the first placeholder. In either case, you may find it more convenient to copy the name from the operator definition and paste it into the placeholder.

   $$\boxed{\;\cdot\,'\rfloor\;}$$

3. In the remaining placeholder, place the operand.

   $$\boxed{\;\underline{0}\,'\;}$$

4. Press = to see the result.

   $$\boxed{\;0\,' = 1\,\blacksquare\;}$$

Tip Just as Mathcad can display a custom operator as if it were a function, you can conversely display a function as if it were an operator.

Arithmetic Operators

To use an arithmetic operator either type its keystroke or choose the operator from the **Calculator** toolbar:

Parentheses (X)

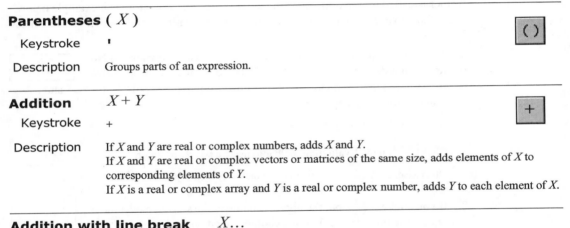

Keystroke   '

Description   Groups parts of an expression.

Addition $X + Y$

Keystroke   +

Description   If X and Y are real or complex numbers, adds X and Y.
                 If X and Y are real or complex vectors or matrices of the same size, adds elements of X to corresponding elements of Y.
                 If X is a real or complex array and Y is a real or complex number, adds Y to each element of X.

Addition with line break $X...$
$+ Y$

Keystroke   [Ctrl] [↵]

Description   Adds in the same manner as Addition, but inserts a line break for cosmetic formatting reasons.

Comments   This formatting feature cannot be used for multiplication or division. It can be used with subtraction if $X - Y$ is written instead as $X + (- Y)$.

Subtraction and Negation $X - Y,\ -X$

Keystroke –

Subtraction

Description   If X and Y are real or complex numbers, subtracts Y from X.
If X and Y are real or complex vectors or matrices of the same size, subtracts elements of Y from corresponding elements of X.

If X is an real or complex array and Y is a real or complex number, subtracts Y from each element of X.

Negation

Description   If X is a real or complex number, reverses the sign of X.
If X is a real or complex array, reverses the sign of each element of X.

Multiplication $X \cdot Y$

Keystroke *

Description   If X and Y are real or complex numbers, multiplies Y by X.
If Y is a real or complex array and X is a real or complex number, multiplies each element of Y by X.
If X and Y are real or complex vectors of the same size, returns the dot product (inner product).
If X and Y are real or complex conformable matrices, performs matrix multiplication.

To change the appearance of multiplication from a dot to a cross, choose **Worksheet Options** from the **Tools** menu, click the Display tab and use drop-down options to make the selection.

Division $\dfrac{X}{z}$

Keystroke /

Description   If X and z are real or complex numbers and z is nonzero, divides X by z.
If X is a real or complex array and z is a nonzero real or complex number, divides each element of X by z.

Inline Division $X \div z$

Keystroke [Ctrl] /

Description   If X and z are real or complex numbers and z is nonzero, divides X by z.
If X is an real or complex array and z is a nonzero real or complex number, divides each element of X by z.

Factorial $n!$

Keystroke !

Description   Returns $n \cdot (n-1) \cdot (n-2) \ldots 2 \cdot 1$ if n is an integer and $n \ge 1$; 1 if $n = 0$.

Complex conjugate $\bar{X}$

Keystroke   **"**

Description   If X is a complex number, reverses the sign of the imaginary part of X.

Absolute value $|x|$

Keystroke   **|**

Description   If z is a real or complex number, $|z|$ returns the absolute value (or modulus or magnitude) $\sqrt{\operatorname{Re}(z)^2 + \operatorname{Im}(z)^2}$ of z.

If $\mathbf{v}$ is real or complex vector, $|\mathbf{v}|$ returns the magnitude (or Euclidean norm or length) $\sqrt{\mathbf{v} \cdot \bar{\mathbf{v}}}$ of $\mathbf{v}$. If all elements in $\mathbf{v}$ are real, this definition is equivalent to $\sqrt{\mathbf{v} \cdot \mathbf{v}}$.

If $\mathbf{M}$ is a real or complex square matrix, $|\mathbf{M}|$ returns the determinant of $\mathbf{M}$.

Square root $\sqrt{z}$

Keystroke   ****

Description   Returns the positive square root for positive z; principal value for negative or complex z.

---

*n*th root $\sqrt[n]{z}$

Keystroke   **[Ctrl] **

Description   Returns the positive nth root for positive z; negative nth root for negative z and odd n; principal value otherwise. n must be an integer, $n \geq 1$.

See also   Exponentiation, Square root

Comments   This operator gives the same values as the **Exponentiation** operator except when $z < 0$ and n is an odd integer and $n \geq 3$ (by special convention).

Reciprocal $\dfrac{1}{z}$

Keystroke   **/ 1**

Scalar Case

Description   Returns the reciprocal (multiplicative inverse) of z, where z is a real or complex number.

Matrix Case

Description   If $\mathbf{M}$ is a real or complex square matrix, the reciprocal of $\mathbf{M}$ is the same as the inverse matrix $\mathbf{M}^{-1}$ (assuming that $\mathbf{M}$ is nonsingular).

See also   Exponentiation

Algorithm   LU decomposition used for matrix inversion (Press *et al.*, 1992)

Exponentiation z^w

Keystroke   ^

Scalar Case

Description   Returns the principal value of *z* raised to the power *w*, where *z* and *w* are real or complex numbers.

See also   nth root

Comments   The principal value is given by the formula $|z|^w \cdot \exp(\pi \cdot i \cdot w)$. In the special case $z < 0$ and $w = 1/n$, where *n* is an odd integer and $n \geq 3$, the principal value has a nonzero imaginary part. Hence, in this special case, Exponentiation does not give the same value as the *n*th root operator (by convention).

Matrix Case

Description   If **M** is a real or complex square matrix and $n \geq 0$ is an integer, $\mathbf{M}^n$ returns the *n*th power of **M** (using iterated matrix multiplication). Under the same conditions, $\mathbf{M}^{-n}$ is the inverse of $\mathbf{M}^n$ (assuming additionally that **M** is nonsingular).

Algorithm   LU decomposition used for matrix inversion (Press *et al.*, 1992)

Equals $c =$

Keystroke   =

Description   Returns numerical value of *c* if *c* is: a variable previously defined in the worksheet; a built-in variable; a globally-defined variable; or a function of several such variables. Appears as an ordinary = on the screen. Not used for symbolic evaluation.

Definition $z := c$, $f(x,y,z,...) := expr$

Keystroke   :

Description   Gives *z* the numerical value *c* from that point onward throughout the worksheet. Gives a function *f(x,y,z,...)* the meaning prescribed by the expression *expr* from that point onward throughout the worksheet. *expr* need not involve *x, y, z, ...* but it usually does; it may involve other built-in or user-defined functions.

See also   Definition (under Evaluation Operators) for example.

Mixed number $k\dfrac{m}{n}$

Keystroke   **[Ctrl] [Shift] +**

Description   If *k, m* and *n* are integers, returns the value of $k + m/n$.

Comments   To display a numerical result as a mixed number, double-click on the result to bring up the Result Format dialog box. Choose Fraction for the result format on the Number Format tab. Click the box next to "Use mixed numbers" so that it is checked.

Vector and Matrix Operators

Most of the operators on the Calculator toolbar also have meaning for vectors and matrices. When you use the addition operator to add two arrays of the same size, Mathcad performs the standard element-by-element addition. Mathcad also uses the conventional arithmetic operators for matrix subtraction, matrix multiplication, integer powers, and determinants.

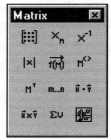

The multiplication symbol means dot product when applied to vectors and matrix multiplication when applied to matrices.

You can also use the vectorize operator (click [▱] on the **Matrix** toolbar) to perform any scalar operation or function element by element on a vector or matrix. See "Performing Calculations in Parallel" on page 61. Figure 17-1 shows some ways to use vector and matrix operators.

Matrix M . . .   **Vectors v and w . . .**

$$M := \begin{pmatrix} 0 & 1 & 2 \\ 3 & 0 & 2 \\ 5 & 3 & 1 \end{pmatrix} \qquad v := \begin{pmatrix} 3+10 \\ 1-4 \\ 5 \cdot 10 \end{pmatrix} \qquad v = \begin{pmatrix} 13 \\ -3 \\ 50 \end{pmatrix} \qquad w := 2 \cdot v \qquad w = \begin{pmatrix} 26 \\ -6 \\ 100 \end{pmatrix}$$

Sum . . .   **Determinant . . .**   **Dot and Cross Product . . .**

$$\sum v = 60 \qquad |M| = 25 \qquad v \cdot w = 5.356 \cdot 10^3 \qquad v \times w = \begin{pmatrix} 0 \\ 0 \\ 0 \end{pmatrix}$$

Inverse . . .

$$M^{-1} = \begin{pmatrix} -0.24 & 0.2 & 0.08 \\ 0.28 & -0.4 & 0.24 \\ 0.36 & 0.2 & -0.12 \end{pmatrix}$$

Transpose . . .

$$w^T = (26 \quad -6 \quad 100)$$

Solve linear system Mx=v with inverse . . .

$$x := M^{-1} \cdot v$$

$$M \cdot M^{-1} = \begin{pmatrix} 1 & 0 & 0 \\ 0 & 1 & 0 \\ 0 & 0 & 1 \end{pmatrix} \qquad x = \begin{pmatrix} 0.28 \\ 16.84 \\ -1.92 \end{pmatrix} \qquad M \cdot x = \begin{pmatrix} 13 \\ -3 \\ 50 \end{pmatrix}$$

Figure 17-1: Vector and matrix operations.

Tip   Operators and functions that expect vectors always expect column vectors. They do not apply to row vectors. To change a row vector into a column vector, use the transpose operator by clicking [▱] on the **Matrix** toolbar.

Insert matrix

Keystroke   [Ctrl]M

Description   Creates a vector or matrix of specified dimensions.

Vector and matrix subscript v_n, $M_{i,j}$

Keystroke   [

Description   If v is a vector, v_n returns the nth element of v.
If M is a matrix, $M_{i,j}$ returns the element in row i and column j of M.

Range variable

Keystroke   ;

Description   Specifies that a variable assume a range of values (for the sake of repeated or iterative calculations).

Dot product $u \cdot v$

Keystroke   *

Description   Returns the dot product (scalar or inner product) of two n-dimensional real or complex vectors u and v.

Cross product $u \times v$

Keystroke   [Ctrl]8

Description   Returns the cross product (vector product) of two 3-dimensional real or complex vectors u and v.

Vector sum Σv

Keystroke   [Ctrl]4

Description   Returns the sum (a scalar) of all elements of a real or complex vector v. (No range variable or vector subscripts are needed.)

Matrix Inverse

Keystroke   ^-1

Description   Returns the multiplicative inverse of a real or complex nonsingular square matrix M.

Algorithm   LU decomposition used for matrix inversion (Press *et al.*, 1992)

Magnitude and Determinant $|x|$

Keystroke |

Description If z is a real or complex number, $|z|$ returns the absolute value (or modulus or magnitude) $\sqrt{\mathrm{Re}(z)^2 + \mathrm{Im}(z)^2}$ of z.

If $\mathbf{v}$ is real or complex vector, returns the magnitude (or Euclidean norm or length) $\sqrt{\mathbf{v} \cdot \overline{\mathbf{v}}}$ of $\mathbf{v}$. If all elements in $\mathbf{v}$ are real, this definition is equivalent to $\sqrt{\mathbf{v} \cdot \mathbf{v}}$.

If $\mathbf{M}$ is a real or complex square matrix, returns the determinant of $\mathbf{M}$.

Algorithm LU decomposition (Press *et al.*, 1992)

Matrix superscript $\mathbf{M}^{\langle n \rangle}$

Keystroke **[Ctrl]6**   M^<>

Description Extracts column n (a vector) from matrix $\mathbf{M}$.

Matrix transpose $\mathbf{M}^{\mathrm{T}}$

Keystroke **[Ctrl]1**   M^T

Description If $\mathbf{M}$ is a vector or matrix, returns a matrix whose rows are the columns of $\mathbf{M}$ and whose columns are the rows of $\mathbf{M}$.

Vectorize $\vec{X}$

Keystroke **[Ctrl] -**

Description Forces operations in expression X to take place element by element. All vectors or matrices in X must be the same size.

$$P := \underline{\mathbf{M} \cdot \mathbf{N}}$$

Comments Mathcad's vectorize operator allows parallel operations to be performed efficiently on each element of a vector or matrix. For example, to

$$P := \overrightarrow{(\mathbf{M} \cdot \mathbf{N})}$$

define a matrix $\mathbf{P}$ by multiplying corresponding elements of the matrices $\mathbf{M}$ and $\mathbf{N}$, you could write $\mathbf{P}_{i,j} = \mathbf{M}_{i,j} \cdot \mathbf{N}_{i,j}$ where i and j are range variables. (This is not matrix multiplication, but rather multiplication element by element.) It's faster, however, to define $\mathbf{P}$ using vectorize:

- Select the whole expression by clicking inside and pressing [Space] until the right-hand side is held between the editing lines.
- Press [Ctrl]– to apply the vectorize operator. Mathcad puts an arrow over the top of the selected expression.

Extending ordinary scalar multiplication to matrices in this fashion, element by element, is referred to as "vectorizing" an expression.

Here are some properties of the vectorize operator:

- The vectorize operator changes the meaning of functions and operators but not constants or variables.

- Operations between an array and a scalar are performed by applying the scalar to each element of the array. For example, if $\mathbf{v}$ is a vector and n is a scalar, applying the vectorize operator to $\mathbf{v}^n$ returns a vector whose elements are the nth powers of the elements of $\mathbf{v}$.

- You cannot use any of the following matrix operations under a vectorize operator: dot product, matrix multiplication, matrix powers, matrix inverse, determinant, or magnitude of a vector. The vectorize operator will transform these operations into element-by-element scalar multiplication, exponentiation, or absolute value, as appropriate.

- The vectorize operator has no affect on operators and functions that *require* vectors or matrices: transpose, cross product, sum of vector elements, and functions like mean. These operators and functions have no scalar meaning.

Picture

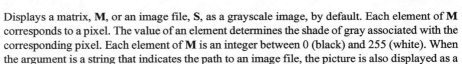

Keystroke   [Ctrl] T

Description   Displays a matrix, $\mathbf{M}$, or an image file, $\mathbf{S}$, as a grayscale image, by default. Each element of $\mathbf{M}$ corresponds to a pixel. The value of an element determines the shade of gray associated with the corresponding pixel. Each element of $\mathbf{M}$ is an integer between 0 (black) and 255 (white). When the argument is a string that indicates the path to an image file, the picture is also displayed as a grayscale image. See "Inserting Pictures" on page 151.

Calculus Operators

To access a calculus operator either type its keystroke, or choose the operator from the **Calculus** toolbar:

Summation

$$\sum_{i\,=\,m}^{n} X$$

Keystroke   [Ctrl] [Shift] 4

Description   Performs iterated addition of X over $i = m, m+1, \ldots, n$. X can be any expression; it need not involve i but it usually does. m and n must be integers. If $m = -\infty$ or $n = \infty$, the evaluation must be performed symbolically.

Example

$$i := 0 \ldots 20 \qquad\qquad x_i := \sin(0.1 \cdot i \cdot \pi)$$

$$\sum_{n=0}^{20} n = 210 \qquad\qquad \prod_{n=0}^{20} (n+1) = 5.109 \cdot 10^{19}$$

$$\sum_{n=0}^{20} x_n = 0 \qquad\qquad \sum_{n=0}^{20} x_n \cdot n = -63.138$$

$$\sum_{n=0}^{20} \sum_{m=0}^{10} n^m = 2.554 \cdot 10^{13}$$

See also   Range sum

Comments   The summation operator has *four* placeholders:

1. The placeholder to the left of the equal sign holds a variable that is the index of summation. It is defined only within the summation operator and therefore has no affect on, and is not influenced by, variable definitions outside the summation operator.

2. Integers, or any expressions that evaluate to integers, go in the placeholders to the right of the equal sign and above the sigma.

3. The remaining placeholder holds the expression you want to sum. Usually, this expression involves the index of summation. If this expression has several terms, first type an apostrophe (') to create parentheses around the placeholder.

4. To evaluate multiple summations, place another summation in the final placeholder of the first summation and use two range variables, as illustrated in the example above.

This use of summation must be carried out over subsequent integers and in steps of one. Use the Range Sum operator to use any range variable you define.

Tip The operation of summing the elements of a vector is so common that Mathcad provides a special operator for it. The vector sum operator (click Σ∪ on the Matrix toolbar) sums the elements of a vector without needing a range variable.

Product

$$\prod_{i\,=\,m}^{n} X$$

Keystroke [Ctrl][Shift]3

Description Performs iterated multiplication of X over $i = m, m + 1, ..., n$. X can be any expression; it need not involve i but it usually does. If $m = -\infty$ or $n = \infty$, the evaluation must be performed symbolically. Works similar to Summation.

See also Range product. See Summation for an example.

Range sum

$$\sum_{i} X$$

Keystroke $

Description Performs iterated addition of X over the range variable i. X can be any expression; it need not involve i but it usually does.

Example

$$i := 0 .. 20 \qquad j := 1 .. 10 \qquad x_i := \sin(0.1 \cdot i \cdot \pi)$$

$$\sum_{i} i = 210 \qquad\qquad \prod_{i} (i + 1) = 5.109 \cdot 10^{19}$$

$$\sum_{i} x_i = 0 \qquad\qquad \sum_{i} x_i \cdot i = -63.138$$

$$y_j := \sum_{i} i^j \qquad\qquad \sum_{i}\sum_{j} i^j = 2.554 \cdot 10^{13}$$

$$y_1 = 210 \qquad\qquad \sum_{j} y_j = 2.554 \cdot 10^{13}$$

$$y_{10} = 2.416 \cdot 10^{13}$$

See also   Summation

Comments   This operator can use any range variable you define as an index of summation:

1. Define a range variable. For example, type **i:1,2;10**.

    $i := 1, 2 .. 10$

2. Click in a blank space. Then click $\sum_n$ on the Calculus toolbar. A summation sign with two placeholders appears.

3. Click on the bottom placeholder and type the name of a range variable.

4. Click on the placeholder to the right of the summation sign and type an expression involving the range variable. If this expression has several terms, first type an apostrophe (**'**) to create parentheses around the placeholder.

5. Press = to get a result.

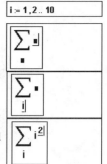

Tip   To enter the expression in the example above using fewer keystrokes, type **i$i^2**.

The **Range sum** operator, unlike the **Summation** operator, cannot stand alone. It requires the existence of a range variable. However, a single range variable can be used with any number of these operators.

Variable Upper Limit of Summation

Mathcad's range summation operator runs through each value of the range variable you place in the bottom placeholder. It is possible, by using Boolean expressions, to sum only up to a particular value. In Figure 17-2, the term $i \le x$ returns the value 1 whenever it is true and 0 whenever it is false. Although the summation operator still sums over each value of the index of summation, those terms for which $i > x$ are multiplied by 0 and hence do not contribute to the summation.

$$i := 0 .. 10$$

$$f(x) := \sum_i i^2 \cdot (i \le x)$$

$$k1 := -4 .. 5$$

$$g(n) := \sum_{j=1}^{n} \sum_{m=1}^{j} m$$

$$f(k1) =$$

0
0
0
0
0
1
5
14
30
55

$$f(0) = 0$$

$$f(5) = 55$$

$$f(-4) = 0$$

$$g(7) = 84$$

$$g(20) = 1.54 \times 10^3$$

Figure 17-2: A variable upper limit of summation.

Range product $\displaystyle\prod_i X$

Keystroke	**#**
Description	Performs iterated multiplication of X over the range variable i. X can be any expression; it need not involve i but it usually does. Works similar to **Range sum**.
See also	Product. See **Range sum** for an example.

Definite integral $\displaystyle\int_a^b f(t)\,dt$

Keystroke	**&**
Description	Returns the definite integral of $f(t)$ over the interval $[a, b]$. a and b must be real scalars. All variables in the expression $f(t)$, except the variable of integration t, must be defined. The integrand, $f(t)$, cannot return an array. $a = -\infty$, $b = \infty$, or both are permitted.
Examples	

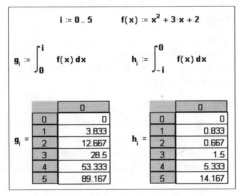

Figure 17-3: Variable limits of integration

As an example, here's how to evaluate the definite integral of $\sin^2(x)$ from 0 to $\pi/4$:

1. Click [icon] on the Calculus toolbar. An integral symbol appears, with placeholders for the integrand, limits of integration, and variable of integration.

    $\displaystyle\int_\blacksquare^\blacksquare \blacksquare\, d\blacksquare$

2. Type your upper and lower limits of integration in the top and bottom placeholders.

    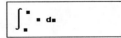

3. Type the expression to be integrated in the placeholder between the integral sign and the "d."

4. Type the variable of integration in the remaining placeholder. Press = for the result.

$$\int_0^{\frac{\pi}{4}} \sin(x)^2 \, dx = 0.143$$

Comments   Here are some important things to remember about integration in Mathcad:

- The limits of integration must be real, but the expression to be integrated can be either real or complex, except for integrals being evaluated with the Infinite Limit algorithm.

- Except for the integrating variable, all variables in the integrand must have been defined elsewhere in the worksheet.

- The integrating variable must be a single variable name.

- If the integrating variable involves units, the upper and lower limits of integration must have the same units.

Note   Like all numerical methods, Mathcad's integration algorithm can have difficulty with ill-behaved integrands. If the expression to be integrated has singularities, discontinuities, or large and rapid fluctuations, Mathcad's solution may be inaccurate.

In some cases, you may be able to find an exact expression for your definite integral or even the indefinite integral (antiderivative) by using Mathcad symbolics.

Variable Limits of Integration

Although the result of an integration is a single number, you can always use an integral with a range variable to obtain results for many numbers at once (as illustrated in Figure 17-3). Such repeated evaluations may take considerable time depending on the complexity of the integrals, the length of the interval, and the value of *TOL*.

Tolerance for Integrals

Mathcad's numerical integration algorithm makes successive estimates of the value of the integral and returns a value when the two most recent estimates differ by less than the value of the built-in variable *TOL*. Figure 17-4 below shows how changing *TOL* affects the accuracy of integral calculations (not to be confused with the mere formatting issue of how many digits to display).

Default tolerance
$$TOL := 0.001 \qquad \int_1^{e^5} \frac{1}{t} \, dt = 5.000000541364253$$

Tighter tolerance
$$TOL := 0.000001 \qquad \int_1^{e^5} \frac{1}{t} \, dt = 5.000000000007783$$

Looser tolerance
$$TOL := 0.1 \qquad \int_1^{e^5} \frac{1}{t} \, dt = 5.011533083011655$$

Figure 17-4: How changing TOL affects the accuracy of integral calculations.

You can change the value of the tolerance by including definitions for *TOL* directly in your worksheet as shown. To see the effect of changing the tolerance, press [Ctrl][F9] to recalculate all the equations in the worksheet.

If Mathcad's approximations to an integral fail to converge to an answer, Mathcad marks the integral with an appropriate error message.

When you change the tolerance, keep in mind the trade-off between accuracy and computation time. If you decrease (tighten) the tolerance, Mathcad will compute integrals more accurately. However, Mathcad will take longer to return a result. Conversely, if you increase (loosen) the tolerance, Mathcad will compute more quickly, but the answers will be less accurate.

Multiple Integrals

You can also use Mathcad to evaluate double or multiple integrals. To set up a double integral, press the ampersand key, [&], twice. Fill in the integrand, the limits, and the integrating variable for each integral. Keep in mind that double integrals take much longer to converge to an answer than single integrals. Wherever possible, use an equivalent single integral in place of a double integral.

Because certain numerical integration methods work best on certain kinds of integrals, Mathcad has an AutoSelect feature for integration. Depending on the kind of integral you are evaluating, Mathcad automatically chooses the most appropriate integration method to use. Using AutoSelect, Mathcad examines the integral and evaluates it using one of the following methods:

- **Romberg**: Romberg trapezoidal approximation with Richard extrapolation—divides the interval into equally spaced intervals.

- **Adaptive:** if the values of *f(x)* vary significantly over the interval, divides the interval into unequally spaced intervals.

- **Infinite Limit**: Integrates using an algorithm appropriate for integrals where one of both of the limits are infinite. The function being integrated must be real.

- **Singular Endpoint**: if *f(a)* and/or *f(b)* is undefined.

If you want to evaluate an integral using a method other than the one chosen during the AutoSelect process, turn off AutoSelect and choose another method. To do so:

1. Type the integral and allow AutoSelect to return a result.

2. Right click on the integral.

3. Click on the method you want to use.

The integral is recalculated using the method you clicked.

Algorithm   Romberg, Kahan transform, QAGS, Clenshaw-Curtis, Gauss-Kronrod formulas (Piessens 1983, Lorczak)

Indefinite integral $\int f(t)\,dt$

Keystroke   **[Ctrl]i**

Description   Returns the indefinite integral (that is, an antiderivative) of *f(t)*. Must be performed symbolically. The integrand, *f(t)*, cannot return an array.

Derivative $\quad \dfrac{d}{dt}f(t)$

Keystroke   **?**

Description   Returns the derivative of $f(t)$ evaluated at t. All variables in the expression $f(t)$ must be defined. The variable t must be a scalar value. The function $f(t)$ must return a scalar.

Examples

> $x := 2 \qquad\qquad y := 10 \qquad\qquad t := 0$
>
> $g(t) := 5 \cdot t^4$
>
> **Derivative**   **Actual result**
>
> $\dfrac{d}{dx}x^5 = 79.99999999999997 \qquad g(x) = 80$
>
> $\dfrac{d}{dx}x^5 \cdot y = 799.9999999999998 \qquad g(x) \cdot y = 800$
>
> $\dfrac{d}{dy}x^5 \cdot y = 31.99999999999998 \qquad x^5 = 32$
>
> $\dfrac{d}{dt}x^5 \cdot y = 0$ (Since expression does not involve t, derivative is zero)

Here's how to evaluate the first derivative of x^3 with respect to x at the point $x = 2$:

1. First define the point at which you want to evaluate the derivative. As a shortcut, type **x:2** .

   > $x := 2$

2. Click below the definition of x. Then click $\boxed{\frac{d}{dx}}$ on the Calculus toolbar. A derivative operator appears with two placeholders.

   > $\dfrac{d}{d\blacksquare}\blacksquare$

3. Type **x** in the bottom placeholder. You are differentiating with respect to this variable. In the placeholder to the right of the $\dfrac{d}{dx}$, enter **x^3**. This is the expression to be differentiated.

   > $\dfrac{d}{dx}x^3$

4. Press = to get the result.

   > $\dfrac{d}{dx}x^3 = 12$

Comments   With Mathcad's derivative algorithm, you can expect the first derivative to be accurate to within 7 or 8 significant digits, provided that the value at which you evaluate the derivative is not too close to a singularity of the function. The accuracy of this algorithm tends to decrease by one significant digit for each increase in the order of the derivative (see nth derivative operator).

The result of differentiating is not a function, but a single number: the computed derivative at the indicated value of the differentiation variable. In the previous example, the derivative of x^3 is not the expression $3x^2$ but $3x^2$ evaluated at $x = 2$. If you want the expression $3x^2$, you will need to use menu symbolics.

Although differentiation returns just one number, you can still define one function as the derivative of another. For example: $f(x) := \frac{d}{dx}g(x)$.

Evaluating $f(x)$ will return the numerically computed derivative of $g(x)$ at x. You can use this technique to evaluate the derivative of a function at many points via range variables.

To change the appearance of the derivative symbol to a partial derivative symbol, choose **Worksheet Options** from the **Tools** menu, click the Display tab and use the drop-down options to make the selection.

There are some important things to remember about differentiation in Mathcad:

- The expression to be differentiated can be either real or complex.
- The differentiation variable must be a single variable name. If you want to evaluate the derivative at several different values stored in a vector, you must evaluate the derivative at each individual vector element (see Figure 17-5).

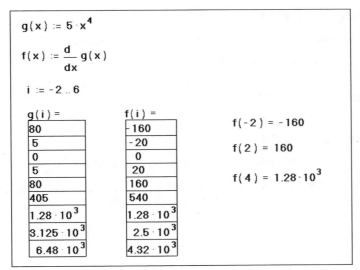

Figure 17-5: Evaluating the derivative of a function at several points.

Algorithm   Modified Ridder's method (Press *et al.*, 1992; Lorczak)

---

*n*th derivative $\dfrac{d^n}{dt^n}f(t)$

Keystroke   **[Ctrl] ?**

Description   Returns the *n*th derivative of $f(t)$ evaluated at t. All variables in $f(t)$ must be defined. The variable t must be a scalar value. The function $f(t)$ must return a scalar. *n* must be an integer between 0 and 5 for numerical evaluation or a positive integer for symbolic evaluation.

Comments	For $n = 1$, this operator gives the same answer as the Derivative operator. For $n = 0$, it simply returns the value of the function itself.
Algorithm	Modified Ridder's method (Press *et al.*, 1992; Lorczak)

Limit $\lim_{t \to a} f(t)$

Keystroke	[Ctrl]L
Description	Returns the two-sided limit of $f(t)$. Must be evaluated symbolically.
Algorithm	Series expansion (Geddes and Gonnet, 1989)

Right-Hand Limit $\lim_{t \to a^+} f(t)$

Keystroke	[Ctrl] [Shift]A
Description	Returns the right-hand limit of $f(t)$. Must be evaluated symbolically.
Algorithm	Series expansion (Geddes and Gonnet, 1989)

Left-Hand Limit $\lim_{t \to a^-} f(t)$

Keystroke	[Ctrl] [Shift]B
Description	Returns the left-hand limit of $f(t)$. Must be evaluated symbolically.
Algorithm	Series expansion (Geddes and Gonnet, 1989)

Evaluation Operators

To access an Evaluation operator either type its keystroke, or choose the operator from the **Evaluation** toolbar:

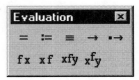

Equals

$$c =$$

Keystroke

=

Description

Returns numerical value of c if c is: a variable previously defined in the worksheet; a built-in variable; a globally-defined variable; or a function of several such variables. Appears as an ordinary = on the screen. Not used for symbolic evaluation.

Definition

$$z := c , \quad f(x,y,z,...) := expr$$

Keystroke

:

Description

Gives z the numerical value c from that point onward throughout the worksheet. Gives a function $f(x,y,z,...)$ the meaning prescribed by the expression *expr* from that point onward throughout the worksheet. *expr* need not involve x, y, z, ... but it usually does; it may involve other built-in or user-defined functions.

Examples

Computing distances between points   *(DEFINITIONS)*

$$x1 := 0 \qquad y1 := 1.5$$
$$x2 := 3 \qquad y2 := 4 \qquad dist(x, y) := \sqrt{x^2 + y^2}$$
$$x3 := -1 \qquad y3 := 1$$

Compute distance from origin: *(EVALUATIONS)*

$$dist(x1, y1) = 1.5$$
$$dist(x2, y2) = 5$$
$$dist(x3, y3) = 1.414$$

Compute distance between points

$$dist(x2 - x1, y2 - y1) = 3.905$$
$$dist(x3 - x1, y3 - y1) = 1.118$$
$$dist(x3 - x2, y3 - y2) = 5$$

Figure 17-6: Example 1.

Comments

You can define arrays in the same way as scalars, with the array name **A** on the left side of a $:=$, and a corresponding array of values to the right.

You can likewise use arrays to define several variables at once, as the previous example shows. The left side of a simultaneous definition is an array whose elements are either names or subscripted variable names. The right side must be an array of values having the same number of rows and columns as the left side. Mathcad defines each variable on the left side with the value of the array in the corresponding position on the right side. Elements on the right side are all

Simultaneous definition of three variables...

$$x := 2$$

$$\begin{bmatrix} \alpha \\ \beta \\ \gamma \end{bmatrix} := \begin{bmatrix} \text{atan}(x) \\ \ln(x) \\ \sqrt{x} \end{bmatrix}$$

$$\alpha = 1.1071487$$
$$\beta = 0.6931472$$
$$\gamma = 1.4142136$$

Swap two variables...

$$A := 1 \qquad B := 2$$

$$\begin{bmatrix} A \\ B \end{bmatrix} := \begin{bmatrix} B \\ A \end{bmatrix}$$

$$A = 2 \qquad B = 1$$

Figure 17-7: Example 2.

evaluated before assigning any of them to the left side. Because of this, nothing on the right side of an expression can depend on what is on the left side. You also cannot have a variable appear more than once on the left side.

When you define a function, Mathcad does not try to evaluate it until you use it later on in the worksheet. If there is an error, the use of the function is marked in error, even though the real problem may be in the definition of the function itself. For example, if $f(x) := 1/x$ and you attempt to evaluate $f(0)$, the error flag occurs not at the definition of $f(x)$ but when Mathcad encounters $f(0)$ for the first time.

Global Definition $\quad z := c, \; f(x,y,z,...) := expr$

Keystroke   ~

Description   Gives z the numerical value c throughout the worksheet regardless of where the global definition is positioned. Likewise, gives a function $f(x,y,z,...)$ the meaning prescribed by the expression $expr$ throughout the worksheet. $expr$ need not involve $x, y, z, ...$ but it usually does; it may involve other built-in or user-defined functions.

Comments   You can globally define arrays in the same way as scalars, with the array name **A** on the left side of a $\equiv$, and a corresponding array of values to the right.

This is the algorithm that Mathcad uses to evaluate all definitions, global and otherwise:

- First, Mathcad takes one pass through the entire worksheet from top to bottom. During this first pass, Mathcad evaluates global definitions only.

- Mathcad then makes a second pass through the worksheet from top to bottom. This time, Mathcad evaluates all definitions made with := as well as all equations containing $\equiv$.

Although global definitions are evaluated before any local definitions, Mathcad evaluates global definitions the same way it evaluates local definitions: top to bottom and left to right. This means that whenever you use a variable to the right of a $\equiv$:

- that variable must also have been defined with a $\equiv$, *and*

- the variable must have been defined *above* the place where you are trying to use it.

Otherwise, the variable is marked in red to indicate that it is undefined.

It is good practice to allow only one definition for each global variable. Although you can define a variable with two different global definitions or with one global and one local definition, this usually makes your worksheet difficult to understand.

Symbolic Equals $c \rightarrow$

Keystroke [Ctrl] .

Description Returns live symbolic "value" of c if c is a variable previously defined in the worksheet, is a built-in variable, is a globally-defined variable, or is a function of several such variables.

Comments The live symbolic equals sign is analogous to the numerical equals sign "=". You can use it to symbolically simplify or factor algebraic expressions, or to symbolically evaluate derivatives, integrals and limits. Note that "$\rightarrow$" applies only to an entire expression (unlike menu symbolics).

Prefix $f\,x$

Keystroke NONE

Description Using the prefix custom operator, $f\,x$ returns the value $f(x)$, where f is either a built-in or user-defined function and x is a real or complex number.

Examples

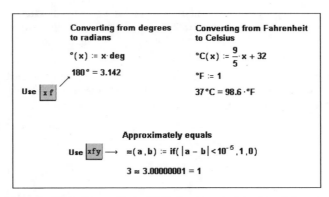

Converting from degrees to radians

$°(\mathbf{x}) := \mathbf{x} \cdot \mathbf{deg}$

$180° = 3.142$

Use $\boxed{x\ f}$

Converting from Fahrenheit to Celsius

$°C(\mathbf{x}) := \dfrac{9}{5} \cdot \mathbf{x} + 32$

$°F := 1$

$37°C = 98.6 \cdot °F$

Approximately equals

Use $\boxed{x f y} \longrightarrow$ $\approx(\mathbf{a},\mathbf{b}) := \mathbf{if}(\,|\mathbf{a} - \mathbf{b}| < 10^{-5}, 1, 0)$

$3 \approx 3.00000001 = 1$

Figure 17-8: Example 1: Defining your own operators.

$\sin\left(\dfrac{\pi}{3}\right) = 0.866$ $\longleftarrow$ Displaying a function the usual way.

$\sin\dfrac{\pi}{3} = 0.866$ $\longleftarrow$ Displaying the same function as if it were an operator *(using the xf button)*.

Figure 17-9: Example 2: Displaying an operator as a function and a function as an operator.

Comments In Figure 17-8, the symbol " $°$ " comes from the Symbol font. First define a function "$°(x)$" as illustrated, then click the Postfix button on the Evaluation toolbar to use postfix notation. For postfix notation, type the name of the operator in the right placeholder and the operand in the left placeholder.

Many publishers prefer to omit parentheses around the arguments to certain functions (*sin* x rather than sin(*x*)). You can do the same thing by treating the *sin* function as an operator with one operand, as in Figure 17-9.

Postfix $x f$

| | |
| x f |

Keystroke   **NONE**

Description   Using the postfix custom operator, $x f$ returns the value *f(x)*, where *f* is either a built-in or user-defined function and x is a real or complex number.

Comments   In Figure 17-8, on page 413, the symbol "°" comes from the Symbol font. First define a function "°(*x*)" as illustrated, then click the postfix button on the Evaluation toolbar to use postfix notation. For postfix notation, type the name of the operator in the right placeholder and the operand in the left placeholder.

Infix $x f y$

| xfy |

Keystroke   **NONE**

Description   Using the infix custom operator, $x f y$ returns the value *f(x,y)*, where *f* is either a built-in or user-defined function and x, y are real or complex numbers.

Comments   In Figure 17-8, on page 413, the symbol "≈" comes from the Symbol font. First define a binary function "≈(*x,y*)" as illustrated, then click the infix button on the Evaluation toolbar to use infix notation. For infix notation, type the name of the operator in the middle placeholder and the operands in the left and right placeholders.

Likewise, in Figure 17-9, on page 413, the binary function "÷(*x,y*)" is defined and then displayed in the more conventional manner: "*x÷y*". Functions and operators are fundamentally the same. Although notation like "÷(*x,y*)" is unconventional, use it if you prefer.

Treefix $_x f_y$

| x^{f}y |

Keystroke   **NONE**

Description   Using the treefix custom operator, $_x f_y$ returns the value *f(x,y)*, where *f* is either a built-in or user-defined function and x, y are real or complex numbers.

Comments   In Figure 17-8, on page 413, the symbol "÷" comes from the Symbol font. First define a binary function "÷(*x,y*)" as illustrated, then click the treefix button on the Evaluation toolbar to use treefix notation. For treefix notation, type the name of the operator in the middle placeholder and the operands in the left and right placeholders.

Boolean Operators

To access a Boolean operator either type its keystroke, or choose the operator from the **Boolean** toolbar:

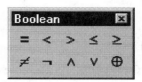

Greater than $\quad x > y,\ S1 > S2$

Keystroke   **>**

Description   For real scalars x and y, returns 1 if $x > y$, 0 otherwise.
For string expressions $S1$ and $S2$, returns 1 if $S1$ strictly follows $S2$ in ASCII order, 0 otherwise.

Less than $\quad x < y,\ S1 < S2$

Keystroke   **<**

Description   For real scalars x and y, returns 1 if $x < y$, 0 otherwise.
For string expressions $S1$ and $S2$, returns 1 if $S1$ strictly precedes $S2$ in ASCII order, 0 otherwise.

Greater than or equal to $\quad x \geq y,\ S1 \geq S2$

Keystroke   **[Ctrl])**

Description   For real scalars x and y, returns 1 if $x \geq y$, 0 otherwise.
For string expressions $S1$ and $S2$, returns 1 if $S1$ follows $S2$ in ASCII order, 0 otherwise.

Less than or equal to $\quad x \leq y,\ S1 \leq S2$

Keystroke   **[Ctrl] (**

Description   For real scalars x and y, returns 1 if $x \leq y$, 0 otherwise.
For string expressions $S1$ and $S2$, returns 1 if $S1$ precedes $S2$ in ASCII order, 0 otherwise.

Not equal to $\quad z \neq w,\ S1 \neq S2$

Keystroke   **[Ctrl] 3**

Description   For scalars z and w, returns 1 if $z \neq w$, 0 otherwise.
For string expressions $S1$ and $S2$, returns 1 if $S1$ is not character by character identical to $S2$, 0 otherwise.

Bold Equals $\quad z = w$

Keystroke   **[Ctrl] =**

Description   Returns 1 if $z = w$, 0 otherwise (also known as Boolean equals). Appears as a bold = on the screen. Also used when typing constraint equations within solve blocks or when typing equations to be solved symbolically.

and	$x \wedge y$	
Keystroke	`[Ctrl] [Shift] 7`	∧

Description $x \wedge y$ returns the value 1 if both x and y are nonzero, and 0 if at least one of x or y is zero.

Comments   The value 0 is regarded as FALSE; any nonzero value (including 1) is regarded as TRUE. The Boolean and operator evaluates the right argument if and only if the left argument is TRUE. $x \wedge y$ is also known as the logical conjunction of x and y.

or	$x \vee y$	
Keystroke	`[Ctrl] [Shift] 6`	∨

Description $x \vee y$ returns the value 1 if at least one of x or y is nonzero, and 0 if both x and y are zero.

Comments   The value 0 is regarded as FALSE; any nonzero value (including 1) is regarded as TRUE. The Boolean or operator evaluates the right argument if and only if the left argument is FALSE. $x \vee y$ is also known as the logical (inclusive) disjunction of x and y.

xor	$x \oplus y$	
Keystroke	`[Ctrl] [Shift] 1`	⊕

Description $x \oplus y$ returns the value 1 if precisely one of x or y is nonzero, and 0 if both x and y are zero or both are nonzero.

Comments   The value 0 is regarded as FALSE; any nonzero value (including 1) is regarded as TRUE. $x \oplus y$ is the same as $(x \vee y) \wedge \neg (x \wedge y)$ and is also known as the logical exclusive disjunction of x and y.

not	$\neg x$	
Keystroke	`[Ctrl] [Shift] 5`	¬

Description $\neg x$ returns the value 0 if x is nonzero and 0 if x is zero.

Comments   The value 0 is regarded as FALSE; any nonzero value (including 1) is regarded as TRUE. $\neg x$ is also known as the logical negation of x.

Programming Operators

To access a Programming operator either type its keystroke, or choose the operator from the **Programming** toolbar:

Special Note: these operators are valid only within a Mathcad programming structure.

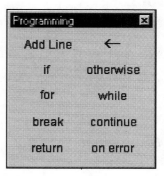

Local Definition $w \leftarrow f(a, b, c, \ldots)$

Keystroke   **{**

Description   Gives w the numerical value of the function $f(a,b,c,\ldots)$ within a program. Outside the program, w remains undefined.

Add Line

Keystroke   **]**

Description   Inserts a line in a program. When you insert the Add Line operator the first time, a program is created (a vertical bar with two placeholders). If you select either of these placeholders and insert the Add Line operator again, more placeholders are created.

Conditional Statement ▪ if ▪

Keystroke   **}**

Description   Within a program, permits evaluation of a statement only when a specified condition is met. You must insert this operator using its toolbar button or equivalent keystroke. Conditional if is not the same as the built-in if function. Do not just type the word "if."

Otherwise   ▪ otherwise

Keystroke   **[Ctrl] [Shift] }**

Description   Within a program, used in conjunction with the if operator to exhaust possibilities not yet covered. You must insert this operator using its toolbar button or equivalent keystroke. Do not just type the word "otherwise."

For Loop

for $\blacksquare \in \blacksquare$

$\blacksquare$

Keystroke	**[Ctrl] [Shift]** ″

for

Description	Within a program, permits evaluation of a sequence of statements a specified number of times. The right-hand placeholder usually contains a range variable. You must insert this operator using its toolbar button or equivalent keystroke. Do not just type the word "for."

While Loop

while $\blacksquare$

$\blacksquare$

Keystroke	**[Ctrl]]**

while

Description	Within a program, permits evaluation of a sequence of statements until a specified condition is met. The right-hand placeholder usually contains a Boolean expression. You must insert this operator using its toolbar button or equivalent keystroke. Do not just type the word "while."

Break

break

Keystroke	**[Ctrl] [Shift]** {

break

Description	Within a for or while loop, halts loop execution. Usually used in conjunction with an if statement, that is, halting occurs if a specified condition occurs. Execution moves to the next statement outside the loop. You must insert this operator using its toolbar button or equivalent keystroke. Do not just type the word "break."
See also	continue and return

Continue

continue

Keystroke	**[Ctrl] [**

continue

Description	Within a for or while loop, halts loop execution, skips remaining steps, and continues at the beginning of the next iteration of the next loop. Usually used in conjunction with an if statement, that is, halting occurs if a specified condition occurs. You must insert this operator using its toolbar button or equivalent keystroke. Do not just type the word "continue."
See also	break and return

Return

return $\blacksquare$

Keystroke	**[Ctrl] [Shift]**	

return

Description	Within a program, halts program execution. Usually used in conjunction with an *if* statement, that is, halting occurs if a specified condition occurs. Also, within a for or while loop, halts loop execution. You must insert this operator using its toolbar button or equivalent keystroke. Do not just type the word "return."
See also	break and continue

On Error   ▮ on error ▮

Keystroke   [Ctrl]'

`on error`

Description   Within a program, permits computation of an alternative expression when an arbitrary numerical error flag is raised. You must insert this operator using its toolbar button or equivalent keystroke. Do not just type the phrase "on error."

Comments   on error executes the right-hand argument first. If no error occurs, it returns the result of the right argument. If an error occurs, then the error is cleared and the left argument is returned.

on error is a general purpose error trap. It is more powerful than using the return statement, coupled with some specific test, to deal with inputs that give rise to numerical error.

Chapter 18
Symbolic Keywords

This chapter lists and describes Mathcad's symbolic keywords. The keywords are listed alphabetically.

Accessing Symbolic Keywords

You can access symbolic keywords in two ways:

- Simply type in the keyword as shown for that keyword, or
- Select the keyword from the **Symbolic** toolbar.

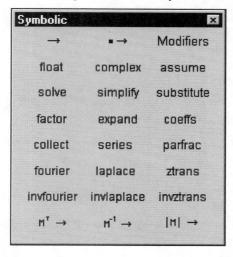

The **Modifiers** toolbar corresponds to symbolic modifiers.

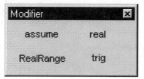

The modifier *assume* is discussed on page 422. The other three modifiers, *real*, *RealRange* and *trig*, are used in some cases with the *simplify* keyword; refer to *simplify* on page 428 to find out how to use these modifiers.

Most of the keywords have equivalent menu choices on the **Symbolics** menu.

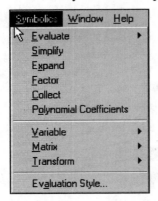

Finding More Information

Refer to the **QuickSheets** under the **Help** menu for examples involving keywords.

Keywords

assume

Syntax   assume, *constraint*

Description   Imposes constraints on one or more variables according to the expression *constraint*. A typical constraint might be that *var* < 10.

assume can also constrain a variable to be real or to fall within a certain range of real values.

Use the following modifiers:

var=real evaluates the expression on the assumption that the variable *var* is real;

var=RealRange(a,b) evaluates on the assumption that var is real and lies between a and b, where a and b are real numbers or infinity (type [**Ctrl**][**Shift**]z to display ∞).

Example

Symbolic evaluation   **Complex evaluation**

$$\int_0^\infty e^{-x^2} \, dx \rightarrow \frac{1}{2} \cdot \sqrt{\pi}$$ $$e^{i \cdot n \cdot \theta} \text{ complex} \rightarrow \cos(n \cdot \theta) + i \cdot \sin(n \cdot \theta)$$

Floating point evaluation

$$\int_0^\infty e^{-x^2} \, dx \text{ float}, 10 \rightarrow .8862269255$$

Constrained evaluation

$$x \cdot \int_0^\infty e^{-\alpha \cdot t} \, dt \text{ assume}, \alpha > 1, \alpha = \text{real} \rightarrow \frac{x}{\alpha}$$

(α is constrained to be greater than 1 and real)

coeffs

Syntax   coeffs, *var*

Description   Finds coefficients of a polynomial when it is written in terms of ascending powers of the variable or subexpression *var*. Mathcad returns a vector containing the coefficients. The first element of the vector is the constant term and the last element is the coefficient of the highest order term in the polynomial.

See also   convert, parfrac for example

Comments   Another way to find the coefficients of a polynomial is to enclose the variable or subexpression *var* between the two editing lines and choose **Polynomial Coefficients** from the **Symbolics** menu.

collect

Syntax   collect, *var1, var2, ... , varn*

Description   Collects terms containing like powers of the variables *var1* through *varn*.

See also   expand for example

Comments   Another way to collect terms is to enclose the expression between the editing lines and choose **Collect** from the **Symbolics** menu

complex

Syntax   complex

Description   Carries out symbolic evaluation in the complex domain. Result is usually of the form $a+i\cdot b$.

See also   assume for example

Comments   Another way to evaluate an expression in the complex domain is to enclose the expression between the editing lines and choose **Evaluate⇒Complex** from the **Symbolics** menu.

convert, parfrac

Syntax   convert, parfrac, *var*

Description   Converts an expression to a partial fraction expansion in the variable *var*.

Example

Expanding expressions to partial fractions

$$\frac{2\cdot x^2 - 3\cdot x + 1}{x^3 + 2\cdot x^2 - 9\cdot x - 18} \text{ convert, parfrac, x} \rightarrow \frac{1}{[3\cdot(x-3)]} + \frac{14}{[3\cdot(x+3)]} - \frac{3}{(x+2)}$$

Use the "coeffs" keyword to treat an expression as a polynomial and write out the coefficients. Specify either a variable or a function as an argument to the keyword.

$$3\cdot b\cdot x^4 - \pi\cdot x^2 + \frac{2}{3}\cdot x - .3\cdot a\cdot b \text{ coeffs, x} \rightarrow \begin{bmatrix} -.3\cdot a\cdot b \\ \frac{2}{3} \\ -\pi \\ 0 \\ 3\cdot b \end{bmatrix}$$

$$\sin(x) + 2\cdot \sin(x)^2 \text{ coeffs, sin}(x) \rightarrow \begin{bmatrix} 0 \\ 1 \\ 2 \end{bmatrix}$$

Comments   The symbolic processor tries to factor the denominator of the expression into linear or quadratic factors having integer coefficients. If it succeeds, it expands the expression into a sum of fractions with these factors as denominators. All constants in the selected expression must be integers or fractions; Mathcad does not expand an expression that contains decimal points.

Another way to convert an expression to a partial fraction is to click on the variable *var* anywhere in the expression. Then choose **Variable⇒Convert to Partial Fraction** from the **Symbolics** menu.

expand

Syntax   expand, *expr*

Description   Expands all powers and products of sums in an expression except for the subexpression *expr*. The argument *expr* is optional. The entire expression is expanded if the argument *expr* is omitted.

Example

Expanding expressions

$$(x + y)^4 \text{ expand } \rightarrow x^4 + 4 \cdot x^3 \cdot y + 6 \cdot x^2 \cdot y^2 + 4 \cdot x \cdot y^3 + y^4$$

$$\cos(5 \cdot x) \text{ expand } \rightarrow 16 \cdot \cos(x)^5 - 20 \cdot \cos(x)^3 + 5 \cdot \cos(x)$$

$$(x + 1) \cdot (y + z) \text{ expand}, x + 1 \rightarrow (x + 1) \cdot y + (x + 1) \cdot z$$

Factoring expressions

$$8238913765711 \text{ factor } \rightarrow (73) \cdot (112861832407)$$

$$\frac{1}{x - 1} + \frac{x}{x + 3} - \frac{2 \cdot x}{x + 2} \text{ factor } \rightarrow \frac{-\left(2 \cdot x^2 - 9 \cdot x - 6 + x^3\right)}{\left[(x - 1) \cdot [(x + 3) \cdot (x + 2)]\right]}$$

$$x^2 - 2 \text{ factor}, \sqrt{2} \rightarrow \left(x + \sqrt{2}\right) \cdot \left(x - \sqrt{2}\right)$$

Collecting terms

$$x^2 - a \cdot y \cdot x^2 + 2 \cdot y^2 \cdot x - x \text{ collect}, x \rightarrow (1 - a \cdot y) \cdot x^2 + \left(2 \cdot y^2 - 1\right) \cdot x$$

$$x^2 - a \cdot y \cdot x^2 + b \cdot y \cdot x - a \cdot x \cdot y \text{ collect}, x, y \rightarrow (1 - a \cdot y) \cdot x^2 + (b - a) \cdot y \cdot x$$

Comments   Another way to expand an expression is to enclose the expression between the editing lines and choose **Expand** from the **Symbolics** menu.

factor

Syntax   factor, *expr*

Description   Factors an expression into a product, if the entire expression can be written as a product.
If the expression is a single integer, Mathcad factors it into powers of primes.
If the expression is a polynomial or rational function, Mathcad factors it into powers of lower-order polynomials or rational functions. The argument *expr* is optional.

See also   expand for example

Comments   If you want to factor an expression over certain radicals, follow the factor keyword with a comma and the radicals.

You may be able to simplify an expression by factoring subexpressions, even if the expression taken as a whole can't be factored. To do so, enclose a subexpression between the editing lines and choose **Factor** from the **Symbolics** menu. You can also use the **Factor** menu command to factor an entire expression, but the **Symbolics** menu commands do not use any previous definitions in your worksheet and do not automatically update.

float

Syntax float, *m*

Description Displays a floating point value with *m* places of precision whenever possible. If the argument *m*, an integer, is omitted, the default precision is 20.

See also assume for example

Comments Another way to perform floating point evaluation on an expression is to enclose the expression between the editing lines and choose **Evaluate⇒Floating Point** from the **Symbolics** menu. In the Floating Point dialog box, specify the number of digits to the right of the decimal point.

fourier

Syntax fourier, *var*

Description Evaluates the Fourier transform of an expression with respect to the variable *var*.

Example

Press [Ctrl] [Shift] . to insert a transform keyword.

$$\text{Dirac}(t) \ \text{fourier}, t \ \rightarrow \ 1$$

$$\frac{3}{1+x^2} \ \text{invfourier}, x \ \rightarrow \ \frac{3}{2} \cdot \exp(-t) \cdot \Phi(t) + \frac{3}{2} \cdot \exp(t) \cdot \Phi(-t)$$

$$\exp(-a \cdot t) \ \text{laplace}, t \ \rightarrow \ \frac{1}{(s+a)}$$

$$\frac{s}{s+a} \ \text{invlaplace}, s \ \rightarrow \ \Delta(t) - a \cdot \exp(-a \cdot t)$$

← $\Delta(t)$ is an impulse at t=0. Although not numerically defined, Mathcad's symbolic processor recognizes this function. $\Delta(t)$ is also known as the Dirac function.

$$\sin\left(\frac{\pi}{2} \cdot t\right) \ \text{ztrans}, t \ \rightarrow \ \frac{z}{(1+z^2)}$$

$$\frac{z}{z-2} \ \text{invztrans}, z \ \rightarrow \ 2^n$$

Comments Mathcad returns a function of ω given by: $\int_{-\infty}^{+\infty} f(t)e^{-i\omega t}dt$ where $f(t)$ is the expression to be transformed.

Mathcad returns a function in the variable ω when you perform a Fourier transform because this is a commonly used variable name in this context. If the expression you are transforming already contains an ω, Mathcad avoids ambiguity by returning a function of the variable ωω instead.

Another way to evaluate the Fourier transform of an expression is to enter the expression and click on the transform variable. Then choose **Transform⇒Fourier** from the **Symbolics** menu.

invfourier

Syntax invfourier, *var*

Description Evaluates the inverse Fourier transform of an expression with respect to the variable *var*.

See also fourier for example

Comments Mathcad returns a function of *t* given by: $\frac{1}{2\pi}\int_{-\infty}^{+\infty} F(\omega)e^{i\omega t}d\omega$ where $F(\omega)$ is the expression to be transformed.

Mathcad returns a function in the variable *t* when you perform an inverse Fourier transform because this is a commonly used variable name in this context. If the expression you are transforming already contains a *t*, Mathcad avoids ambiguity by returning a function of the variable *tt* instead.

Another way to evaluate the inverse Fourier transform of an expression is to enter the expression and click on the transform variable. Then choose **Transform⇒Inverse Fourier** from the **Symbolics** menu.

invlaplace

Syntax	invlaplace, *var*
Description	Evaluates the inverse Laplace transform of an expression with respect to the variable *var*.
See also	fourier for example
Comments	Mathcad returns a function of *t* given by: $\dfrac{1}{2\pi i}\displaystyle\int_{\sigma-i\infty}^{\sigma+i\infty}F(s)e^{st}dt$ where $F(s)$ is the expression to

be transformed and all singularities of $F(s)$ are to the left of the line $\text{Re}(s) = \sigma$.

Mathcad returns a function in the variable *t* when you perform an inverse Laplace transform because this is a commonly used variable name in this context. If the expression you are transforming already contains a *t*, Mathcad avoids ambiguity by returning a function of the variable *tt* instead.

Another way to evaluate the inverse Laplace transform of an expression is to enter the expression and click on the transform variable. Then choose **Transform⇒Inverse Laplace** from the **Symbolics** menu.

invztrans

Syntax	invztrans, *var*
Description	Evaluates the inverse *z*-transform of an expression with respect to the variable *var*.
See also	fourier for example
Comments	Mathcad returns a function of *n* given by a contour integral around the origin: $\dfrac{1}{2\pi i}\displaystyle\int_{C}F(z)z^{n-1}dz$

where $F(z)$ is the expression to be transformed and C is a contour enclosing all singularities of the integrand.

Mathcad returns a function in the variable *n* when you perform an inverse *z*-transform since this is a commonly used variable name in this context. If the expression you are transforming already contains an *n*, Mathcad avoids ambiguity by returning a function of the variable *nn* instead.

Another way to evaluate the inverse *z*-transform of an expression is to enter the expression and click on the transform variable. Then choose **Transform⇒Inverse Z** from the **Symbolics** menu.

laplace

Syntax	laplace, *var*
Description	Evaluates the Laplace transform of an expression with respect to the variable *var*.
See also	fourier for example
Comments	Mathcad returns a function of *s* given by: $\displaystyle\int_{0}^{+\infty}f(t)e^{-st}dt$, where $f(t)$ is the expression to be transformed.

Mathcad returns a function in the variable s when you perform a Laplace transform since this is a commonly used variable name in this context. If the expression you are transforming already contains an s, Mathcad avoids ambiguity by returning a function of the variable ss instead.

Another way to evaluate the Laplace transform of an expression is to enter the expression and click on the transform variable. Then choose **Transform$\Rightarrow$Laplace** from the **Symbolics** menu.

series

Syntax   series, $var=z, m$

Description   Expands an expression in one or more variables, var, around the point z. The order of expansion is m. Arguments z and m are optional. By default, the expansion is taken around zero and is a polynomial of order six.

Example

Generating a series around the point x=0:

$$\ln(x + y) \ \text{series}, x \ \rightarrow \ \ln(y) + \frac{x}{y} - \frac{1}{2}\cdot\frac{x^2}{y^2} + \frac{1}{3}\cdot\frac{x^3}{y^3} - \frac{1}{4}\cdot\frac{x^4}{y^4} + \frac{1}{5}\cdot\frac{x^5}{y^5}$$

Generating a series for sin(x) with order 6:

$$\sin(x) \ \text{series}, x, 6 \ \rightarrow \ x - \frac{1}{6}\cdot x^3 + \frac{1}{120}\cdot x^5$$

Generating a series around the point x=1 and y=0 but show only those terms whose exponents sum to less than 3:

$$e^x + y \ \text{series}, x = 1, y, 3 \rightarrow \exp(1) + \exp(1)\cdot(x - 1) + y + \frac{1}{2}\cdot\exp(1)\cdot(x - 1)^2$$

$\uparrow$

Press [Ctrl] = for the equal sign.

Comments   Mathcad finds Taylor series (series in nonnegative powers of the variable) for functions that are analytic at 0, and Laurent series for functions that have a pole of finite order at 0. To develop a series with a center other than 0, the argument to the series keyword should be of the form $var=z$, where z is any real or complex number. For example, series, $x=1$ expands around the point $x=1$. Press **[Ctrl] =** for the equal sign.

To expand a series around more than one variable, separate the variables by commas. The last line in the example above shows an expression expanded around x and y.

Another way to generate a series expansion is to enter the expression and click on a variable for which you want to find a series expansion. Then choose **Variable$\Rightarrow$Expand to Series** from the **Symbolics** menu. A dialog box will prompt you for the order of the series. This command is limited to a series in a single variable; any other variables in the expression will be treated as constants. The results also contain the error term using the O notation. Before you use the series for further calculations, you will need to delete this error term.

When using the approximations you get from the symbolic processor, keep in mind that the Taylor series for a function may converge only in some small interval around the center. Furthermore, functions like sin or exp have series with infinitely many terms, while the polynomials returned by Mathcad have only a few terms (how many depends on the order you select). Thus, when you approximate a function by the polynomial returned by Mathcad, the approximation will be reasonably accurate close to the center, but may be quite inaccurate for values far from the center.

simplify

Syntax

simplify

Description

Simplifies an expression by performing arithmetic, canceling common factors, and using basic trigonometric and inverse function identities.

To control the simplification, use the following modifiers:

assume=real simplifies on the assumption that all the indeterminates in the expression are real;

assume=RealRange(*a,b*) simplifies on the assumption that all the indeterminates are real and are between *a* and *b*, where *a* and *b* are real numbers or infinity ([**Ctrl**]*Z*);

trig, simplifies a trigonometric expression by applying only the following identities:

$$\sin(x)^2 + \cos(x)^2 = 1 \qquad \cosh(x)^2 - \sinh(x)^2 = 1,$$

but does not simplify the expression by simplifying logarithms, powers, or radicals.

Example

$$\frac{x^2 - 3 \cdot x - 4}{x - 4} + 2 \cdot x - 5 \text{ simplify } \rightarrow 3 \cdot x - 4$$

$$e^{2 \ln(a)} \text{ simplify } \rightarrow a^2$$

$$\sin(\ln(a \cdot b))^2 \text{ simplify } \rightarrow 1 - \cos(\ln(a) + \ln(b))^2$$

$$\sin(\ln(a \cdot b))^2 \text{ simplify , trig } \rightarrow 1 - \cos(\ln(a \cdot b))^2$$

$$\left(2^b\right)^c \text{ simplify } \rightarrow \left(2^b\right)^c$$

$$\left(2^b\right)^c \text{ simplify , assume = real } \rightarrow 2^{b \cdot c} \quad \text{<-- Press [Ctrl] = for the equal sign.}$$

$$\sqrt{x^2} \text{ simplify } \rightarrow \text{csgn}(x) \cdot x$$

$$\sqrt{x^2} \text{ simplify , assume = RealRange}(-10, -5) \rightarrow -x \quad \text{<-- Press [Ctrl] = for the equal sign.}$$

Comments

You can also simplify an expression by placing it between the two editing lines and choosing **Simplify** from the **Symbolics** menu. This method is useful when you want to simplify parts of an expression. Mathcad may sometimes be able to simplify parts of an expression even when it cannot simplify the entire expression. If simplifying the entire expression doesn't give the answer you want, try selecting subexpressions and choosing **Simplify** from the **Symbolics** menu. If Mathcad can't simplify an expression any further, you'll just get the original expression back as the answer.

In general, when you simplify an expression, the simplified result will have the same numerical behavior as the original expression. However, when the expression includes functions with more than one branch, such as square root or the inverse trigonometric functions, the symbolic answer may differ from a numerical answer. For example, simplifying asin(sin(θ)) yields θ, but this equation holds true numerically in Mathcad only when θ is a number between −π/2 and π/2.

solve

Syntax   solve, *var*

Description   Solves an equation for the variable *var* or solves a system of equations for the variables in a
                  vector *var*.

Examples

$$A1 = \frac{L}{r^2} + 2 \cdot C \text{ solve}, r \rightarrow \begin{bmatrix} \frac{1}{(A1 - 2 \cdot C)} \cdot \sqrt{(A1 - 2 \cdot C) \cdot L} \\ \frac{-1}{(A1 - 2 \cdot C)} \cdot \sqrt{(A1 - 2 \cdot C) \cdot L} \end{bmatrix}$$

$a := 34$

$$\frac{1}{2} \cdot x^2 + x = -2 + a \text{ solve}, x \rightarrow \begin{bmatrix} -1 + \sqrt{65} \\ -1 - \sqrt{65} \end{bmatrix}$$ Use [Crtr] = for the equal sign.

$$\frac{\alpha \cdot f + 1}{f - \beta} = e^{-\alpha} \text{ solve}, f \rightarrow \frac{-(1 + \exp(-\alpha) \cdot \beta)}{(\alpha - \exp(-\alpha))}$$

$$x^3 - 5 \cdot x^2 - 4 \cdot x + 20 > 0 \text{ solve}, x \rightarrow \begin{bmatrix} (-2 < x) \cdot (x < 2) \\ 5 < x \end{bmatrix}$$

$e^t + 1 \text{ solve}, t \rightarrow i \cdot \pi$ You don't need =0 when finding roots.

Figure 18-1: Solving equations, solving inequalities, and finding roots.

Using the "solve" keyword (press [Ctrl]+[Shift]+Period):

$$\begin{bmatrix} x + 2 \cdot \pi \cdot y = a \\ 4 \cdot x + y = b \end{bmatrix} \text{ solve}, \begin{bmatrix} x \\ y \end{bmatrix} \rightarrow \begin{bmatrix} \frac{1}{(-1 + 8 \cdot \pi)} \cdot (2 \cdot \pi \cdot b - a) \\ \frac{-(-4 \cdot a + b)}{(-1 + 8 \cdot \pi)} \end{bmatrix}$$

Using a solve block:

Given $x + 2 \cdot \pi \cdot y = a$ <- Use [Ctrl]= to type the equal sign.

         $4 \cdot x + y = b$

$$\text{Find}(x, y) \rightarrow \begin{bmatrix} \frac{1}{(-1 + 8 \cdot \pi)} \cdot (2 \cdot \pi \cdot b - a) \\ \frac{-(-4 \cdot a + b)}{(-1 + 8 \cdot \pi)} \end{bmatrix}$$

Figure 18-2: Solving a system of equations symbolically.

Comments   Solving equations symbolically is far more difficult than solving them numerically. The symbolic
                  solver sometimes does not give a solution. Many problems can only be solved via numerical
                  approach and many more yield symbolic solutions too lengthy to be useful.

Another way to solve for a variable is to enter the equation, click on the variable you want to solve for in an equation, and choose **Variable⇒Solve** from the **Symbolics** menu.

You can use either the symbolic solve keyword or a solve block, as illustrated above, to solve a system of equations symbolically. No initial guess values are necessary for symbolic schemes.

substitute

Syntax   substitute, *var1*= *var2*

Description   Replaces all occurrences of a variable *var1* with an expression or variable *var2*.
Press [**Ctrl**] = for the equal sign.

Example

To substitute x for z in the expression below, use the "substitute" keyword and an argument indicating which variable to replace with which expression. Use [Ctrl] = for the equal sign in the argument.

$$z^2 + \frac{2}{z} \text{ substitute}, z = x \quad \rightarrow \quad x^2 + \frac{2}{x}$$

Substituting f(sin(x)) for y:

$$\sqrt{1 + y^2} \text{ substitute}, y = f(\sin(x)) \quad \rightarrow \quad \sqrt{1 + f(\sin(x))^2}$$

Comments   Mathcad does not substitute a variable for an entire vector or a matrix. You can, however, substitute a scalar expression for a variable that occurs in a matrix.
To do so, follow these steps:

1. Select the expression that will replace the variable and choose **Copy** from the **Edit** menu.

2. Click on an occurrence of the variable you want to replace and choose **Variable⇒Substitute** from the **Symbolics** menu. You can also use this menu command to perform a substitution in any expression.

ztrans

Syntax   ztrans, *var*

Description   Evaluates the *z*-transform of an expression with respect to the variable *var*.

See also   fourier for example

Comments   Mathcad returns a function of *z* given by: $\sum_{n=0}^{+\infty} f(n)z^{-n}$, where $f(n)$ is the expression to be transformed.

Mathcad returns a function in the variable *z* when you perform a *z*-transform since this is a commonly used variable name in this context. If the expression you are transforming already contains a *z*, Mathcad avoids ambiguity by returning a function of the variable *zz* instead.

Another way to evaluate the *z*-transform of an expression is to enter the expression and click on the transform variable. Then choose **Transform⇒Z** from the **Symbolics** menu.

Appendices

- Appendix A: Special Functions
- Appendix B: SI Units
- Appendix C: CGS units
- Appendix D: U.S. Customary Units
- Appendix E: MKS Units
- Appendix F: Predefined Variables
- Appendix G: Suffixes for Numbers
- Appendix H: Greek Letters
- Appendix I: Arrow and Movement Keys
- Appendix J: Function Keys
- Appendix K: ASCII codes
- Appendix L: References

Appendix A: Special Functions

Mathcad sometimes returns a symbolic expression in terms of a function that isn't one of Mathcad's built-in functions.

You can define many of these functions in Mathcad. See the "Other Special Functions" topic in the QuickSheets under the Help menu for examples.

The list below gives definitions for these functions. Except for Ei, erf, and Zeta, all of which involve infinite sums, and also W, you can use such definitions to calculate numerical values in Mathcad.

Function Definitions

Name	Definition

Euler's constant

$$\gamma = \lim_{n \to \infty}\left(\sum_{k=1}^{n}\frac{1}{k} - \ln(n)\right) = 0.57721566\ldots$$

Hyperbolic cosine integral

$$\mathrm{Chi}(x) = \gamma + \ln(x) + \int_0^x \frac{\cosh(t) - 1}{t}\,dt$$

Cosine integral

$$\mathrm{Ci}(x) = \gamma + \ln(x) + \int_0^x \frac{\cos(t) - 1}{t}\,dt$$

Dilogarithm function

$$\mathrm{dilog}(x) = \int_1^x \frac{\ln(t)}{1 - t}\,dt$$

Dirac delta (unit impulse) function

$$\mathrm{Dirac}(x) = 0 \quad \text{if } x \text{ is not zero.}$$

$$\int_{-\infty}^{\infty} \mathrm{Dirac}(x)\,dx = 1$$

Exponential integral

$$\mathrm{Ei}(x) = \gamma + \ln(x) + \sum_{n=1}^{\infty} \frac{x^n}{n \cdot n!} \quad (x > 0)$$

Complex error function

$$\mathrm{erf}(z) = \frac{2}{\sqrt{\pi}} \sum_{n=0}^{\infty} \frac{(-1)^n z^{2n+1}}{n!(2n+1)} \quad \text{(for complex } z\text{)}$$

Fresnel cosine integral

$$\mathrm{FresnelC}(x) = \int_0^x \cos\left(\frac{\pi}{2}t^2\right) dt$$

Fresnel sine integral

$$\mathrm{FresnelS}(x) = \int_0^x \sin\left(\frac{\pi}{2}t^2\right) dt$$

Incomplete elliptic integral of the second kind

$$\mathrm{LegendreE}(x, k) = \int_0^x \left(\frac{1 - k^2 \cdot t^2}{1 - t^2}\right)^{1/2} dt$$

Complete elliptic integral of the second kind

$$\mathrm{LegendreEc}(k) = \mathrm{LegendreE}(1, k)$$

Associated complete elliptic integral of the second kind

$$\mathrm{LegendreEc1}(k) = \mathrm{LegendreEc}(\sqrt{1 - k^2})$$

Incomplete elliptic integral of the first kind	$\mathrm{Legendre\,F}(x, k) = \int_0^x \dfrac{1}{\sqrt{(1 - t^2)(1 - k^2 \cdot t^2)}}\,dt$

Complete elliptic integral of the first kind

$$\mathrm{Legendre\,Kc}(k) = \mathrm{Legendre\,F}(1, k)$$

Associated complete elliptic integral of the first kind

$$\mathrm{Legendre\,Kc1}(k) = \mathrm{Legendre\,Kc}(\sqrt{1 - k^2})$$

Incomplete elliptic integral of the third kind

$$\mathrm{Legendre\,Pi}(x, n, k) = \int_0^x \frac{1}{\sqrt{(1 - n^2 \cdot t^2)}\sqrt{(1 - t^2)(1 - k^2 \cdot t^2)}}\,dt$$

Complete elliptic integral of the third kind

$$\mathrm{Legendre\,Pic}(n, k) = \mathrm{Legendre\,Pi}(1, n, k)$$

Associated complete elliptic integral of the third kind

$$\mathrm{Legendre\,Pic1}(k) = \mathrm{Legendre\,Pic}(n, \sqrt{1 - k^2})$$

Digamma function

$$\mathrm{Psi}(x) = \frac{d}{dx}\ln(\Gamma(x))$$

Polygamma function

$$\mathrm{Psi}(n, k) = \frac{d^n}{dx^n}\mathrm{Psi}(x)$$

Hyperbolic sine integral

$$\mathrm{Shi}(x) = \int_0^x \frac{\sinh(t)}{t}\,dt$$

Sine integral

$$\mathrm{Si}(x) = \int_0^x \frac{\sin(t)}{t}\,dt$$

Lambert W function

$\mathrm{W}(x)$ is the principal branch of a function satisfying $\mathrm{W}(x) \cdot \exp(\mathrm{W}(x)) = x$.
$\mathrm{W}(n, x)$ is the nth branch of $\mathrm{W}(x)$.

Riemann Zeta function

$$\mathrm{Zeta}(x) = \sum_{n=1}^{\infty} \frac{1}{n^x} \quad (x > 1)$$

Comments

The Psi function and Γ appear frequently in the results of *indefinite* sums and products. If you use a single variable name rather than a full range in the index placeholder of a summation or product, and you choose **Evaluate Symbolically** or another symbolic evaluation command, Mathcad will attempt to calculate an indefinite sum or product of the expression in the main placeholder. The indefinite sum of $f(i)$ is an expression $S(i)$ for which $S(i + 1) - S(i) = f(i)$.

The indefinite product of $f(i)$ is an expression $P(i)$ for which $\dfrac{P(i + 1)}{P(i)} = f(i)$.

Appendix B: SI Units

Base Units

m (meter), *length*   kg (kilogram), *mass*   s (second), *time*
A (ampere), *current*   K (kelvin), *temperature*   cd (candela), *luminosity*
mole or mol, *substance*

Angular Measure

$rad = 1$ $deg = \frac{\pi}{180} \cdot rad$ $sr = 1 \cdot sr$

Length

$cm = 0.01 \cdot m$ $km = 1000 \cdot m$ $mm = 0.001 \cdot m$
$ft = 0.3048 \cdot m$ $in = 2.54 \cdot cm$ $yd = 3 \cdot ft$
$mi = 5280 \cdot ft$

Mass

$gm = 10^{-3} \cdot kg$ $tonne = 1000 \cdot kg$ $lb = 453.59237 \cdot gm$
$mg = 10^{-3} \cdot gm$ $ton = 2000 \cdot lb$ $slug = 32.174 \cdot lb$
$oz = \frac{lb}{16}$

Time

$min = 60 \cdot s$ $hr = 3600 \cdot s$ $day = 24 \cdot hr$
$yr = 365.2422 \cdot day$

Area, Volume

$hectare = 10^4 \cdot m^2$ $acre = 4840 \cdot yd^2$ $L = 0.001 \cdot m^3$
$mL = 10^{-3} \cdot L$ $fl\_oz = 29.57353 \cdot cm^3$ $gal = 128 \cdot fl\_oz$

Velocity, Acceleration

$mph = \frac{mi}{hr}$ $kph = \frac{km}{hr}$ $g = 9.80665 \cdot \frac{m}{s^2}$

Force, Energy, Power

$N = kg \cdot \frac{m}{s^2}$ $dyne = 10^{-5} \cdot N$ $lbf = g \cdot lb$
$kgf = g \cdot kg$ $J = N \cdot m$ $erg = 10^{-7} \cdot J$
$cal = 4.1868 \cdot J$ $kcal = 1000 \cdot cal$ $BTU = 1.05506 \cdot 10^3 \cdot J$
$W = \frac{J}{s}$ $kW = 1000 \cdot W$ $hp = 550 \cdot \frac{ft \cdot lbf}{s}$

Pressure, Viscosity

$Pa = \frac{N}{m^2}$ $psi = \frac{lbf}{in^2}$ $atm = 1.01325 \cdot 10^5 \cdot Pa$

$\text{in\_Hg} = 3.37686 \cdot 10^3 \cdot \text{Pa}$ $\text{torr} = 1.33322 \cdot 10^2 \cdot \text{Pa}$ $\text{stokes} = 10^{-4} \cdot \dfrac{m^2}{s}$

$\text{poise} = 0.1 \cdot \text{Pa} \cdot s$

Electrical

$C = A \cdot s$ $V = \dfrac{J}{C}$ $mV = 10^{-3} \cdot V$

$kV = 10^3 \cdot V$ $\Omega = \dfrac{V}{A}$ $k\Omega = 10^3 \cdot \Omega$

$M\Omega = 10^6 \cdot \Omega$ $S = \dfrac{1}{\Omega}$ $\text{mho} = \dfrac{1}{\Omega}$

$H = \dfrac{V}{A} \cdot s$ $\mu H = 10^{-6} \cdot H$ $mH = 10^{-3} \cdot H$

$\mu A = 10^{-6} \cdot A$ $mA = 10^{-3} \cdot A$ $kA = 10^3 \cdot A$

$F = \dfrac{C}{V}$ $pF = 10^{-12} \cdot F$ $nF = 10^{-9} \cdot F$

$\mu F = 10^{-6} \cdot F$ $Wb = V \cdot s$

$Oe = \dfrac{1000}{4 \cdot \pi} \cdot \dfrac{A}{m}$ $T = \dfrac{Wb}{m^2}$ $\text{gauss} = 10^{-4} \cdot T$

Frequency, Activity

$Hz = \dfrac{1}{s}$ $kHz = 10^3 \cdot Hz$ $MHz = 10^6 \cdot Hz$

$GHz = 10^9 \cdot Hz$ $Bq = \dfrac{1}{s}$ $Hza = 2 \cdot \pi \cdot Hz$

Temperature

$R = 0.556 \cdot K$

Dose

$Gy = \dfrac{J}{kg}$ $Sv = \dfrac{J}{kg}$

Luminous Flux, Illuminance

$lm = cd \cdot sr$ $lx = \dfrac{cd \cdot st}{m^2}$

Appendix C: CGS units

Base Units

cm (centimeter), *length*   gm (gram), *mass*   sec (second), *time*

coul (coulomb), *charge*   K (kelvin), *temperature*

Angular Measure

rad = 1

$$\deg = \frac{\pi}{180} \cdot \text{rad}$$

Length

m = 100 · cm   km = 1000 · m   mm = 0.1 · cm

ft = 30.48 · cm   in = 2.54 · cm   yd = 3 · ft

mi = 5280 · ft

Mass

kg = 1000 · gm   tonne = 1000 · kg   lb = 453.59237 · gm

mg = 10^{-3} · gm   ton = 2000 · lb   slug = 32.174 · lb

$oz = \dfrac{lb}{16}$

Time

min = 60 · sec   hr = 3600 · sec   day = 24 · hr

yr = 365.2422 · day

Area, Volume

hectare = $10^8 \cdot \text{cm}^2$ acre = 4840 · yd^2 liter = 1000 · cm^3

mL = cm^3 fl_oz = 29.57353 · cm^3 gal = 128 · fl_oz

Velocity, Acceleration

$mph = \dfrac{mi}{hr}$ $kph = \dfrac{km}{hr}$ $g = 980.665 \cdot \dfrac{cm}{sec^2}$

$c = 2.997925 \cdot 10^{10} \cdot \dfrac{cm}{sec}$ $c\_ = c \cdot \dfrac{sec}{m}$

Force, Energy, Power

$dyne = gm \cdot \dfrac{cm}{sec^2}$ newton = 10^5 · dyne   lbf = g · lb

kgf = g · kg   erg = dyne · cm   joule = 10^7 · erg

cal = 4.1868 · 10^7 · erg   BTU = 1.05506 · 10^{10} · erg   kcal = 1000 · cal

$watt = \dfrac{joule}{sec}$ kW = 1000 · watt $hp = 550 \cdot \dfrac{ft \cdot lbf}{sec}$

Pressure, Viscosity

$$Pa = 10 \cdot \frac{dyne}{cm^2} \qquad psi = \frac{lbf}{in^2} \qquad atm = 1.01325 \cdot 10^5 \cdot Pa$$

$$in\_Hg = 3.38638 \cdot 10^3 \cdot Pa \qquad torr = 1.33322 \cdot 10^2 \cdot Pa \qquad stokes = \frac{cm^2}{sec}$$

$$poise = 0.1 \cdot Pa \cdot sec$$

Electrical

These are CGS-esu units, based only on mass, length, and time. The "stat" units are defined in terms of dyne, cm, and sec.

$$statamp = dyne^{0.5} \cdot cm \cdot sec^{-1} \qquad statcoul = dyne^{0.5} \cdot cm \qquad statvolt = dyne^{0.5}$$

$$statohm = sec \cdot cm^{-1} \qquad statsiemens = cm \cdot sec^{-1} \qquad statfarad = cm$$

$$statweber = dyne^{0.5} \cdot cm \qquad stathenry = sec^2 \cdot cm^{-1} \qquad stattesla = dyne^{0.5} \cdot cm \cdot sec^{-2}$$

Frequency

$$Hz = \frac{1}{sec} \qquad kHz = 10^3 \cdot Hz \qquad MHz = 10^6 \cdot Hz$$

$$GHz = 10^9 \cdot Hz \qquad Hza = 2 \cdot \pi \cdot Hz$$

Temperature

$$R = 0.556 \cdot K$$

Conversions to SI Units

$$amp = \frac{c}{10} \cdot statamp \qquad volt = \frac{watt}{amp} \qquad ohm = \frac{volt}{amp}$$

$$coul = amp \cdot sec \qquad farad = \frac{coul}{volt} \qquad henry = volt \cdot \frac{sec}{amp}$$

Appendix D: U.S. Customary Units

Base Units

ft (foot), *length*   lb (pound), *mass*   sec (second), *time*

coul (coulomb), *charge*   K (kelvin), *temperature*

Angular Measure

rad = 1

$$\text{deg} = \frac{\pi}{180} \cdot \text{rad}$$

Length

$$\text{in} = \frac{\text{ft}}{12} \qquad\qquad \text{m} = \frac{\text{ft}}{0.3048} \qquad\qquad \text{yd} = 3 \cdot \text{ft}$$

$$\text{cm} = 0.01 \cdot \text{m} \qquad\qquad \text{mi} = 5280 \cdot \text{ft} \qquad\qquad \text{km} = 1000 \cdot \text{m}$$

$$\text{mm} = 0.001 \cdot \text{m}$$

Mass

$$\text{slug} = 32.174 \cdot \text{lb} \qquad\qquad \text{oz} = \frac{\text{lb}}{16} \qquad\qquad \text{ton} = 2000 \cdot \text{lb}$$

$$\text{kg} = \frac{\text{lb}}{0.45359237} \qquad\qquad \text{tonne} = 1000 \cdot \text{kg} \qquad\qquad \text{gm} = 10^{-3} \cdot \text{kg}$$

$$\text{mg} = 10^{-3} \cdot \text{gm}$$

Time

$$\text{min} = 60 \cdot \text{sec} \qquad\qquad \text{hr} = 3600 \cdot \text{sec} \qquad\qquad \text{day} = 24 \cdot \text{hr}$$

$$\text{yr} = 365.2422 \cdot \text{day}$$

Area, Volume

$$\text{acre} = 4840 \cdot \text{yd}^2 \qquad\qquad \text{hectare} = 10^4 \cdot \text{m}^2 \qquad\qquad \text{fl\_oz} = 29.57353 \cdot \text{cm}^3$$

$$\text{liter} = 0.035 \cdot \text{ft}^3 \qquad\qquad \text{mL} = 10^{-3} \cdot \text{liter} \qquad\qquad \text{gal} = 128 \cdot \text{fl\_oz}$$

Velocity, Acceleration

$$\text{mph} = \frac{\text{mi}}{\text{hr}} \qquad\qquad \text{kph} = \frac{\text{km}}{\text{hr}} \qquad\qquad \text{g} = 32.174 \cdot \frac{\text{ft}}{\text{sec}^2}$$

Force, Energy, Power

$$\text{lbf} = \text{g} \cdot \text{lb} \qquad\qquad \text{newton} = \text{kg} \cdot \frac{\text{m}}{\text{sec}^2} \qquad\qquad \text{dyne} = 10^{-5} \cdot \text{newton}$$

$$\text{kgf} = \text{g} \cdot \text{kg} \qquad\qquad \text{joule} = \text{newton} \cdot \text{m} \qquad\qquad \text{erg} = 10^{-7} \cdot \text{joule}$$

$$\text{cal} = 4.1868 \cdot \text{joule} \qquad\qquad \text{kcal} = 1000 \cdot \text{cal} \qquad\qquad \text{BTU} = 1.05506 \cdot 10^3 \cdot \text{joule}$$

$$\text{watt} = \frac{\text{joule}}{\text{sec}} \qquad\qquad \text{hp} = 550 \cdot \frac{\text{ft} \cdot \text{lbf}}{\text{sec}} \qquad\qquad \text{kW} = 1000 \cdot \text{watt}$$

Pressure, Viscosity

$$psi = \frac{lbf}{in^2}$$

$$Pa = \frac{newton}{m^2}$$

$$atm = 1.01325 \cdot 10^5 \cdot Pa$$

$$in\_Hg = 3.386 \cdot 10^3 \cdot Pa$$

$$torr = 1.333 \cdot 10^2 \cdot Pa$$

$$stokes = \frac{cm^2}{sec}$$

$$poise = 0.1 \cdot Pa \cdot sec$$

Electrical

$$volt = \frac{watt}{amp}$$

$$mV = 10^{-3} \cdot volt$$

$$KV = 10^3 \cdot volt$$

$$ohm = \frac{volt}{amp}$$

$$mho = \frac{1}{ohm}$$

$$siemens = \frac{1}{ohm}$$

$$\Omega = ohm$$

$$K\Omega = 10^3 \cdot ohm$$

$$M\Omega = 10^6 \cdot ohm$$

$$henry = \frac{weber}{amp}$$

$$\mu H = 10^{-6} \cdot henry$$

$$mH = 10^{-3} \cdot henry$$

$$amp = \frac{coul}{sec}$$

$$\mu A = 10^{-6} \cdot amp$$

$$mA = 10^{-3} \cdot amp$$

$$KA = 10^3 \cdot amp$$

$$farad = \frac{coul}{volt}$$

$$pF = 10^{-12} \cdot farad$$

$$nF = 10^{-9} \cdot farad$$

$$\mu F = 10^{-6} \cdot farad$$

$$weber = volt \cdot sec$$

$$oersted = \frac{1000}{4 \cdot \pi} \cdot \frac{amp}{m}$$

$$tesla = \frac{weber}{m^2}$$

$$gauss = 10^{-4} \cdot tesla$$

Frequency

$$Hz = \frac{1}{sec}$$

$$kHz = 10^3 \cdot Hz$$

$$MHz = 10^6 \cdot Hz$$

$$GHz = 10^9 \cdot Hz$$

$$Hza = 2 \cdot \pi \cdot Hz$$

Temperature

$$R = 0.556 \cdot K$$

Appendix E: MKS Units

Base Units

m (meter), *length*   kg (kilogram), *mass*   sec (second), *time*

coul (coulomb), *charge*   K (kelvin), *temperature*

Angular Measure

$rad = 1$

$$deg = \frac{\pi}{180} \cdot rad$$

Length

$cm = 0.01 \cdot m$ $km = 1000 \cdot m$ $mm = 0.001 \cdot m$

$ft = 0.3048 \cdot m$ $in = 2.54 \cdot cm$ $yd = 3 \cdot ft$

$mi = 5280 \cdot ft$

Mass

$gm = 10^{-3} \cdot kg$ $tonne = 1000 \cdot kg$ $lb = 453.59237 \cdot gm$

$mg = 10^{-3} \cdot gm$ $ton = 2000 \cdot lb$ $slug = 32.174 \cdot lb$

$oz = \frac{lb}{16}$

Time

$min = 60 \cdot sec$ $hr = 3600 \cdot sec$ $day = 24 \cdot hr$

$yr = 365.2422 \cdot day$

Area, Volume

$hectare = 10^4 \cdot m^2$ $acre = 4840 \cdot yd^2$ $liter = (0.1 \cdot m)^3$

$mL = 10^{-3} \cdot liter$ $fl\_oz = 29.57353 \cdot cm^3$ $gal = 128 \cdot fl\_oz$

Velocity, Acceleration

$$mph = \frac{mi}{hr}$$ $$kph = \frac{km}{hr}$$ $$g = 9.80665 \cdot \frac{m}{sec^2}$$

Force, Energy, Power

$$newton = kg \cdot \frac{m}{sec^2}$$ $dyne = 10^{-5} \cdot newton$ $lbf = g \cdot lb$

$kgf = g \cdot kg$ $joule = newton \cdot m$ $erg = 10^{-7} \cdot joule$

$cal = 4.1868 \cdot joule$ $kcal = 1000 \cdot cal$ $BTU = 1.05506 \cdot 10^3 \cdot joule$

$$watt = \frac{joule}{sec}$$ $kW = 1000 \cdot watt$ $$hp = 550 \cdot \frac{ft \cdot lbf}{sec}$$

Pressure, Viscosity

$$Pa = \frac{newton}{m^2} \qquad psi = \frac{lbf}{in^2} \qquad atm = 1.01325 \cdot 10^5 \cdot Pa$$

$$in\_Hg = 3.38638 \cdot 10^3 \cdot Pa \qquad torr = 1.33322 \cdot 10^2 \cdot Pa$$

$$stokes = 10^{-4} \cdot \frac{m^2}{sec}$$

$$poise = 0.1 \cdot Pa \cdot sec$$

Electrical

$$volt = \frac{watt}{amp} \qquad mV = 10^{-3} \cdot volt \qquad kV = 10^3 \cdot volt$$

$$ohm = \frac{volt}{amp} \qquad mho = \frac{1}{ohm} \qquad siemens = \frac{1}{ohm}$$

$$\Omega = ohm \qquad k\Omega = 10^3 \cdot ohm \qquad M\Omega = 10^6 \cdot ohm$$

$$henry = \frac{weber}{amp} \qquad \mu H = 10^{-6} \cdot henry \qquad mH = 10^{-3} \cdot henry$$

$$amp = \frac{coul}{sec} \qquad \mu A = 10^{-6} \cdot amp \qquad mA = 10^{-3} \cdot amp$$

$$kA = 10^3 \cdot amp \qquad farad = \frac{coul}{volt} \qquad pF = 10^{-12} \cdot farad$$

$$nF = 10^{-9} \cdot farad \qquad \mu F = 10^{-6} \cdot farad \qquad weber = volt \cdot sec$$

$$oersted = \frac{1000}{4 \cdot \pi} \cdot \frac{amp}{m} \qquad tesla = \frac{weber}{m^2} \qquad gauss = 10^{-4} \cdot tesla$$

Frequency

$$Hz = \frac{1}{sec} \qquad kHz = 10^3 \cdot Hz \qquad MHz = 10^6 \cdot Hz$$

$$GHz = 10^9 \cdot Hz \qquad Hza = 2 \cdot \pi \cdot Hz$$

Temperature

$$R = 0.556 \cdot K$$

Appendix F: Predefined Variables

Mathcad's predefined variables are listed here with their default starting values.

Constant=Value	Meaning
$\pi = 3.14159...$	Pi. Mathcad uses the value of π to 15 digits. To type π, press [Ctrl][Shift]p.
$e = 2.71828...$	The base of natural logarithms. Mathcad uses the value of e to 15 digits.
$\infty = 10^{307}$	Infinity. This symbol represents values larger than the largest real number representable in Mathcad (about 10^{307}). To type ∞, press [Ctrl][Shift]Z.
$\% = 0.01$	Percent. Use in expressions like **10*%** (appears as $10 \cdot \%$) or as a scaling unit at the end of an equation with an equal sign.
CTOL $= 10^{-3}$	Constraint tolerance used in solving and optimization functions: how closely a constraint must be met for a solution to be considered acceptable.
CWD $=$ "[system path]"	String corresponding to the working folder of the worksheet.
FRAME $= 0$	Counter for creating animation clips.
in$n = 0$	Input variables (**in0**, **in1**, etc.) in a Mathcad component in a MathConnex system. See the *MathConnex User's Guide* for details.
ORIGIN $= 0$	Array origin. Specifies the index of the first element in arrays.
PRNCOLWIDTH $= 8$	Column width used in writing files with *WRITEPRN* function.
PRNPRECISION $= 4$	Number of significant digits used when writing files with the *WRITEPRN* function.
TOL $= 10^{-3}$	Tolerance used in numerical approximation algorithms (integrals, equation solving, etc.): how close successive approximations must be for a solution to be returned. For more information, see the sections on the specific operation in question.

Appendix G: Suffixes for Numbers

The table below shows how Mathcad interprets numbers (sequences of alpha-numerics beginning with a number and ending with a letter).

Radix

Suffix	Example	Meaning
b, B	100001b	Binary
h, H	8BCh	Hexadecimal
o, O	1007o	Octal

Units and other

Suffix	Example	Meaning
i *or* j	4i, 1j, 3 + 1.5j	Imaginary
K	−273K	Standard absolute temperature unit
L	−2.54L	Standard length unit
M	2.2M	Standard mass unit
Q	−100Q	Standard charge unit
S	6.97S	Standard substance unit in SI unit system
T	3600T	Standard time unit
C	125C	Standard luminosity unit in SI unit system

Note Because Mathcad by default treats most expressions involving a number followed immediately by a letter to mean implied multiplication of a number by a variable name, you will need to backspace over the implied multiplication operator to create expressions like **4.5M**.

Appendix H: Greek Letters

To type a Greek letter into an equation or into text, press the Roman equivalent from the table below, followed by [**Ctrl**]**G**. Alternatively, use the Greek toolbar.

Name	Uppercase	Lowercase	Roman equivalent
alpha	A	α	A
beta	B	β	B
chi	X	χ	C
delta	Δ	δ	D
epsilon	E	ε	E
eta	H	η	H
gamma	Γ	γ	G
iota	I	ι	I
kappa	K	κ	K
lambda	Λ	λ	L
mu	M	μ	M
nu	N	ν	N
omega	Ω	ω	W
omicron	O	o	O
phi	Φ	φ	F
phi (alternate)		φ	J
pi	Π	π	P
psi	Ψ	ψ	Y
rho	P	ρ	R
sigma	Σ	σ	S
tau	T	τ	T
theta	Θ	θ	Q
theta (alternate)	ϑ		J
upsilon	Y	υ	U
xi	Ξ	ξ	X
zeta	Z	ζ	Z

Note   The Greek letter π is so commonly used that it has its own keyboard shortcut: [**Ctrl**][**Shift**]**P**.

Appendix I: Arrow and Movement Keys

Keys	Actions
[↑]	Move crosshair up. In math: move editing lines up. In text: move insertion point up to previous line.
[↓]	Move crosshair down. In math: move editing lines down. In text: move insertion point down to next line.
[←]	Move crosshair left. In math: select left operand. In text: move insertion point one character to the left.
[→]	Move crosshair right. In math: select right operand. In text: move insertion point one character to the right.
[PgUp]	Scroll up about one-fourth the height of the window.
[PgDn]	Scroll down about one-fourth the height of the window.
[Shift][↑]	In math: move crosshair outside and above expression. In text: highlight from insertion point up to previous line.
[Shift][↓]	In math: move crosshair outside and below expression. In text: highlight from insertion point down to next line.
[Shift][←]	In math: highlight parts of an expression to the left of the insertion point. In text: highlight to left of insertion point, character by character.
[Shift][→]	In math: highlight parts of an expression to the right. In text: highlight to right of insertion point, character by character.
[Ctrl][↑]	In text: move insertion point to the beginning of a line.
[Ctrl][↓]	In text: move insertion point to the end of a line.
[Ctrl][←]	In text: move insertion point left to the beginning of a word.
[Ctrl][→]	In text: move insertion point to the beginning of next word.
[Ctrl][↵]	Insert a hard page break. In math: insert addition with line break operator. In text: set the width of the text region.
[Ctrl][Shift][↑]	In text: highlight from insertion point up to the beginning of a line.
[Ctrl][Shift][↓]	In text: highlight from insertion point to end of the current line.
[Ctrl][Shift][←]	In text: highlight left from insertion point to the beginning of a word.
[Ctrl][Shift][→]	In text: highlight from insertion point to beginning of the next word.
[Space]	In math: cycles through different states of the editing lines.
[Tab]	In text: moves the insertion point to the next tab stop. In math or plot: move to next placeholder.
[Shift][Tab]	In math or plot: move to previous placeholder.
[Shift][PgUp]	Move up to previous pagebreak.
[Shift][PgDn]	Move down to next pagebreak.
[Home]	Move to beginning of previous region. In text, move to beginning of current line.
[End]	Move to next region. In text, move to end of current line.

[Ctrl][Home]	Scroll to beginning of worksheet. In text, move insertion point to beginning of text region or paragraph.
[Ctrl][End]	Scroll to end of worksheet. In text, move insertion point to end of text region or paragraph.
[↵]	In text: start new line. In equation or plot: move crosshair below region, even with left edge of region.

Appendix J: Function Keys

Keys	Actions
[F1]	Help.
[Shift][F1]	Context sensitive help.
[F2]	Copy selected region to clipboard.
[F3]	Cut selected region to clipboard.
[F4]	Paste contents of clipboard.
[Ctrl][F4]	Close worksheet or template.
[Alt][F4]	Close Mathcad.
[F5]	Open a worksheet or template.
[Ctrl][F5]	Search for text or math characters.
[Shift][F5]	Replace text or math characters.
[F6]	Save current worksheet.
[Ctrl][F6]	Make next window active.
[Ctrl][F7]	Inserts the prime symbol (').
[F7]	Open a new worksheet.
[F9]	Recalculate a selected region.
[Ctrl][F9]	Recalculate worksheet

Note These function keys are provided mainly for compatibility with earlier Mathcad versions. Mathcad also supports standard Windows keystrokes for operations such as file opening, [Ctrl]O], and saving, [Ctrl]S], copying, [Ctrl]C], and pasting, [Ctrl]V]. Choose **Preferences** from the **Tools** menu and check "Use standard Windows shortcut keys" on the General tab to enable all Windows shortcuts.

Appendix K: ASCII codes

Decimal ASCII codes from 32 to 255. Nonprinting characters are indicated by "*npc*."

Code	Character	Code	Character	Code	Character	Code	Character	Code	Character
32	[space]	80	P	130	‚	182	¶	230	æ
33	!	81	Q	131	ƒ	183	·	231	ç
34	"	82	R	132	„	184	¸	232	è
35	#	83	S	133	...	185	¹	233	é
36	$	84	T	134	†	186	º	234	ê
37	%	85	U	135	‡	187	»	235	ë
38	&	86	V	136	ˆ	188	¼	236	ì
39	'	87	W	137	‰	189	½	237	í
40	(	88	X	138	Š	190	¾	238	î
41	)	89	Y	139	‹	191	¿	239	ï
42	*	90	Z	140	Œ	192	À	240	ð
43	+	91	[	141–4	*npc*	193	Á	241	ñ
44	,	92	\	145	'	194	Â	242	ò
45	-	93	]	146	'	195	Ã	243	ó
46	.	94	^	147	"	196	Ä	244	ô
47	/	95	_	148	"	197	Å	245	õ
48	0	96	`	149	•	198	Æ	246	ö
49	1	97	a	150	–	199	Ç	247	÷
50	2	98	b	151	—	200	È	248	ø
51	3	99	c	152	~	201	É	249	ù
52	4	100	d	153	™	202	Ê	250	ú
53	5	101	e	154	š	203	Ë	251	û
54	6	102	f	155	›	204	Ì	252	ü
55	7	103	g	156	œ	205	Í	253	ý
56	8	104	h	157–8	*npc*	206	Î	254	þ
57	9	105	i	159	Ÿ	207	Ï	255	ÿ
58	:	106	j	160	*npc*	208	Ð		
59	;	107	k	161	¡	209	Ñ		
60	<	108	l	162	¢	210	Ò		
61	=	109	m	163	£	211	Ó		
62	>	110	n	164	¤	212	Ô		
63	?	111	o	165	¥	213	Õ		
64	@	112	p	166	¦	214	Ö		
65	A	113	q	167	§	215	×		
66	B	114	r	168	¨	216	Ø		
67	C	115	s	169	©	217	Ù		
68	D	116	t	170	ª	218	Ú		
69	E	117	u	171	«	219	Û		
70	F	118	v	172	¬	220	Ü		
71	G	119	w	173	-	221	Ý		
72	H	120	x	174	®	222	Þ		
73	I	121	y	175	¯	223	ß		
74	J	122	z	176	°	224	à		
75	K	123	{	177	±	225	á		
76	L	124			178	²	226	â		
77	M	125	}	179	³	227	ã		
78	N	126	~	180	´	228	ä		
79	O	127–9	*npc*	181	µ	229	å		

Appendix L: References

Abramowitz, M., and I. Stegun. *Handbook of Mathematical Functions*. New York: Dover, 1972.

Devroye, L. *Non-uniform Random Variate Distribution*. New York: Springer-Verlag, 1986.

Friedman, J. H. "A Variable Span Smoother." *Tech Report No. 5*. Laboratory for Computational Statistics. Palo Alto: Stanford University.

Geddes, K. and G. Gonnet. "A New Algorithm for Computing Symbolic Limits Using Generalized Hierarchical Series." *Symbolic and Algebraic Computation (Proceedings of ISSAC '88)*. Edited by P. Gianni. From the series *Lecture Notes in Computer Science*. Berlin: Springer-Verlag, 1989.

Golub, G. and C. Van Loan. *Matrix Computations*. Baltimore: John Hopkins University Press, 1989.

Hairer, E. and G. Wanner. *Solving Ordinary Differential Equations II: Stiff and Differential-Algebraic Problems*. Berlin: Springer-Verlag, 2nd rev. ed., 1996.

Knuth, D. *The Art of Computer Programming: Seminumerical Algorithms*. Reading: Addison-Wesley, 1997.

Lorczak, P. *The Mathcad Treasury*. A Mathsoft E-book. Cambridge: Mathsoft, Inc.

Nash, J.C. *Compact Numerical Methods For Computers*. Bristol: Adam Hilger Ltd., 1979.

Niven, I. and H. Zuckerman. *An Introduction to the Theory of Numbers*. New York: John Wiley & Sons, 1972.

Piessens, R., E. de Doncker-Kapenga, C. W. Überhuber and D. K. Kahaner, QUAD-PACK, *A Subroutine Package for Automatic Integration*, Springer-Verlag, 1983.

Press, W.H., W.T. Flannery, S.A.Teukolsky, and B.P.Vetterling. *Numerical Recipes in C*. Cambridge University Press, New York, 1992.

Polak, E. *Optimization – Algorithms and Consistent Approximations*. New York: Springer-Verlag, 1997.

Singleton, R. *Communications of ACM*. Vol. 11, no. 11. November, 1986.

Wilkinson, J.H. and C. Reinsch. *Handbook for Automatic Computation*. Vol. II, *Linear Algebra*. New York: Springer-Verlag, 1971.

Winston, W. *Operations Research: Applications and Algorithms*. Belmont: Wadsworth, 1994.

Index

↵ (Enter key) 1
→ (symbolic equal sign) 196
→ (vectorize operator) 61
 94–95, 245
% 442
( ) (parentheses) 46
, 317, 371
:= (definition) 17, 99
= (evaluating expression) 17, 101
∞ (infinity) 442
2D plots, creating 21
3D Plot Format dialog box 184
absolute value 396
accessing Mathcad from other applications 248
accessing other applications from Mathcad 216
acos function 260
acosh function 260
acot function 260
acoth function 261
acsc function 261
acsch function 261
activation 8
ActiveX 243, 248
adaptive smoothing of data 149
add line 417
addition 394
    with line break 394
Ai function 261
Airy functions 261, 264
aligning
    output tables 59
    regions 80
    text 70
and function 416
angle function 262
Animate command 121
animation
    compressing AVI files 121
    creating 121
    playback 122
    saving 121
    speed 121–122
antisymmetric tensor function 388
APPENDPRN function 262
application component
    SmartSketch 226
application components
    Axum/S-PLUS 224
    Data Acquisition control (DAC) 229

    Excel 222
    MATLAB 226
approximations
    root of expression 125
arccosecant 261
arccosine 260
arccotangent 260
arcsecant 262
arcsine 263
arctangent 263
area
    collapsing 86
    deleting 87
    expanding 86
    inserting 85
    locking and unlocking 86
    naming 86
    password protecting 85–86
arg function 262
arguments
    of functions 106
arithmetic mean 317
arithmetic operators
    absolute value 396
    addition 394
    addition with line break 394
    complex conjugate 396
    division 395
    exponentiation 396–397
    factorial 395
    multiplication 395
    negation 395
    nth root 396
    parentheses 394
    range variable 399
    square root 396
    subtraction 395
arrays
    calculations by element 61
    copying and pasting 59
    creating 53
    defining with range variables 54
    displaying in results 58
    extracting a row or column 57
    graphical display of 62
    importing data into 220
    nested 63, 113
    operators for 398
    ORIGIN used with 57
arrow keys, for editing 13, 445
ASCII codes

entering in strings 35
table 447
ASCII data
importing and exporting 215
asec function 262
asech function 262
asin function 263
asinh function 263
assume keyword 422
atan function 263
atan2 function 263
atanh function 263
augment function 258, 263
Author's Reference 23, 29, 93
Auto (on status bar) 118
automatic calculation mode 118
automating
Mathcad from other applications 243
autoscaling of axis limits 169
AutoSelect
in solving 132
overriding 132
AVI files
compression 121
creating 121
hyperlinking from worksheet 122
playback 122
Axum/S-PLUS component 224
background color 83
bar plots (3D)
formatting 184
base of results (decimal/octal/binary) 113
base units 115
bei function 264
ber function 264
Bessel functions
Ai function 261
bei function 264
ber function 264
Bi function 264
I0 function 294
I1 function 295
In function 298
J0 function 300
J1 function 301
Jn function 291–292, 301
js function 302
K0 function 302
K1 function 302
Kn function 302
updates 5

Y0 function 387
Y1 function 387
Yn function 387
ys function 387
beta distribution 276, 330, 341, 348
Bi function 264
binary data
importing and exporting 215
binary numbers 34, 113
binomial distribution 277, 330, 341, 348
bitmaps
color palettes 155
copying from the Clipboard 153
creating pictures from 152
blank lines, inserting or deleting 82
blank pages in printouts 92
blank space between regions 13
BMP files 85, 152
bold equals 415
bookmarks 27
Boolean comparison
strict 5
Boolean operators 130
and function 416
bold equals 415
greater than 415
greater than or equal to 415
less than 415
less than or equal to 415
not equal to 415
not function 416
or function 416
xor function 416
border around a region 13
boundary value 266, 323, 356, 368
boundary value problems 142
break statement 237, 418
breaking equations 202
bspline function 265
B-splines 146
built-in functions
listed by type 249
built-in variables 100
bulleted paragraphs 70
Bulstoer function 140
Bulstoer function 266
bulstoer function 265
bvalfit function 144, 266
C_DILLA folder, activation 9
CAD drawings 226
Calc on message line 119

calculation 17
    controlling 118
    disabling for individual equation 120
    equations 17, 100
    locking area 85
    order in worksheets 101
    result format 112
    units in 115
calculator, using Mathcad as 16
calculus operators
    definite integral 405
    derivative 408
    indefinite integral 407
    left-hand limit 410
    limit 410
    nth derivative 409
    product 403
    range product 405
    range sum 403
    right-hand limit 410
    summation 402
calling Mathcad from other applications 248
Cauchy distribution 277, 330, 342, 348
ceil function 267
Celsius 111, 117
CFFT function 269
cfft function 268
CGS units 116, 436
characters, deleting or inserting in math 42
Chebyshev polynomials 381
Check In 96
Check Out 96
Chi function 432
chi-squared distribution 277, 331, 342, 349
cholesky function 269
Ci function 432
Clipboard 48, 202
closing a worksheet 22
closing Mathcad
    See exiting Mathcad
cnorm function 254
cnper function 270
coeffs keyword 423
Collaboratory 29
collapsing an area 86
collect keyword 423
colon (:) as definition symbol 17, 99
color
    Electronic Book annotation 26
    equation highlight 83
    in equations 51

    in text 69
    of worksheet background 83
color images
    displaying 151
color palettes for bitmaps 155
colormap 308, 368
colormap files 186
cols function 270
column 34
column vectors
    See vectors
combin function 270
combinatorics functions
    combin function 270
    permut function 333
combining matrices
    augment function 263
    stack function 373
common logarithm 310
complex conjugate 396
complex keyword 423
complex numbers
    arg function 262
    csgn function 274
    display of 113
    entering 34
    Im function 297
    imaginary unit symbol 113
    Re function 349
    signum function 370
    vector field plots 182
complex threshold 113
Component Wizard 217
components
    application-based 216
    customizing 247
    deleting 247
    inserting 217
    overview of 216
    redistributing 247
    scripted 243
    See also application components
computing results 17, 100
concat function 271
cond1 function 271
cond2 function 271
conde function 271
condi function 271
condition number of matrix 271
conditional
    functions 256

statement 234
conditional function *if* 296
conditional statement if 417
confluent hypergeometric function 319, 336
conjugate, complex 396
constants
    changing the font style of 50
    See also numbers *and* predefined variables
constraint
    in solve blocks 130
    tolerance 131
constraints in solve blocks 286, 327, 331
contacting Mathsoft 9
context menu
    See pop-up menu
continue statement 418
contour plots
    creating 181
    formatting 184
    See also plots, 3D
controls 245
    changing the appearance of 246
    inserting 245
Controls, customized 243
convert keyword 201
Convert to Partial Fraction command 201
convert, parfrac keyword 423
copy and paste 15, 118, 156
copying
    expressions 48
    from E-book 26
    regions 15
    results 118
copying regions 15
corr function 271
correlation coefficient 271
cos function 272
cosh function 272
cosine integral 432
cot function 272
coth function 272
covariance 276
crate function 272
CreateMesh function 273
CreateSpace function 273
creating
    2D plots 161
    3D plots 175
    contour plots 181
    E-book 93
    hyperlinks 89

popup window 89
Portable Document Format (PDF) files 93
region tags 90
space curve 178
surface plots 176, 179
text regions 65
variables 17
vector field plots 182
worksheet templates 77
creating arrays 53
cross product 399
crosshair for insertion 13
csc function 274
csch function 274
csgn function 274
csort function 274
cspline function 274
CTOL variable 131, 286, 327, 331, 442
cube root 114
cubic spline interpolation 145
cumint function 275
cumprn function 276
cumulative distribution functions 254
cumulative probability
    See probability distribution
curve fitting
    functions for 147
    polynomial 147
    using cubic splines 145
Curve Fitting and Smoothing Functions 250
cvar function 276
cyl2xyz function 276
δ function 388
dashed selection rectangle 14
data
    entering into a table 55
Data Acquisition control (DAC) 229
data files
    exporting from an array 60
    functions for reading and writing 250
    importing data from 220
    reading from 215
    writing to 215
data input 220
Data Tables
    creating from a file 219
database, importing from 220
databases, exchanging data with 222, 226
DataTable component 220
date in header or footer 85
dbeta function 276

dbinom function 277
dcauchy function 277
dchisq function 277
debugging a worksheet 123
decimal places
    in displayed results 113
    internal precision 112
decimal points
    numerical calculation 113
default formats
    2D plots 170
    3D plots 184
    numerical results 112
    template 79
    worksheet layout 77
defining
    complex numbers 34
    functions 106
    global variables 102
    local variables in program 232
    multiple definitions of variable 101
    numbers 33
    programs 231
    range variables 103
    See also creating
    strings 35
    units 111, 115
    variables 17, 99
definite integral 205, 405
definition 397, 411
    global 412
    local 417
definition symbol (:=) 17, 99
degrees, converting to radians 117, 256
deleting
    blank lines 82
    characters in math 42
    equations 16
    hard page breaks 84
    hyperlinks 90
    operators 45
    parentheses 47
    parts of an expression 49
    regions 16
    text 65
delta function 388, 432
derivative 408
derivatives
    symbolic 204
determinant 209, 400
Developer's Reference 23, 29, 230, 244–245, 248

device-independent bitmap 154
dexp function 277
dF function 277
dgamma function 278
dgeom function 278
dhypergeom function 278
diag function 278
dialects (spell-checker) 75
DIB
    See device-independent bitmap
dictionaries (spell-checker) 75
Differential Equation Solve Blocks
    E-book in Web Library 6
differential equation solvers
    Bulstoer function 266
    bulstoer function 265
    bvalfit function 266
    multigrid function 323
    Odesolve function 327, 331
    Radau function 347
    radau function 346
    relax function 356
    Rkadapt function 359
    rkadapt function 358
    rkfixed function 326, 360
    sbval function 368
    Stiffb function 375
    stiffb function 374
    Stiffr function 376
    stiffr function 376
differential equation solvers, command-line 136
differential equations 133
    higher order 133, 135
    partial 144
    second order
        differential equations
            second order 133
    slowly varying solutions 141
    smooth systems 140
    stiff systems 141
differential equations, evaluating only the final value 141
differentiation 408–409
differentiation variable 408
dilog function 432
dilogarithm function 432
dimensions 110
Dirac function 432
disabling equations 120
display of arrays 58
display of operators 391

displayed precision
    See decimal places
division 395
division, inline 395
DLLS, building 243
dlnorm function 278
dlogis function 278
dnbinom function 279
dnorm function 279
dot product 399
double integrals 405
Down One Level command 63
downloads 32
dpois function 279
drag and drop 15, 26, 48, 156–157
dragging regions 15
drawings
    See pictures
dt function 279
dunif function 280
dweibull function 280
ε function 388
e, base of natural logarithms 100, 307, 442
e, value of 36
E-book 93
    creating 93
    searching for information in 25
E-books 23
    finding on the Web 26
Edit Go to Page command 13
Edit Links command 158
editing equations
    annotated example 41
    changing a number 42
    changing a variable or function name 42
    compared to word processors 41
    deleting an operator 45
    deleting parentheses 47
    deleting parts of expression 49
    inserting an operator 42
    making expression an argument to a function 48
    moving parts of an expression 48
    moving/rearranging equations 80
editing lines 41
eff function 280
Ei function 432
eigenanalysis 280–281, 290–291
eigenvals function 280
eigenvalues 259
eigenvec function 281
eigenvecs function 281

eigenvectors 259
Electronic Book
    copying information from 26
    moving around in 25, 27
    toolbar 25, 27
Electronic Books 91
elliptic integral 432
Email 97
endpoints for ranges 105
engineering notation 113
Enter key 1
equal sign (=)
    in numerical calculations 101
    in solve blocks 128
    symbolic calculations 196, 206–207
equality constraints 130
equals 397, 411
    bold 415
equations
    as constraints in solve blocks 130
    breaking 202
    calculating results 17, 100
    color 51
    disabling calculation for 120
    dragging and dropping 48
    effect of range variables in 105
    errors in 123
    font 50
    global definitions 102
    in text 72
    locking in area 85–86
    order of evaluation 101, 118
    processing and calculating 17, 118
    properties 120
    solving for root 125
    solving symbolically 206–208
    solving with solve blocks 127
    styles 50
    units in 109
    variable definition 99
equations, solving 286, 327, 331, 364
erf function 281, 432
erfc function 282
ERR variable 320
ERR variable and *Minerr* 131
error function 282
error messages
    correcting 124
    in equations 123
    tracing the source of 123
    with units 110

Euclidean norm 400
Euler's constant 432
Euler's gamma function 388
Evaluate Complex command 201
Evaluate Floating Point command 201
Evaluate in Place option 202
Evaluate Symbolically command 201–202
evaluation operators
    definition 411
    equals 411
    global definition 412
    infix 414
    postfix 414
    prefix 413
    symbolic equals 413
    treefix 414
Excel
    Excel component 222
exchanging data with other applications 216
exiting Mathcad 22
exp function 282
Expand command 201
expand keyword 201, 424
expand nested arrays 113
Expert Solver 127
expfit function 282
exponential
    notation, entering 34
    notation, in displayed results 113
exponential distribution 277, 333, 342, 357
exponential function 282
exponential integral 432
exponentiation
    matrix case 396–397
    scalar case 396–397
exporting
    components as MCM 247
    worksheets as RTF 95
exporting data 215
expression type functions
    IsArray function 300
    IsScalar function 300
    IsString function 300
    UnitsOf function 382
expressions
    applying a function to 48
    converting to partial fractions 201
    correcting errors in 124
    deleting parts of 49
    error messages in 123
    evaluating 100

    expanding 201
    moving parts of 48
    selecting several 80
    simplifying 202
    symbolic evaluation of 196–197
Extension Packs 249
extrapolation 338
F (function) keys, table of 446
F distribution 277, 333, 342, 357
Φ function 389
Factor command 201
factor keyword 424
factorial 395
Fahrenheit 111, 117
fast Fourier transform 283, 285
Features In-depth 23
FFT function 285
fft function 283
fhyper function 285
file access functions 250
    APPENDPRN function 262
    GETWAVINFO function 291
    LoadColormap function 308
    READ_BLUE function 349
    READ_GREEN function 350
    READ_HLS function 350
    READ_HLS_HUE function 350
    READ_HLS_LIGHT function 351
    READ_HLS_SAT function 351
    READ_HSV function 351
    READ_HSV_HUE function 351
    READ_HSV_SAT function 351
    READ_HSV_VALUE function 352
    READ_IMAGE function 352
    READ_RED function 353
    READBMP function 350
    READPRN function 352
    READRGB function 353
    READWAV function 354
    SaveColormap function 368
    WRITE_HLS function 384
    WRITE_HSV function 384
    WRITEBMP function 384
    WRITEPRN function 385
    WRITERGB function 385
    WRITEWAV function 386
File Input component 219
File Output component 219
File Send command 97
files
    opening 77

reading data from 250
saving 22
See also data files
See also worksheets
finance
    cnper function 270
    crate function 272
    cumint function 275
    cumprn function 276
    eff function 280
    fv function 288
    fvadj function 288
    fvc function 288
    ipmt function 299
    irr function 299
    mirr function 322
    nom function 324
    nper function 325
    npv function 325
    pmt function 335
    ppmt function 338
    pv function 340
    rate function 347
Find function 128, 208, 286, 327, 331
first order differential equation 136
float keyword 425
floor function 287
font
    changing in header or footer 85
    changing in math 50
    changing in text 68
footers 84
for loop 235
for loop statement 418
Format Header/Footer command 84
Format Style command 71
formatting
    2D plots 168
    3D plots 184
    numbers in matrices 59
    operators 391
    results 112
    symbolic 202
    worksheets 83
Formatting toolbar 12
    math styles 51
    text styles 71
fourier keyword 210, 425
Fourier transform functions
    fft function 283
Fourier transforms

alternate form 285
CFFT function 269
cfft function 268
FFT function 285
fft function 283
ICFFT function 295
icfft function 295
IFFT function 297
ifft function 297
symbolic 210
fractions
    displaying results as 113
FRAME for animation 121
frequency
    Fourier analysis 283
    statistical counts 292
Fresnel cosine integral 432
FresnelC function 432
FresnelS function 432
functions
    applying to an expression 48
    built-in 249
    colormap 186
    defining 19, 106
    file access 250
    inserting 249
    interpolation 145
    list of categories 249
    optimization 125
    other special 432
    piecewise continuous 256
    prediction 145
    recursive 108
    regression 147
    See also built-in functions
    smoothing 149
    solving 125
    to find roots of expressions 125
    uniform polyhedra 252
    user-defined 36, 106
fv function 288
fvadj function 288
fvc function 288
Γ function 388
gamma (Euler's constant) 432
gamma distribution 278, 334, 342, 358
gamma function 388
Gauss hypergeometric function 285
Gaussian distribution 254, 279, 335, 344, 364
gcd function 289
generalized

regression 148
genfit function 289
geninv function 290
genvals function 290
genvecs function 291
geometric distribution 278, 334, 343, 358
geometric mean 291
Getting Started Primers 23
GETWAVINFO function 291
Given function 286, 327, 331
Given, in solve blocks 128, 208
global definition 412
global definitions 102
gmean function 291
graphics, inserting 151
graphing
 data 166
 expressions 164
 functions 164, 176
 in 2D 161
 in 3D 175
 uniform polyhedra 252
 vector 166
graphs
 creating 21, 175, 252
 formatting 21
 resizing 162
 See also plots, 2D
greater than 415
greater than or equal to 415
greatest common divisor 289
greatest integer function 287
Greek letters
 in equations 36
 in text 67
 table of 444
Greek toolbar 37, 67, 444
guess
 for solve blocks 128
guidelines for aligning regions 81
hard page breaks 84
harmonic mean 294
HBK files 24
headers and footers 84
Heaviside step function 389
Help
 Author's Reference 29
 context-sensitive 28
 Developer's Reference 29
 online 28
 See also Resource Center *and* technical support

Her function 292
Hermite polynomial 292
hexadecimal numbers 34
highlighting equations 83
highpass filter 389
hist function 292
histogram 292
histogram function 293
history of browsing in Electronic Book 25
hlookup function 294
hmean function 294
HTML 93
 Positioning 94
HTML/MathML 95
hyperbolic cosine integral 432
hyperbolic functions
 cosh function 272
 coth function 272
 csch function 274
 sech function 369–370
 sinh function 371
 tanh function 380
hyperbolic sine integral 433
hypergeometric 278, 285, 319, 334, 336, 343, 358
hyperlinks
 deleting 90
 editing 90
 to other file types 91
 to regions 90
 to worksheets 89
hysical 23
i (imaginary unit) 34
I0 function 294
I1 function 295
ibeta function 295
ICFFT function 295
icfft function 295
identity function 296
if conditional statement 417
if function 256, 296
if statement 234
IFFT function 297
ifft function 297
Im function 297
image file
 BMP format 152
 in headers and footers 85
Image files
 reading from and writing to 215
Image Processing Functions 253
imaginary Bessel Kelvin function 264

imaginary numbers
    entering 34
    symbol for 34, 113
imaginary value 113
implied multiplication 41, 109, 443
importing data 215, 220
importing data from a database 220
impulse function 388, 432
In function 298
incompatible units (error message) 110
incomplete
    beta function 295
    elliptic integral 432
    gamma function 388
increments for ranges 105
indefinite integral 205, 407
indented paragraphs 70
index variables
    See range variables
inequalities
    as constraints in solve blocks 130
infinity (∞) 36, 442
infix 414
Inline division 395
inner product 399
in-place activation 156
Input Table component 55
input to a component 216
Insert 44
Insert Area command 85
Insert Function command 249
Insert Hyperlink command 89
Insert key 42, 66
Insert Link command 89
Insert Math Region command 73
insert matrix 399
Insert Matrix command
    to create array 53
    to resize array 54
Insert Object command 15, 118, 156
Insert Reference command 88
Insert Unit command 110, 115
inserting
    blank lines 82
    equations in text 72
    functions 48
    graphic objects 155
    graphics computationally linked 158
    hyperlinks 89
    math region 73
    minus sign in front of expression 46

    parentheses around expression 46
    pictures 151
    text 65
    units 110
    worksheet 88
inserting a component 217
insertion point 16
installation instructions 7
integral transforms
    Fourier 210
    Laplace 210
    z 210
integrals
    indefinite 205
    symbolic evaluation of 205
integration 405, 407
IntelliMouse support 13, 194
intercept function 298
International System of units (SI) 116
Internet
    Collaboratory 29
interp function 298
interpolation
    cubic spline 145
    functions 145
    linear 145
interpolation functions
    bspline function 265
    cspline function 274
    interp function 298
    linterp function 306
    lspline function 311, 313
    pspline function 339
interrupting calculations in progress 120
inverse
    cumulative distributions 254
    Fourier transform 210
    Laplace transform 210
    z-transform 210
inverse cumulative probability
    See inverse probability distribution
inverse hyperbolic functions
    acosh function 260
    acoth function 261
    acsch function 261
    asech function 262
    asinh function 263
    atanh function 263
inverse of matrix 399
inverse probability distribution functions
    qbeta function 341

qbinom function 341
qcauchy function 342
qchisq function 342
qexp function 342
qF function 342
qgamma function 342
qgeom function 343
qhypergeom function 343
qlnorm function 343
qlogis function 343
qnbinom function 344
qnorm function 344
qpois function 344
qt function 345
qunif function 345
qweibull function 345
inverse trigonometric functions
    acos 260
    acot function 260
    acsc function 261
    angle function 262
    asec function 262
    asin 263
    atan function 263
    atan2 function 263
invfourier keyword 210, 425
invlaplace keyword 210, 426
invztrans keyword 210, 426
ipmt function 299
irr function 299
IsArray function 300
ise 6
IsScalar function 300
IsString function 300
iteration
    in programs 235
    with range variables 19
iwave function 300
j (imaginary unit) 34
J0 function 300
J1 function 301
Jac function 301
Jacobi polynomial 301
Jacobian matrix 141, 374
JavaScript 244
Jn function 291–292, 301
JPEG 94
js function 302
JScript 244
K0 function 302
K1 function 302

keywords, symbolic 197, 421
    assume 422
    coeffs 423
    collect 423
    complex 423
    convert, parfrac 423
    expand 424
    factor 424
    float 425
    fourier 425
    invfourier 425
    invlaplace 426
    invztrans 426
    laplace 426
    series 427
    simplify 428
    solve 429
    substitute 430
    ztrans 430
Kn function 302
knots 265
Kronecker's delta function 388
ksmooth function 149, 303
Kummer function 319, 336
kurt function 303
kurtosis 303
Lag function 303
Laguerre polynomial 303
Lambert W function 433
laplace keyword 210, 426
Laplace transforms 210
Laplace's equation 144, 323, 356
last function 304
lcm function 304
least common multiple 304
least integer function 267
least squares
    <function>regress 354
    genfit function 289
    intercept function 298
    linfit function 305
    loess function 308, 368
    slope function 371
    stderr function 374
Leg function 304
Legendre function 285
Legendre polynomial 304
LegendreE function 432
LegendreEc function 432
LegendreEc1 function 432
LegendreF function 433

LegendreKc function 433
LegendreKc1 function 433
LegendrePi function 433
LegendrePic function 433
LegendrePic1 function 433
length function 304
less than 415
less than or equal to 415
lgsfit function 305
limit 410
    left-hand 410
    right-hand 410
limits
    axis 21
    default range 21
limits, evaluating 206
line break
    in text 66
line function 305
linear
    equations 286, 327, 331
    independence 347
    interpolation 145, 306
    prediction 145, 338
    programming 127, 315, 321
    regression 147, 354
    system solver and optimizer 127
    systems of equations 127
linfit function 305
link
    See also hyperlinks
    to objects 155
    to other worksheets 88–89
linterp function 145, 306
list box control 245
literal subscripts 37
ln (natural log) function 307
lnfit function 308
LoadColormap function 186, 308
local definition 417
local result format 20
lockable area
    See area
locked calculations 85–86
locking and unlocking an area 86
loess function 308, 368
log and exponential functions
    exp function 282
    ln function 307
    log function 310
log function 310

logfit function 310
logistic distribution 334, 343, 362
lognormal distribution 334, 343, 362
long equations 202
lookup function 310
looping
    for loop 235
    while loop 236
lowpass filter 389
lsolve 127
lsolve function 311
lspline function
    one-dimensional case 311
    two-dimensional case 313
LU decomposition 314
lu function 314
magnitude 400
mailing worksheets 97
mantissa 287
manual mode 118
margins 83
match function 314
Math Optimization command 213
Math Options command 100
math region 33
math styles
    applying 51
    Constants 50
    editing 50
    saving 52
    Variables 50
Math toolbar 12, 37
Mathcad
    accessing from other applications 248
Mathcad 6, 7, or 8 78
Mathcad Enterprise 6, 96
Mathcad OLE automation objects 248
Mathcad Web Library 32
Mathcad Web site 9
Mathcad's Object Model 23
MathML 93
MathML, content 94
MathML, presentation 94
Mathsoft controls 245
Mathsoft home page 27
Mathsoft, contacting 9
MATLAB component 226
matrices
    adding/deleting rows or columns 54
    as array elements 63
    calculations by element 61

creating with components 216
defining by formula 54
defining with two range variables 54
definition of 34
determinant 209
displayed as pictures 151
displayed as scrolling output tables 58
extracting a column 56
extracting elements 56
limits on size 53, 59
numbering elements 57
operators for 398
ORIGIN used with 57
plotting in contour plot 182
start with row and column zero 57
subscripts 56
matrix
    changing size 54
Matrix Determinant command 209–210
Matrix display style 113
matrix function 314
Matrix Invert command 210
matrix operators
    combining 263, 373
    cross product 399
    determinant 400
    dot product 399
    insert matrix 399
    inverse 399
    magnitude 400
    picture 401
    raising to a power 396–397
    subscript 399
    sum 399
    superscript 400
    transpose 400
    vectorize 400
Matrix Transpose command 209–210
max function 315
Maximize function 315
MCD file 77
MCM file 247
MCT file 77
mean function 317
Measurement Computing
    supported data acquisition devices 229
measurement for the ruler 82
medfit function 317
median function 318
medsmooth function 318
metafile 154

mhyper function 319, 336
Microsoft Internet Explorer 27, 244
Microsoft Office 158
min function 320
Minerr function 131, 320
Minimize function 321
minus sign 395
    inserting in front of expression 46
MIP
    See mixed integer programming
mirr function 322
mixed integer programming 132
mixed number 397
mixed numbers
    displaying results as 113
MKS units 116, 440
mod function 323
mode
    See manual mode
mode function 323
modifiers, symbolic 421
modulus 400
moving
    crosshair 13, 445
    editing lines 42, 445
    insertion point 42, 445
    regions 15
moving regions 15
multigrid function 145, 323
multiple integrals 405
multiple roots
    finding with *polyroots* 125, 127
    finding with solve blocks 131
multiplication 40, 395, 399, 403, 405
    implied 41, 109, 443
multivalued functions 114
names of variables and functions 36
National Instruments
    supported data acquisition devices 229
natural logarithm 307
negating an expression 46
negation 395
negative binomial distribution 279, 335, 344, 363
nested arrays
    defining 63
    displaying 63
    expanding 63, 113
New Features 4
nom function 324
nonlinear
    equations 286, 327, 331, 364

regression 289, 305
nonlinear systems of equations 127
nonscalar value (error message) 104
norm1 function 324
norm2 function 324
normal distribution 254, 279, 335, 344, 364
norme function 325
normi function 325
not equal to 415
not function 416
notations in this *User's Guide* 1
nper function 325
npv function 325
nth derivative 409
nth root 396
nudging regions 15, 80
nudging with arrows 80
num2str function 326
number format
 See result format
number theory functions
 gcd function 289
 lcm function 304
 mod function 323
numbered paragraphs 70
numbers 33
 binary 34, 113
 complex 34
 decimal 113
 displayed as zero 113
 exponential notation for 34, 113
 format for computed results 112
 formatting 20, 112
 hexadecimal 34
 imaginary 34
 octal 34, 113
 radix (base) for results 113
numerical methods
 root finding 125
 solving and optimization 132
numol 138
object linking and embedding
 See OLE
Object Model in Mathcad 23
objects
 embedding 155
 linking 155
octal numbers 34, 113
ODBC component 220
Odesolve function 133, 327, 331
OLE

automation 243, 248
 drag and drop 157
 editing links 158
 in-place activation 156, 158
 scripting objects 244
 via components 216
on error statement 239, 419
online resources 23
OpenGL 175
operator placeholder 45
operators
 arithmetic 394
 Boolean 415
 calculus 402
 changing the display of 391
 defined 38
 deleting 45
 derivative 204
 evaluation 411
 for vectors and matrices 398
 indefinite integral 205
 inserting 42
 matrix 398
 programming 417
 replacing 45
 toolbars 12
 vector sum 403
optimization
 Maximize function 315
 Minerr function 320
 Minimize function 321
Optimize Palette command 155
optimizers 127
or function 416
order
 of polynomial regression 147
 of worksheet evaluation 102
ORIGIN variable 57
otherwise statement 417
output from a component 216
output table 58
 alignment 59
 resizing 59
 versus matrix display style 113
overlapping regions 82
overtyping text 66
page
 breaks, inserting and deleting 84
 headers and footers 84
 length 84
 numbering 85

Page Setup dialog box 83, 91
palettes, color, for bitmaps 155
parabolic heat
    solving 136
paragraphs 65
    bullets 70
    hanging indent 70
    indenting 70
    numbers 70
    properties 69
    tab stops 70
    text alignment in 70
parametric plot
    creating 164
parametric surface plots
    creating 180–181
    See also plots, 3D
parentheses 394
    deleting from expression 47
    inserting into an expression 46
partial differential equations 144, 323, 356
    second order
        olve blocks 135
        tial differential equations
            second order 135
partial fractions 423
password protecting an area 85
    hiding an area 86
Paste command 15, 157
Paste Special command 154, 157
pasting
    bitmaps 153
    device-independent bitmaps 153
    from Clipboard 48, 153
    metafiles 153
    OLE objects 157
pbeta function 330
pbinom function 330
pcauchy function 330
pchisq function 331
PDE solve block 135
PDE, solving with a solve block 135
Pdesolve 135
Pdesolve function 135
Pearson's correlation coefficient 271
pending computations 118–119
percent 442
permut function 333
personal
    dictionary (spell-checker) 75
pexp function 333

pF function 333
pgamma function 334
pgeom function 334
phypergeom function 334
pi
    entering 37
    value 36
pi (3.14159...) 42, 100, 442, 444
picture 401
picture operator 63, 151
pictures
    border on 154
    creating from bitmap file 152
    creating from matrix 151
    creating using SmartSketch 226
    formatting 154
    pasted from Clipboard 153
    resizing 154
piecewise continuous functions
    δ function 388
    ε function 388
    Φ function 389
    if function 296
    sign function 370
placeholder 16, 33
placeholder for an operator 45
Playback command 122
plnorm function 334
plogis function 334
plots 3D
    graphing functions 176
plots, 2D
    autoscaling of axis limits 169
    changing perspective 171
    copying format from existing plot 170
    creating 21, 162
    default formats 170
    formatting 168
    graphing expressions 163
    graphing functions 163
    graphing vectors 166
    multiple traces on 164
    read-out of coordinates 172
    reference lines in 169
    resizing 162
    setting axis or data limits 169
    setting default formats 170
    Show Markers 169
    titles and labels 168
    traces on 164
    tracing coordinates on 172

zooming 171
plots, 3D 175
    3D Plot Format dialog box 185
    3D Plot Wizard 175
    annotations 191
    backplanes 185
    color 186, 190
    colormaps 186–187
    contour lines 188
    contour plots 181
    converting 191
    creating 175
    examples 176, 179
    fill color 186
    filling contours 187
    fog 184
    formatting 184
    graphic annotations on 191
    lighting 190
    line color 189
    lines 188
    multiple plots on 184
    OpenGL graphics 175
    parametric surface plots 180–181
    point color 190
    point symbols 190
    QuickPlot 175
    resizing 162
    rotating 193
    space curves 178
    spinning 193
    surface plots 176, 179
    text on 191
    titles 186
    uniform polyhedra 252
    vector field plots 182
    wireframe 188
    zooming 193–194
pmt function 335
pnbinom function 335
PNG 94
pnorm function 335
Poisson distribution 279, 338, 344, 366
Poisson's equation 144, 324, 356
pol2xy function 337
polar plots
    creating 162
    formatting 168
    See also plots, 2D
polygamma function 433
polyhedra 252

Polyhedron 335
Polyhedron function 335
PolyLookup function 336
polynomial
    finding roots of 286, 327, 331, 337, 364
    finding the roots of 127
    regression 147, 289, 305, 308, 354, 368
polyroots function 127, 337
popup hyperlink 89
pop-up menu
    3D plots 191
    animation playback 122
    Input Table component 56
    MathSoft Control component 246
    Scriptable Object Component 245
    SmartSketch component 226
    solving 132
    Web browsing 27
popup menu
    component 218
    Data Acquisition control 229
    MATLAB component 226
    OBDC component 221
popup window, creating 89
Portable Document Format (PDF), creating 93
postfix 414
ppmt function 338
ppois function 338
precision, internal 112
predefined variables 100
predict function 338
prediction, linear 145
prefix 413
prime notation
    inside a solve block 133
principal branch of function 114
Print Preview command 92
printing 22
    and calculation of worksheet 119
    and pagination 84
    blank pages in 83, 92
    color 83
    page settings for 83
    print preview 92
    wide worksheets 91
PRNCOLWIDTH variable 442
PRNPRECISION variable 442
probability density functions
    dbeta function 276
    dbinom function 277
    dcauchy function 277

dchisq function 277
dexp function 277
dF function 277
dgamma function 278
dgeom function 278
dhypergeom function 278
dlnorm function 278
dlogis function 278
dnbinom function 279
dnorm function 279
dpois function 279
dunif function 280
dweibull function 280
probability distribution functions
   pbeta function 330
   pbinom function 330
   pcauchy function 330
   pchisq function 331
   pexp function 333
   pF function 333
   pgamma function 334
   pgeom function 334
   phypergeom function 334
   plnorm function 334
   plogis function 334
   pnbinom function 335
   pnorm function 335
   ppois function 338
   pt function 340
   punif function 340
   pweibull function 341
processing equations 17, 118
   results of 118
product 395, 399, 403, 405
programming operators
   add line 417
   break 418
   continue 418
   for 418
   if 417
   local definition 417
   on error 419
   otherwise 417
   return 418
   while 418
programs 231
   adding lines 232
   break statement 237
   controlling or interrupting 237
   defining 231
   error handling 239

for loop 235
generating symbolic results 233
if statement 234
local assignment 231
looping 235
nested 241
on error statement 239
output of 231
recursion 242
return statement 238
statements 232
subroutines 241
symbolic evaluation of 233
while loop 236
properties
   of components 218
   of controls 221
   region 83, 90
protecting a worksheet 87
Psi function 433
Psin function 433
pspline function 339
pt function 340
punif function 340
pv function 340
pweibull function 341
pwrfit function 341
qbeta function 341
qbinom function 341
qcauchy function 342
qchisq function 342
qexp function 342
qF function 342
qgamma function 342
qgeom function 343
qhypergeom function 343
qlnorm function 343
qlogis function 343
qnbinom function 344
qnorm function 344
qpois function 344
QR decomposition 344
qr function 344
qt function 345
quadratic equation solving 132
QuickPlot 163, 175
QuickSheets 23
   storing custom operators 392
qunif function 345
qweibull function 345
Radau 140

Radau function 347
radau function 346
radians
    converting to degrees 117, 256
    trig functions 256
radix of displayed results 113
random number generators
    rbeta function 348
    rbinom function 348
    rcauchy function 348
    rchisq function 349
    rexp function 357
    rF function 357
    rgamma function 358
    rgeom function 358
    rhypergeom function 358
    rlnorm function 362
    rlogis function 362
    rnbinom function 363
    rnd function 363
    rnorm function 364
    root function 364
    rpois function 366
    rt function 367
    runif function 367
    rweibull function 367
range product 405
range sum 403
range variable creation 399
range variables
    array calculations with 61
    creating arrays with 54
    defining 19, 103, 105
    fundamental principle for 105
    how Mathcad evaluates equations with 105
    setting endpoints and increments 105
rank function 347
rate function 347
rbeta function 348
rbinom function 348
rcauchy function 348
rchisq function 349
Re function 349
READ_BLUE function 349
READ_GREEN function 350
READ_HLS function 350
READ_HLS_HUE function 350
READ_HLS_LIGHT function 351
READ_HLS_SAT function 351
READ_HSV function 351
READ_HSV_HUE function 351

READ_HSV_SAT function 351
READ_HSV_VALUE function 352
READ_IMAGE function 352
READ_RED function 353
READBIN 215
READBMP function 350
READPRN function 352
READRGB function 353
READWAV function 354
real Bessel Kelvin function 264
recursion 108
Reference Table 23
Reference Tables 23
references
    and relative paths 89
    to other worksheets 88
regions 13
    aligning 80
    blank space between 13
    copying 15
    deleting 16
    dragging 15
    dragging across documents 15
    equation 13
    hyperlinking to 90
    locking 85
    moving 15
    overlapping 82
    properties 90
    properties of 14
    protecting from editing 87
    putting borders around 13
    selecting 14
    separating 82
    tags, creating 90
    text 18, 65
    unlocking 86
    viewing 13, 82
region-to-region hyperlinking 90
regress function
    one-dimensional case 354
    two-dimensional case 355
regression
    functions 147
    generalized 148
    localized 147
    multivariate 147
    polynomial 147
    using linear combinations of functions 148
regression functions
    expfit function 282

genfit function 289
intercept function 298
lgsfit function 305
line function 305
linfit function 305
lnfit function 308
loess function 308, 368
logfit function 310
medfit function 317
pwrfit function 341
regress function 354
sinfit function 371
slope function 371
stderr function 374
Relative button 94
relative paths
    for references 89
relax function 145, 356
Release Notes 32
Repaginate Now command 84
replacing characters in math or text 74
replacing operators 45
reports
    for a solve block 132
resizing
    graphs 162
    pictures 154
Resource Center
    accessing worksheets on Web 26
    Web browsing in 26
Resources Window
    bookmarks 27
Resources window 23
resources, online 23
result format 112
Result Format dialog box 20
results
    calculating 17
    calculating with equations 100
    complex 114
    copying 118
    formatting 20, 112
    units in 115
    wrapping 202
return statement 238, 418
reverse function 357
rexp function 357
rF function 357
rgamma function 358
rgeom function 358
rhypergeom function 358

Riccati equation 286, 327, 331
rich text format (RTF) 95
Riemann Zeta function 433
right page margin 83
Rkadapt function 359
rkadapt function 358
rkfixed function 136, 326, 360
rlnorm function 362
rlogis function 362
rnbinom function 363
rnd function 254, 363
rnorm function 364
root function 125, 364
roots
    finding 125
    finding multiple with solve blocks 131
    finding symbolically 206–207
    numerical approximations used 125
    of polynomials 127
round function 366
round-trip HTML 95
row vector 34
row vectors
    See vectors
rows function 366
rpois function 366
rref function 366
rsort function 367
rt function 367
RTF file 77
    See also rich text format
ruler
    for formatting a worksheet 81
    for formatting text 70
    measurement system 70
Runge-Kutta initial-value solver 136
runif function 367
rweibull function 367
Save as Web Page 93
Save Layout As button 94
SaveColormap function 186, 368
saving
    new file 22
    templates 79
    worksheets 22, 77
sbval function 143, 368
scalar 33
scalar product 399
scatter plots (3D)
    formatting 184
    See also plots, 3D

scientific notation 113
scripable object components 243
Scriptable Object component 243
    protection when opening 248
scripting languages, supported 244
search
    E-book 26
    in equations 73
    in text 73
search function 369
sec function 369
sech function 369–370
seed for random number generator 363
selecting
    graphs 162
    math expression 43
    page break 84
    regions 14
    text 66
selection rectangle 14
semicolon, in range variable definitions 104
Separate Regions command 82, 84
separating overlapping regions 82, 84
series keyword 427
SharePoint 96
Sharepoint 6
SharePoint Repository 96
Shi function 433
Show Border option 155
Si function 433
sign function 370
signum function 370
Simplify command 202
simplify keyword 202, 428
simultaneous equations, solving 286, 327, 331
simultaneous equations, solving numerically 127
sin function 370–371
sine integral 433
sinfit function 371
singular matrix 311
singular value decomposition 379–380
sinh function 371
skew function 371
skewness 371
slope function 371
SmartSketch component 158, 226
smooth systems (differential equations) 140
smoothing functions
    ksmooth function 303
    medsmooth function 318
    supsmooth function 378

smoothing of data 149
soft page breaks 84
solve block 286, 327, 331
solve blocks 127, 133, 135
    constraints in 130
    definition of 127
    expressions allowed in 130
    finding multiple solutions 131
    Given in 128
    reports for 132
    tolerance 131
    using to solve differential equations 133, 135
    using to solve numerically 127
    using to solve symbolically 208
Solve command 430
solve keyword 206–207, 429
Solving and Optimization Extension Pack 127
solving equations 127
    AutoSelect of algorithm 132
    linear systems 132
    nonlinear systems 132
    See also solve blocks
    with *root* function 125
    with solve blocks 127, 208
    with Solve for Variable 206
    with solve keyword 206
solving functions
    Find 286
    Find function 327, 331
    Maximize function 315
    Minerr function 320
    Minimize function 321
    polyroots function 337
    root function 364
sorting functions
    csort function 274
    reverse function 357
    rsort function 367
    sort function 372
space curves
    creating 178
    See also plots, 3D
spaces, inserting or deleting 82
special functions
    eff function 280
    erf function 281
    erfc function 282
    fhyper function 285
    Γ function 388
    Her function 292
    ibeta function 295

Jac function 301
Lag function 303
Leg function 304
mhyper function 319, 336
other
    complete elliptic integral
        of the first kind 433
        of the second kind 432
        of the third kind 433
    complex error function 432
    cosine integral 432
    digamma 433
    dilogarithm 432
    Dirac delta 432
    Euler's constant 432
    exponential integral 432
    Fresnel cosine integral 432
    Fresnel sine integral 432
    hyperbolic cosine integral 432
    hyperbolic sine integral 433
    incomplete elliptic integral
        of the first kind 433
        of the second kind 432
        of the third kind 433
    Lambert W 433
    polygamma 433
    Riemann Zeta 433
    sine integral 433
    Tcheb function 381
    Ucheb function 381
spell-checking 74
sph2xyz function 373
spherical Bessel functions 302, 387
spline functions 145–146, 311
spreadsheets, exchanging data with 216
square root 396
stack function 258, 373
stack overflow error 108
standard deviation 374
standard error 374
standard normal distribution 254
statistics
    cubic spline interpolation 145
    cumulative distribution functions 254
    generalized linear regression 148
    interpolation 145
    inverse cumulative distributions 254
    linear interpolation 145
    linear prediction 145
    linear regression 147

multivariate polynomial regression 147
polynomial regression 147
probability density functions 254
statistics functions
    corr function 271
    cvar function 276
    gmean function 291
    hist function 292
    histogram function 293
    hmean function 294
    kurt function 303
    mean function 317
    median function 318
    mode function 323
    skew function 371
    Stdev function 374
    stdev function 374
    Var function 382
    var function 382
stderr function 374
Stdev function 374
stdev function 374
step function 389
step size
    for differential equation solving 141
    for iteration 105
Stiffb function 375
stiffb function 374
Stiffr function 376
stiffr function 376
str2num function 377
str2vec function 377
string functions
    concat function 271
    error function 282
    num2str function 326
    search function 369
    str2num function 377
    str2vec function 377
    strlen function 377
    substr function 378
    vec2str function 382
strings
    arguments to file access functions 250
    as elements of vectors 35
    defining 35
    editing 44
    evaluating 35
    variables 35
strlen function 377
Student's t distribution 340, 345, 367

styles
  math 50
  text 71
submatrix function 378
subroutines 241
subscript button 69
subscripts
  in text 69
  literal 37
  non-numeric 37
  ORIGIN used with 57
  start with zero 57
substitute keyword 430
substr function 378
subtraction 395
summation 394, 402
superscript 400
  to get column from matrix 57
superscript button 69
supsmooth function 149, 378
surface plots
  creating 176, 178–179
  formatting 184
  parametric 180–181
  See also plots, 3D
svd function 379
svds function 380
symbolic
  equal sign 196
  evaluation 196
  evaluation of programs 233
  keywords 197
symbolic equals 413
symbolic keywords 421
  assume 422
  coeffs 423
  collect 423
  complex 423
  convert, parfrac 423
  expand 424
  factor 424
  float 425
  fourier 425
  invfourier 425
  invlaplace 426
  invztrans 426
  laplace 426
  series 427
  simplify 428
  solve 429
  substitute 430

  ztrans 430
symbolic modifiers 421
symbolics menu 422
Symbolics menu commands 201
Symbolics menu, using 201
system requirements for Mathcad 7
t distribution 340, 345, 367
tab stops in a worksheet 81
tables of data 55
tabs in a paragraph 70
tag
  region, creating 90
tan function 380
tanh function 380
Tcheb function 381
Technical Support 32
technical support 9
temperature conversions 111, 117
templates 77
  creating new 79
  modifying 79
  used to save calculation mode 118
  using to create a worksheet 77
tensor 388
text 65
  alignment 70
  bullets in 70
  changing font 68
  color 69
  editing 68
  entering 18
  Greek letters in 67
  inserting equations in 72
  moving 67
  moving insertion point in 66
  Occupy Page Width option 68
  Push Regions Down As You Type option 69
  regions 65
  selecting 66
  spell-checking 74
  styles 71
  tools 73
text box 18, 65
text regions 65
  changing width 67
  creating 18, 65
  editing 68
  how to exit 18, 65
text ruler 70
text styles 71
  applying 71

creating 72
modifying 71
text tools 73
tilde (~), used in global definitions 102
time in header or footer 85
Tip of the Day 29
TOL variable 100, 286, 327, 331, 364, 442
and solve blocks 131
tolerance
constraint (CTOL) 286, 327, 331
convergence (TOL) 364
See TOL variable *and* CTOL variable
toolbar
Boolean 415
calculator 394
calculus 402
evaluation 411
Formatting 12
Math 12
matrix and vector 398
programming 417
standard 12
toolbars
customizing 12
Electronic Book 25, 27
programming 232
Web 27
Tools
text 73
top-to-bottom evaluation 101
tr function 381
trace 381
traces, on 2D plots 164
tracing the source of an error 123
trailing zeros 113
transforms
Fourier (numerical) 283, 285
Fourier (symbolic) 210, 425
Laplace 210, 426
wavelet 383
z 210, 430
transpose 400
transpose of matrix 209
treefix 414
trigonometric functions
cos function 272
cot function 272
csc function 274
sec function 369
sin function 370–371
tan function 380

with degrees and radians 117
trunc function 381
truncation
thresholded 5
truncation and round-off functions
ceil function 267
floor function 287
round function 366
trunc function 381
Tutorials
23
tutorials 23
two-point boundary value problems 142
typing over text 66
U.S. Customary units 116
Ucheb function 381
undefined variables 101, 103
undo 4
uniform distribution 280, 340, 345, 367
uniform polyhedra 252
units
alternative definitions 115
base units 115
CGS system 116
common sources of error 110
converting calculated results 116
default 109
defining 111, 115
dimensional consistency 110
errors in dimensions 110
in calculated values 115
in equations 109
metric 116
MKS system 115
placeholder 115
prefixes 116
SI 116
simplifying 113
U.S. customary 116
UnitsOf function 111, 382
Up One Level command 63
update
window manually 119
worksheet window 119
URL
Mathsoft home page 27
Use Default Palette command 155
user-defined functions 106
evaluating variables in 107
valid names 36
Var function 382

var function 382
Variable Differentiate command 204
Variable Integrate command 205
Variable Solve command 207
variables
    changing the font style of 50
    defining 17, 99
    global definitions of 102
    in red 103, 123
    matrices 34, 53
    names 36
    predefined 100
    range variables 19, 103
    string 35
    undefined 123
    vectors 34
variance of a data set 382
VBScript 244
vec2str function 382
vector
    changing size 54
    definition of 34
vector and matrix functions
    augment function 263
    cholesky function 269
    cols function 270
    cond1 function 271
    cond2 function 271
    conde function 271
    condi function 271
    CreateMesh function 273
    CreateSpace function 273
    cyl2xyz function 276
    diag function 278
    eigenvals function 280
    eigenvec function 281
    eigenvecs function 281
    geninv function 290
    genvals function 290
    genvecs function 291
    hlookup function 294
    identity function 296
    last function 304
    lookup function 310
    lsolve function 311
    lu function 314
    match function 314
    matrix function 314
    max function 315
    min function 320
    norm1 function 324

norm2 function 324
norme function 325
normi function 325
pol2xy function 337
Polyhedron function 335
PolyLookup function 336
qr function 344
rank function 347
rows function 366
rref function 366
sph2xyz function 373
stack function 373
submatrix function 378
svd function 379
svds function 380
tr function 381
vlookup function 383
xyz2cyl function 386
xyz2pol function 386
xyz2sph function 386
vector and matrix functions functions
    length function 304
vector and matrix subscript 399
vector field plots
    creating 182
    from complex matrices 182
    See also plots, 3D
vector norm 400
vector product 399
vector sum 399
vector sum operator 403
vectorize 400
vectorize operator 61
    effect of 61
    how to type 61
    properties of 61, 401
vectors
    as array elements 63
    calculations by element 61
    column vectors 398
    displayed as scrolling output tables 58
    graphing 166
    numbering elements 57
    operators for 398
    ORIGIN used with 57
    row 398
    start with element zero 57
    subscripts 56
    undefined elements filled with zeros 57
    vectorize operator 61
View Animate command 121

View Zoom command 13
Visual Basic Scripting Edition 244
vlookup function 383
W function 433
wait message 119
WAV files
    reading from and writing to 215
wave function 383
wavelet transform functions
    iwave function 300
    wave function 383
Web Library 32
Web pages
    creating from worksheets 93
    formatting 94
Web pages, creating from worksheets 93
Web toolbar 27
Weibull distribution 280, 341, 345, 367
while loop statement 418
while loops 236
windows
    update results manually 119
    working with 13
    zooming in and out of 13
Windows keystrokes 13, 446
wireframe, in 3D plots 188
Wizards
    for inserting 3D plots 175
    for inserting a component 217
word processor 39
worksheet ruler 81
worksheets
    closing 22
    creating 77
    exporting as RTF 95
    formatting 83
    gathering in an E-book 93
    hyperlinking 89
    in popup window 89
    including by reference 88
    opening 78
    opening from Internet 27
    order of evaluation 101
    printing 22, 91

    protecting 87
    referencing in another worksheet 88
    saving 22, 77–78
    saving as templates 79
    saving in an earlier format 78
    sending by Email 97
World Wide Web
    accessing 27
    bookmarks for browsing 27
    Collaboratory 29
    Mathsoft home page 27
    toolbar 27
WRITE_HLS function 384
WRITE_HSV function 384
WRITEBIN 215
WRITEBMP function 384
WRITEPRN function 385
WRITERGB function 385
WRITEWAV function 386
Wythoff symbol for a polyhedron 183
xor function 416
X-Y plots
    creating 21, 162
    formatting 168
    See also plots, 2D
xyz2cyl function 386
xyz2pol function 386
xyz2sph function 386
Y0 function 387
Y1 function 387
y-intercept 298
Yn function 387
ys function 387
zero threshold 113
zeros of expressions or functions
    See roots
Zeta function 433
zooming
    2D plots 171
    3D plots 194
    windows 13
ztrans keyword 210, 430
z-transforms 210